German, Dutch, and Scandinavian Literatures

Library of Congress Classification
2009

Prepared by the Policy and Standards Division

LIBRARY OF CONGRESS
Cataloging Distribution Service
Washington, D.C.

This edition cumulates all additions and changes to Subclass PT through Weekly List 2008/51, dated December 17, 2008. Additions and changes made subsequent to that date are published in weekly lists posted on the World Wide Web at

<http://www.loc.gov/aba/cataloging/classification/weeklylists/>

and are also available in Classification Web, the online Web-based edition of the Library of Congress Classification.

Library of Congress Cataloging-in-Publication Data

Library of Congress.
Library of Congress classification. PT. German, Dutch, and Scandinavian literatures / prepared by the Policy and Standards Division. — 2009 ed.
p. cm.
"This edition cumulates all additions and changes to subclass PT through Weekly list 2008/51, dated December 17, 2008. Additions and changes made subsequent to that date are published in weekly lists posted on the World Wide Web ... and are also available in Classification Web, the online Web-based edition of the Library of Congress classification" — T.p. verso.
Includes index.
ISBN: 978-0-8444-1228-3
1. Classification, Library of Congress. 2. Classification—Books—German literature. 3. Classification—Books—Dutch literature. 4. Classification—Books—Scandinavian literature. I. Library of Congress. Policy and Standards Division. II. Title. III. Title: German, Dutch, and Scandinavian literatures.

Z696.U5P84 2009 025.4'683931—dc22 2009004701

For sale by the Library of Congress Cataloging Distribution Service,
101 Independence Avenue, S.E., Washington, DC 20541-4912.
Product catalog available on the Web at **www.loc.gov/cds**.

PREFACE

The first edition of subclass PT - Part 1, *German Literature*, was published in 1938 and was reprinted in 1966 with supplementary pages of additions and changes. A second edition was published in 1989. The first edition of subclass PT - Part 2, *Dutch and Scandinavian Literature*, was published in 1941 and was reprinted in 1966 with supplementary pages of additions and changes. A second edition was published in 1992. The 2000 edition of subclass PT was the first in which both parts were published together in a single volume, with the title *German, Dutch, and Scandinavian Literatures*. A 2005 edition cumulated additions and changes that were made during the period 2000-2005. This 2009 editions cumulates additions and changes that have been made between 2005 and 2008.

In editions of the Library of Congress classification schedules published since 2004, classification numbers or spans of numbers that appear in parentheses are formerly valid numbers that are now obsolete. Numbers or spans that appear in angle brackets are optional numbers that have never been used at the Library of Congress but are provided for other libraries that wish to use them. In most cases, a parenthesized or angle-bracketed number is accompanied by a "see" reference directing the user to the actual number that the Library of Congress currently uses, or a note explaining Library of Congress practice.

Access to the online version of the full Library of Congress Classification is available on the World Wide Web by subscription to *Classification Web*. Details about ordering and pricing may be obtained from the Cataloging Distribution Service at

<http://www.loc.gov/cds/>

New or revised numbers and captions are added to the Library of Congress Classification schedules as a result of development proposals made by the cataloging staff of the Library of Congress and cooperating institutions. Upon approval of these proposals by the weekly editorial meeting of the Policy and Standards Division of the Acquisitions and Bibliographic Access Directorate, new classification records are created or existing records are revised in the master classification database. Weekly lists of newly approved or revised classification numbers and captions are posted on the World Wide Web at

<http://www.loc.gov/aba/cataloging/classification/weeklylists/>

Janis Young, cataloging policy specialist in the Policy and Standards Division, is responsible for coordinating the overall intellectual and editorial content of class P and its various subclasses. Kent Griffiths, assistant editor of classification schedules, creates new classification records and their associated index terms, and maintains the master database.

Barbara B. Tillett, Chief
Policy and Standards Division

January 2009

OUTLINE

PT1-4897	German literature
PT1-80	Literary history and criticism
PT83-(873)	History of German literature
PT175-230	Medieval
PT236-405	Modern
PT500-597	Poetry
PT605-709	Drama
PT711-871	Prose
PT(881)-(951)	Folk literature
PT923-937	Faust legend
PT1100-1479	Collections
PT1100-1141	General
PT1151-1241	Poetry
PT1251-1299	Drama
PT1301-1360	Prose
PT1371-(1374)	Early to 1950. Old and Middle High German
PT1375-1479	Middle High German
PT1501-2688	Individual authors or works
PT1501-1695	Middle High German, ca. 1050-1450/1500
PT1701-1797	1500-ca. 1700
PT1799-2592	1700-ca. 1860/70
PT1891-2239	Goethe
PT1891-2017	Works
PT2026-(2039)	Translations
PT(2044)-2239	Biography and criticism
PT2600-2653	1860/70-1960
PT2660-2688	1961-2000
PT2700-2728	2001-
PT3701-3971	Provincial, local, colonial, etc.
PT3701-3746	East Germany
PT4801-4897	Low German literature
PT5001-5980	Dutch literature
PT5001-5348	Literary history and criticism
PT5001-5112	General
PT5121-5185	Special periods
PT5201-5243	Poetry
PT5250-5295	Drama
PT5300-5348	Prose
PT(5351)-5395	Folk literature
PT5398	Juvenile literature (General)
PT5400-5547	Collections
PT5400-5409	General

OUTLINE

	Old Norse literature: Old Icelandic and Old Norwegian - Continued
PT7220-7262.5	Collections
PT7230-7252	Poetry
PT7255-7262.5	Prose
PT7261-7262.5	Sagas
PT7263-7296	Individual sagas and historical works
PT7298-7309	Religious works
PT7312-7318	Scientific and learned literature
PT7326-7338	Individual authors or works before 1540
PT7351-7550	Modern Icelandic literature
PT7351-7418	Literary history and criticism
PT(7420)-(7438)	Folk literature
PT7442	Juvenile literature (General)
PT7450-7495	Collections
PT7500-7511	Individual authors or works
PT7500-7501	16th-18th centuries
PT7510-7511	19th-20th centuries
PT7512-7513	21st century
PT7520-7550	Provincial, local, foreign
PT7581-7599	Faroese literature
PT7581-7592	Literary history and criticism
PT7593-7596.5	Collections
PT7597	Local
PT7598-7599	Individual authors or works
PT7601-8260	Danish literature
PT7601-7869	Literary history and criticism
PT7721-7762	Special periods
PT7770-7794	Poetry
PT7800-7832	Drama
PT7835-7869	Prose
PT(7900)-7930	Folk literature
PT7935	Juvenile literature (General)
PT7945-8046	Collections
PT7975-7994	Poetry
PT7999-8020	Drama
PT8021-8046	Prose
PT8050-8177.36	Individual authors or works
PT8050	Medieval
PT8060-8098	16th-18th centuries

OUTLINE

	Danish literature
	Individual authors and works
	16th-18th centuries - Continued
PT8070-8094.5	Holberg, Ludvig
PT8100-8167	19th century
PT8102-8120	Andersen, Hans Christian
PT8145-8157	Oehlenschläger, Adam Gottlob
PT8174-8175	1900-1960
PT8176-8176.36	1961-2000
PT8177-8177.36	2001-
PT8205-8260	Provincial, local, foreign
PT8301-9155	Norwegian literature
PT8301-8574	Literary history and criticism
PT(8420)-8456	Special periods
PT8460-8489	Poetry
PT8500-8534	Drama
PT8540-8574	Prose
PT(8600)-(8637)	Folk literature
PT8640	Juvenile literature (General)
PT8650-8733	Collections
PT8675-8695	Poetry
PT8699-8718	Drama
PT8719-8723	Prose
PT8750-8952.36	Individual authors or works
PT8750-8775	16th-18th centuries
PT8800-8942	19th century
PT8851-8900	Ibsen, Henrik
PT8949-8950	1900-1960
PT8951-8951.36	1961-2000
PT8952-8952.36	2001-
PT9000-9094	Landsmaal or New Norwegian
PT9000-9019	Literary history and criticism
PT9025-9055	Collections
PT9064-9094	Individual authors
PT9100-9155	Provincial, local, foreign
PT9201-9999	Swedish literature
PT9201-9499	Literary history and criticism
PT9320-9370	Special periods
PT9375-9404	Poetry
PT9415-9449	Drama
PT9460-9499	Prose

	Swedish literature - Continued
PT(9509)-(9542)	Folk literature
PT9544	Juvenile literature (General)
PT9547-9639	Collections
PT9565-9570	Translations
PT9580-9599	Poetry
PT9605-9625	Drama
PT9626-9639	Prose
PT9650-9877.36	Individual authors or works
PT9650-9651	Medieval
PT9674-9715	16th-18th centuries
PT9725-9850	19th century
PT9759-9771	Lagerlöf, Selma
PT9800-9817	Strindberg, Johan August
PT9820-9838	Tegnér, Esaias
PT9870-9875	1900-1960
PT9876-9876.36	1961-2000
PT9877-9877.36	2001-
PT9950-9999	Provincial, local, foreign

German literature
Literary history and criticism
Cf. PN821+ Germanic literature
Periodicals
1.A1-.A3 International
1.A4-Z American and English
2 French
3 German
5 Italian
7 Scandinavian
8 Spanish and Portuguese
9 Other
(11-19) Yearbooks
see PT1+
Societies
21.A1-.A3 International
21.A4-Z American and English
22 French
23 German
25 Italian
27 Scandinavian
28 Spanish and Portuguese
29 Other
31 Congresses
Collections
Cf. PF3112.9+ Chrestomathies
35 Monographs, studies, etc. By various authors
36 Festschriften. By honoree, A-Z
41 Encyclopedias. Dictionaries
43 Pictorial atlases
45 Theory and principles of the study of German literature
47 History of literary history
49 Philosophy. Psychology. Aesthetics
Including national characteristics in literature
50 Finance
Including government support of literature
Study and teaching
51 General
53 General special
By period
55 Middle ages to 1600
57 17th and 18th centuries
59 19th century
61 20th century
62 21st century
63.A-Z By region or country, A-Z
65.A-Z By school, A-Z

Literary history and criticism -- Continued
Biography of teachers, critics, and historians
67.A2 Collective
67.A3-Z Individual, A-Z
Subarrange each by Table P-PZ50
Criticism
For criticism, unless specifically German see PN80+
(69) Periodicals
see PN80
71 Treatises. Theory. Canon
73 History
74 Special topics (not A-Z)
e.g. Textual criticism
75 Collections of essays in criticism
By period
76 Medieval to 1600
77 17th century
78 18th century
79 19th century
80 20th century
81 21st century
History of German literature
General
Treatises in German
83 Early works to 1800
84 Works, 1800-1850
Including later editions of works of this period
85 Works, 1850-
89 Works by Catholic authors or treating of Catholic literature
91 Treatises in English
93 Treatises in other languages
Compends
German
95 Through 1900
96 1901-
English
98 Through 1900
99 1901-
101 Other languages
103 Outlines, syllabi, tables, atlases, charts, questions and answers, etc.
107 Single addresses, essays, lectures, etc.

History of German literature
General -- Continued
109 Dialect literature. Dialects in literature
Class here treatises dealing with the literature written completely or incidentally in the various dialects of the German language
For treatises restricted to a particular dialect, prefer classification with that dialect
For treatises dealing with the dialects as they appear in literature, from a linguistic or phraseological point of view see PF5011
Special topics
109.5 Awards, prizes
110.A-Z Special, A-Z
110.A5 Andreas-Gryphius-Preis
110.B47 Berliner Literaturpreis
110.B73 Bremer-Literaturpreis
110.C37 Carl-Zuckmayer-Medaille
110.C57 Christian-Wagner-Preis
110.G4 Georg-Büchner-Preis
110.G48 Geschwister-Scholl-Preis
110.G75 Grillparzer-Preis
110.H45 Heinrich-Heine-Preis
110.I53 Ingeborg-Bachmann-Preis
110.J6 Johann Peter Hebel-Preis
110.J65 Joseph-Breitbach-Preis
110.K5 Kleist-Preis
110.L55 Literaturpreis der Konrad-Adenauer-Stiftung
110.M39 Max Geilinger-Preis
110.M67 Mörike-Preis
110.N4 Nelly-Sachs-Preis
110.S35 Schillerpreis
110.T5 Thomas-Dehler-Preis
110.T84 Tukan-Preis
110.W37 Walter-Bauer-Literaturpreis
110.W54 Wilhelm Raabe-Literaturpreis
111 Relations to history, civilization, culture, etc.
112 Relations to art, music, painting, etc.
Relations to foreign literature
115 General
Special
117 Ancient
Cf. PA3012, PA3071, PA6023, Classical literature
Oriental
Cf. PJ312+ Oriental philology
119 General
120.A-Z Special. By language, A-Z

History of German literature
Special topics
Relations to foreign literature -- Continued

123.A-Z By country or language, A-Z
e.g.
123.F7 France
123.G7 Great Britain
123.I8 Italy
123.L3 Latin
123.N6 Norway
123.S58 Slavic countries
123.S7 Spain
123.S8 Sweden
123.U6 United States
125 Translations
127 German literature by foreign authors (General)
For individual authors, see PT1501+; PT3919+
129 Various aspects, forms, etc.
e.g. Evolution of the different forms: poetry, drama, etc.; Psychology, etc.
Special subjects not limited to one period or form
134.A-Z A - L
134.A48 Allusions
134.A53 Androgyny
134.A55 Animals
134.A7 Arcadia
134.A74 Architecture, Domestic
134.A88 Autobiography
134.B62 Body, Human
134.B65 Books and reading
134.B67 Boredom
134.B69 Boundaries
134.C48 Cities and towns
134.C485 Clocks
134.C49 Clothing and dress
134.C5 Cockaigne. Schlaraffenland. Fool's Paradise
134.C7 Creativity
134.D4 Death
134.D45 Déjà vu
134.D46 Denial (Psychology)
134.D66 Doppelgängers. Doubles
134.E3 Eccentrics
134.E32 Education
134.E36 Ego (Psychology)
134.E56 Emotions
134.E68 Erotic literature
134.E7 Esthetics

History of German literature
Special subjects not limited to one period or form
A-L -- Continued

134.E75 Ethics
134.E82 Exiles
134.E83 Existentialism
134.F3 Faithfulness
134.F35 Family
134.F64 Folly
134.F66 Food
134.F75 Friendship
134.G33 Gardens
134.G4 Genius
134.G46 Geography
134.G8 Grail
134.G85 Grief
134.H36 Happiness
134.H43 Heart
134.H45 Heresy
134.H5 History
134.H7 Holy Roman empire
134.H72 Homeland. "Heimat"
134.H73 Homosexuality
134.H75 Honor
134.H85 Human beings
Human body see PT134.B62
134.I34 Identity (Psychology)
134.I4 Industrial arts
Inns see PT148.T34
134.I5 Inwardness. "Innerlichkeit"
134.I7 Irony
134.K5 Kinship
134.K73 Krkonoše (Czechoslovakia and Poland). Riesengebirge
134.L15 Labor. Working class
134.L2 Laments
134.L23 Last Supper
134.L27 Laughter
134.L3 Law
135 Legends. Mythology
Cf. PT204+
137 L - N
137.L47 Libel and slander
137.L5 Liberty
137.L53 Liminality
137.L6 Loneliness
137.L65 Love
137.M2 Machinery

History of German literature
Special subjects not limited to one period or form
L-N -- Continued

137.M24 Marriage
137.M245 Marseille (France)
137.M25 Mathematics
137.M27 Meditation
137.M3 Melancholy
137.M34 Memory
137.M4 Metaphor
137.M53 Midlife crisis
137.M64 Money
137.M95 Myth
139 Nature
143 N - R
(143.N5) Nibelungen
see PT1604
143.O23 Obituaries
143.O24 Occultism
143.O25 Occupations
143.O44 Old age
143.O74 Organ (Musical instrument)
143.O75 Orientalism
143.P25 Pain
143.P28 Parody
143.P3 Pastoral literature
143.P33 Pathos
143.P35 Peasants' War, 1524-1525
143.P4 Pessimism. "Weltschmerz"
143.P43 Photography
143.P46 Pluralism
143.P64 Polarity
143.P65 Politics
143.P655 Poor
143.P66 Popular culture
143.P67 Possessiveness
143.R37 Rape
143.R4 Realism
147 Religion
148 R - Z
148.R65 Romanticism
148.S3 Science
148.S34 Self. Identity (Psychology)
148.S45 Sentimentalism
Slander see PT137.L47
148.S66 Snow
148.S7 Social life

History of German literature
Special subjects not limited to one period or form
R-Z -- Continued

148.S712 Social mobility
148.S715 Sound
148.S72 Speech
148.S73 Split self
148.S75 The State
148.S78 Subconsciousness
148.S8 Supernatural
148.T34 Taverns (Inns)
148.T37 Technology
148.T54 Theater
148.T57 Time
(148.T65) Topography
see PT134.G46
148.T67 Torture
148.T8 Trials, Legal
148.T83 Trojan War
148.T86 Truthfulness and falsehood
148.U85 Utopias
148.V3 Vampires
148.W3 War
148.W47 Werewolves
148.W55 Wills
148.W65 Work
Working class see PT134.L15

Special countries and races
149.A2 General. Exoticism
149.A3-Z Special, A-Z
Under each country:

.x	*General*
.x2A-.x2Z	*Local, A-Z*

149.A35 Africa
149.A45 Alps
149.A5 America
149.A85 Australia
149.B55 Blacks
149.B6 Bohemia
149.F7 France
149.G24 Galicia (Poland and Ukraine)
Germany. Germans
149.G3 General
149.G4 Local, A-Z
e.g.
149.G4B7 Bremen
149.G94 Gypsies. Romanies

History of German literature
Special countries and races
Special, A-Z -- Continued

149.I6 India
149.I8 Italy
149.J3 Japan
149.J38 Jerusalem
149.J4 Jews
149.O34 Oceania
149.P6 Poland
Romanies see PT149.G94
149.R66 Romania
149.R87 Russia
149.S6 Slavs
149.S7 Spain
149.S9 Swiss
149.T9 Turkey
151.A3-Z Treatment of special classes, A-Z
151.A8 Artists
151.B4 Beggars
151.C6 Children
151.C7 Clergy
Cf. PT151.P7 Priests
151.C8 Criminals
151.D92 Dwarfs
151.H4 Hermits
151.M65 Mothers
151.M8 Musicians
151.N8 Nuns
151.P4 Peasants
151.P5 Physicians
151.P62 Poachers
151.P7 Priests
151.R65 Romanies
151.U5 Unmarried mothers
151.V3 Vagabonds
151.W53 Widows
151.W7 Women
151.Y6 Youth
153.A-Z Individual characters, A-Z
153.B56 Bluebeard (Legendary character)
153.C37 Cassandra (Legendary character)
153.D64 Don Juan (Legendary character)
153.G46 Geneviève, of Brabant (Legendary character)
153.O76 Orpheus (Greek mythology)
155 Biography (Collective)
Individual see PT1501+

History of German literature
Biography (Collected) -- Continued
159 Memoirs. Letters
162 Iconography: Portraits, monuments, etc.
163 Literary landmarks. Homes and haunts of authors
167 Women authors. Literary relations of women
169 Jewish authors
170.A-Z Other classes of authors, A-Z
By period
171 General works covering more than one period or parts of more than one period
Medieval
General (to 1500/1520)
175 Treatises. Compends
179 Special subjects (not elsewhere provided for under forms, etc.)
183 Old High German (to ca. 1050)
Middle High German (ca. 1050-1500/1520)
187 General works
1050-1350
191 General works
193 11th-12th centuries (1050-1180)
195 13th century (1180-1300)
1350-1500/20
197 General works
199 14th century
201 15th century
Special forms
Poetry see PT175+
Epic poetry
202 General works
203 Court epic
203.5 Spielmannsepik
203.7 Biblical epic
Hero legends
204 General
Including treatises on the Germanic "heldensage"
Cf. PT7188, PT7261+, Scandinavian sagas
205 Special topics (not A-Z)
Special cycles
Beowulf legend see PR1580+
(205.5) Nibelungen legend
see PT1589+

History of German literature
By period
Medieval
Special forms
Epic poetry
Hero legends
Special cycles -- Continued
206 Wolfdietrich-Hugdietrich-Ortnit (or Hartungen) legend
Comprehensive works only
For the individual poems, see PT1543.H7, PT1629.O8, PT1679.W9
Dietrich von Bern
Including Ermanarich, Etzel (Attila), etc.
207 General
For individual authors and works in Middle High German see PT1501+
Cf. PF3987.H5+ Hildebrandslied
Cf. PT7233+ Edda
Cf. PT7296.T4+ Thidreks saga
209.A-Z Special characters, A-Z
Dietrich von Bern see PT207+
209.E3 Ecke
Ermanarich see PT207+
Etzel see PT207+
212.A-Z Other hero legends, A-Z
212.A4 Alexander
212.A76 Arminius, Prince of the Cherusci
212.C53 Charlemagne
212.G3 Gawain
Hilde-Gudrun see PT1529
212.T75 Tristan
212.W3 Walthari (Walter of Aquitane)
212.W6 Wieland (Wayland the Smith)
213 Minor narrative poetry (Schwankdichtung)
214 Special topics (not A-Z)
Lyric poetry
215 General works
217 Minnesingers
(219) Meistersingers
see PT245
221 Religious poetry
225 Didactic poetry
227 Other
e.g. "Spruchdichtung"
(229) Drama
see PT621

History of German literature
By period
Medieval
Special forms -- Continued
230 Prose. Prose romances
Modern
236 General
Special topics see PT111
238 Early modern to 1700
Renaissance and Reformation (ca. 1440 to 1648)
241 General works
Special topics
245 Meistersingers
246 Other topics (not A-Z)
Special periods
Reformation, 1517-1556/1618
251 General works
255 Special topics (not A-Z)
261 Thirty Years' war, 1618-1648
17th-18th centuries (to 1740)
271 General works
275 Special topics (not A-Z)
The literary societies
279.A1 General
279.A3-Z By society, A-Z
(281) Foreign relations
see PT115+
18th (-19th) century (1700-1800/1870)
285 General works
289 Special topics (not A-Z)
Special subdivisions of the period
1700-1750/1770
293 General works
295 Special topics (not A-Z)
296 Contemporary works
297 Gottsched. Bodmer. Breitinger. Nicolai. Bremer beiträge
The age of Frederick the Great. Prussian poets
301 General works
304 Contemporary works
307 Klopstock. Lessing. Wieland
1750/1770-1800/1830. The classic age
311 General works
313 Special topics (not A-Z)
314 Göttinger bund
317 Period of Herder. "Sturm und drang"
321 Goethe and Schiller

History of German literature
By period
Modern -- Continued
19th century
Cf. PT285+ 18th and early 19th centuries
Cf. PT311+ Late 18th and early 19th centuries
341 General works
345 Special topics (not A-Z)
Special subdivisions of the period
1789/1800-1830/50
351 Treatises
354 Contemporary works
Romanticism
361 General works
363.A-Z Special topics, A-Z
363.A4 Aesthetics
363.A8 Art criticism
363.A82 Artists
363.B5 Bible
363.B56 Blindness
363.C44 Children
363.C5 Cities and towns
363.C55 Classical civilization
363.C57 Closure (Rhetoric)
363.D6 Doppelgängers
363.D7 Dramas
363.D8 Dreams
363.E26 Economics
363.E3 Education. Educators
363.E5 England
363.E55 Enthusiasm
363.E8 Ethics
363.F3 Fairy tales. "Märchen"
363.F45 Feminism
363.G6 Gothic horror tales. Nachtstücke
363.I5 India
363.I7 Irony
363.L3 Landscape
363.L7 Love
363.M4 Metaphor
363.M5 Mines and mineral resources
363.M8 Music
363.N27 Nationalism
363.N3 Nature
363.N48 Netherlands
363.N5 Nihilism
363.N6 Nomads. Wanderers

History of German literature
By period
Modern
19th century
Special subdivisions of the period
1789/1800-1830/50
Romanticism
Special topics, A-Z -- Continued

363.P5 Philosophy
363.P6 Poetics
363.P62 Poets
363.P7 Prose poems
363.P8 Pseudoromanticism
363.R3 Race
363.R35 Religion
363.R4 Rhine River and Valley
363.R6 Romance philology
363.R7 Romantisch (The word)
363.S2 Salons
363.S3 Science
363.S6 Social problems
363.S8 The State
363.S9 Switzerland
363.T5 Theater
363.T7 Translating
Wanderers see PT363.N6
363.W37 War
363.W6 Women
365.A-Z Relation to special persons, A-Z
e.g.
365.H4 Heine
365.N5 Nietzsche
(371) Patriotic poetry
see PT573.P7
373 The Swabian school
Cf. PT3804+ Provincial literature
375 The Austrian poets
381 Young Germany
384.A-Z Special relations, A-Z
384.F7 France
384.G7 Great Britain
384.S3 Saint-Simonianism
(386) Political poetry
see PT573.P7
391 1830/50-1870/80
395 1870/80-1900
20th century

History of German literature
By period
Modern
20th century -- Continued
401 General works
405 Special topics (not A-Z)
21st century
411 General works
415 Special topics (not A-Z)
Special forms
Poetry
500 Periodicals. Societies. Collections
501 Treatises
503 Compends
507 Popular poetry. Volkslied
509.A-Z Special topics, A-Z
509.A6 Anthologies
509.B58 Blue
509.C64 Cologne (Germany)
509.C66 Concentration camps
509.E5 Endings
509.G4 Gesellschaftslieder
509.H58 History
509.H7 Household poem
509.K4 Klagelied
509.L36 Language and languages
509.M3 Martinslieder
509.N3 Nature. Landscape
509.N5 Night
509.P54 Philosophy
509.R4 Religion
509.S7 Spartacus
509.S8 Swan-knight legend
509.S9 Symbolism
509.T5 Time
509.U54 Unicorns
509.W3 War
509.W5 Winiliod
509.W6 Women. Women poets
509.Z8 Zuccalmaglio and the Volkslied
(511) Special regions or places, A-Z
see PT3801+
Special periods
Medieval see PT175+
Modern
General
521 Treatises. Compends

History of German literature
Special forms
Poetry
Special periods
Modern
General -- Continued
523 Special topics (not A-Z)
16th century
525 Treatises. Compends
527 Special topics (not A-Z)
17th century
529 Treatises. Compends
531 Special topics (not A-Z)
18th century
533 Treatises. Compends
535 Special topics (not A-Z)
19th century
537 Treatises. Compends
539 Special topics (not A-Z)
To 1850
541 Treatises. Compends
543 Special topics (not A-Z)
1850-1900
545 Treatises. Compends
547 Special topics (not A-Z)
20th century
551 Treatises. Compends
553 Special topics (not A-Z)
21st century
555 Treatises. Compends
557 Special topics (not A-Z)
Special forms of poetry
561 Epic
(569) Popular poetry
see PT507
Lyric
571 General
573.A-Z Special subjects, A-Z
573.A44 Alienation (Social psychology)
573.B75 Bridges
(573.C5) Children
see PT577.C5
573.C6 Cosmology
573.D4 Death
573.E4 Elegiac
573.L27 Larks
573.L3 Law

History of German literature
Special forms
Poetry
Special forms of poetry
Lyric
Special subjects, A-Z -- Continued
Legends see PT135
573.L6 Love
573.M3 Melancholy
573.M6 Moon
573.N28 Narration (Rhetoric)
573.N3 Nature. Landscape
573.P3 Pastoral
573.P7 Political. Patriotic. Historical
573.P8 Primitivism
573.R4 Religious
573.S6 Social problems
573.S86 Stone
573.W3 War
577.A-Z Special classes, A-Z
577.C5 Children
577.L3 Laboring class. Working class
577.S7 Soldiers
577.S8 Students
581.A-Z Special by form, A-Z
581.B3 Ballad
581.C64 Concrete poetry
581.D5 Dithyrambus
581.E7 Epigramm
Spruch; Gnome
581.F7 Free verse
581.G3 Gazel
581.H5 Heroide
581.H9 Hymn
581.I4 Idyll
581.L6 Loblied
581.M3 Madrigal
581.M4 Makame
581.O3 Ode
581.P8 Priamel
581.R5 Riddle
581.S6 Sonnet
591 Didactic
595 Prose poems
597 Other
e.g. Parody, Travesty, Society verse, Anacreontic verse

History of German literature
Special forms -- Continued
Drama
For technique of drama see PN1660+
For history and study of the German stage see PN2640+
605 Periodicals. Societies. Collections
History
General
611 Treatises
613 Compends
619 Special topics (not A-Z)
e.g. Exhibitions
By period
621 Medieval. Origins to 1500
Modern
General
626 Treatises
628 Special topics (not A-Z)
16th century. Humanism. Reformation
631 Treatises
633 Special topics (not A-Z)
17th-18th centuries
636 Treatises
638 Special topics (not A-Z)
18th (-19th) century
641 Treatises
643 Special topics (not A-Z)
19th century
651 Treatises
653 Special topics (not A-Z)
To 1850/70
656 Treatises
658 Special topics (not A-Z)
1850/70-1900
661 Treatises
663 Special topics (not A-Z)
20th century
666 Treatises
668 Special topics (not A-Z)
21st century
669 Treatises
669.5 Special topics (not A-Z)
Special types
671 Tragedy
676 Comedy
681 Drama (Schauspiel)

History of German literature
Special forms
Drama
Special types -- Continued

686 Tragicomedy
688 Pastoral drama
691 Romantic drama
693 Historical drama
694 Religious drama
(695) Melodrama
see ML
696 Farces
697.A-Z Other, A-Z
697.C3 Carnival drama
697.I5 Interludes
697.J4 Jesuit drama
697.R3 Radio plays
701 Folk drama
709 Children's plays
Cf. PN3169.A+ Amateur theater

Prose
General
711 Treatises
713 Compends
717 Special topics (not A-Z)
Short story, Novelle see PT747.S6
Special periods
Medieval see PT230
Modern
721 General
723 16th century. Renaissance. Reformation
725 17th-18th centuries
728 18th century
731 19th century
735 20th century
738 21st century
Prose fiction
For technique see PN3355+
General
741 Treatises
743 Compends
744 Digests, synopses, etc.
747.A-Z Special kinds, A-Z
747.A38 Adventure stories
"Artist" novel see PT747.K77
747.A8 Autobiographic fiction
747.D4 Detective and mystery stories

History of German literature
Special forms
Prose
Prose fiction
Special kinds, A-Z -- Continued

747.D5 Dime novels. Groschenromane
747.E6 Entwicklungsromane. Bildungsromans
747.E7 Epistolary fiction. Brieromane
747.F3 Fantastic fiction
747.G56 Ghost stories
747.H5 Historical fiction
747.K77 Künstlerroman. "Artist" novel
747.K8 Kunstmärchen. Fairy tales
(747.L8) Lügendichtungen
see PT851
747.P4 Peasant tales. "Dorfgeschichte"
747.P5 Picaresque fiction
747.P76 Protest literature
747.P79 Psychological fiction
747.R7 Robinsonades, Avanturieres, etc.
747.R75 Romans à clef. Schlüsselromane
Schelmenroman see PT747.P5
747.S3 School (Schulromane)
747.S34 Science fiction
747.S6 Short story, Novelle
747.S7 Social romance
747.S74 Sports stories
749.A-Z Special topics, A-Z
749.A56 Anti-Nazi movement
749.B47 Berlin
749.B56 Biography
749.B7 Brigands and robbers
749.D39 Death
749.D4 Decadence
749.F4 Festivals
749.F74 Freemasonry
749.H64 Holocaust, Jewish (1939-1945)
749.I6 Individualism
749.J39 Jesus Christ
749.J4 Jews
749.L66 Loneliness
749.L7 Love
749.M35 Manners and customs
749.M46 Middle class
749.M5 Militarism
749.M66 Motherhood
749.N27 National socialism

History of German literature
Special forms
Prose
Prose fiction
Special topics, A-Z -- Continued

749.N3 Nationalism
749.N36 Nature
749.N6 Nobility
749.R4 Religion
749.S3 Schools
749.S48 Sex
749.S6 Social conditions
749.S7 Soldiers
749.U87 Utopias
(749.W3) Wagner
see ML410
749.W6 Women
Special periods
(751) Medieval
see PT230
753 15th-16th centuries. Reformation
756 General works
17th-18th centuries
759 18th century
19th century
763 General works
766 To 1850/70
771 1850/70-1900
772 20th century
774 21st century
801 Oratory
811 Letters
831 Essays
841 Dialogue
851 Wit and humor. Satire
871 Miscellaneous
(873) Juvenile literature
see PT1021
Folk literature
For general works on folk literature, see GR
(881) Periodicals. Societies. Collections
History
(883) General works
By period
887 Origins. Medieval (to ca. 1500/1600)
(889) Modern (1500/1600-)
(890.A-Z) Special topics, A-Z

Folk literature
History
Special topics, A-Z -- Continued
(890.S4) Schinderhannes
By form
(891) Poetry
see PT507
(893) Drama
see PT701
(895) Prose
see PT883+
Collections
(901) General
Chapbooks. "Volksbücher"
903 General works. History
Collections
see PT882-(895)
905 Reprints
see PT882-(895)
For reprints not in chapbook form see PT901+
906 Originals
see PT882+
Special chapbooks
Originals and reprints
907.A-Z Prose tales, A-Z
908 Poetry. Ballads
(911) Poetry
see PT1201+
(913) Drama
see PT1287+
(915) Legends (Sagen. Heldensagen)
(919.A-Z) By region or place, A-Z
(921) Fairy tales (Märchen), including translations
For juvenile editions, see PZ8, PZ24, PZ34, etc.
Special characters, heroes, fairies, etc.
Faust legend
923 Volksbücher
Historia D. Johannis Faust, ca. 1575 (Wolfenbüttel manuscript)
923.A15 Editions. By date
Historia von d. Johann Fausten, 1587
923.A2 Editions. By date
923.A3 Edition of 1589, n.p., n. printer (with Erfurt stories)
923.A4 Edition of 1590 (with additional chapters)
923.A5 Widman's edition, 1599
923.A6 Revised by Pfitzer, 1674

Folk literature
Collections (of texts exclusively)
Special characters, heroes, fairies, etc.
Faust legend
Volksbücher
Historia von d. Johann Fausten, 1587 -- Continued

923.A7 Faustbuch der Christlich Meynenden, 1725
Christoph Miethen, supposed author
923.A8A-.A8Z Other versions. By editor, A-Z
923.A9-Z Translations. By language and date
Popular drama. Puppet plays
925.A1 Collections. By date
925.A2 Separate editions. By date
925.A5-Z Translations. By language and date
927 Folk songs, ballads, etc.
History of Wagner, disciple of Faust
929.A2 Volksbuch and later revisions. By date
929.A3 Puppet plays
929.A4 English version
929.A5 Dutch version
937 History and criticism
941.A-Z Other than Faust, A-Z
Class here medieval folk literature only. For general or modern literature, see GR
Eulenspiegel
941.E8 Texts
941.E9 History and criticism
Finkenritter
941.F5 Texts
941.F6 History and criticism
Friedrich, Graf von Isenberg, ca. 1190-1226
941.F83 Texts
941.F84 History and criticism
Geneviève of Brabant
941.G4 Texts
941.G5 History and criticism
Heinrich der Löwe
941.H4 Texts
941.H5 History and criticism
Hug Schapler
941.H8 Texts
941.H82 History and criticism
Matthias Tobias
941.M3 Texts
941.M4 History and criticism
Rübezahl
941.R7 Texts

Folk literature
Collections (of texts exclusively)
Special characters, heroes, fairies, etc.
Other than Faust, A-Z
Rübezahl -- Continued
941.R8 History and criticism
Schildbürger
941.S3 Texts
941.S4 History and criticism
Siegfried
941.S5 Texts
941.S6 History and criticism
Tannhäuser
941.T2 Texts
941.T3 History and criticism
Vlad III, Prince of Wallachia; Dracula
941.V55 Texts
941.V552 History and criticism
(951) Individual tales
Cf. PT907+ Chapbooks
1021 Children's literature (General)
For special genres, see the genre
Collections of German literature
General (including general modern)
1100 Early through 1800
1101 1801-
1105 Minor. Selections. Anthologies
1107 Selections from women authors
1109.A-Z Special classes of authors, A-Z
1109.C3 Catholic authors
Cf. PT89
1109.C5 Child authors
1109.G74 Greek authors
1109.I5 Immigrant writings
1109.J4 Jewish authors
1109.M45 Mentally ill
1109.M55 Minority authors
1109.P47 Physicians
1109.W6 Women
1110.A-Z Special topics (Prose and verse), A-Z
1110.A4 Aeronautics
1110.A5 Alpine regions
1110.A6 Artisans
1110.A7 Atomic warfare
1110.A8 Austria
1110.A84 Automobiles
1110.B24 Baden

Collections of German literature
General (including general modern)
Special topics (Prose and verse), A-Z -- Continued

1110.B3	Bavaria
1110.B4	Berlin
1110.B56	Black Forest
1110.B64	Bohemia
1110.B68	Bosnia and Hercegovina
1110.B8	Burgenland
1110.C4	Children
1110.C44	Christmas
1110.C57	City and town life
1110.C6	Constance, Lake
1110.C65	Country life
1110.D7	Dreams
1110.E3	Education
1110.E4	Elbe River
1110.E95	Europa (Greek mythology)
1110.F3	Family
1110.F35	Fathers
1110.F7	Franconia
1110.F74	Friedrich, Graf von Isenberg
1110.G38	Germans in foreign countries
1110.G4	Germany
1110.G72	Graubünden (Switzerland)
1110.G76	Graz (Austria)
1110.H35	Hansa towns
1110.H4	Heidelberg
1110.H46	Hesse
1110.H5	Historical. Patriotic
1110.H85	Human ecology
1110.I5	Immortality
1110.I7	Iran
1110.I8	Italy
1110.J4	Jews
1110.K42	Kiel (Germany)
1110.K44	Kleist, Heinrich von
1110.L3	Labor
1110.L5	Liberty
1110.L54	Life
1110.L6	Love
1110.M45	Minden (North Rhine-Westphalia, Germany)
1110.M56	Months
1110.M6	Mothers
1110.M8	Munich
1110.N3	Nationalism
1110.N4	New Year

Collections of German literature
General (including general modern)
Special topics (Prose and verse), A-Z -- Continued

1110.N43 New York (N.Y.)
1110.N47 Night
1110.O4 Old age
1110.P3 Palatinate
1110.P35 Peace
1110.P4 Peasants
1110.P43 Peasants' War, 1595-1597
1110.P57 Poaching
1110.P6 Poland
1110.P65 Portugal
1110.P75 Prague
1110.P83 Prussia, East
1110.R34 Railroads
1110.R37 Reading
1110.R4 Religion
1110.R45 Revolutionary literature
1110.R6 Rome
1110.R8 Ruhr Valley
1110.S14 Saale River Region
1110.S18 Sausages
1110.S19 Saxony
1110.S2 Saxony, Lower
1110.S28 Schleswig-Holstein
1110.S3 Schwabing
1110.S35 Sea stories
1110.S4 Self-sacrifice
1110.S44 Separation
1110.S5 Silesia
1110.S7 Stalin
1110.S8 Summer
1110.S85 Swabia
1110.S87 Switzerland
1110.S9 Sylt
1110.T3 Tailors
1110.T4 Teachers
Travels see PT1110.V69
1110.V46 Venice
1110.V69 Voyages and travels
1110.W33 Weddings
1110.W35 Weimar
1110.W4 Westphalia
1110.W45 Wienerwald
1110.W47 Wiesbaden
1110.W49 Wine

Collections of German literature
General (including general modern)
Special topics (Prose and verse), A-Z -- Continued
1110.W5 Winter
1110.W6 Women
1110.W65 Worpswede, Germany
1110.W8 Württemberg
1110.Z8 Zürich
(1111) Translations from foreign literatures into German
see PN, PQ, PR, etc.
Translations of German literature
1112 Polyglot
1113 English
1114 French
1115 Italian
1116.A-Z Other languages, A-Z
By period
To 1500 see PT1371+
1121 (15th-) 16th century
1126 (16th-) 17th century
1131 (17th-) 18th century
(18th-) 19th century
1136.A2 Annuals. Yearbooks. Serials
1136.A3-Z General works
(19th-) 20th century
1141.A2 Annuals. Yearbooks. Serials
Cf. AY17+
1141.A3-Z General works
(20th-) 21st century
1142 Annuals. Yearbooks. Series
1143 General works
Local divisions see PT3801+
Poetry
General
1151 Early through 1800
1153 1801-
1155 Selections, anthologies, etc.
Including textbooks
1156 Selections from women poets
1158 Concordances, dictionaries, indexes, etc.
(1159) Translations from foreign literatures into German
see PN, PA-PT
Translations into foreign languages
1160.A2 Polyglot
By language
English
1160.E5 General

	Collections of German literature
	Poetry
	Translations into foreign languages
	By language
	English -- Continued
	Special
1160.E6	Ballads
1160.E7	Other special forms
1160.E8A-.E8Z	By translator, A-Z
	French
1160.F5	General
	Special
1160.F6	Ballads
1160.F7	Other special forms
1160.F8A-.F8Z	By translator, A-Z
	Italian
1160.I5	General
	Special
1160.I6	Ballads
1160.I7	Other special forms
1160.I8A-.I8Z	By translator, A-Z
	Portuguese
1160.P5	General
	Special
1160.P6	Ballads
1160.P7	Other special forms
1160.P8A-.P8Z	By translator, A-Z
	Russian
1160.R5	General
	Special
1160.R6	Ballads
1160.R7	Other special forms
1160.R8A-.R8Z	By translator, A-Z
	Spanish
1160.S5	General
	Special
1160.S6	Ballads
1160.S7	Other special forms
1160.S8A-.S8Z	By translator, A-Z
1161.A-Z	Other languages, A-Z
	By period
	Early to 1400 see PT1391+
	Modern
	General see PT1151+
	15th-17th centuries
	Meistersingers
1163.A2	Contemporary collections

Collections of German literature
Poetry
By period
Modern
15th-17th centuries
Meistersingers -- Continued
1163.A5-Z Modern collections
Other collections
1165.A2 Contemporary collections. By compiler or title
1165.A5-Z Modern collections
1167 (17th-) 18th centuries
1169 Serials collections, 18th-19th centuries. By date-letter.
Subarrange by title, e.g.
Class here Musenalmanache and similar collections of the late 18th and early 19th centuries
1169.D70M8 1770. Musenalmanach, Göttingen, 1770-1804
1169.E11A5 1811. Alpenrosen, 1811-1830
(18th-) 19th century
1171 General collections
Special periods
1172 To 1850/60
1173 1850/60-1900
(19th-) 20th century
1174 General collections
1175.A-Z Serials collections. By title, A-Z
Cf. AY17+
(20th-) 21st century
1176 General collections
1177.A-Z Serials collections, By title, A-Z
Special kinds
Epic
1179 General
1181.A-Z Special, A-Z
1181.B4 Beast epics
1181.C6 Comic
1181.R4 Religious
1185 Ballads
Translations see PT1160+
Lyric
1187 General
Special
(1189) Medieval
see PT1419+
(1190) (15th-) 16th century
see PT1163+
(1192) 17th century
see PT1163+

Collections of German literature
Poetry
Special kinds
Lyric
Special -- Continued
(1193) 18th century
see PT1167+
(1194) 19th century
see PT1171+
(1195) 20th century
see PT1174+
Volkslied
Cf. ML, Music
1199 Periodicals. Societies
Collections
General
1201 Early to 1770. By editor or title
Including editions of manuscript collections, reprints of broadsides and early editions
Later, 1770-
1203 Comprehensive
e.g.
1203.A7 Arnim's Des Knaben Wunderhorn
(1204) By period
see PT1201+
1205.A-Z By region or place, A-Z
e.g.
Cf. PT3801+ German literature by region, etc.
1205.A8 Austria
1205.B3 Bavaria
1205.C7 Cologne
1205.C9 Czechoslovakia
1205.E8 Erzgebirge
1205.G3 Galicia
1205.H3 Hanover
1205.L8 Luxemburg
1205.N2 Nassau
1205.P2 Palatinate
1205.P8 Prussia
1205.R5 Rhine
1205.S3 Schleswig-Holstein
1205.S8 Styria
1205.S85 Swabia
1205.S9 Switzerland
1205.T9 Tyrol
1205.V5 Vienna
1205.V7 Voralberg

Collections of German literature
Poetry
Special kinds
Volkslied
Collections
By region or place, A-Z -- Continued
1205.W4 Westphalia
By subject
Historico-politico
1206 Medieval to 1600
1207 Medieval and modern
1209 (15th-) 16th century. Reformation, etc.
1211 (16th-) 17th century. Thirty years' war, etc.
1213 (17th-) 18th century. Seven years' war, etc.
1217 (18th-) 19th century
1221 (19th-) 20th century
1222 (20th-) 21st century
(1225.A-Z) Special persons, A-Z
For political figures see PT1206+
For other persons see PT1231.A+
(1227) Songs of special armies
see PT1231.S6
1229 Religious poetry
1231.A-Z Other special, A-Z
1231.A3 Aeronautics
1231.A4 Agriculture
1231.A5 Album verses
1231.A7 Arts
1231.B5 Blind
1231.B7 Brecht, Bertold
1231.B73 Büchner, Georg, 1813-1837
1231.B75 Building
1231.B8 Butterflies
1231.C38 Cathedrals
1231.C48 Children
1231.C5 Children's songs
1231.C53 Christmas
1231.C55 Cities and towns
1231.C57 Clocks and watches
1231.C6 Consolation
1231.D43 Death
1231.D7 Drinking songs. Drinking customs
1231.D8 Dürer, Albrecht, 1471-1528. Knight, Death and the Devil
1231.E2 Easter
1231.E7 Erotic poetry
1231.F6 Flowers

Collections of German literature
Poetry
Special kinds
By subject
Other special, A-Z -- Continued

1231.F8 Freemasonry
1231.G34 Gall, Saint, ca. 550-ca. 630
1231.G38 Gastronomy
1231.G7 Grace (at meals)
1231.H35 Happiness
1231.H36 Harvesting
1231.H5 Hiking. "Wanderlieder"
1231.H6 Horsemanship
1231.H8 Humor
1231.H85 Hunting
1231.J4 Jews
1231.L2 Labor
1231.L4 Legends, Germanic
1231.L6 Love
1231.M45 Melancholy
1231.M5 Miners
1231.M6 Moors and heaths
1231.M7 Mothers
1231.N3 Nature
1231.N5 Night
1231.P4 Peasants
Places
1231.P6 General collections
1231.P7A-.P7Z By region or country, A-Z
1231.P8 Police
1231.R4 Reinig, Christa
1231.S3 Saints' days
1231.S31-.S39 Special saints
1231.S36 Martinslieder
1231.S4 Seas and sailors
1231.S6 Soldiers' songs
1231.S8 Students
1231.T3 Tannhäuser
1231.T45 Theater
1231.T6 Tobacco
1231.T8 Trades. Arbeiterlieder
Travels see PT1231.V69
1231.T82 Trees
1231.V56 Violets
1231.V69 Voyages and travels
1231.W5 Winter

Collections of German literature
Poetry
Special kinds -- Continued
1232.A-Z Particular ballads and songs, A-Z
By first word of title
Other forms
1233 Didactic poetry
1235 Epigrams
1237 Fables in verse
Cf. PT1356 Fables in prose
1239 Gnomic verse
1241.A-Z Minor forms, A-Z
1241.B7 Brettl-lieder (Chansons)
1241.C3 Canzone
1241.C6 Concrete poetry
1241.C65 Couplets
1241.E6 Elegies
1241.I6 Idylls
1241.L55 Limericks
1241.M3 Madrigals
1241.N6 Nonsense verses
1241.O22 Occasional verse
1241.O3 Odes
1241.P7 Prose poems
1241.S4 Schüttelreim (Spoonerisms)
1241.S6 Sonnets
Drama
Comprehensive
1251 Early through 1800
1253 1801-
1255 Selected plays. Anthologies
Translations
(1256) From foreign literature into German
see PA-PT
From German into foreign languages
1257 Polyglot
1258 English
1259 French
1260.A-Z Other languages, A-Z
By period
(1262) Medieval
see PT1435+
1263 16th century. Reformation
1264 17th century
1265 18th century
1266 19th century
20th century

Collections of German literature
Drama
By period
20th century -- Continued
1268.A-.Z8 General works
1268.Z9 Copyright deposit. Uncataloged
1268.Z99 Plays in typewritten form
1269 21st century
Special kinds
Tragedies
1271 General works
1273.A-Z Translations. By language, A-Z
Comedies
1275 General works
1277.A-Z Translations. By language, A-Z
Drama (Schauspiel)
1279 General works
1281.A-Z Special forms, subjects, etc., A-Z
1281.B8 "Bürgerliches" drama
1281.H5 Historical drama
(1281.M6) Motion picture plays
see PN1997
1281.P4 Peasants' War, 1524-1525
1281.R3 Radio plays
1281.R4 Religious drama
1281.R5 "Ritterdrama"
1281.S3 "Schicksalsdrama"
1283.A-Z Minor forms, A-Z
1283.F2 Farces
1283.I5 Interludes, etc.
1283.P3 Parodies
1285 Amateur drama
Popular drama. Folk-drama
Cf. PT925.A1+ Faust legend (drama)
1287 General works
Special
1289 Christmas plays. "Krippenspiele"
1290 Passion plays
Cf. PN3241 Oberammergau play
1291.A-Z Other special, A-Z
(1297) Puppet plays
see PN1981; PT925
Shadow plays see PN6120.S5
1299.A-Z Individual plays, A-Z
Prose
Comprehensive
1301 Early through 1800

Collections of German literature
Prose
Comprehensive -- Continued
1303 1801-
1305 Selections, anthologies, etc.
(1306) Translations from foreign literatures into German
see PA-PT
Translations from German into other languages
1307 Polyglot
1308.A-Z English. By translator, A-Z
1309.A-Z French. By translator, A-Z
1310.A-Z Other languages, A-Z
By period
(1311) Old High German
see PF3985+
(1312) Middle High German
see PT1479
1313 (15th-) 16th century. Reformation
1314 (16th-) 17th century
1315 (17th-) 18th century
1316 (18th-) 19th century
1318 (19th-) 20th century
1319 (20th-) 21st century
Prose fiction
Comprehensive
1321 Early through 1800
1323 Recent, 1801-
1324 Selections, anthologies, etc.
(1325) Translations from foreign literatures into German
see PA-PT
Translations from German into other languages
1326 Polyglot
1327 English
1328 French
1329.A-Z Other languages, A-Z
By period
(1330) Middle High German
see PT1479
(1331) 15th-18th centuries
see PT1313
1332 19th century
1334 20th century
1335 21st century
Short stories. "Novellen"
1337 Comprehensive collections. Serials
1338 Minor (including school texts)

Collections of German literature
Prose fiction
Short stories. "Novellen" -- Continued

(1339) Translations
see PT1326+

1340.A-Z Special forms, subjects, etc., A-Z
1340.C45 Children
1340.C5 Christmas
1340.D4 Detective and mystery stories
Dorfgeschichte see PT1340.P43
1340.F33 Family
1340.F35 Fantastic fiction
1340.G39 Gay men
1340.H6 Horror tales
1340.H7 House plants
1340.H8 Hunting stories
1340.K8 Kunstmärchen. Fairy tales
1340.L3 Lawyers. Judges
1340.L6 Love stories
1340.M4 Men
1340.M57 Money
1340.M6 Mothers
1340.P43 Peasant tales. Dorfgeschichte
1340.P6 Pomerania
1340.R6 Romantic
1340.S35 Schools
1340.S36 Science fiction
1340.S4 Sequels
1340.S55 Skis and skiing
1340.S6 Sports stories
1340.S8 Students
1340.T45 Third Reich
Travels see PT1340.V65
1340.V5 Violence
1340.V65 Voyages and travels
1340.W35 War
1340.W4 Weimar Republic
1340.W65 Women

(1341) Chapbooks
see PT905+, PT923+

Oratory
1344 Through 1800
1345 1801-

Letters
1348 Collections. Selections
By period
1349 Through 1800

Collections of German literature
Letters
By period -- Continued
1350 1801-
1352.A-Z Special, A-Z
1352.B5 Birthday letters
1352.C5 Children (Letters to or from children)
1352.C55 Christmas letters
1352.E4 Emigrants
1352.L8 Love letters
1352.M7 Mothers (letters to or from mothers)
1352.N4 New Year letters
1352.W8 Women's letters
1354 Essays
1356 Fables (in prose)
Cf. PT1237 Poetry
1358 Wit and humor
1359 Minor collections
For less literary productions see PN6193+
1360 Miscellaneous
Cf. PN6246, PN6253, PN6263, etc.
By period
To 1500
Collections comprising both Old and Middle High German works
1371 General
1372 Selections, anthologies, etc.
(1373) Translations
see PT1383+
(1374) Old High German (to ca. 1100)
see PF3985+
Middle High German
Collections
1375 Comprehensive
1377 Selections, anthologies, etc.
Cf. PF4069 Readers
Special periods
1379 To 1300/1350
1380 14th-15th centuries
1381 15th century
Translations
1383 Modern Germany
1384 English
1385.A-Z Other. By language, A-Z
By form
Poetry
General collections

Middle High German
Collections
By form
Poetry
General collections -- Continued
1391 Comprehensive
1392 Selections, anthologies, etc.
Translations
1394 Modern German
1396 English
1397.A-Z Other. By language, A-Z
Special periods
1399 To 1300/50
1401 14th-15th centuries
1402 15th century
1405.A-Z Special regions, A-Z
Special forms
Epic
1411 Comprehensive (Collections and selections)
Popular epics
1413.A-Z Collections. By title or editor, A-Z
1413.A4 Ambraser Heldenbuch
1413.D5 Dietrich cycle
1413.H3 Hagen. Heldenbuch
1413.H4 Heldenbuch. Frankfort am Main, 1590
1413.K3 Kaspar von der Rön. Heldenbuch
1413.P5 Piper. Spielmannsdichtung
1413.S73 Strassburger Heldenbuch
1414.A-Z Translations. By language and translator, A-Z
Special epics
see the titles in PT1501+
1415 Court epics
1417 Other (Narrative poetry)
1417.3.A-Z Translations. By language, A-Z
1418 Adaptations, paraphrases, tales
Juvenile literature see PZ31+
Lyric
Minnesingers
1419.A-Z Medieval collections
1419.B3 Basel. Universität Bibliothek. MSS. (N.1.3.)
1419.C3 Carmina burana
Cf. PA8133.S8 Latin
1419.H2 Haagsche liedernhandschrift
For German songs only
Cf. PT5559.H2 Dutch
1419.H4 Heidelberger liederhandschrift, Grosse
1419.H5 Heidelberger liederhandschrift, Kleine

Middle High German
Collections
By form
Poetry
Special forms
Lyric
Minnesingers
Medieval collections -- Continued

1419.J3 Jenaer liederhandschrift
1419.K6 Königsteiner Liederbuch
(1419.M3) Manesse's liederhandschrift
see PT1419.H4
1419.S73 Sterzinger Miszellaneen-Handschrift
1419.W4 Weingarten liederhandschrift
1421 Modern collections
Translations
1424 Modern German
1425 English
1426.A-Z Other. By language, A-Z
(1427) (14th-) 15th century
see PT1163
1429.A-Z Other special, A-Z
1429.D5 Didactic
1429.M5 Minnereden
1429.P6 Political
1429.R4 Religious
Drama, ca. 1300-1600
1435 Comprehensive
1436 Minor. Selections, anthologies, etc.
1437 Translations
Special
Mysteries
1438 Comprehensive
1439 Medieval and early modern collections
e.g. Erlauer spiele, Sterzinger spiele, etc.
1440 Modern selections
1441 Translations
Easter plays
1443 General
1444.A-Z Special. By place or title, A-Z
e.g.
1444.L8 Lucerne
Passion plays
1446 General
1448.A-Z Special. By place or title, A-Z
e.g.
1448.F7 Friedberg

Middle High German
Collections
By form
Drama, ca. 1300-1600
Special
Mysteries
Passion plays -- Continued
1450 Marienklagen
Modern survivals, imitations, etc.
Cf. PT1290 Popular and folk drama
1452 General
1453.A-Z Special. By place or title, A-Z
Oberammergau see PN3235+
Christmas plays
1455 General
1456.A-Z Special plays, A-Z
1457 Modern survivals, imitations, etc.
Cf. PT1289 Popular and folk drama
1457.A2 General
1457.A5-Z Special, A-Z
Minor festival plays
Epiphany
1459.A2 General works
1459.A5-Z Special plays
Ascension
1460.A2 General works
1460.A5-Z Special plays
Corpus Christi (Fronleichnam)
1461.A2 General works
1461.A5-Z Special plays
1462 Other
Plays from the Old Testament
1464.A2 General
1464.A5-Z Special plays
Plays from the New Testament
1466.A2 General
1466.A5-Z Special plays
Legends and miracles dramatized
1468 General
1469.A-Z Special plays. By saint or title, A-Z
1471 Other
e.g. Frau Jutten; Weltgerichtspiel
Moralities
1473.A2 General
1473.A5-Z Special plays
1475 Fastnachtsspiele
1477 Translations

Middle High German
Collections
By form
Drama, ca. 1300-1600
Special -- Continued
Low German drama see PT4837+
1479 Prose
Translations
see PT1112+ General
Individual authors or works
Middle High German, ca. 1050-1450/1500
Subarrange authors by Table P-PZ38 unless otherwise specified
Subarrange works by Table P-PZ43 unless otherwise specified
1501 A - Az
Der Ackermann aus Böhmen see PT1548.J53
Adam und Eva see PT1566.L9
(1501.A24) Ältere Judith (Middle High German poem)
see PT1548.J77
1501.A26-.A263 Afra, Saint. Legend (Table P-PZ43)
1501.A27 Albert, von Stade, d. ca. 1260 (Table P-PZ38)
Albrecht, author of Der jüngere Titurel see PT1501.A4
Albrecht von Eyb see PT1517.E8
1501.A3 Albrecht von Halberstadt, fl. 1210-1218 (Table P-PZ38)
1501.A35 Albrecht von Johannsdorf, fl. 1190 (Table P-PZ38)
1501.A4 Albrecht von Scharfenberg, 13th cent. (Table P-PZ40 modified)
1501.A4A61-.A4Z458 Separate works. By title
1501.A4M5 Merlin
1501.A4T4 Titurel, Der jüngere (authorship doubtful)
Alexanderlied see PT1560+
1501.A59-.A593 Alexius, Saint. Legend (Table P-PZ43)
Cf. PT1556+ Konrad von Würzburg
1501.A62-.A623 Alpharts tod (Table P-PZ43)
Alsfelder passionsspiel see PT1448.A+
1501.A65 Altswert, meister (Table P-PZ38)
1501.A67-.A673 Anegenge (Das jüngere Anegenge) (Table P-PZ43)
Cf. PT1517.E9
1501.A7-.A713 Annolied (Table P-PZ43a)
1501.A72-.A723 Antichrist (Table P-PZ43)
Apollonius von Tyrland see PT1537.H84
Der arme Heinrich see PT1534.A6+
1501.A74 Arnold, priest, 12th cent. (Table P-PZ38)
1501.A75-.A753 Artus-Hof (Table P-PZ43)
1501.A9 Ava, d. 1127 (Table P-PZ38)
1503 B - Bi

Individual authors or works
Middle High German, ca. 1050-1450/1500
B - Bi -- Continued

1503.B2-.B23 Barlaam (Poem by Otto II, bp. of Freising) (Table P-PZ43)
Barthel Regenbogen see PT1637.R4
1503.B3-.B33 Baumgarten geistlicher Herzen (Table P-PZ43)
1503.B5 Beheim, Michael, b. 1416 (Table P-PZ38)
1503.B66-.B663 Berliner Weltgerichtsspiel (Table P-PZ43)
1503.B7 Berthold von Holle, 13th cent. (Table P-PZ38)
1503.B8 Berthold von Regensburg, d. 1272 (Table P-PZ38)
1505 Bible
Class here poetical paraphrases and Bible stories only
1505.B27 Complete
1505.B28 Selections
Old Testament
1505.B29 General works
Complete or several parts
1505.B3 Pentateuch
1505.B31 Genesis
1505.B32 Exodus
1505.B33 Judges
1505.B335 Ruth
1505.B34 Samuel
1505.B35 Kings
1505.B355 Job
1505.B36 Psalms
1505.B37 Proverbs
Prophets
Including Minor Prophets or selections
1505.B38 General
1505.B381 Isaiah
1505.B382 Jeremiah
1505.B383 Ezekiel
1505.B384 Daniel
1505.B39 Other canonical books
1505.B398 Apocrypha. Maccabees, etc.
New Testament
1505.B4 General
Complete or several parts
1505.B41 Selection
Gospels
1505.B42 General works
1505.B43 Matthew
1505.B44 Mark
1505.B45 Luke
1505.B46 John

Individual authors or works
Middle High German, ca. 1050-1450/1500
Bible
New Testament -- Continued

1505.B47 Acts
Epistles
1505.B48 General works
Complete or several parts
1505.B481 Romans
1505.B482 Corinthians
1505.B483 Ephesians
1505.B484 Galatians
1505.B485 Philippians
1505.B486 Colossians
1505.B487 Thessalonians
1505.B488 Timothy. Titus
1505.B489 Philemon
1505.B49 Hebrews
1505.B491 James
1505.B492 Peter
1505.B493 John
1505.B494 Jude
1505.B5 Revelation
Cf. PT1537.H5 Heinrich von Hesler
1505.B6 Apocrypha. Gospel of Nicodemus, etc.
Cf. PT1537.H5 Heinrich von Hesler
1505.B9 Historienbibeln
(1505.Z5) History and criticism (General)
see BS460.G3
1507 Bi - Br
1507.B3-.B33 Biterolf und Dietleib (Table P-PZ43)
1507.B7 Boner, Ulrich, 14th cent. (Table P-PZ38)
1507.B74 Bote, Hermann, ca. 1465-1520 (Table P-PZ40)
Brandan, Saint, Legend see PT1511.B5+
1509 Brant, Sebastian, 1458-1521 (Table P-PZ39 modified)
1509.A61-.Z48 Separate works. By title
Subarrange each work by Table P-PZ43 unless otherwise specified
1509.N2-.N79 Narrenschiff
1509.N2 Editions. By date
Including the anonymous revised editions
1509.N23 Extracts, partial refacimentos, etc.
1509.N25 Low German versions. By date
1509.N28A-.N28Z Modern German versions. By author, A-Z
Translations
1509.N31-.N39 Latin (alphabetically by translator)
1509.N4 Latin and English

Individual authors or works
Middle High German, ca. 1050-1450/1500
Brant, Sebastian, 1458-1521
Separate works. By title
Narrenschiff
Translations -- Continued

1509.N41-.N49 English (alphabetically by translator)
Barclay's translation see PR2209.B3
1509.N51-.N59 French (alphabetically by translator)
1509.N71-.N79 Other languages (alphabetically)
1509.Z7 Grammar. Syntax
1509.Z8 Versification
1509.Z9 Glossaries
1511 Bra - Bro
1511.B5-.B53 Brendan, Saint. Legend (Table P-PZ43)
1511.B54-.B543 Brief an die Frau von Plauen (Table P-PZ43)
1511.B545-.B5453 British Library. Manuscript. Arundel 164, fol. 108v-121v (Table P-PZ43)
1511.B56-.B563 British Library. Manuscript. Harleian 3971 (Table P-PZ43)
1512 Bru - Bz
1512.B25 Brun von Schonebeck, 13th cent. (Table P-PZ38)
1512.B3-.B33 Das buch der beispiele (Translation of Bidpai) (Table P-PZ43)
Bühel, Hans von see PT1533.H7
Büheler, Hans der see PT1533.H7
1512.B8 Burkhart von Hohenfels, fl. 1226-1229 (Table P-PZ38)
1513 C - Cz
(1513.C3) Carmina burana
see PT1419.C3
1513.C4-.C43 Catonis disticha (Table P-PZ43)
1513.C57-.C573 Christherre-Chronik (Table P-PZ43)
1513.C65-.C653 Codex Esterházy (Table P-PZ43)
1513.C7 Colin, Philipp, 14th cent. (Table P-PZ38)
Joint author with Claus Wisse, PT1679.W85
(1513.C8) Crescentia
see PT1551.K2
1515 D - Dz
1515.D25 Damen, Hermann, ca. 1255-1307 or 9
Daniel von dem blühenden thal (von Blumenthal) see PT1653.D3+
1515.D3 Dankrotzheim, Konrad, d. 1444 (Table P-PZ38)
1515.D35-.D353 Darmstädter Gedicht über das Weltende (Table P-PZ43)
David von Augsburg, d. 1271 see BV5070+
1515.D4-.D43 Dietrichs erste ausfahrt (Table P-PZ43)
Dietrichs flucht see PT1537.H25
1515.D5-.D53 Dietrich und seine gesellen (Table P-PZ43)
1515.D6-.D63 Dietrich und Wenezlan (Table P-PZ43)

Individual authors or works
Middle High German, ca. 1050-1450/1500
D - Dz -- Continued

1515.D7 Dietrich von der Glezze, 13th cent. (Table P-PZ38)
Disticha Catonis see PT1513.C4+
1515.D74-.D743 Dresden. Sächsische Landesbibliothek. MSS. (Cod. germ. chart. M68 (d)) (Table P-PZ43)
1515.D84-.D843 Dresdener Heldenbuch (Table P-PZ43)
Dukus Horant see PJ5129.A15+
1515.D9-.D93 Dulciflorie (Table P-PZ43)
1517 E - Ez
1517.E12 Eberhard von Cersne (Table P-PZ38)
1517.E15 Ebernant, of Erfurt, fl. 1200 (Table P-PZ38)
1517.E16 Ebner, Christina, 1277-1356 (Table P-PZ38)
Eckenlied. Ecke. Ecken aussfart
Cf. PT209.E3
1517.E18 Texts. By date
1517.E2A-.E2Z Modern versions. By editor, A-Z
1517.E22 Criticism
Edelstein see PT1507.B7
1517.E35 Egen von Bamberg, 14th cent. (Table P-PZ38)
Egenolf, von Staufenberg, d. ca. 1324 see PT1651.S78
Egerer fronleichnamsspiel see PT1461.A2+
1517.E37 Ehingen, Georg van, 1428-1508 (Table P-PZ38)
1517.E4 Eilhard von Oberge, 12th cent. (Table P-PZ38)
1517.E42-.E423 Eisenacher Zehnjungfrauenspiel (Table P-PZ43)
1517.E43 Elisabeth, countess of Nassau-Saarbrücken, d. 1456 (Table P-PZ38)
1517.E45-.E453 Elizabeth of Hungary, Saint, Life of. Leben der heiligen Elisabeth (Table P-PZ43)
Biography in verse written about 1300
Ems, Rudolf von see PT1647+
Eneide see PT1540.E6+
Engelhart und Engeltrut see PT1556.E6+
1517.E5 Enikel, Jansen, 13th cent. (Table P-PZ38)
Eraclius see PT1631.O8
Erec see PT1534.E7+
Erlauer spiele see PT1446+
1517.E65-.E653 Die erlösung (Table P-PZ43)
Ernst, Herzog see PT1543.H32+
Eschenbach, Ulrich von see PT1661.U3
Eschenbach, Wolfram von see PT1682+
Eulenspiegel see PT941.E8+
Evangelium Nicodemi see PT1505.B6
Exodus see PT1505.B32
1517.E8 Eyb, Albrecht von, 1420-1475 (Table P-PZ38)

Individual authors or works
Middle High German, ca. 1050-1450/1500
E - Ez -- Continued
1517.E9 Ezzo von Bamberg, 11th cent. (Table P-PZ38)
Cf. PT1501.A67+ Anegenge (Das jüngere)
Ezzolied (Anegenge) see PT1517.E9
1519 F - Fr
1519.F15-.F153 Facetus (Table P-PZ43)
Fastnachtsspiele see PT1475
1519.F3 Fleck, Konrad, 13th cent. (Table P-PZ38)
Flore und Blancheflur see PT1519.F3
1519.F4 Folz, Hans, 15th cent. (Table P-PZ38)
Frau Jutten (Play) see PT1471
1519.F7 Frauenlob, d. 1318 (Table P-PZ38)
Freiberg, Heinrich von see PT1537.H4
1521 Freidank, 13th cent. (Table P-PZ37)
1522 Freid - Fz
1522.F3 Fressant, Hermann, 14th cent. (Table P-PZ38)
Friedberger passionsspiel see PT1448.F7
1522.F4 Friedrich von Hausen, d. 1190 (Table P-PZ38)
1522.F5-.F53 Friedrich von Schwaben (Epic poem) (Table P-PZ43)
1522.F6 Friedrich von Sunburg, 13th cent. (Table P-PZ38)
Fronleichnamsspiele see PT1461.A2+
1522.F8 Füetrer, Ulrich, 15th cent. (Table P-PZ38)
Fussesbrunnen, Konrad von see PT1555.K2
1524 G - Go
Garel von dem blüenden tal see PT1636.P2
Gauriel von Muntabel see PT1555.K6
(1524.G4) Geiler, Johannes, von Kaisersberg
see BX890
1524.G47-.G473 Geistlicher Spiegel der armen sündigen Seele (Table P-PZ43)
Genesis see PT1505.B31
Gerhard, Der gute see PT1647.G92+
Gericht, Jüngste see PT1664.V77+
1524.G5-.G53 Gesta Romanorum (Table P-PZ43)
Middle High German texts
Cf. PA8320+ Medieval Latin literature
Glichesaere see PT1536.H8
1524.G6-.G63 Göttweiger Trojanerkrieg (Table P-PZ43)
1524.G65-.G653 Goldemar (Table P-PZ43)
Goldene schmiede see PT1556.G8+
Gottesfreund in Oberland see PT1567.M7
1524.G8 Gottfried von Neifen, fl. 1234-1255 (Table P-PZ38)
Gottfried von Strassburg, 13th cent.
(Tristan, only known work)
1525.A1 Anonymous editions. By date

Individual authors or works
Middle High German, ca. 1050-1450/1500
Gottfried von Strassburg, 13th cent. -- Continued

1525.A2 Editions. By editor, A-Z
1525.A21-.A29 Selections. By editor
Translations
1525.A3-.A39 Modern German
1525.A4-.A49 English
1525.A5-.A59 French
1525.A6-.A69 Other languages (alphabetically)
Biography and criticism
1526.A1-.Z3 General and textual criticism
1526.Z4 Language, metrics, etc.
1526.Z5 Dictionaries
1526.Z7 Glossaries
1527 Gott - Gu
Gregorius see PT1534.G7+
1527.G43 Grissaphan, Georgius, 14th cent. (Table P-PZ38)
Gudrun
1528.A1 Anonymous editions. By date
1528.A2 Editions. By editor, A-Z
1528.A21-.A29 Selections. By editor
Translations
1528.A3-.A39 Modern German
1528.A4-.A49 English
1528.A5-.A59 French
1528.A6-.A69 Other languages (alphabetically)
1529 Criticism
1529.A1-.Z3 General and textual criticism
1529.Z5 Language, metrics, etc.
1529.Z7 Dictionaries, glossaries, etc.
1530 Gud - Gz
1530.G5 Gundacker von Judenburg, 13th cent. (Table P-PZ38)
1533 H - Hart
1533.H2 Hadamar von Laber, 14th cent. (Table P-PZ38)
1533.H3 Hadlaub, Johannes, fl. 1300 (Table P-PZ38)
1533.H35-.H353 Das Häslein (Table P-PZ43)
1533.H37 Hätzler, Klara, 15th cent. (Table P-PZ38)
1533.H38 Hage, Hartwig von dem (Table P-PZ38)
1533.H4 Hagen, Gotfrid, d. ca. 1301 (Table P-PZ38)
Die halbe bier see PT1556.H2+
Halberstadt, Albrecht von see PT1501.A3
1533.H64 Haller, Heinrich, fl. 1455-1471 (Table P-PZ38)
1533.H68 Hans, Brother, fl. ca. 1400 (Table P-PZ38)
1533.H7 Hans von Bühel, fl. 1400-1412 (Table P-PZ38)
1533.H75 Hartlieb, Johann, fl. 1450 (Table P-PZ38)

Individual authors or works
Middle High German, ca. 1050-1450/1500
H - Hart -- Continued

1533.H9 Hartmann, der arme, fl. ca. 1140 (Table P-PZ38)
Author of Rede vom glouven

Hartmann von Aue, 12th cent.
Collected works

1534.A1 Anonymous editions. By date

1534.A2A-.A2Z By editor, A-Z

1534.A25 Selections, extracts, etc. By date

Translations

1534.A3A3-.A3A39 Modern German versions. By translator alphabetically

1534.A3A4-.A3Z Other. By language, A-Z

1534.A4-Z Separate works

1534.A4 Lyrical poems

1534.A45 Büchlein (1st and 2d)

1534.A5 Lieder

1534.A59 Criticism

Other works. By title

1534.A6-.A9 Der arme Heinrich

1534.A6A-.A6Z Editions. By editor, A-Z

Translations

1534.A7 English

1534.A71-.A79 Other

1534.A8 Criticism

(1534.A9) Dictionaries
see PT1535.Z82

Erec

1534.E7A-.E7Z Editions. By editor, A-Z

Translations

1534.E8 English

1534.E81-.E89 Other

1534.E9 Criticism

Dictionaries see PT1535.Z83

Gregorius

1534.G7A-.G7Z Editions. By editor, A-Z

1534.G73A-.G73Z Translations. By language, A-Z

1534.G8 Criticism

Dictionaries see PT1535.Z84

Iwein

1534.I2A-.I2Z Editions. By editor, A-Z

Translations

1534.I3 English

1534.I31-.I39 Other

1534.I5 Criticism

(1534.I9) Dictionaries
see PT1535.Z85

Individual authors or works
Middle High German, ca. 1050-1450/1500
Hartmann von Aue, 12th cent. -- Continued
Biography and criticism
1535.A1-.Z3 General works
1535.Z4 Language. Metrics, etc.
Dictionaries, glossaries, etc. By date
1535.Z8 General
1535.Z81 Poems
1535.Z82 Arme Heinrich
1535.Z83 Erec
1535.Z84 Gregorius
1535.Z85 Iwein
1536.H15 Hartmann von Starkenburg, 13th cent. (Table P-PZ38)
Haslau, Konrad von see PT1555.K3
Hausen, Friedrich von see PT1522.F4
1536.H2 Hayden, Gregor, fl. 1450 (Table P-PZ38 modified)
1536.H2A61-.H2A78 Separate works. By title
Salomon und Markolf see PT1651.S27+
Heidelberger liederhandschriften see PT1419.H4
1536.H24-.H243 Heidin (Table P-PZ43)
1536.H3-.H33 Die heilige regel für ein vollkommenes leben (Table P-PZ43)
1536.H4-.H43 Heimonskinder (Table P-PZ43)
Reinolt von Montelban; Renout van Montalbaen
1536.H8 Heinrich der Glichesaere, 12th cent. (Table P-PZ38)
For Isengrînes nôt (lost) preserved in a revised form entitled "Reinhart Fuchs," by an unknown author of the 14th century see PT1637.R6+
1537.H2 Heinrich der Teichner, fl. 1350-1375 (Table P-PZ38)
1537.H25 Heinrich der Vogler, ca. 1282 (Table P-PZ38)
Supposed author of "Dietrichs flucht" and "Rabenschlacht"
1537.H3 Heinrich von Beringen, 12th cent. (Table P-PZ38)
1537.H33 Heinrich von Burgus, 13th cent. (Table P-PZ38)
1537.H35 Heinrich von dem Türlin, fl. 1220 (Table P-PZ38)
1537.H4 Heinrich von Freiberg, fl. 1300 (Table P-PZ38)
1537.H5 Heinrich von Hesler, fl. 1300 (Table P-PZ38)
Heinrich von Kaufringer see PT1551.K4
1537.H6 Heinrich von Krolewitz, 13th cent. (Table P-PZ38)
1537.H65 Heinrich von Langenstein, 1325 (ca.)-1397 (Table P-PZ40)
Heinrich von Miessen, known as Frauenlob see PT1519.F7
1537.H7 Heinrich von Melk, fl. 1160 (Table P-PZ38)
1537.H8 Heinrich von Morungen, 13th cent. (Table P-PZ38)
1537.H83 Heinrich von Mügeln, fl. 1346-1371 (Table P-PZ38)
1537.H84 Heinrich von Neustadt, fl. 1312 (Table P-PZ38)
1537.H85 Heinrich von Nördlingen, fl. ca. 1340 (Table P-PZ38)
1537.H88 Heinrich von Rugge, 12th cent. (Table P-PZ38)

Individual authors or works
Middle High German, ca. 1050-1450/1500 -- Continued

1540-1541	Heinrich von Veldeke, 12th cent.
	Collected works
1540.A1	Anonymous editions. By date
1540.A2A-.A2Z	By editor, A-Z
1540.A5-Z	Separate works
1540.A5-.A6	Lieder (Table P-PZ43a)
1540.E6-.E7	Eneide (Table P-PZ43a)
1540.S5-.S6	Servatius (Table P-PZ43a)
	Biography and criticism
1541.A1-.Z3	General works
1541.Z4	Language, metrics, etc.
1541.Z5	Dictionaries, glossaries, etc.
1542.H3	Heinrich Clûzênere, 13th cent. (Table P-PZ38)
	Heinrich Laufenberg see PT1563.L2
	Helmbrecht see PT1679.W4
1543.H2	Herbort von Fritzlar, fl. 1190-1217 (Table P-PZ38)
1543.H25	Herger, 12th cent. (Table P-PZ38) Author of poems formerly ascribed to Spervogel
1543.H27	Hermann, Bruder, 13th cent. (Table P-PZ38)
1543.H29	Hermann monk, of Salzburg, 14th cent. (Table P-PZ38)
	Hermann von Sachsenheim see PT1651.S2
1543.H3	Herrand von Wildonie, 1248-1278 (Table P-PZ38)
1543.H32-.H329	Herzog Ernst (Romances) Arrange by letter under which the version is known
1543.H35	Hiltbolt von Schwangau (Table P-PZ38)
1543.H47	Hirschvelder, Bernhard, fl. 1454-1502 (Table P-PZ38)
1543.H5-.H53	Historie von Herzog Leopold und seinem Sohn Wilhelm von Österreich (Table P-PZ43)
	Holle, Berthold von see PT1503.B7
1543.H7-.H73	Hugdietrich (Table P-PZ43)
1543.H8	Hugo von Langenstein, fl. 1282-1319 (Table P-PZ38)
	Hugo von Montfort see PT1568.M4
1545	Hugo von Trimberg, fl. 1260-1309 (Table P-PZ39) Author of "Der renner" and "Der sammler" (lost)
1548	Hu - Jz
1548.H97-.H973	Hystoria von dem wirdigen ritter sant Wilhelm (Table P-PZ43)
1548.I6	Ingold, meister, 15th cent. (Table P-PZ38)
	Isengrînes nôt see PT1536.H8
	Iwein see PT1534.I2+
1548.J14-.J143	Jagd auf einen edden Fasan (Table P-PZ43)
	Jans Enikel see PT1517.E5
	Jenaer liederhandschrift see PT1419.J3
1548.J2	Jeroschin, Nicolaus von, fl. 1335-1347 (Table P-PZ38)
1548.J3-.J33	Johan ûz dem virgiere (Poem) (Table P-PZ43)

Individual authors or works
Middle High German, ca. 1050-1450/1500
Hu - Jz -- Continued

	Johann von Michelsberg, Ritterfahrt des see PT1537.H4
	Johann von Morsheim see PT1568.M6
1548.J46	Johann von Soest, 1448-1506 (Table P-PZ38)
1548.J49	Johann von Vippach, 14th cent. (Table P-PZ38)
1548.J5	Johann von Würzburg, fl. 1314 (Table P-PZ38)
	Johann Hartlieb see PT1533.H75
1548.J53	Johannes, von Tepl, ca. 1350-1414 or 5 (Table P-PZ38)
1548.J54	Johannes Brunwart, von Augheim, Ritter, 13th cent. (Table P-PZ38)
	Johannes Geiler von Kaisersberg see BX890
	Johannes Hadlaub see PT1533.H3
	Johannes Rothe see PT1645.R8
	Johannes Schiltberger see G370.S3
	Johannes Tauler see BV5070+
1548.J6	Johannes von Frankenstein, fl. 1300 (Table P-PZ38)
	Johannes von Saaz see PT1548.J53
	Johannes von Salzburg see PT1543.H29
	Johannsdorf, Albrecht von see PT1501.A35
1548.J77-.J773	Judith (Ältere Judith) (Table P-PZ43)
1548.J78-.J783	Judith (Jüngere Judith) (Table P-PZ43)
1548.J79-.J793	Judith (13th century poem) (Table P-PZ43)
1548.J85	Junge Meissner, 13th/14th cent. (Table P-PZ38)
	Jungfrauen, spiel von den Klugen und Thörichten see PT1466.A2+
1551.K2-.K24	Kaiserchronik (Table P-PZ43a) Cf. PT1553 Konrad, pfaff
	Kaiserberg, Geiler von see BX890
1551.K25-.K253	Karel ende Elegast (Table P-PZ43)
1551.K3-.K33	Karlmeinet (Table P-PZ43)
1551.K335-.K3353	Karlsruhe-Badische Landesbibliothek. MSS. (408) (Table P-PZ43)
1551.K34	Karoch, Samuel, fl. 1466-1476 (Table P-PZ38)
	Kaspar von der Rön, fl. 1474 see PT1413.K3
1551.K4	Kaufringer, Heinrich, 14th cent. (Table P-PZ38)
	Kindheit, Jesu see PT1555.K2
	Die klage see PT1626.N5+
1551.K46-.K463	Kleine Lucidarius (Seigfried Helbling) (Table P-PZ43) Cf. PT1566.L8+ Lucidarius
	Die kleine Rosengarten see PT1563.L3+
1551.K48-.K483	Kloster der Minne (Table P-PZ43)
1551.K56-.K563	König im Bade (Table P-PZ43)
1551.K6-.K63	König Rother (Table P-PZ43)
1551.K7-.K73	König vom Odenwalde (Table P-PZ43)

Individual authors or works
Middle High German, ca. 1050-1450/1500 -- Continued

1551.K8-.K83 Königin von Frankreich (Table P-PZ43)
For Schondoch's poem see PT1651.S35
Cf. PT1533.H7 Hans van Bühel, Königstochter von Frankreich

1553 Konrad, pfaff, 12th cent. (Table P-PZ37)

1555.K2 Konrad von Fussesbrunnen, fl. 1162-1187 (Table P-PZ38)

1555.K3 Konrad von Haslau, 13th cent. (Table P-PZ38)

1555.K4 Konrad von Heimesfurt, 13th cent. (Table P-PZ38)

1555.K43 Konrad von Helmsdorf, 14th cent. (Table P-PZ38)

1555.K45 Konrad von Landegg, fl. 1271-1304 (Table P-PZ38)

1555.K5 Konrad von Megenberg, 14th cent. (Table P-PZ38)

1555.K6 Konrad von Stoffel, 13th cent. (Table P-PZ38)

Konrad von Würzburg, d. 1287

Collected works

1556.A1 Anonymous editions. By date

1556.A2A-.A2Z By editor, A-Z

1556.A3A-.A3Z Selections, extracts, etc. By editor, A-Z

1556.A4A-.A4Z Translations. By language, A-Z

1556.A5 Lieder

1556.A59 Criticism

1556.A6 Selected works. By date

1556.A7-.W4 Separate works

1556.A7-.A73 Alexius (Table P-PZ43)

1556.E6-.E63 Engelhart (Engelhard) und Engeltrut (Table P-PZ43)

1556.G8-.G83 Goldene schmiede (Table P-PZ43)

1556.H2-.H23 Die halbe bir (doubtful authorship) (Table P-PZ43)

1556.H4-.H43 Das Herze (Herzmähre, Herzemaere) (Table P-PZ43)

1556.K2-.K23 Kaiser Otte (Otte (Otto) mit dem barte) (Table P-PZ43)

1556.K5-.K53 Klage der kunst (Table P-PZ43)

1556.P3-.P33 Pantaleon (Table P-PZ43)

1556.P5-.P53 Partonopier und Meliur (Table P-PZ43)

1556.S2-.S23 Sant (Sanct) Nicolaus (authorship spurius) (Table P-PZ43)

1556.S3-.S33 Schwanritter (Table P-PZ43)

1556.S5-.S53 Silvester (Table P-PZ43)

1556.T7-.T73 Der Trojanische krieg (Trojanerkrieg) (Table P-PZ43)

1556.T9-.T93 Turnei von Nantheiz (Nanteis) (Table P-PZ43)

1556.W4-.W43 Der wërlte lôn (Der welt lohn) (Table P-PZ43)

Biography and criticism

1557.A1-.Z3 General

1557.Z4 Language, metrics, etc.

1557.Z6 Dictionaries, vocabularies, etc.

1557.Z7 Glossaries

1559 Konrad A - Lam

Konrad Dankrotzheim see PT1515.D3

Individual authors or works
Middle High German, ca. 1050-1450/1500
Konrad A - Lam -- Continued
Konrad Fleck see PT1519.F3
1559.K6 Konrad Muskatblüt, fl. 1453-1458 (Table P-PZ38)
Not to be confused with Muskatblüt, fl. 1420, PT1568.M9
1559.K64-.K643 Kopenhagener Weltgerichtsspiel (Table P-PZ43)
1559.K7-.K72 Kreuzenstein passion play (Table P-PZ43a)
1559.K73-.K733 Die Kreuzfahrt Ludwigs des Frommen (Table P-PZ43)
Der Kreuziger see PT1548.J6
Krolewitz, Heinrich von see PT1537.H35
Die Krone (Diu crône) see PT1537.H35
1559.K78 Kuchimeister, Christian, 14th cent. (Table P-PZ38)
Kudrun see PT1528+
1559.K8 Kürenberg, 12th cent. (Table P-PZ38)
Laber, Hadamar von see PT1533.H2
Lamprecht der pfaffe, 12th cent.
"Alexander," only known work
1560.A1 Anonymous editions. By date
1560.A2A-.A2Z Editions. By editor, A-Z
1560.A21-.A29 Selections. By editor
Translations
1560.A3-.A39 Modern German
1560.A4-.A49 English
1560.A5-.A59 French
1560.A6-.A69 Other languages (alphabetically)
Biography and criticism
1561.A1-.Z3 General and textual criticism
1561.Z4 Language, metrics, etc.
1561.Z5 Dictionaries, vocabularies
1561.Z7 Glossaries
1563 Lamp - Lich
Langenstein, Hugo von see PT1543.H8
1563.L15-.L153 Lanzelot (Prose romance) (Table P-PZ43)
1563.L2 Laufenberg, Heinrich, d. 1460 (Table P-PZ38)
1563.L3-.L33 Laurin (Table P-PZ43)
1563.L4-.L43 Laurin und Walberan (Table P-PZ43)
Lichtenstein, Ulrich von, fl. 1255
Collected works
1564.A1 Anonymous editions. By date
1564.A2 By editor
1564.A3A-.A3Z Translations (Collected or selected). By language, A-Z
1564.A4 Selected works. Selections. By date
1564.A5-Z Separate works. By title
1564.A5 Lieder
1564.F6-.F63 Frauenbuch (Table P-PZ43)
1564.F7-.F73 Frauendienst (Table P-PZ43)

Individual authors or works
Middle High German, ca. 1050-1450/1500
Lichtenstein, Ulrich von, fl. 1255 -- Continued
Biography and criticism

1565.A2 Dictionaries, indexes, etc. By date
1565.A3-.A39 Autobiography, journals, memoirs. By title
1565.A4 Letters (Collections). By date
1565.A41-.A49 Letters to and from particular individuals. By correspondent (alphabetically)
1565.A5-.Z39 General works
1565.Z4 Language, metrics, etc.
1565.Z5 Dictionaries
1566 Lic - Lz
1566.L27-.L273 Liebende und die Burg der Ehre (Table P-PZ43)
1566.L28-.L283 Liebesfreuden und -leiden (Table P-PZ43)
1566.L29-.L293 Lied vom Hürnen Seyfrid (Table P-PZ43)
1566.L3-.L33 Die lilie (Table P-PZ43)
1566.L37 Lirer, Thomas, 12th? cent. (Table P-PZ38)
1566.L5-.L53 Livländische Reimchronik (Table P-PZ43)
1566.L55-.L553 Das Lob Salomons (Middle High German poem) (Table P-PZ43)
1566.L6-.L61 Lof der reinster vrowen, 13th cent. (Table P-PZ43a)
1566.L7-.L73 Lohengrin (Table P-PZ43)
1566.L75-.L753 Lorengel (Table P-PZ43)
1566.L8-.L83 Lucidarius (Table P-PZ43)
Cf. PT1551.K46+ Kleine Lucidarius (Siegfried Helbling)
Lübecker fronleichnamsspiel see PT1461.A2+
1566.L9 Lutwin, 13th cent. (Table P-PZ38)
Luzerner osterspiel see PT1444.L8
1567 M - Mönch
1567.M17-.M173 Das Märterbuch (Poem) (Table P-PZ43)
1567.M2-.M23 Der Maget krône (Table P-PZ43)
1567.M3-.M33 Mai und Beaflor (Table P-PZ43)
Cf. PT1636.P2 Der Pleier
Manesse's liederhandschrift see PT1419.H4
1567.M4-.M43 Maria Magdalena (Epic poem) (Table P-PZ43)
Marienklagen see PT1450
Marienlob, Das rheinische see PT1566.L6+
1567.M5 Der Marner, fl. 1231-1267 (Table P-PZ38)
1567.M6 Maximilian I, emperor of Germany, 1459-1519 (Table P-PZ38 modified)
Separate works. By title
1567.M6A7 Theuerdank
1567.M6A75 Der weiss kunig
Meissen, Heinrich von see PT1519.F7
1567.M63-.M64 Memento mori (Table P-PZ43a)

Individual authors or works
Middle High German, ca. 1050-1450/1500
M - Mönch -- Continued
1567.M65-.M653 Menschlich biede fart (Table P-PZ43)
1567.M67-.M673 Merigarto (11th century fragment) (Table P-PZ43)
Merlin see PT1501.A4M5
1567.M7 Merswin, Rulman, 1307-1382 (Table P-PZ38)
Cf. BV5070+ Mysticism
1567.M716-.M718 Minneburg (Table P-PZ43a)
1567.M72-.M723 Minnelehre (Table P-PZ43)
Mönch von Salzburg see PT1543.H29
1567.M73-.M733 Mönch Felix (Table P-PZ43)
1568.M4 Montfort, Hugo, graf von, 1357-1423 (Table P-PZ38)
1568.M55-.M553 Morant und Galie (Table P-PZ43)
1568.M57-.M573 Moriz von Craûn (Romance) (Table P-PZ43)
Morolf see PT1651.S25+
1568.M6 Morsheim, Johann von, d. 1516 (Table P-PZ38)
Morungen, Heinrich von see PT1537.H8
Mügeln, Heinrich von see PT1537.H83
1568.M85 Münster, Sebastian, 1489-1552 (Table P-PZ38)
1568.M9 Muskatblüt, fl. 1420 (Table P-PZ38)
Not to be confused with Konrad Muskatblüt, PT1559.K6
1569 N - Nei
Narrenschiff see PT1509.N2+
Neidhart von Reuenthal, 13th cent.
1570.A1 Anonymous editions. By date
1570.A2A-.A2Z Editions. By editor, A-Z
Translations
1570.A3-.A39 Modern German
1570.A4-.A49 English
1570.A5-.A59 French
1570.A6-.A69 Other languages (alphabetically)
Criticism
1571.A1-.Z3 General and textual criticism
1571.Z5 Language, metrics, etc.
1571.Z7 Dictionaries, glossaries, etc.
1572.N2-.N23 Neidhart Fuchs (Table P-PZ43)
Neifen, Gottfried von see PT1524.G8
Nibelungenlied
Editions
1575.A1 Manuscripts. Facsimiles (A-W, a-m)
Subarrange by letter under which the manuscript is known, e.g. Edition of manuscript A or h: A 1856; h 18
Printed editions
1575.A5-Z By editor, A-Z
1576 Editions of fragments

Individual authors or works
Middle High German, ca. 1050-1450/1500
Nibelungenlied
Editions
Printed editions -- Continued
School editions. Selections

1578.A1 German
Subarrange by editor

1578.E5 English
Subarrange by editor

1578.F5 French
Subarrange by editor

Translations

1579.A1 Modern German

1579.A3 English
Subarrange by translator, if given, or date

1579.A5 French

1579.A6-.A7 Other, A-Z

1580 Paraphrases, adaptations, etc.

(1581) Juvenile
see PZ8.1, PZ14.1, PZ24.1, PZ34.1, etc.

(1582) Dramatizations

1583 Parodies. Travesties

Translations (as subject, comparative studies, etc.)

1585.A2 General

1585.A3-Z By language, A-Z

1587 Illustrations to the Nibelungenlied

Criticism, interpretation, etc.

1589 General
Including treatises on the unity of the poem, "Lieder theories," "Nibelungenfrage," etc.

Sources and origins

(1591) General
see PT1589

Special

1592 Particular sagas or cycles of sagas

1595 Mythological and historical characters

1595.A2 General

1595.A5-Z Special, A-Z

1595.K47 Kriemhild

1595.R8 Rüdiger von Bechelaren

1595.S5 Siegfried

1599 Authorship

1601 Style and composition. Technique

1603.A-Z Comparison with other epics, A-Z

1604 Nibelungen myth in folklore and literature

Special topics

Individual authors or works
Middle High German, ca. 1050-1450/1500
Nibelungenlied
Criticism, interpretation, etc.
Special topics -- Continued

1605 History. Geography
1607 Civilization
1608.A-Z Other, A-Z
1608.H8 Humor
1608.L7 Loyalty
1608.P64 Politics
1608.R48 Revenge
1608.S67 Sports
1608.S9 Symbolism
1608.W8 Women

Study and teaching
1609.A2 General and Germany
1609.A3-Z Other countries, A-Z

Textual criticism. Relation of manuscripts
1611 General
1612.A-Z Special manuscripts, A-W, a-m
Arrange by author, A-Z
Cf. note under PT1575.A1
1613 Special "aventiuren"
1615 Special passages

Linguistic treatises
Grammar
1617 General
1618 Phonology, morphology, syntax, word-order, dialect, etc.
1621 Versification
1621.Z5 Rhyme glossaries

Die Klage
1624.A1 Editions. By date
1624.A51-Z Criticism

1626.N5-.N53 Nicholas, Saint, bp. of Myra. Legend (Table P-PZ43)
Nicholas von Wyle see PT1695.W8
Nicodemus, Evangelium see PT1505.B6
Nicolaus von Jeroschin see PT1548.J2
Nithart von Reuental see PT1570+

1629 O - Or
Oberammergauer passionsspiel see PN3235+
Oberge, Eilhart von see PT1517.E4
Offenbarung Johannes see PT1505.B5
1629.O7-.O73 Orendel (Orendel und Bride) (Table P-PZ43)
1629.O8-.O83 Ortnit (Table P-PZ43)

1631 Os - Oz

Individual authors or works
Middle High German, ca. 1050-1450/1500
Os - Oz -- Continued
Osterspiele see PT1443+
1631.O7-.O73 Oswald, Saint, King. Legend (Table P-PZ43)
Oswald von Wolkenstein see PT1695.W4
1631.O8 Otte, German poet, fl. 1200 (Table P-PZ38)
Otto II, Bp. of Freising, d. 1220 see PT1503.B2+
Otto mit dem barte see PT1556.K2+
1631.O9 Otto von Botenlauben, graf von Henneberg, fl. ca. 1197-1234 (Table P-PZ38)
1633 P - Pl
Pantaleon see PT1556.P3+
Paraphrase des Buches Daniel see PT1505.B384
Paraphrase des Buches Hiob see PT1505.B355
Partonopier und Meliur see PT1556.P5+
Parzival see PT1682.P2+
1633.P4-.P43 Das Passional (Table P-PZ43)
By the unknown author of the Väterbuch, PT1664.V3
Passionspiele see PT1446+
1633.P7-.P73 Pfaff vom Kalenberg (Pfarrer vom Kalenberg) (Table P-PZ43)
1633.P75-.P753 Pfaffe mit der Schnur (Table P-PZ43)
1633.P8 Philipp, bruder, 14th cent. (Table P-PZ38)
1633.P87-.P873 Physiologus (Table P-PZ43)
(1633.P9) Pilgerfahrt des träumenden mönche
see PQ1483.G3G4+
1636 Pl - Pz
1636.P2 Der Pleier, fl. 1260-1280 (Table P-PZ38)
Including Garel vom blüenden tal, Meleranz, and Tandareis und Flordibel
1636.P4-.P43 Portimunt (Table P-PZ43)
1636.P48 Preining, Jörg, b. 1450? (Table P-PZ38)
1636.P5 Prischuch, Thomas, fl. 1404-1460 (Table P-PZ38)
1636.P6-.P63 Das Puechel ist von geistleicher Gemahelschaft (Table P-PZ43)
1636.P7 Püterich, Jakob, von Reichertshausen, 1400-1469 (Table P-PZ38)
1637 R - Ro
Rabenschlacht see PT1537.H25
Redentiner osterspiel see PT4846.R35
Regel für ein vollkommenes leben see PT1536.H3+
1637.R4 Regenbogen, Barthel, 13th cent. (Table P-PZ38)
1637.R48-.R483 Reine Sibille (Prose romance) (Table P-PZ43)
1637.R5-.R53 Reinfried von Braunschweig (13th century poem) (Table P-PZ43)

Individual authors or works
Middle High German, ca. 1050-1450/1500
R - Ro -- Continued

1637.R6-.R63 Reinhart Fuchs (Table P-PZ43)
Cf. PT1536.H8 Heinrich der Glichesaere
1637.R8 Reinmar der Alte, d. ca. 1207 (Table P-PZ38)
1637.R84 Reinmar von Brennenberg, 13th cent. (Table P-PZ38)
1637.R87 Reinmar von Zweter, 13th cent. (Table P-PZ38)
Reinolt von Montelban see PT1536.H15
Der renner see PT1545
Reuenthal, Neidhart von see PT1570+
1637.R93 Ringoltingen, Thüring von, ca. 1415-1483 or 4 (Table P-PZ38)
1637.R95-.R953 Rittertreue (Table P-PZ43)
(1640) Rolandslied
see PT1553
1643 Rosenblüt, Hans, 15th cent. (Table P-PZ39)
1645.R4-.R43 Rosengarten ("Der grosse Rosengarten"; "Rosengarten zu Worms") (Table P-PZ43)
Rosengarten, Der kleine see PT1563.L3+
1645.R8 Rothe, Johannes, d. 1434 (Table P-PZ38)
Rother, König see PT1551.K6+
Rudolf von Ems, d. ca. 1254
Collected works
1647.A1 Anonymous editions. By date
1647.A2A-.A2Z By editor, A-Z
1647.A3A-.A3Z Translations. By language, A-Z
1647.A4A-.A4Z Selections, extracts, etc. By editor
1647.A5-Z Separate works
1647.A7-.A73 Alexander (Table P-PZ43)
1647.B4-.B43 Barlaam und Josaphat (Table P-PZ43)
1647.E9 Eustachius (lost)
1647.G92-.G93 Der gute Gerhard (Table P-PZ43a)
1647.W3-.W4 Weltchronik (Table P-PZ43a)
1647.W6-.W63 Willehalm (Wilhelm) von Orlens (Table P-PZ43)
Biography and criticism
1648.A1-.Z3 General. Textual criticism
1648.Z4 Language, metrics, etc.
1648.Z5 Dictionaries, vocabularies, etc.
1648.Z7 Glossaries
1650.R78 Rüdiger, von Hünchoven, 13th cent. (Table P-PZ38)
1650.R8 Rudolf von Fenis, fl. 1158-1192 (Table P-PZ38)
1650.R85 Ruprecht von Würzburg, 13th cent. (Table P-PZ38)
Saaz, Johannes von see PT1548.J53
1651.S17 Sachsendorf, Ulrich von, 13th cent. (Table P-PZ38)
1651.S2 Sachsenheim, Hermann von, d. 1458 (Table P-PZ38)
1651.S23-.S233 Der Saelden hort (Table P-PZ43)

Individual authors or works
Middle High German, ca. 1050-1450/1500 -- Continued
Sängerkrieg auf der Wartburg see PT1679.W3+
1651.S25-.S253 Salman und Morolf (Spielmannsepos) (Table P-PZ43)
1651.S26-.S263 Salomo und Morolf (Spruchgedicht) (Table P-PZ43)
1651.S27-.S273 Salomon und Markolf (Table P-PZ43)
Poem by Gregor Hayden, ca. 1450
Salzburg, Mönch see PT1543.H29
Der sammler see PT1545
1651.S275-.S2753 Sanct Brandan (Middle High German poem) (Table P-PZ43)
1651.S29-.S3 Sankt Trudperter Hohes Lied (Table P-PZ43a)
1651.S33 Schiller, Jörg, 15th cent. (Table P-PZ38)
Schmiede, Der goldene see PT1556.G8+
1651.S34 Schmieher, Peter, 15th cent. (Table P-PZ38)
Schnepper, Hans see PT1643
1651.S35 Schondoch, 14th cent. (Table P-PZ38)
Schonebeck, Brun von see PT1512.B25
1651.S37 Segen, Johan van (Table P-PZ38)
1651.S38 Seifried, fl. 1352 (Table P-PZ38)
Servatius (Legend) see PT1540.S5+
Seuse, Heinrich see BV5070+
1651.S45 Sibote von Erfurt (Table P-PZ38)
1651.S47-.S473 Sibyllen Weissagung (Table P-PZ43)
1651.S5 Sigeher, 13th cent. (Table P-PZ38)
1651.S6-.S63 Sigenot (Table P-PZ43)
Solomon
see Salman; Salomon
1651.S65 Spechtshart, Hugo, of Reutlingen, 1285-1359 or 1360 (Table P-PZ38)
1651.S7-.S713 Der Sperber (Table P-PZ43a)
Spervogel see PT1543.H25
1651.S72-.S723 Spiegel des Sunders (Table P-PZ43)
1651.S74-.S743 St. Anselmi Fragen an Maria (Table P-PZ43)
1651.S75 Stagel, Elsbeth, ca. 1300-1366 (Table P-PZ38)
1651.S78 Staufenberg, Egenolf von, 14th cent. (Table P-PZ38)
1651.S8 Steinhöwel, Heinrich, 1412-1482? (Table P-PZ38)
1651.S84 Steinmar, Berthold, von Klingau 1251-1293 (Table P-PZ38)
Sterzinger spiele see PT1439
1651.S89-.S893 Stiftsbibliothek Sankt Gallen. Manuscript. Cod. Sang. 1164 (Table P-PZ43)
Stoffel, Konrad von see PT1555.K6
Strassburg, Gottfried von see PT1525+
Der Stricker, 13th cent.
Collected works
1653.A1 Anonymous editions. By date
1653.A2A-.A2Z By editor, A-Z

Individual authors or works
Middle High German, ca. 1050-1450/1500
Der Stricker, 13th cent. -- Continued

1653.A3A-.A3Z Translations. By language, A-Z
1653.A4A-.A4Z Selections, extracts, etc. By editor, A-Z
1653.A5-Z Separate works, A-Z
1653.B5-.B53 Bispel (Table P-PZ43)
1653.D3-.D33 Daniel vom blühenden tal (Table P-PZ43)
1653.K4-.K43 Karl der Grosse (Table P-PZ43)
1653.P2-.P23 Der pfaffe Amis (Table P-PZ43)
Biography and criticism
1654.A1-.Z3 General. Textual criticism
1654.Z4 Language, metrics, etc.
1654.Z5 Dictionaries, vocabularies, etc.
1654.Z7 Glossaries
1656.S8 Suchensinn, fl. 1390 (Table P-PZ38)
1656.S82 Suchenwirt, Peter, 14th cent. (Table P-PZ38)
1656.S85 Süsskind von Trimberg, 13th cent. (Table P-PZ38)
1656.S86-.S87 Summa theologiae (Middle High German poem) (Table P-PZ43a)
Suso, Heinrich see BV5070+
1656.S9-.S93 Syon filia (Tohter Syon) (Table P-PZ43)
1658 T - Tot
Tandareis see PT1636.P2
1658.T3 Tannhäuser. Minnesinger. 13th cent. (Table P-PZ38)
Cf. PT941.T2+
(1658.T35) Tauler, Johannes
see BV5080+
1658.T38-.T383 Teufels netz (Table P-PZ43)
Theoderich der Grosse see PT207+
Theuerdank see PT1567.M6A7
1658.T39-.T393 Thomas Aquinas, Saint, 1225?-1274. Summa theologica. Middle High German translation (Table P-PZ43)
1658.T4 Thomasin von Zerclaere, fl. 1215-1216 (Table P-PZ38)
Till Eulenspiegel see PT941.E8+
1658.T5 Tilo von Kulm, fl. 1331-1338 (Table P-PZ38)
For Gedicht von siben ingesigeln, Paraphrase des Buches Hiob see PT1505.B355
1658.T55-.T553 Tirol und Fridebrant (Table P-PZ43)
Titurel see PT1682.T2+
(1658.T6) Titurel, Der jüngere
see PT1501.A4T4
(1659) Totentänze
see N7720
1660 Tot - Tz
1660.T4-.T43 Treves. Stadtbibliothek MSS. (810/1338) (Table P-PZ43)
Trimberg, Hugo von see PT1545

Individual authors or works
Middle High German, ca. 1050-1450/1500
Tot - Tz -- Continued
Tristan
see PT1517.E4; PT1525+; PT1537.H4; PT1661.U5
1660.T65-.T653 Tristan als Mönch (Table P-PZ43)
Trojanischer krieg
see PT1543.H2, PT1661.U5
1660.T69 Trutmann, Anton (Table P-PZ38)
1660.T78 Tünger, Augustin, b. 1455 (Table P-PZ38)
Türheim, Ulrich von see PT1661.U5
Türlin, Heinrich von see PT1537.H35
Türlin, Ulrich von see PT1661.U2
1660.T79-.T793 Der Tugenden Buch (Table P-PZ43)
1660.T8-.T83 Tundals vision (Fragment of a rimed paraphrase; Albers Tundalus) (Table P-PZ43)
1661 U - Uz
Ulenspiegel see PT941.E8+
Ulrich Boner see PT1507.B7
1661.U2 Ulrich von dem Türlin, fl. 1269 (Table P-PZ38)
1661.U3 Ulrich von Eschenbach, 13th cent. (Table P-PZ38)
1661.U4 Ulrich von Gutenburg, fl. 1172-1200 (Table P-PZ38)
Ulrich von Lichtenstein see PT1564+
1661.U44 Ulrich von Pottenstein, fl. 1398-1416 (Table P-PZ38)
Ulrich von Sachsendorf see PT1651.S17
1661.U45 Ulrich von Singenberg, fl. 1209-1228 (Table P-PZ38)
1661.U5 Ulrich von Türheim, 13th cent. (Table P-PZ38)
1661.U7 Ulrich von Winterstetten, 13th cent. (Table P-PZ38)
1661.U8 Ulrich von Zatzikhoven, fl. ca. 1200 (Table P-PZ38)
Urstende see PT1555.K4
1664 V - Vz
1664.V2-.V3 Väterbuch (Table P-PZ43a)
The author (unknown) wrote also the Passional, PT1633.P4
Veldeke, Heinrich von see PT1540+
1664.V4-.V43 Vienna. Nationalbibliothek. MSS. (2722) (Table P-PZ43)
1664.V5 Vintler, Hans, d. 1419 (Table P-PZ38)
Vogelweide, Walther von der see PT1670+
Vogler, Heinrich der see PT1537.H25
1664.V6 Volcnant von Erlach, ca. 1168-ca. 1230 (Table P-PZ38)
1664.V74 Volmar, fl. ca. 1250 (Table P-PZ38)
1664.V75-.V753 Vom Rechte (Table P-PZ43)
1664.V77-.V773 Von dem jungesten tage (Poem) (Table P-PZ43)
1664.V775-.V7753 Von dem üblen Weibe (Table P-PZ43)
1664.V7755-.V77553 Von deme Gîre (Table P-PZ43)
1664.V7768-.V77683 Von einem Schatz (Table P-PZ43)
1664.V777-.V7773 Von einer edlen Amme (Table P-PZ43)

Individual authors or works
Middle High German, ca. 1050-1450/1500
V - Vz -- Continued
1664.V78-.V783 Von unsers herren liden (Poem) (Table P-PZ43)
1664.V8-.V83 Von zwein studenten (Novelle) (Table P-PZ43)
1664.V87-.V873 Vorauer Novelle (Table P-PZ43)
1664.V88 Vorster, Johannes, d. 1444 (Table P-PZ38)
1664.V9-.V93 Vrône Botschaft ze der Christenheit (Table P-PZ43)
1667 W - Walther
Der wälsche gast see PT1658.T4
Walther von der Vogelweide, 12th cent.
Poems
1670.A1 Anonymous editions. By date
1670.A1A-.A1Z Editions. By editor
1670.A2 Selections. By editor
1670.A25 Interpolations, continuations, additions. By author
Translations
1670.A3 Modern German
1670.A5-Z Other languages, A-Z
Subarrange by translator
Biography and criticism
1671 General. Life and works
1672 Birthplace, homes and haunts, relations to contemporaries, religious and political views, etc.
1672.Z3 Anniversaries, celebrations. By date
1672.Z5 Iconography. Monuments
1672.Z9 Treatment in literature, fiction, drama, etc.
For individual authors, see PA-PT
Criticism, interpretation, etc.
1673 General
1674 Special
Sources, manuscripts, chronology of works, etc.
Textual criticism
1675.A2 General
1675.A3-Z Special
1676 Dictionaries. Concordances
Language. Style
1677.A2 General works
1677.A4-Z Grammar
1678 Versification
1679.W2 Walther von Rheinau, fl. ca. 1300 (Table P-PZ38)
1679.W3-.W313 Wartburgkrieg (Table P-PZ43)
Weihnachtsspiele see PT1455+
Der weiss kunig see PT1567.M6A75
1679.W33-.W333 Weltgerichtsspiel (Table P-PZ43)
1679.W35 Wernher, priest (or pfaffe), fl. 1172 (Table P-PZ38)
1679.W36 Wernher, Bruder, ca. 1220-ca. 1266 (Table P-PZ38)

Individual authors or works
Middle High German, ca. 1050-1450/1500 -- Continued

1679.W4 Wernher der Gartenaere, 13th cent. (Table P-PZ38)
1679.W43 Wernher (Swiss poet), 14th cent. (Table P-PZ38)
1679.W435 Wernher vom Niederrhein, 12th cent. (Table P-PZ38)
1679.W44 Wernher von Elmendorf, fl. ca. 1171 (Table P-PZ38)
1679.W445 Wernher von Honberg, graf, 1284-1320 (Table P-PZ38)
Wernher von Tegernsee see PT1679.W445
Widwilt see PT1501.A75+
1679.W5 Wierstraat, Christianus, 15th cent. (Table P-PZ38)
Wigalois see PT1679.W8
1679.W52-.W523 Wigamur (Table P-PZ43)
1679.W53 Der wilde mann, pseud. (Table P-PZ38)
1679.W55-.W553 Wilhalm von Orlens (Poem) (Table P-PZ43)
Wilhelm von Orange see PT1682.W4+
Willehalm see PT1682.W4+
Willehalm von Orlens see PT1647.W6+
1679.W6 Winsbeke (Table P-PZ38)
1679.W65-.W653 Winsbekin (Table P-PZ43)
Winterstetten, Ulrich von see PT1661.U7
1679.W8 Wirnt von Gravenberg, 13th cent. (Table P-PZ38)
1679.W85 Wisse, Claus, 14th cent. (Table P-PZ38)
Wissenhere, Michel see PT1695.W9
1679.W86 Wittenweiler, Heinrich, 15th cent. (Table P-PZ38)
1679.W88 Witzlav III, prince of Rügen, d. 1325 (Table P-PZ38)
1679.W9-.W93 Wolfdietrich (Table P-PZ43)
Wolfram von Eschenbach, 12th cent.
1682.A1 Collected works. By date
1682.A2A-.A2Z Collected works. By editor, A-Z
1682.A21-.A29 Selections, extracts, etc. By editor
Translations (Collected)
Subarrange by translator or editor
1682.A3-.A39 Modern German
1682.A4-.A49 English
1682.A5-.A59 French
1682.A6-.A69 Other languages (alphabetically)
Separate works
Lieder
1682.L2 Editions. By date
Translations
1682.L4 Modern German
1682.L6 Other. By language
Subarrange by translator
1682.L8 Criticism
Parzival (including editions of Parzival and Titurel)
1682.P2A-.P2Z Editions. By editor, A-Z
1682.P4 Selections

Individual authors or works
Middle High German, ca. 1050-1450/1500
Wolfram von Eschenbach, 12th cent.
Separate works
Parzival (including editions of Parzival and Titurel) -- Continued
Translations
1682.P6 Modern German
1682.P8 Other. By language
Subarrange by translator
(1682.P9) Criticism
see PT1688+
Titurel
Cf. PT1501.A4T4 Der jüngere Titurel
1682.T2 Editions
Cf. PT1682.P2A+ Parzival and Titurel collectively
Translations
1682.T4 Modern German
1682.T6A-.T6Z Other. By language, A-Z
Subarrange by translator
1682.T8 Criticism
Trojanerkrieg see PT1524.G6+
Willehalm
Cf. PT1537.H4 Heinrich von Freiberg
Cf. PT1661.U5 Ulrich von Türheim
1682.W4 Editions. By date
Translations
1682.W5 Modern German
1682.W6 Other. By language
Subarrange by translator
1682.W8 Criticism
Biography
1685 General works. Life, times, relations
1686 General special
1687 Special topics (by author)
Criticism, interpretation, etc.
Including criticism of Parzival alone
1688 General
Special
1689.A2 Sources
1689.A3 Chronology. Dates of compositions
1689.A5-.Z4 Special characters, A-Z
1689.Z5 Other special (by author)
Textual criticism
1690.A2 General
1690.A5-Z Special passages
1691 Language, grammar, style

Individual authors or works
Middle High German, ca. 1050-1450/1500
Wolfram von Eschenbach, 12th cent.
Criticism, interpretation, etc. -- Continued

1692 Versification
1692.Z5 Indexes of rimes
1693 Lexicography
1693.Z5 Dictionaries
1695.W4 Wolkenstein, Oswald von, 1367-1445 (Table P-PZ38)
1695.W6-.W63 Der Württemberger (Table P-PZ43)
1695.W8 Wyle, Niclas von, fl. 1447-1478 (Table P-PZ38)
1695.W9 Wyssenhere, Michel, 15th cent. (Table P-PZ38)
Zatzikhoven, Ulrich von see PT1661.U8
Zerclaere, Thomasin von see PT1658.T4
Zweter, Reinmar von see PT1637.R87

1500-ca. 1700

1701 Anonymous works (Table P-PZ28)
1702.A2 Aal, Johannes, d. 1551 (Table P-PZ40)
1702.A23 Abele, Matthias, d. 1677 (Table P-PZ40)
1703-1704 Abraham a Sancta Clara, 1644?-1709 (Table P-PZ36)
1705.A2 Abschatz, Johann Erasmus Assmann, freiherr von, 1646-1699 (Table P-PZ40)
1705.A3 Ackermann, Johannes, 16th cent. (Table P-PZ40)
1705.A317 Adelphus, Johannes, 16th cent. (Table P-PZ40)
1705.A35 Albert, Henrich, 1604-1651 (Table P-PZ40)
1705.A4 Albertinus, Aegidius, 1560-1620 (Table P-PZ40)
1705.A5 Alberus, Erasmus, d. 1553 (Table P-PZ40)
1705.A54 Albinus, Michael, 1610-1653 (Table P-PZ40)
1705.A6 Andreä, Johann Valentin, 1586-1654 (Table P-PZ40)
Angelus Silesius see PT1791.S2
1705.A65 Anton Ulrich, Duke of Brunswick-Wolfenbüttel, 1633-1714 (Table P-PZ40)
1705.A7 Assig, Hans von, 1650-1694 (Table P-PZ40)
1707 Ayrer, Jacob, d. 1605 (Table P-PZ39)
1709.B15 Bähr, Johann, 1655-1700 (Table P-PZ40)
Balde, Jacob see PA8463.B2
1709.B3 Barth, Kaspar von, 1587-1658 (Table P-PZ40)
1709.B43 Beckh, Johann Joseph, 1635-ca. 1692 (Table P-PZ40)
Beer, Johann, 1655-1700 see PT1709.B15
1709.B45 Bernardt, Georg, 1595-1660 (Table P-PZ40)
1709.B55 Birken, Sigmund von, 1626-1681 (Table P-PZ40)
1709.B57 Blaimhofer, Maximilian, b. 1759 (Table P-PZ40)
1709.B6 Bohse, August, 1661-1742 (Table P-PZ38)
1709.B73 Brandmüller, Johannes, 1593-1664 (Table P-PZ40)
1709.B78 Brunner, Andreas, 1589-1650 (Table P-PZ40)
1709.B8 Brunner, Thomas, d. 1570 (Table P-PZ40)
Callenbach, Franz see PT1832.C7

Individual authors or works
1500-ca. 1700 -- Continued

1711.C2 Canitz, Friedrich Rudolf Ludwig, freiherr von, 1654-1699 (Table P-PZ40)
1711.C45 Chryseus, Johann, 16th cent. (Table P-PZ40)
1711.C5 Clauert, Hans, d. 1566 (Table P-PZ40)
1711.C7 Cochlaeus, Johannes, 1479-1552 (Table P-PZ40)
1711.C84 Culmann, Leonhard, 1498?-1562 (Table P-PZ40)
1711.C9 Czepko, Daniel von, 1605-1660 (Table P-PZ40)
1712 D - Dac
1713 Dach, Simon, 1605-1659 (Table P-PZ39)
1714.D25 Daniel von Soest
1714.D3 Dedekind, Friedrich, d. 1598 (Table P-PZ40)
1714.D45 Dilherr, Johann Michael, 1604-1669 (Table P-PZ40)
1714.D84 Dürer, Hieronymus, 1641-1704 (Table P-PZ40)
1715.E2 Eberlin, Johann, von Günzburg, ca. 1465-ca. 1530 (Table P-PZ38)
(1715.E3) Eck, Johann, 1486-1543
see BR-BX; for biography, see BX4705.E24
1715.E4 Eckstein, Ulrich, called Utz, 1528-1558 (Table P-PZ40)
1715.E6 Emser, Hieronymus, 1477 or 78-1527 (Table P-PZ40)
Cf. BR-BX
1715.E65 Engelbrecht, Anton, ca. 1485-1558 (Table P-PZ40)
1715.E8 Ernst, Jacob Daniel, 1640-1707 (Table P-PZ40)
Faust legend see PT923+
1717.F4 Feinler, Gottfried, fl. 1676-1700 (Table P-PZ40)
Filidor, der dorfferer see PT1793.S7
Fischart, Johann, ca. 1550-1590?
1720.A1 Works. By date
1720.A2 Selected works. By date
1720.A3-Z Selections, extracts, etc. By editor, A-Z
1721 Translations. By language
Subarrange by translator
1722.A-Z Separate works, A-Z
Affenteurliche und ungeheurliche geschichtschrift see PT1722.G4
1722.A7 Allerpraktik grossmutter
1722.B5 Bienenkorb
1722.E4 Ehzuchtbüchlein
1722.E8 Eulenspiegel
1722.F3 Flöhhaz
Gargantua und Pantagruel see PT1722.G4
1722.G4 Geschichtklitterung
1722.G5 Glückhafft schiff von Zürich
1722.J4 Jesuitenhütlein
1722.P4 Peter von Stauffenberg
Philosophisch ehzuchtbüchlein see PT1722.E4

Individual authors or works
1500-ca. 1700
Fischart, Johann, ca. 1550-1590?
Separate works -- Continued
1722.P6 Podagrammisch trostbüchlein
1723 Biography. Life and works
1724 Criticism
1724.A-.Z3 General
1724.Z5 Language. Grammar
1724.Z7 Metrics. Versification
1724.Z9 Dictionaries, vocabularies, etc.
1725 Fisch - Flem
1726 Fleming, Paul, 1609-1640 (Table P-PZ39)
1727.F32 Franck, Michael, Peter and Sebastian (collectively) (Table P-PZ40)
Cf. ML3103 Music
1727.F33 Franck, Michael, 1609-1667 (Table P-PZ40)
1727.F35 Franck, Peter, 1616-1675 (Table P-PZ40)
1727.F37 Franck, Sebastian, 1606-1668 (Table P-PZ40)
1727.F39 Frischlin, Jakob, 1557-1621 (Table P-PZ40)
1727.F4 Frischlin, Nicodemus, 1547-1590 (Table P-PZ38)
Cf. PA8520.F85 Latin literature
1729.G2 Gart, Thiebold, fl. 1540 (Table P-PZ40)
1729.G22 Gauch, Jacob, 1640-1690 (Table P-PZ40)
1729.G3 Gengenbach, Pamphilus, fl. 1509-1524 (Table P-PZ40)
1729.G4 Gerbel, Nicolaus, ca. 1485-1560 (Table P-PZ40)
1729.G5 Gerhardt, Paulus, 1607-1676 (Table P-PZ40)
Cf. BV330.G4 Hymn writers
Cf. M2061 Music
Cf. ML3186 Music
Gorgias, Johann, 1640-1684 see PT1794.V46
1729.G7 Graff, Jörg, 16th cent. (Table P-PZ40)
1729.G8 Greflinger, Georg, ca. 1620-1677 (Table P-PZ40)
1729.G83 Greiffenberg, Catharina Regina von, 1633-1694 (Table P-PZ40)
Grimmelshausen, Hans Jacob Christoffel von, 1625-1676
1731.A1 Collected works. By date
1731.A3 Selected works
Cf. PT1731.A9 Simplicianische schriften
1731.A4A-.A4Z Translations. By language, A-Z
1731.A5A-.A5Z Selections. By editor, A-Z
Separate works

Individual authors or works
1500-ca. 1700
Grimmelshausen, Hans Jacob Christoffel von, 1625-1676
Separate works -- Continued
1731.A6-.A8 Simplicissimus ("Der abenteurliche Simplicissimus," "Simplicius Simplicissimus," etc.)
The first edition (1669) contained five books. Its popularity was so great that the author hurriedly wrote a sixth book which appeared separately in 1669 as a continuation and was later published in the same volume as the original work
1731.A6 Editions. By date
1731.A63 Abridged editions. By date
1731.A65 Selected books. By date
1731.A7 Translations. By language and date
1731.A8 Continuatio des abendtheurlichen Simplicissimi, 1669
1731.A9 Simplicianische schriften
Editions of all or several of the continuations and of minor works in which Simplicissimus appears
Minor works
1731.B3 Bärnhäuter (Der erste beernhäuter)
1731.C7 Courasche
Der deutsche Michel see PT1731.M6
1731.D4 Dietwald und Amelinde
1731.E9 Ewigwährender kalendar
1731.F6 Fliegender wandersmann
Translation of F. Baudouin's L'homme dans la lune, Paris, 1648, which was a translation of "The man in the moon . . . by Domingo Gonsales," by Francis Godwin, London, 1638
Cf. PT1731.S2 Satyrische gesicht
1731.G2 Galgenmannhlein
1731.G4 Gaukeltasche
1731.J7 Joseph (Des vortrefflich keuschen Josephs lebensbeschreibung)
Later editions include Masai
1731.K8 Kurtze und kurtzweilige reise-beschreibung nach der obern monds-welt
Cf. PT1731.S2 Satyrische gesicht
1731.M4 Melcher
1731.M6 Michel (Dess weltberuffenen Simplicissimi pralerey . . . mit seinem teutschen Michel)
1731.M8 Musai
Cf. PT1731.J7 Joseph
1731.P7-.P9 Proximus und Lympida (Table P-PZ43a)
1731.R2 Rathstübel Plutonis
1731.R3 Ratio status

	Individual authors or works
	1500-ca. 1700
	Grimmelshausen, Hans Jacob Christoffel von, 1625-1676
	Separate works
	Minor works -- Continued
	Reise-beschreibung see PT1731.K8
1731.S2	Satyrische gesicht und Traumgeschicht
	The title of a 1660 collection containing: Von dir und mir, Der fliegende wanders-mann and Kurtze und kurtzweilige reise-beschreibung
1731.S3	Satyrischer pilgram
	Schwartz und weiss see PT1731.S3
1731.S4	Simplicissimus als arzt
1731.S7	Springinsfeld (Der seltzame Springinsfeld)
	Der stolze Melcher see PT1731.M4
1731.T8	Traumgeschicht von dir und mir
	Cf. PT1731.S2 Satyrische gesicht
	Trutz Simplex see PT1731.C7
1731.V4	Verkehrte welt
1731.V7	Vogelnest
1732	Biography and criticism
1733.G8	Grob, Johann, 1643-1697 (Table P-PZ40)
	Gryphius, Andreas, 1616-1664
1734.A1	Collected works. By date
1734.A17	Collected poems. By date
1734.A3A-.A3Z	Translations. By language, A-Z
1734.A5-Z	Separate works
1735	Biography and criticism
1736.G2	Gryphius, Christian, 1649-1706 (Table P-PZ40)
	Günther, Johann Christian, 1695-1723 see PT2281.G9
1736.G8	Gwalther, Rudolf, 1519-1586 (Table P-PZ40)
1737.H13	Hainzmann, Johann Christoph, fl. 1681-1690 (Table P-PZ40)
1737.H15	Hallmann, Johann Christian, d. 1704 (Table P-PZ40)
1737.H16	Hamersteten, Augustin von d. 1525 (Table P-PZ38)
1737.H18	Happel, Eberhard Werner, 1647-1690 (Table P-PZ40)
1737.H2	Harsdörfer, Georg Philipp, 1607-1658 (Table P-PZ40)
1737.H3	Haugwitz, August Adolf von, 1645-1706 (Table P-PZ40)
1737.H35	Hayneccius Martin, 1544-1611 (Table P-PZ40)
1737.H38	Heermann, Johann, 1585-1647 (Table P-PZ40)
1737.H4	Heinrich Julius, duke of Brunswick-Wolfenbüttel, 1564-1613 (Table P-PZ40)
1737.H52	Hellwig, Johann, 1609-1674 (Table P-PZ40)
1737.H6	Herman, Nicolaus, d. 1561 (Table P-PZ40)
1737.H65	Hertzog, Bernhard, 16th cent. (Table P-PZ40)
1737.H7	Hock, Theobald, b. 1573 (Table P-PZ40)
1737.H77	Hoffmann, Gottfried, 1658-1712 (Table P-PZ40)

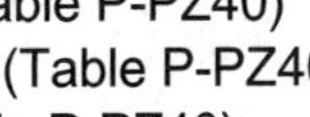

Individual authors or works
1500-ca. 1700 -- Continued

1737.H8 Hofmann von Hofmannswaldau, Christian, 1617-1679 (Table P-PZ40)
1737.H83 Hollonius, Ludwig, 16th cent. (Table P-PZ40)
1737.H85 Hoyer, Frau Anna (Owens) 1584-1655 (Table P-PZ40)
1739 Hutten, Ulrich von, 1488-1523 (Table P-PZ39 modified)
For Hutten and the Reformation see BR350.H8
For Latin works see PA8530+
Criticism
For biography see PA8535
1739.Z481-.Z489 Periodicals. Societies. Serials
1739.Z49 Dictionaries, indexes, etc. By date
Autobiography, journals, memoirs see PA8535
Letters (Collections) see PA8535
Letters to and from particular individuals see PA8535
1739.Z5A5-.Z5Z General works
1741.I8 Israël, Samuel, d. 1633 (Table P-PZ40)
1741.J64 Johann II, Prince, Count Palatine, 1492-1557 (Table P-PZ40)
1741.K34 Kaldenbach, Christoph (Table P-PZ40)
1741.K4 Kirchoff, Hans Wilhelm, 16th cent. (Table P-PZ40)
1741.K48 Kitscher, Johannes von (Table P-PZ40)
1741.K5 Klaj, Johann, 1616?-1656 (Table P-PZ38)
1741.K55 Klesch, Daniel, 1619-1697 (Table P-PZ40)
1741.K6 Knaust, Heinrich, fl. 1557 (Table P-PZ40)
1741.K65 Knorr von Rosenroth, Christian, 1636-1689 (Table P-PZ40)
1741.K7 Kongehl, Michael, 1646-1710 (Table P-PZ40)
1741.K74 Kormart, Christoph, 1644-1701 (Table P-PZ40)
1741.K8 Krüger, Bartholomaus, fl. 1587 (Table P-PZ40)
1741.K88 Kuefstein, Haus Ludwig, freiherr von, 1587-1657 (Table P-PZ40)
1741.K9 Kuhlmann, Quirin, 1651-1689 (Table P-PZ38)
1741.K94 Kydt, Johann Heinrich (Table P-PZ40)
(1743.L3) Lauremberg, Johann
see PT4847.L3, Low German literature
1743.L34 Laurentius, von Schnifis, 1633-1702 (Table P-PZ40)
1743.L47 Lehmann, Christoph, 1568-1638 (Table P-PZ40)
1743.L5 Leibnitz, Gottfried Wilhelm, freiherr von, 1646-1716 (Table P-PZ40)
Cf. B2550+ Leibnitz as philosopher
Lied von hürnen Seyfrid see PT1791.S55+
1743.L64 Linck, Wenzeslaus, 1483-1547 (Table P-PZ40)
1743.L7 Lindener, Michael, d. 1562 (Table P-PZ40)
Loën, Johann Michael freiherr von see PT2424.L63
1744 Logau, Friedrich von, 1604-1655 (Table P-PZ37)
1745.L5 Lohenstein, Daniel Casper von, 1635-1683 (Table P-PZ38)

Individual authors or works
1500-ca. 1700 -- Continued

1746	Luther, Martin, 1483-1546 (Table P-PZ39 modified) Class here literary works and criticism only Cf. BR323.492+ Religion Cf. Z8528 Bibliography
	Criticism
1746.Z481-.Z489	Periodicals. Societies. Serials
1746.Z49	Dictionaries, indexes, etc. By date
(1746.Z5A3)	This number not used
(1746.Z5A4)	This number not used
(1746.Z5A41-.Z5A49)	This number not used
1746.Z5A5-.Z5Z	General works
1747.M15	Mahler, Johannes, d. 1634 (Table P-PZ40)
1747.M19	Manuel, Hans Rudolf, 1525-1571 (Table P-PZ40)
1747.M2	Manuel, Niklaus, 1484?-1530 (Table P-PZ40)
1747.M25	Marschalk, Nikolaus, ca. 1470-1525 (Table P-PZ40)
	Megerle, Ulrich see PT1703+
1747.M295	Meier, Joachim, 1661-1732 (Table P-PZ40)
1747.M298	Melisso, 1691-1721 (Table P-PZ40)
1747.M325	Metzger, Ambrosius, 1573-1632 (Table P-PZ40)
1747.M34	Mitternacht, Johann Sebastian, 1613-1679 (Table P-PZ40)
1747.M35	Möller, Johann, 1623-1680 (Table P-PZ40)
1747.M4	Montanus, Martin, fl. 1557 (Table P-PZ40)
1747.M5	Morhof, Daniel Georg, 1639-1691 (Table P-PZ40)
1747.M7	Moscherosch, Johann Michael, 1601-1669 (Table P-PZ40)
1747.M73	Moscherosch, Quirin, 1623-1675 (Table P-PZ40)
1747.M8	Mühlpfort, Heinrich 1639-1681 (Table P-PZ40)
1748	Murer, Jodocus, 1530-1580 (Table P-PZ39)
1749	Murner, Thomas, 1475-1537 (Table P-PZ39)
1750	Mur - Mus
1751	Musculus, Andreas, 1514-1581 (Table P-PZ39)
1753.M9	Myllius Martin, d. 1521 (Table P-PZ40)
1753.N4	Neukirch, Benjamin, 1665-1729 (Table P-PZ40)
1753.N5	Neumark, Georg, 1621-1681 (Table P-PZ40)
1753.N54	Neunmann, Jochum (Table P-PZ40)
1753.N65	Niege, Georg, 1525-1589 (Table P-PZ40)
1753.N86	Nunnenbeck, Lienhard (Table P-PZ40)
1753.O7	Olearius, Adam, d. 1671 (Table P-PZ40)
1755-1756	Opitz, Martin, 1597-1639 (Table P-PZ36)
1757.P24	Pape, Ambrosius, 1553-1612 (Table P-PZ40)
1757.P26	Pastorius, Francis Daniel, 1651-1719 (Table P-PZ40) For his biography see F152
1757.P3	Pauli, Johannes, 16th cent. (Table P-PZ40)
1757.P35	Paumgartner, Balthasar, der jüngere, d. 1600 or 1601 (Table P-PZ40)
1757.P38	Peters, Friedrich, 1549-1617 (Table P-PZ40)

Individual authors or works
1500-ca. 1700 -- Continued
1757.P4 Peucker, Nicolaus, d. 1674 (Table P-PZ40)
Pfaff (Pfarrer) vom Kalenberg see PT1633.P7+
1757.P43 Pfeilschmidt, Andreas, 16th cent. (Table P-PZ40)
1757.P55 Pinxner, Andreas, b. 1674 (Table P-PZ40)
1757.P7 Pontus und Sidonia (Romance)
1757.P76 Post, Hermann, 1693-1762 (Table P-PZ40)
1757.P786 Praetorius, Johannes, 1630-1680 (Table P-PZ40)
1757.P787 Prem, Wolf (Table P-PZ40)
1757.P79 Printz, Wolfgang Caspar, 1641-1717 (Table P-PZ40)
1757.P8 Probst, Peter, d. 1576 (Table P-PZ40)
1757.P83 Pronner, Leo, ca. 1550-1630 (Table P-PZ40)
1757.P88 Puschman, Adam, 1532-1600 (Table P-PZ40)
1759.R14 Rabener, Justus Gottfried, 1634-1699 (Table P-PZ40)
1759.R15 Rachel, Joachim, 1618-1669 (Table P-PZ40)
1759.R2 Rebhun, Paul, d. 1546 (Table P-PZ40)
1759.R4 Reuter, Christian, b. 1665 (Table P-PZ40)
1759.R435 Reutter, Leonart, fl. 1550 (Table P-PZ40)
1759.R46 Riemer, Johannes, 1648-1714 (Table P-PZ40)
1759.R47 Rinckhart, Martin, 1586-1649 (Table P-PZ40)
1759.R5 Ringwaldt, Bartholomäus, ca. 1530-1599 (Table P-PZ40)
1759.R6 Rist, Johannes, 1607-1667 (Table P-PZ38)
1759.R7 Röling, Johann, 1634-1679 (Table P-PZ40)
1759.R79 Rollenhagen, Gabriel, 1583-1619 (Table P-PZ40)
1759.R8 Rollenhagen, Georg, 1542-1609 (Table P-PZ40)
1759.R83 Römoldt, Johannes, 16th cent. (Table P-PZ40)
1759.R9 Ruf, Jacob, d. 1558 (Table P-PZ40)
Sachs, Hans, 1494-1576
Collected works
1761.A1-.A6 Comprehensive editions
Older editions and facsimiles
1761.A1 First folio, 5v., 1558-1579
1761.A2 Second folio (v. I-III), 1560-1577
1761.A3 Third folio (v. I-III), 1570-1588
(Title edition of v. III, pub. Nürnberg, 1628)
1761.A4 Fourth folio (v. I-III), 1589-1591
1761.A5 Kempten edition, 5v., 1612-1616
1761.A6 Modern editions. By date
1761.A7 Miscellaneous works. By date
1761.A8-.Z8 Selected works. By editor
1761.Z9 Selections, extracts, etc. By date
Special forms
Poetical works. Lieder, Schwänke, Fabeln, etc.
Collections and selections
1762.A1 General. By date
Special

Individual authors or works
1500-ca. 1700
Sachs, Hans, 1494-1576
Special forms
Poetical works. Lieder, Schwänke, Fabeln, etc.
Collections and selections
Special -- Continued
1762.A3 Meistergesänge
1762.A4 Spruchgedichte
For editions omitting the dramatic works, originally included in the Spruchgedichte
1762.A5 Other
1762.A7-Z Separate works
Dramatic works
Collections and selections
1763.A1 General. By date
Special
1763.A2 Tragedies
1763.A3 Comedies
1763.A4 Fastnachtsspiele. Carnival plays. By date
1763.A7-Z Separate plays, A-Z
e.g.
1763.H4 Henno
1763.H8 Das lied vom hürnen Seufrid
Prose works
1764.A1 Collections and selections. By date
1764.A3-Z Separate works, A-Z
1767.A-Z Translations. By language, A-Z
Subarrange by translator, A-Z
1768 Doubtful or spurious works
1769 Imitations. Adaptations
1770 Illustrations of the works
Biography and criticism
Bibliography see Z8774
1771 Periodicals. Societies. Collections
1772 General works. Literary biography. Life and works
1773 Biographical details
Sources, Love and marriage, etc.
1774 Relations to contemporaries
1775 Anniversaries. Celebrations. Festschriften
1776 Memorial addresses, poetry, fiction, drama, opera, in honor of Sachs or based upon his life
1777 Iconography
1778 Authorship: Manuscripts, sources, forerunners, associates, followers, allusions
1779 Chronology of his works
Criticism

Individual authors or works
1500-ca. 1700
Sachs, Hans, 1494-1576
Biography and criticism
Criticism -- Continued
1780 General and miscellaneous
1781.A-Z Special topics, A-Z
1781.A4 Allegory
1781.F3 Fastnachtsspiel
1781.G4 Genre elements
1781.N8 Nuremberg
1781.R4 Reformation
1781.S7 Sprichwort
1782 Textual criticism
Language. Style
1783 General works
1784 Dictionaries. Concordances
Grammar
1785 General
1786 Special
1787 Versification
1788 Dialect
1789 Representation on the stage
Cf. PT1776 Memorial drama
1791.S15 Sandrub, Lazarus, fl. 1618 (Table P-PZ40)
1791.S18 Schallenberg, Christoph von, 1561-1597 (Table P-PZ40)
1791.S19 Schechner, Jörg, 1500-1573 (Table P-PZ40)
1791.S2 Scheffler, Johann, 1624-1677 (Table P-PZ40)
1791.S3 Scheit, Caspar, d. 1565 (Table P-PZ38 modified)
1791.S3A61-.S3A78 Separate works. By title
1791.S3A65 Frölich heimfart
1791.S3A67 Grobianus
Translation of Dedekind's work
1791.S3A7 Lobrede von wegen des meyen
1791.S3A73 Musica
1791.S3A76 Todten dantz
1791.S33 Scherffer, Wencel, 1603-1674 (Table P-PZ38)
1791.S336 Schirmer, David, 1623-1687 (Table P-PZ40)
1791.S338 Schmidt, Bernhard, 1535-1592 (Table P-PZ40)
1791.S339 Schnebelin, Johann Andreas, d. 1705 (Table P-PZ40)
1791.S34 Schoch, Johann Georg (Table P-PZ40)
1791.S35 Schottelius, Justus George, 1612-1676 (Table P-PZ38)
1791.S38 Schumann, Valentin, 16th cent. (Table P-PZ40)
1791.S4 Schupp, Johann Balthasar, 1610-1661 (Table P-PZ38 modified)
1791.S4A61-.S4A78 Separate works. By title
1791.S4A61 Aurora

Individual authors or works
1500-ca. 1700
Schupp, Johann Balthasar, 1610-1661
Separate works. By title -- Continued

1791.S4A62 Bücher-dieb
1791.S4A63 Calendar
1791.S4A64 Chromio und Lagasso
1791.S4A65 Corinna
1791.S4A66 Deutsche gedichte
1791.S4A67 Deutscher Lucianus
1791.S4A68 Der freund in der not
1791.S4A69 Geplagter Hiob
1791.S4A7 Ninivitischer buss-spiegel
1791.S4A71 Der rachsüchtige Lucidor
(1791.S4A72) Regentenspiegel
see PT1791.S4A76
1791.S4A73 Register der sünden und laster
1791.S4A74 Relation aus dem Parnasso
1791.S4A75 Sabbathschänder
1791.S4A76 Salomo, oder Regentenspiegel
1791.S42 Schwartzenbach, Onoferus, d. 1574 (Table P-PZ38)
1791.S43 Schwarz, Sibylle, 1621-1638 (Table P-PZ38)
1791.S45 Schwarzenberg, Johann, freiherr von, d. 1528 (Table P-PZ38)
1791.S5 Schwieger, Jacob, 1624-ca. 1667 (Table P-PZ38)
For the "Geharnschte Venus" formerly ascribed to him see PT1793.S7
1791.S53 Scultetus, Andreas, 17th cent. (Table P-PZ40)
Siegfried
1791.S55 Das lied vom hürnen Seyfrid
Cf. PT941.S5+ Folk literature
Cf. PT1763.H8 Sachs, Hans
Silesius, Angelus see PT1791.S2
1791.S66 Sophie Elisabeth, Duchess, consort of August, Duke of Braunschweig-Lüneburg, 1613-1676 (Table P-PZ40)
1791.S8 Spangenberg, Wolfhart, ca. 1570-1637? (Table P-PZ38)
1792 Spee, Friedrich von, 1591-1635 (Table P-PZ37)
1793.S52 Speer, Daniel, 1637- (Table P-PZ40)
1793.S58 Sprenger, Balthasar, fl. 1505-1509 (Table P-PZ40)
1793.S7 Stieler, Kaspar von, 1632-1707 (Table P-PZ40)
1793.S74 Stockfleth, Heinrich Arnold, 1643-1708 (Table P-PZ40)
1793.S76 Stoppe, Daniel, 1697-1747 (Table P-PZ40)
1793.S94 Suevus Sigismundus, 1526-1596 (Table P-PZ40)
1793.T4 Thomasius, Christian, 1655-1728 (Table P-PZ40)
1793.T5 Thym, Georg, d. 1560 (Table P-PZ40)
1793.T9 Türckis, Damian, fl. 1607-1634 (Table P-PZ40)
1793.U5 Ulenhart, Niklas, fl. 1617 (Table P-PZ40)

Individual authors or works
1500-ca. 1700 -- Continued

1794.V46 Veriphantor, 1640-1684 (Table P-PZ40)
1794.V7 Voith, Valten, 16th cent. (Table P-PZ40)
1795.W18 Wagner, Johannes, d. 1590 (Table P-PZ40)
1795.W2 Waldis, Burkard, ca. 1490-ca. 1556 (Table P-PZ40)
1795.W25 Weber, Georg, fl. 1650 (Table P-PZ40)
Cf. ML54.7 Music
1795.W3 Weckherlin, Georg Rodolf, 1584-1653 (Table P-PZ38)
1795.W4 Weise, Christian, 1642-1708 (Table P-PZ40)
1795.W5 Welsch gattung (16th century poem)
1795.W56 Werder, Dietrich von dem, 1584-1657 (Table P-PZ40)
1795.W57 Werdum, Ulrich von, 1632-1681 (Table P-PZ40)
1795.W6 Wernicke, Christian, 1661-1725 (Table P-PZ38)
1795.W7 Wickram, Jörg, 16th cent. (Table P-PZ40)
1795.W72 Wieland, Johann Sebastian, 1590-1635? (Table P-PZ40)
1795.W75 Wild, Sebastian, fl. 1547-1583 (Table P-PZ40)
1795.W77 Das Windschiff aus Schlaraffenland
1797.Z4 Zesen, Philipp von, 1619-1689 (Table P-PZ40)
1797.Z5 Ziegler und Kliphausen, Heinrich Anshelm von, 1663-1696 (Table P-PZ40)
Zimmerische chronik see DD176.A2
1797.Z6 Zinkgref, Julius Wilhelm, 1591-1635 (Table P-PZ40)

1700-ca. 1860/70

1799 Anonymous works (Table P-PZ28)
1801.A15 Abt, Anton, 1841-1895 (Table P-PZ40)
Adlersfeld, Frau Eufemia (Ballestrem di Castellengo) see PT2601.D64
1801.A4 Ahlborn, Frau Luise (Jäger), 1834-1911 (Table P-PZ40)
Albers, Paul see PT2601.L14
1801.A55 Albert, Michael, 1836-1893 (Table P-PZ40)
1801.A6 Albrecht, Johann Friedrich Ernst, 1752-1814 (Table P-PZ40)
1801.A7 Alexander, Count of Württemberg, 1801-1844 (Table P-PZ40)
Alexander, Robert see PT2457.R56
Alexis, Willibald see PT2285.A+
1802.A3 Allmers, Hermann, 1821-1902 (Table P-PZ40)
1802.A35 Alxinger, Johann Baptist von, 1755-1797 (Table P-PZ40)
1802.A4 Amalie, Princess of Saxony, 1794-1870 (Table P-PZ40)
Amyntor, Gerhard von see PT1885.G4
1802.A6 Angely, Louis, 1788-1835 (Table P-PZ40)
1802.A63 Anneke, Mathilde Franziska Giesler, 1817-1884 (Table P-PZ40)
1803 Anzengruber, Ludwig, 1839-1889 (Table P-PZ39)
1805.A6 Apel, Johann August, 1771-1816 (Table P-PZ40)
1805.A72 Archenholz, Johann Wilhelm, 1743-1812 (Table P-PZ40)

Individual authors or works
1700-ca. 1860/70 -- Continued
Armand see PT2532.S3
Armin see PT1889.G6
1807 Arndt, Ernst Moritz, 1769-1860 (Table P-PZ39)
Cf. DB, DD, etc.
Arnim, Bettina (Brentano) von, 1785-1859
1808.A4 Collections and selections. By date
1808.A4A14 Minor selections. By date
Separate works
1808.A4A15 Clemens Brentanos frühlingskranz
1808.A4A18 Dies buch gehört dem könig
1808.A4A2 Gespräche mit dämonen
1808.A4A3-.A4A39 Goethes briefwechsel mit einem kinde (and translations)
e.g.
1808.A4A32 English
1808.A4A5-.A4A59 Günderode (and translations)
1808.A4A6 Ilius Pamphilius und die Ambrosia
Correspondence
1808.A4A8 General and miscellaneous. By date
1808.A4A81-.A4A89 Special persons
e.g.
1808.A4A84 Friedrich Wilhelm IV, King of Prussia
1808.A4A86 Goethe
Class here Briefwechsel mit Goethe, not to be confused with PT1808.A4A3+
1808.A4A9-Z Biography and criticism
Arnim, Gisela von see PT2281.G15
Arnim, Ludwig Achim, freiherr von, 1781-1831
1809.A1 Collected works. By date
1809.A11-.A14 Selected works. By editor (or publisher)
1809.A15 Novels (Collections. By editor)
Cf. PT1809.L3 Landhausleben
1809.A17 Poems (Collections. By date)
Drama (Collections and selections)
1809.A18 Schaubühne (original and later editions)
1809.A19 Other collections and selections. By editor
Translations
1809.A2-.A29 English. By translator
1809.A3-.A39 French. By translator
1809.A5-.A59 Other. By language (alphabetically)
1809.A61-.Z4 Separate works
1809.A7 Ariels offenbarungen
1809.A8 Armuth, reichtum, schuld und busse der gräfin Dolores
Bertholds erstes und zweites leben see PT1809.K8
1809.F8 Fürst Ganzgott und Sänger Halbgott

Individual authors or works
1700-ca. 1860/70
Arnim, Ludwig Achim, freiherr von, 1781-1831
Separate works -- Continued
Gedichte see PT1809.A17
1809.G4 Gesänge der liedertafel. Bd. 1
No more published
1809.G6 Die gleichen (Schauspiel)
Die gräfin Dolores see PT1809.A8
1809.H3 Halle und Jerusalem
1809.H6 Hollins liebeleben
1809.I8 Isabella von Ägypten
1809.K5 Die kirchenordnung (Novelle)
Des Knaben Wunderhorn see PT1203.A7
1809.K7 Kriegslieder. Erste sammlung
No more published
1809.K8 Die kronenwächter
1809.L3 Landhausleben (Erzählungen). 1. bd
No more published
1809.M3 Die majoratsherren (Novelle)
1809.O8 Owen Tudor, eine reisegeschichte (Novelle)
1809.R3 Raphael und seine nachbarinnen (Novelle)
Schaubühne see PT1809.A18
1809.T6 Der tolle invalide auf dem Fort Ratonneau (Novelle)
1809.T7 Tröst einsamkeit
1809.V4 Die verkleidungen des französischen hofmeisters (Novelle)
1809.W5 Die wintergarten
1809.Z5A2 Letters. By date
1809.Z5A3-.Z5Z Biography and criticism
Arnold, Hans see PT1828.B7
1810.A4 Arnold, Ignaz Theodor Ferdinand Cajetan, 1774-1812 (Table P-PZ40)
Arter, Emil see PT2453.R5
1810.A8 Assing, Frau Rosa Maria (Varnhagen von Ense), 1783-1840 (Table P-PZ40)
1810.A82 Aston, Louise, 1814-1871 (Table P-PZ40)
Auerbach, Berthold, 1812-1882
1812.A3 Collected works. By date
1812.A3A51-.A3Z4 Separate works
1812.A3A55 Adam und Eva
1812.A3A8 Auf der höhe
1812.A3B3 Barfüssele
1812.A3B7 Brigitta
1812.A3D4 Deutsche abende
1812.A3D5 Dichter und kaufmann
1812.A3D6 Diethelm von Buchenberg

Individual authors or works
1700-ca. 1860/70
Auerbach, Berthold, 1812-1882
Separate works -- Continued
1812.A3D7 Drei einzige töchter
1812.A3E4 Edelweiss
1812.A3F6 Die forstmeister
1812.A3F7 Die Frau Professorin
1812.A3J5 Joseph im schnee
1812.A3J6 Joseph und Benjamin
1812.A3L3 Das landhaus am Rhein
1812.A3L4 Landolin von Reutershöfen
1812.A3N3 Nach dreissig jahren; neue dorfgeschichten
1812.A3N4 Neues leben
1812.A3S3 Schwartzwälder dorfgeschichten
1812.A3S6 Spinoza (Novel)
1812.A3W3 Waldfried
1812.A3Z3 Zur guten stunde
1812.A3Z6 Correspondence
Biography and criticism
1812.A3Z8 General works
1812.A3Z9 Criticism
1812.A5 Auersperg, Anton Alexander, graf von, 1806-1876 (Table P-PZ40)
1812.A8 Auffenberg, Joseph, freiherr von, 1798-1857 (Table P-PZ40)
1812.A83 August, Duke of Saxe-Gotha and Altenburg, 1772-1822 (Table P-PZ40)
1812.A9 Ayrenhoff, Cornelius Hermann von, 1733-1819 (Table P-PZ40)
1815.B2 Babo, Joseph Marius, 1756-1822 (Table P-PZ40)
1815.B225 Bacheracht, Therese von, 1804-1852 (Table P-PZ40)
1815.B227 Baczko, Ludwig von, 1756-1823 (Table P-PZ40)
1815.B23 Bärmann, Georg Nicolaus, 1785-1850 (Table P-PZ40)
1815.B25 Bässler, Ernst Ferdinand, 1816-1879 (Table P-PZ40)
1815.B3 Baggesen, Jens, 1764-1826 (Table P-PZ40)
1815.B5 Bahrdt, Karl Friedrich, 1741-1792 (Table P-PZ40)
Ballestrem, Eufemia, gräfin von see PT2601.D64
1815.B6 Ballheim, Beda von, fl. 1891 (Table P-PZ40)
1815.B7 Bandlow, Heinrich, 1855- (Table P-PZ40)
1816.B4 Bauer, Edmund, fl. 1846 (Table P-PZ40)
1816.B42 Bauer, Klara, 1836-1876 (Table P-PZ40)
1816.B44 Bauer, Ludwig Cölestin, 1832-1910 (Table P-PZ40)
Bauernfeld, Eduard von, 1802-1890
1816.B5 Collected works. By date
1816.B5A15 Collected plays
1816.B5A17 Collected poems

Individual authors or works
1700-ca. 1860/70
Bauernfeld, Eduard von, 1802-1890 -- Continued
1816.B5A18 Collected novels
1816.B5A19 Collected essays
1816.B5A3-.B5Z29 Separate works
Translations
1816.B5Z3-.B5Z39 English
1816.B5Z4-.B5Z49 French
1816.B5Z6-.B5Z69 Other. By language (alphabetically)
1816.B5Z8-.B5Z9 Biography and criticism
1816.B75 Baumgarten-Crusius, Detlev Karl Wilhelm, 1786-1845 (Table P-PZ40)
Bayer, Robert von see PT2603.A9
1816.B9 Bayersdorfer, A. (Table P-PZ40)
1817.B2 Bechstein, Ludwig, 1801-1860 (Table P-PZ40)
1817.B24 Bechtolsheim, Julie von, 1752-1847 (Table P-PZ40)
1817.B3 Beck, Karl Isidore, 1817-1879 (Table P-PZ40)
1817.B37 Becker, Ludwig, 1808-1861 (Table P-PZ40)
1817.B4 Becker, Nicolaus, 1809-1845 (Table P-PZ40)
Beer, A.T. see PT1819.B3
1817.B5 Beer, Michael, 1800-1833 (Table P-PZ40)
Behrens, Bertha see PT2603.E34
1817.B8 Benedix, Roderich, 1812-1873 (Table P-PZ40)
1818.B2 Bentzel-Sternau, Christian Ernst, graf von, 1767-1849 (Table P-PZ40)
Bereslas, Ferdinand see PT1815.B25
1818.B26 Bermann, Moritz, 1823-1895 (Table P-PZ40)
Bernays, Isaak see PT2463.S8
Bernhard, Marie see PT2603.E7
1818.B4 Bernhardi, August Ferdinand, 1769-1820 (Table P-PZ40)
1818.B42 Bernhardi, Sophie (Tieck), 1775-1833 (Table P-PZ40 modified)
1818.B42A61-.B42Z458 Separate works. By title
1818.B42E8 Evremont
Berthen Juta see PT2281.G57
Berthold, Ernst, 1797-1870 see PT2457.R58
Berthold, Franz see PT2453.R16
1818.B45 Berthold, Gustav Adolf, 1818-1894 (Table P-PZ40)
1818.B46 Berthold, Karl Adam, 1835-1885 (Table P-PZ40)
1818.B5 Berthold, Theodor Gottfried Johann, 1814-1909 (Table P-PZ40)
Bertram, Dr. see PT2513.S4
1818.B6 Bertuch, Friedrich Justin, 1747-1822 (Table P-PZ40)
1818.B7 Bethusy-Huc, Valeska (von Reiswitz-Kaderzin) gräfin von, 1849- (Table P-PZ40)

Individual authors or works

1700-ca. 1860/70 -- Continued

1818.B8 Beyrich, Frau Clementine (Helm), 1825-1896 (Table P-PZ40)

1819.B15 Biedermann, Charles, 1856-1901 (Table P-PZ40)

1819.B2 Biernatzki, Johann Christoph, 1795-1840 (Table P-PZ40)

1819.B23 Bilderbeck, Ludwig Benedict Franz, freiherr von, b. 1766 (Table P-PZ40)

For works in French see PQ1957.B47

1819.B25 Billig, Gustav, 1813-1888 (Table P-PZ40)

1819.B3 Binzer, August Daniel, freiherr von, 1793-1868 (Table P-PZ40)

1819.B33 Binzer, Emilie von, 1801-1891 (Table P-PZ40)

1819.B4 Birch-Pfeiffer, Charlotte, 1800-1868 (Table P-PZ40)

1819.B5 Bischoff, Josef Eduard Konrad, 1828-1911 (Table P-PZ40)

1819.B6 Bitzius, Albert, 1797-1854 (Table P-PZ40)

1819.B65 Blaul, Friedrich, 1809-1863 (Table P-PZ40)

1819.B67 Bloch, Eduard, 1831-1895 (Table P-PZ40)

1819.B7 Blomberg, Hugo, freiherr von, 1820-1871 (Table P-PZ40)

1819.B8 Blüthgen, Viktor, 1844-1920 (Table P-PZ40)

Blum, Adolph see PT1887.G8

1820.B2 Blum, Hans, 1841-1910 (Table P-PZ40)

1820.B3 Blum, Frau Lodoiska von, 1841- (Table P-PZ40)

1820.B4 Blumauer, Aloys, 1755-1798 (Table P-PZ40)

1820.B44 Blumenhagen, Wilhelm, 1781-1839 (Table P-PZ40)

1820.B46 Blumenreich, Frau Franziska, 1849- (Table P-PZ40)

1820.B5 Blumenthal, Oskar, 1852- (Table P-PZ40)

Later plays in collaboration with Gustav Kadelburg

1820.B6 Bode, Johann Joachim Christoph, 1730-1793 (Table P-PZ40)

1820.B7 Bodenstedt, Friedrich Martin von, 1819-1892 (Table P-PZ40)

1820.B8 Bodmer, Johann Jakob, 1698-1783 (Table P-PZ40)

1820.B83 Boehlendorff, Casimir Ulrich, 1775-1825 (Table P-PZ40)

1821 Börne, Ludwig, 1786-1837 (Table P-PZ39)

1823.B2 Börnstein, Heinrich, 1805-1892 (Table P-PZ40)

1823.B3 Boettger, Adolf, 1815-1870 (Table P-PZ40)

1823.B4 Boie, Heinrich Christian, 1744-1806 (Table P-PZ40)

Bolanden, Conrad von see PT1819.B5

1823.B6 Bolgiani, Valeska (Müller), 1830-1876 (Table P-PZ40)

1823.B65 Bonaventura, pseud. (Table P-PZ40)

Author of Nachtwachen

Friedrich Wilhelm Joseph von Schelling, supposed author

Clemens Maria Brentano, supposed author

Friedrich Gottlob Wetzel, supposed author

1823.B7 Borkenstein, Hinrich, 1705-1777 (Table P-PZ40)

1823.B75 Bormann, Edwin, 1851-1912 (Table P-PZ40)

Individual authors or works
1700-ca. 1860/70 -- Continued

1823.B8 Bouterwek, Friedrich, 1766-1828 (Table P-PZ40)
Boy-Ed, Frau Ida see PT2603.O92
1824.B3 Brachmann, Louise, 1777-1822 (Table P-PZ40)
1824.B4 Brachvogel, Albert Emil, 1824-1878 (Table P-PZ40)
1824.B5 Brackel, Ferdinande, freiin von, 1835-1905 (Table P-PZ40)
1824.B52 Bräker, Ulrich, 1735-1798 (Table P-PZ40)
1824.B55 Brandes, Johann Christian, 1735-1799 (Table P-PZ40)
1824.B57 Brandrup, Frau Marie Wilhelmine Emilie (Remus), 1844-1907 (Table P-PZ40)
1824.B7 Braun von Braunthal, Karl Johann, 1802-1866 (Table P-PZ40)
1824.B75 Brawe, Joachim Wilhelm von, 1738-1758 (Table P-PZ40)
1824.B77 Breden, Christiane (Friderik), 1844-1901 (Table P-PZ40)
1824.B8 Breier, Eduard, 1811-1886 (Table P-PZ40)
1824.B9 Breitinger, Johann Jakob, 1701-1776 (Table P-PZ38)
1824.B95 Brentano, Christian, 1784-1851 (Table P-PZ40)
Brentano, Clemens Maria, 1778-1842
1825.A1 Collected works. By date
1825.A11A-.A11Z Selected works. By editor, A-Z
1825.A15 Collected novels
1825.A16 Miscellaneous prose
1825.A18 Collected poems
1825.A19 Collected dramas
Translations
1825.A2-.A29 English. By translator
1825.A3-.A39 French. By translator
1825.A5-.A59 Other. By language (alphabetically)
1825.A61-.Z4 Separate works
1825.A7 Aloys und Imelde (Drama)
Aus der chronika eines fahrenden schülers see PT1825.C4
Bogs wunderbare geschichte see PT1825.W8
1825.C4 Chronika eines fahrenden schülers
1825.C6 Claudia
1825.D7 Die drei nüsse
Frühlingskranz see PT1808.A4A15+
Gedichte see PT1825.A18
1825.G3 Geschichte vom braven Kasperl und dem schönen Annerl
1825.G6 Gockel, Hinkel und Gackeleia
1825.G7 Godwi, oder Das steinerne bild der mutter (Roman)
Der goldfaden see PT1795.W7
1825.G8 Die gründung Prags (Drama)
1825.G9 Gustav Wasa (parody on Kotzebue's play)
Kasperl und Annerl see PT1825.G3

Individual authors or works
1700-ca. 1860/70
Brentano, Clemens Maria, 1778-1842
Separate works -- Continued
Des knaben wunderhorn see PT1203.A7
1825.L8 Die lustigen musikanten (Singspiel)
Märchen see PZ31+
Nachtwachen see PT1823.B65
1825.P7 Ponce de Leon (Lustspiel)
1825.R6 Romanzen vom rosenkranz (Verse)
1825.S3 Satiren und poetische spiele
1825.S4 Die schachtel mit der friedenspuppe (Novelle)
1825.S6 Spanische und italienische novellen
Uhrmacher Bogs wunderbare geschichte see PT1825.W8
Valeria, oder Vaterlist see PT1825.P7
1825.V5 Victoria und ihre geschwister
1825.W8 Wunderbare geschichte von Bogs dem uhrmacher
1825.Z5A2 Letters. By date
1825.Z5A3-.Z5Z Biography and criticism
1827.B17 Brentano, Fritz, 1840- (Table P-PZ40)
1827.B2 Brentano, Sophie, 1776-1800 (Table P-PZ40)
1827.B3 Brentano, Frau Sophie (Schubart), 1773?-1806 (Table P-PZ40)
Wife of Clemens Brentano, 1803-1806
Cf. PT1825.Z5A2 Correspondence of Brentano and Sophie Mereau
1827.B4 Bretzner, Christoph Friedrick, 1748-1807 (Table P-PZ40)
1827.B5 Breusing, Hermann, b. 1815 (Table P-PZ40)
1827.B6 Brinckman, John, 1814-1870 (Table P-PZ40)
1827.B63 Brinkman, Karl Gustaf von, 1764-1847 (Table P-PZ40)
1827.B8 Brobergen, Lotte von, d. 1784 (Table P-PZ40)
1828.B2 Brockes, Barthold Heinrich, 1680-1747 (Table P-PZ40)
1828.B4 Bronikowski, Alexander August Ferdinand von Oppeln-, 1788-1834 (Table P-PZ40)
1828.B45 Bronner, Franz Xaver, 1758-1850 (Table P-PZ40)
1828.B5 Bruckbräu, Friedrich Wilhelm, 1792-1874 (Table P-PZ40)
1828.B55 Brückner, Johann Jakob, 1762-1811 (Table P-PZ40)
1828.B56 Brun, Friederike, 1765-1835 (Table P-PZ40)
Buchholz, Wilhelmine see PT2526.S3
1828.B6 Büchner, Georg, 1813-1837 (Table P-PZ38)
1828.B7 Bülow, Frau Babette (Eberty) von, 1850- (Table P-PZ40)
1828.B75 Bülow, Frida Sophie Luise, freifräulein von, 1857-1909 (Table P-PZ40)
1828.B8 Bülow, Margarethe von, 1860-1884 (Table P-PZ40)
Bürger, Gottfried August, 1747-1794
1829.A1 Collected works. By date

Individual authors or works
1700-ca. 1860/70
Bürger, Gottfried August, 1747-1794 -- Continued

1829.A17	Collected poems. By date
	Translations
1829.A2-.A29	English. By translator
1829.A3-.A39	French. By translator
1829.A5-.A59	Other. By language (alphabetically)
1829.A6	Selected works. Selections. By date
1829.A7-.Z4	Separate works
1829.L4	Lenore (Table P-PZ43)
1829.P4	Des pfarrers Tochter von Taubenhain (Table P-PZ43)
1829.R3	Raubgraf (Table P-PZ43)
1829.W5	Der wilde jäger (Table P-PZ43)
1829.Z5A2	Letters
1829.Z5A3-.Z5Z	Biography and criticism
	Bürger, Hugo see PT2424.L8
1831.B2	Bürstenbinder, Elisabeth, 1838-1918 (Table P-PZ40)
1831.B5	Bulthaupt, Heinrich Alfred, 1849-1905 (Table P-PZ40)
1831.B7	Burgsdorff, Wilhelm von, 1772-1822 (Table P-PZ40)
	Burow, Julie see PT2445.P47
(1832.B2)	Busch, Wilhelm, 1832-1908 see PT2603.U8
1832.B24	Busch-Schücking, Katharina, 1791-1831 (Table P-PZ40)
1832.B3	Buschman, Gotthard, freiherr von, 1810-1888 (Table P-PZ40)
	Byr, Robert see PT2603.A9
1832.C7	Callenbach, Franz, 1663-1743 (Table P-PZ38)
1832.C8	Campe, Joachim Heinrich, 1746-1818 (Table P-PZ40)
1833.C2	Canz, Wilhelmine Friederike Gottliebe, 1815-1901 (Table P-PZ40)
1833.C25	Cardauns, Hermann, 1847-1925 (Table P-PZ40)
	Carmen Sylva see PT1858.E4
	Carus, Theodor see PT1818.B5
1833.C3	Caspari, Karl Heinrich, 1815-1861 (Table P-PZ40)
1833.C4	Castelli, Ignaz Franz, 1781-1862 (Table P-PZ40)
1834	Chamisso, Adelbert von, 1781-1838 (Table P-PZ39 modified)
1834.A61-.Z48	Separate works. By title Subarrange each work by Table P-PZ43 unless otherwise specified
	Peter Schlemihl
1834.P4	German texts. By date
1834.P4A-.P4Z	School texts. By editor
1834.P5	Dramatizations
1834.P6A-.P6Z	Translations. By language, A-Z
1834.P7	Criticism

Individual authors or works
1700-ca. 1860/70 -- Continued
Charles, Jean see PT1824.B7
1837.C2 Chézy, Wilhelmine Christiane (von Klencke) von, 1783-1856 (Table P-PZ40)
1837.C315 Christiani, Rudolph, 1798-1858 (Table P-PZ40)
1837.C32 Christlich Meynender, 18th cent. (Table P-PZ40)
Chrusen, P.P. see PT2545.U6
1837.C35 Claar, Emil, 1842- (Table P-PZ40)
1837.C5 Claudius, Matthias, 1740-1815 (Table P-PZ40)
1837.C52 Clauren, H. (Heinrich), 1771-1854 (Table P-PZ40)
1838.C2 Cölln, Eduard, 1831-1891
Cohn, Moritz see PT2605.O328
Colenfeld, A. von see PT1889.G65
1838.C3 Collin, Heinrich Joseph von, 1772-1811 (Table P-PZ40)
1838.C4 Collin, Matthäus von, 1779-1824 (Table P-PZ40)
Conrad, G. see PT1885.G33
1838.C5 Conrad, Michael Georg, 1846- (Table P-PZ40)
Constant, W. see PT2583.W85
1838.C6 Contessa, Carl Wilhelm Salice-, 1777-1825 (Table P-PZ40)
1838.C65 Cornelius, Peter, 1824-1874 (Table P-PZ40)
Cf. ML410.C8 Music
Corvinus, Jakob see PT2451
1839.C2 Cramer, Johann Andreas, 1710-1777 (Table P-PZ40)
1839.C3 Cramer, Karl Friedrich, 1752-1807 (Table P-PZ40)
1839.C4 Cramer, Karl Gottlob, 1758-1817 (Table P-PZ40)
1839.C5 Cranz, August Friedrich, 1737-1801 (Table P-PZ40)
1839.C6 Cremeri, Benedikt Dominik Anton, 1762-1795 (Table P-PZ40)
Cron, Clara see PT2553.W75
1839.C8 Cronegk, Johann Friedrich von, 1731-1758 (Table P-PZ38)
1840 Cu - Dah
1840.C28 Cünzer, Carl Borromäus (Table P-PZ40)
1841 Dahn, Felix Ludwig Sophus, 1834-1912 (Table P-PZ39)
1842.D3 Dalberg, Wolfgang Heribert, freiherr von, 1750-1806 (Table P-PZ40)
Damberger, Christian Friedrich see PT2534.T37
1842.D7 Damitz, Karl von (Table P-PZ40)
Daniel, Vetter see PT2526.S5
1842.D75 Daumer, Georg Friedrich, 1800-1875 (Table P-PZ40)
Debeck, Dr. see PT2461.S6
1843.D2 Decken, Auguste von der, 1828-1908 (Table P-PZ40)
1843.D3 Deinhardstein, Johann Ludwig, 1794-1859 (Table P-PZ40)
Dellarosa, Ludwig see PT1887.G8
1843.D4 Demme, Hermann Christoph Gottfried, 1760-1822 (Table P-PZ40)
1843.D7 Denis, Michael, 1729-1800 (Table P-PZ40)

Individual authors or works
1700-ca. 1860/70 -- Continued

	Desiderius, Pius see PT2510.S4
1843.D9	Destouches Joseph Anton von, 1767-1832 (Table P-PZ40)
	Detlef, Carl see PT1816.B42
1844.D2	Devrient, Eduard, 1801-1877 (Table P-PZ40)
1844.D3	Devrient, Otto, 1838-1894 (Table P-PZ40)
	Dewall, Johannes van see PT2388.K7
1844.D58	Diepenbrock, Carl Joseph, 1808-1884 (Table P-PZ40)
1844.D7	Dincklage-Campe, Emmy von, 1825-1891 (Table P-PZ40)
1844.D8	Dincklage-Campe, Friedrich, freiherr von, 1839-1918 (Table P-PZ40)
1845	Dingelstedt, Franz, freiherr von, 1814-1881 (Table P-PZ39)
	Dito und Idem see PT1858.E4
1846.D15	Dittmarsch, Karl, 1819-1893 (Table P-PZ40)
1846.D3	Döring, Georg, 1789-1833 (Table P-PZ40)
1846.D4	Dohm, Frau Hedwig, 1833-1919 (Table P-PZ40)
1846.D5	Domeier, Frau Anna Luise, 1847?- (Table P-PZ40)
1846.D7	Dorer, Edmund, 1831-1890 (Table P-PZ40)
	Dranmor see PT2504.S9
1846.D8	Dreves, Lebrecht, 1816-1870 (Table P-PZ40)
1846.D9	Drollinger, Carl Friedrich, 1688-1742 (Table P-PZ40)
1846.D93	Dronke, Ernst, 1822-1891 (Table P-PZ40)
	Droste-Hülshoff, Annette Elisabeth, freiin von, 1797-1848
1848.A1	Collected works. By date
1848.A14	Miscellaneous collections. Unpublished material
1848.A7-.Z3	Separate works
1848.Z4	Letters
1848.Z5	Biography and criticism
1849.D3	Duboc, Édouard, 1822-1910 (Table P-PZ40)
	Duffek, Nikolaus see PT2458.R5
1849.D44	Dulk, Albert Friedrich Benno, 1819-1884 (Table P-PZ40)
1849.D5	Duller, Eduard, 1809-1853 (Table P-PZ40)
1849.D64	Durach, J.B. (Johann Baptist), 1766-1832 (Table P-PZ40)
	Durangelo, R. see PT2461.R7
	Düringsfeld, Ida von see PT2453.R3
1849.D7	Dusch, Johann Jakob, 1725-1787 (Table P-PZ40)
1851.E2	Eberhard, Christian August Gottlob, 1769-1845 (Table P-PZ40)
1851.E5	Ebers, Georg Moritz, 1837-1898 (Table P-PZ40)
1851.E6	Ebert, Karl Egon, 1801-1882 (Table P-PZ40)
1853	Ebner von Eschenbach, Maria, freifrau, 1830-1916 (Table P-PZ39)
1855.E2	Eckardt, Ludwig, 1827-1871 (Table P-PZ40)
1855.E3	Eckermann, Johann Peter, 1792-1854 (Table P-PZ38) Cf. PT2013.E3+
1855.E4	Eckstein, Ernst, 1845-1900 (Table P-PZ40)

Individual authors or works
1700-ca. 1860/70 -- Continued
Ehrich, Gärtner see PT1851.E2
1856 Eichendorff, Joseph Karl Benedikt, freiherr von, 1788-1857 (Table P-PZ39)
1858.E2 Eichrodt, Ludwig, 1827-1892 (Table P-PZ40)
1858.E25 Eisler, Moritz, 1818-1890 (Table P-PZ40)
Elbe, A. von der see PT1843.D2
1858.E3 Elcho, Rudolf, 1839-1922? (Table P-PZ40)
1858.E36 Elisabeth, Empress, consort of Franz Joseph I, Emperor of Austria, 1837-1898 (Table P-PZ40)
1858.E4 Elisabeth, queen of Romania, 1843-1916 (Table P-PZ40)
"Dito und Idem" (pseudonym of Queen Elizabeth and M. Kremitz)
Elling, Franz von see PT2436.M6
Elmar, Karl see PT2533.S4
1858.E5 Elsholtz, Franz von, 1791-1872 (Table P-PZ40)
1858.E55 Elz, Alexander, fl. ca. 1858 (Table P-PZ40)
1858.E6 Emerich, Friedrich Joseph, 1773-1802 (Table P-PZ40)
End, Jörg von see PT2526.S4
1858.E7 Engel, Johann Jakob, 1741-1802 (Table P-PZ40)
1858.E73 Engel, Moritz Erdmann, 1767-1836 (Table P-PZ40)
1858.E75 Engelhardt, Karl August, 1768-1834 (Table P-PZ40)
1858.E755 Engels, Friedrich, 1820-1895 (Table P-PZ40)
Eritis sicut Deus see PT1833.C2
Erlburg, L. von see PT2515.S7
1858.E8 Eschenburg, Johann Joachim, 1743-1820 (Table P-PZ40)
1858.E84 Essellen, Christian, 1823-1859 (Table P-PZ40)
Essenther, Franziska see PT1820.B46
1858.E92 Ewald, Johann Joachim, b. 1727 (Table P-PZ40)
Eyth, Max von, 1836-1906 see PT2609.Y7
1861.F2 Felder, Franz Michael, 1839-1869 (Table P-PZ40)
Fels, Egon see PT2349.H75
1861.F4 Feuchtersleben, Ernst, freiherr von, 1806-1849 (Table P-PZ40)
Filidor see PT2436.M49
1861.F43 Fischer, Johann Georg, 1816-1897 (Table P-PZ40)
1861.F45 Fitger, Arthur Heinrich Wilhelm, 1840-1909 (Table P-PZ40)
1861.F65 Flach, Josephine Adelheid Mathilde, 1826- (Table P-PZ40)
1861.F67 Fleck, Clara, 1838- (Table P-PZ40)
1861.F7 Follen, August Adolf Ludwig, 1794-1855 (Table P-PZ40)
1861.F75 Follen, Charles Theodore Christian, 1796-1840 (Table P-PZ40)
Fontane, Theodor, 1819-1898
1863.A1 Collected works. By date
1863.A15 Collected novels and stories. By date
1863.A17 Collected poems. By date

Individual authors or works
1700-ca. 1860/70
Fontane, Theodor, 1819-1898 -- Continued
1863.A6 Selected works. Selections. By date
1863.A61-.Z3 Separate works. By title
Subarrange each work by Table P-PZ43
1863.Z4 Autobiography
1863.Z5 Letters
1863.Z6 Biography
1863.Z7 Criticism
1865.F15 Forster, Georg, 1754-1794 (Table P-PZ38)
Fouqué, La Motte see PT2389
1865.F2 François, Luise von, 1817-1893 (Table P-PZ40)
1865.F25 Frankl, Ludwig August, 1810-1894 (Table P-PZ40)
Franz, Henrietta see PT2445.P43
Franzos, Karl Emil see PT2611.R3
Frapan, Ilse see PT2601.K7
1865.F7 Freericks, Minna, 1826-1911 (Table P-PZ40)
Freese, Heinrich see PT2463.S8
Freier, Gustav see PT2388.L3
Freiligrath, Ferdinand, 1810-1876
1867.A1 Collected works. By date
Translations
1867.A1995 Polyglot. By date
1867.A2-.A29 English. By translator, if given, or date
1867.A3-.A39 French. By translator, if given, or date
1867.A5-.A59 Other. By language
1867.A6 Selected works. Selections. By date
1867.A61-.Z48 Separate works. By title
Subarrange each work by Table P-PZ43
1867.Z4 Letters
1867.Z5 Biography
1867.Z6 Criticism
1869.F4 Frenzel, Karl Wilhelm Theodor, 1827-1914 (Table P-PZ40)
Frey, Bernhard see PT2603.E7
1869.F45 Frey, Friedrich Hermann, 1839-1911 (Table P-PZ40)
1872.F3 Frey, Jakob, 1824-1875 (Table P-PZ40)
1872.F5 Freydorf, Frau Alberta (von Cornberg) von, 1846- (Table P-PZ40)
Freyer, Gustav see PT2388.L3
1873 Freytag, Gustav, 1816-1895 (Table P-PZ39)
1875.F24 Friedrich, Friedrich, 1828-1890 (Table P-PZ40)
1875.F6 Fröhlich, Abraham Emanuel, 1796-1865 (Table P-PZ40)
1875.F64 Frölich, Frau Henriette (Rauthe), 1768-1819 (Table P-PZ40)
1875.F7 Frommel, Emil, 1828-1896 (Table P-PZ40)
1875.F84 Fuchs, Adolf, 1805-1885 (Table P-PZ40)

Individual authors or works
1700-ca. 1860/70 -- Continued
1875.F9 Fulda, Fürchtegott Christian, b. 1768 (Table P-PZ40)
1875.F96 Fürnstein, Anton, 1783-1841 (Table P-PZ40)
1875.F97 Fuseli, Henry, 1741-1825 (Table P-PZ40)
Galen, Philipp see PT2390.L5
Gall, Louise von see PT2512.S22
1877.G5 Garve, Christian, 1742-1798 (Table P-PZ40)
1877.G7 Gaudy, Franz Bernhard Heinrich Wilhelm, freiherr von, 1800-1840 (Table P-PZ40)
1880.G4 Geib, August, 1842-1879 (Table P-PZ40)
1881 Geibel, Emanuel, 1815-1884 (Table P-PZ39)
1882.G3 Geiger, Carl Ignaz, 1756-1791 (Table P-PZ40)
1882.G4 Gelbcke, Ferdinand Adolf, 1812-1892 (Table P-PZ40)
1883 Gellert, Christian Fürchtegott, 1715-1769 (Table P-PZ39 modified)
Biography and criticism
(1883.Z5A5-.Z5Z) This number not used
1883.Z6 General works
1885.G2 Gemmington, Eberhard Friedrich, freiherr von, 1726-1791 (Table P-PZ40)
1885.G25 Gemmington, Otto Heinrich, freiherr von, 1755-1836 (Table P-PZ38)
1885.G3 Genée, Rudolph, 1824-1914 (Table P-PZ40)
Gensichen, Otto Franz see PT2613.E456
1885.G33 Georg, prince of Prussia, 1826-1902 (Table P-PZ40)
George, Amara see PT2372.K8
1885.G35 Georgi, Karl August, 1802-1867 (Table P-PZ40)
1885.G4 Gerhardt, Dagobert von, 1831-1910 (Table P-PZ40)
1885.G45 Gerlach (Table P-PZ40)
1885.G5 Gerle, Wolfgang Adolf, 1781-1846 (Table P-PZ40)
1885.G6 Gerok, Karl, 1815-1890 (Table P-PZ40)
1885.G7 Gerstäcker, Friedrich Wilhelm Christian, 1816-1872 (Table P-PZ40)
1885.G8 Gerstenberg, Heinrich Wilhelm von, 1737-1823 (Table P-PZ40)
1885.G85 Gessler, Friedrich, 1844-1891 (Table P-PZ40)
1886 Gessner, Salomon, 1730-1788 (Table P-PZ39 modified)
1886.A61-.Z48 Separate works. By title
1886.D2 Daphnis (Table P-PZ43)
1886.E6 Erast (Table P-PZ43)
1886.E7 Der erste schiffer (Table P-PZ43)
1886.I5 Idyllen (Table P-PZ43)
1886.I6 Neue idyllen (Table P-PZ43)
1886.N2 Die nacht (Table P-PZ43)
1886.T6 Der tod Abels (Table P-PZ43)
1887.G15 Gildemeister, Otto, 1823-1902 (Table P-PZ40)

Individual authors or works
1700-ca. 1860/70 -- Continued
1887.G2 Gilm zu Rosenegg, Hermann von, 1812-1864 (Table P-PZ38)
1887.G3 Giseke, Robert, 1827-1890 (Table P-PZ40)
1887.G6 Glaser, Adolf, 1829-1916 (Table P-PZ40)
1887.G7 Glassbrenner, Adolf, 1810-1876 (Table P-PZ40)
1887.G76 Glatz, Jakob (Table P-PZ40)
1887.G8 Gleich, Joseph Alois, 1772-1841 (Table P-PZ40)
1888 Gleim, Johann Wilhelm Ludwig, 1719-1803 (Table P-PZ39)
1889.G2 Glück, Barbara Elisabeth, 1814-1894 (Table P-PZ40)
1889.G3 Glümer, Claire von, 1825-1906 (Table P-PZ40)
1889.G4 Gmeiner, Christiane, 1839 or 40-1912 (Table P-PZ40)
Godin, Frau Amélie (Speyer) Linz see PT2424.L53
1889.G5 Göckingk, Leopold Friedrich Günther von, 1748-1828 (Table P-PZ38)
1889.G55 Goedeke, Karl, 1814-1887 (Table P-PZ40)
1889.G6 Goedsche, Hermann Ottomar Friedrich, 1815-1878 (Table P-PZ40)
1889.G65 Goerling, Adolph, 1821-1877 (Table P-PZ40)
1889.G7 Görlitz, Karl, 1830-1890 (Table P-PZ40)
1889.G8 Görner, Karl August, 1806-1884 (Table P-PZ40)
1889.G9 Görres, Johann Joseph von, 1776-1848 (Table P-PZ40)
Goethe, Johann Wolfgang von, 1749-1832
Collected works
Editions to 1867
By date-letter for the first volume
1891.A70-.A99 1770-1799
1891.B00-.B66 1800-1866
Editions, 1867-
By date-letter for the first volume
1891.B67-.B99 1869-1899
1891.C00-.C99 1900-1999
1891.D00-.D99 2000-2099
(1891.Z5) Critical and annotated editions
Translations see PT2026+
1892.A2 Selections. Anthologies. Quotations
Cf. PT1896, PT2026.A2, etc.
Partial editions. Selected works
1892.A3-.Z3 General. By editor
1893 By period
For the earlier incomplete editions published by Goethe or unauthorized reprints of the same see PT1891
To 1775 or 1778. Der junge Goethe
1893.A1 General. By editor, A-Z
1893.A2 Childhood. Youth to 1765
1893.A3 Leipzig. Frankfurt. 1765-1770

Individual authors or works
1700-ca. 1860/70
Goethe, Johann Wolfgang von, 1749-1832
Collected works
Partial editions. Selected works
By period
To 1775 or 1778. Der junge Goethe -- Continued

1893.A4 Strassburg, 1770-1771
1893.A5 Wetzlar. Frankfurt. 1772-1775
1893.A6 Weimar, 1775-1786
1893.A7 Italian journey, 1786-1788
Cf. PT2001.C1+ Italienische reise
1893.A8 1788-1805. Goethe and Schiller
1893.A9 Later years. 1805-1832
1894 Poems and dramas
General
1894.A1 By date
1894.A2A-.A2Z By editor, A-Z
Poems
1894.A3 Comprehensive editions. By date
1894.A4-Z Editions with commentaries. By editor, A-Z
Translations see PT2026+
1895 Selections. Anthologies. Quotations
see PT1892.A2
1895.A2 By editor, publisher, A-Z
1895.A3 School editions
(1895.A5-Z) By period
see PT1893
Special forms
Lyric see PT1894
1895.B2 Balladen
1895.B3 Criticism
1895.E7 Elegien
1895.S8 Sonette
1896 Minor collections. Almanacs, birthday books, etc.
Cf. PT1892.A2, PT2026.A2, etc.
1898 Particular groups as arranged in the "Ausgabe letzter hand"
1898.A5 An personen
1898.A6 Antiker form sich nähernd
Balladen see PT1895.B2
1898.C3 Cantaten
Elegien see PT1895.E7
1898.E6 Epigrammatisch
1898.E7 Epigramme, Sechzehn
Epigramme, Venezianische see PT1898.V3
1898.G4 Gesellige lieder

Individual authors or works
1700-ca. 1860/70
Goethe, Johann Wolfgang von, 1749-1832
Poems and dramas
Poems
Selections. Anthologies. Quotations
Particular groups as arranged in the "Ausgabe letzter hand" -- Continued

1898.G6 Gott, gemüt und welt
1898.G7 Gott und welt
1898.I6 Invektiven
1898.K8 Kunst
1898.L8 Lyrisches
1898.P3 Parabolisch
Sonette see PT1895.S8
1898.S2 Sprichwörtlich
1898.S3 Sprüche in reimen
Cf. PT1898.G6 Gott, gemüt und welt
Cf. PT1898.S2 Sprichwörtlich
Cf. PT1898.Z2 Zahme Xenien
1898.V3 Venezianische epigramme
1898.V4 Vermischte gedichte
1898.V5 Vier jahreszeiten
1898.V7 Votivtafeln (by Goethe and Schiller)
1898.W3 Weissagungen des Bakis
1898.W4 West-östlicher divan
1898.W5 Criticism
1898.X2 Xenien (by Goethe and Schiller)
1898.Z2 Zahme Xenien
1898.Z5 Other selections not comprised in PT1895 or PT1898.A-Z2. By editor
1899 Special poems
e.g.
Cf. PT1911 Epic poems
1899.E5 Elegie, September, 1823
1899.E8 Erlkönig
1899.G4 Die geheimnisse
1899.K6 Kleine blumen
1899.Z3 Die zauberflöte
1899.Z9 Poems designated by first word
1899.Z9W7 "Worte die der dichter spricht"
1900 Spurious poems
Cf. PT2017.A+ Spurious works
1901 Imitations, parodies, travesties
Cf. PT2018 Imitations in general
(1902) Art, illustrations, music
Illustrations see PT2022

	Individual authors or works
	1700-ca. 1860/70
	Goethe, Johann Wolfgang von, 1749-1832
	Poems and dramas
	Poems
	Art, illustrations, music
	Musical compositions
	see M and ML
	Criticism, interpretation, etc.
1904	General works
1906	Special
	Particular groups of poems see PT1898
	Particular poems see PT1899
1907	Textual criticism
	Cf. PT2219+ General
(1908)	Language
	see PT2225+
(1909)	Versification
	see PT2235
(1910)	Study and teaching
	see PT2150
1911	Epic poems
	Collections
1911.A1	By date
1911.A1A-.A1Z	By editor, A-Z
1911.A2-Z	Separate works
1911.A3	Achilleis
1911.E8	Der ewige Jude
1911.H2-.H7	Hermann und Dorothea
1911.H2	Text editions. By date
1911.H2A-.H2Z	Editions. By editor, A-Z
1911.H4A-.H4Z	School editions. By editor, A-Z
1911.H7	Criticism
1911.J3	Die jagd (projected poem)
1911.N3	Naturgedicht (projected poem)
1911.R2-.R7	Reineke Fuchs
1911.R2	Text editions. By date
1911.R2A-.R2Z	Editions. By editor, A-Z
1911.R4A-.R4Z	School editions. By editor, A-Z
1911.R7	Criticism
1911.W5	Wilhelm Tell (projected poem)
1912	Criticism, interpretation, etc.
1914	Dramatic works
	Collections
1914.A1	Text editions. By date
(1914.A1A-.A1Z)	Editions. By editor
	Translations see PT2026+

Individual authors or works
1700-ca. 1860/70
Goethe, Johann Wolfgang von, 1749-1832
Poems and dramas
Dramatic works -- Continued
Selected plays
General
1914.A2 Text editions. By date
(1914.A2A-.A2Z) Editions. By editor
By period
1914.A3 To 1786
1914.A4 1786-1832
(1914.A5) Selections, anthologies
see PT1892.A2
Minor groups
1914.A7 Festspiele
1914.A8 Maskenzüge
1914.A83 Prologues, theaterreden, etc.
1914.A85 Fragments
1914.A87 Translations
Criticism
For criticism of particular groups, see the group
General see PT1964+
Separate works
1915.A8 Die aufgeregten
1915.B8 Der bürgergeneral
1915.C2 Claudine von Villa Bella
Clavigo
1915.C5 Texts. By date
1915.C5A-.C5Z Texts. By editor
1915.C6 School editions. By editor
1915.C8 Criticism
Egmont
1915.E1 Texts. By date or editor
1915.E2 Acting editions. By editor
1915.E3 School editions. By editor
1915.E4 Criticism
1915.E6 Elpenor
1915.E7 Des Epimenides erwachen
1915.E8 Erwin und Elmire
1915.F3 Fastnachtsspiel
Faust
Editions
1916.A1 Complete editions (Parts 1-2). By date
(1916.A2) Complete editions. By editor
1916.A3 Acting editions. By editor
1916.A4 School editions. By editor

Individual authors or works
1700-ca. 1860/70
Goethe, Johann Wolfgang von, 1749-1832
Poems and dramas
Dramatic works
Separate works, A-Z
Faust
Editions -- Continued

1916.A5 Collections of omitted passages
Translations see PT2026+
1916.A6 Selections, anthologies. By date
Separate parts
1917.A1 The "Urfaust"
1917.A2 Faust. Ein fragment
Faust. First part
1917.A4 Editions. By date
1917.A4A-.A4Z Critical editions. By editor, A-Z
1917.A6A-.A6Z School editions. By editor, A-Z
Omitted passages see PT1916.A5
Translations see PT2026+
Selections see PT1916.A6
Special parts
1917.A8 Zueignung
1917.A81 Vorspiel
1917.A82 Prolog in Himmel
1917.A83-.A87 Separate acts, 1-5
1917.A88 Walpurgisnacht
Faust. Second part
1919.A1 Editions. By date
1919.A1A-.A1Z Critical editions. By editor
(1919.A2) Acting editions
see PT1919.A2
1919.A3A-.A3Z School editions. By editor, A-Z
(1919.A5) Omitted passages, including "Helena"
see PT1916.A5
Selections, quotations see PT1916.A6
1919.A71-.A75 Editions of special acts, 1-5
1919.A8 Editions of special episodes
1920 Imitations. Paraphrases. Adaptations
1921 Parodies, travesties, etc.
(1922) Music, Opera
see M and ML
1923 Illustrations (without text or with quotations)
Illustrated editions see PT1916+
1924 History and criticism of illustrations
Criticism, interpretation, etc.
1925 General works

Individual authors or works
1700-ca. 1860/70
Goethe, Johann Wolfgang von, 1749-1832
Poems and dramas
Dramatic works
Separate works, A-Z
Faust
Criticism, interpretation, etc. -- Continued
General special

(1927) Philosophy
see PT1925

1928 Sources. Origins

1928.A1 Collections of sources

1928.A2-.Z8 General treatises

1928.Z9-.Z99 Special sources (alphabetically)

1928.Z95 Lucien of Samosata

1928.Z96 Paracelsus

1928.Z98 Winckler, Nikolaus

1929 Characters

1929.A2 General

1929.A5-Z Special

1929.B3 Baccalaureus

Faust see PT1925+

1929.G7 Gretchen

1929.H6 Homunculus

Mephistopheles see PT1925+

1929.W65 Women

1930 Other general special

1931 Comparative criticism. Relations to other works and subjects

(1931.5) Collections of plays, novels and poems on Faust
see PN6071.F33

Translations (as subject)
Cf. PT2020 General works

1932.A2 General

1932.A5-Z By language
e.g.

1932.E5 English (General)

1932.E6-.E79 English translators (alphabetically)
e.g.

1932.E77 Taylor, Bayard

1932.F8 French

1933 Faust on the stage
Cf. PT1968+ Criticism of dramatic representation
Cf. PT2173.A+ Criticism, by country

Individual authors or works
1700-ca. 1860/70
Goethe, Johann Wolfgang von, 1749-1832
Poems and dramas
Dramatic works
Separate works, A-Z
Faust
Criticism, interpretation, etc. -- Continued

1934 Film adaptations
Appreciation of Faust
1935.A2 General and in Germany
1935.A5-Z Special countries, A-Z
1935.E5 England
1935.F8 France
Criticism of special parts, acts, and scenes
1937.A1 The "Urfaust"
1937.A2 Faust (Fragment)
Faust. First part
1938 General
1939 Special
1939.A1 Zueignung
1939.A2 Vorspiel
1939.A3 Prolog in Himmel
1939.B1-.B5 Separate acts, 1-5
1939.C2 Separate scenes. By title, A-Z
1939.C2E2 Zum Erdgeist
Subarrange by author, using successive cutter numbers
1939.C2W2 Wald und höhle
Subarrange by author, using successive cutter numbers
1939.C2W3 Walpurgisnacht
Subarrange by author, using successive cutter numbers
Faust. Second part
1940 General
1941 Special parts
1941.A1-.A5 Act 1-5
Cf. PT2082 Relation to women
Cf. PT2184.W7 Female characters in his works; Das Ewig-Weibliche
1941.B5 Classische Walpurgisnacht
1942 Textual criticism
For special parts see PT1937+
Language
1945 General works
1946 Dictionaries

Individual authors or works
1700-ca. 1860/70
Goethe, Johann Wolfgang von, 1749-1832
Poems and dramas
Dramatic works
Separate works, A-Z
Faust
Criticism, interpretation, etc.
Language -- Continued
1947 Grammar
1948 Versification
1951.F5 Die fischerin
1951.G4 Die geschwister
1951.G8 Götter, helden und Wieland
Götz von Berlichingen
1952.A1 Editions. By date
1952.A2A-.A2Z Acting editions. By editor, A-Z
1952.A3A-.A3Z School editions. By editor, A-Z
Translations see PT2026+
Criticism
1952.A5 Sources
1952.A6-Z Treatises
1953.G7 Gross-Cophta
1953.H3 Hanswursts hochzeit
Hausgenossen, Die ungleichen see PT1963.U6
Iphigenie auf Delphos see PT1958.I6
Iphigenie auf Tauris
Editions
For complete editions containing various versions see PT1954.A2A+
Prose versions
1954.A1 Version of 1779 (Ms. of K. Bibliothek, Berlin)
1954.A11 Lavater's copy, 1780 (Irregular verses)
1954.A12 Strassburg ms. 1780 (Lost)
1954.A13 Version of 1781 (Six mss.; Oldenburg ms. edited by Stahr, 1839)
Final version in verse
1954.A2 Text editions. By date
1954.A2A-.A2Z Critical editions. By editor, A-Z
1954.A3A-.A3Z School editions. By editor, A-Z
1954.A4A-.A4Z Selections, extracts, etc. By editor, A-Z
Translations see PT2026+
Criticism, interpretation, etc.
1955 General
1956 Special

Individual authors or works
1700-ca. 1860/70
Goethe, Johann Wolfgang von, 1749-1832
Poems and dramas
Dramatic works
Separate works, A-Z -- Continued

1958.I6	Iphigenie in Delphi (projected play) "Iphigenie auf Delphos," "Iphigenie von Delphi," etc. Only outline of play preserved
1958.J3	Jahrmarktsfest zu Plundersweilern
1958.J5	Jery und Bätely
1958.K8	Künstlers apotheose
1958.K9	Künstlers erdewallen
1958.L3	Die laune des verliebten
1958.L5	Lila
1958.M2	Mahomet
	Maskenzüge see PT1914.A8
1958.M5	Die mitschuldigen
1958.N2	Die natürliche tochter
1958.N3	Nausikaa (Fragment)
1958.N4	Neueröffnetes puppenspiel
1958.N5	Das neueste von Plundersweilern
1958.P3	Paläofron und Neoterpe
1958.P4	Pandora
1958.P45	Pater Brey
	Plundersweilern, Jahrmarktsfest zu see PT1958.J3
	Plundersweilern, Das neueste see PT1958.N5
1958.P6	Prolog zu den neuesten offenbarungen Gottes
1958.P7	Prometheus
1958.P8	Proserpina
	Puppenspiel, Neueröffnetes see PT1958.N4
1958.S2	Satyros; oder, Der vergötterte waldteufel
1958.S4	Scherz, list und rache
1958.S7	Stella
1958.T3	Tancred
1961	Torquato Tasso (Table P-PZ41 modified)
1961.A3	School editions
1963.T4	Der triumph der empfindsamkeit
1963.U6	Die ungleichen hausgenossen
1963.V3	Die vögel
1963.V6	Vorspiele
	Walpurgisnacht see PT1917.A88
1963.W3	Was wir bringen
1963.Z3	Zauberflöte. Zweiter theil (Fragment)
	Criticism, interpretation, etc. of Goethe's dramatic works
1964	General

Individual authors or works
1700-ca. 1860/70
Goethe, Johann Wolfgang von, 1749-1832
Poems and dramas
Dramatic works
Criticism, interpretation, etc. of Goethe's dramatic works -- Continued
1965 General special
e.g. Technique
1966 Special topics
Plots, suspense, time relations, unities, etc.
Dramatic representation of Goethe's plays
1968 In Germany
Cf. PT1933 Faust on the stage in Germany
Cf. PT1956 Ighigenie auf Tauris
(1969) In other countries
see PT2173
Works in prose and prose fiction
1970.A1 Collections. By date
1970.A1A-.A1Z Collections. By editor, A-Z
Translations see PT2026+
1970.A2 Selections, anthologies, etc.
1970.A3 Partial editions. Selected works. Miscellaneous
1971.A1 Works of fiction
Collections see PT1970.A1
1971.A3-Z Separate works
Aus meinem leben, Dictung und wahrheit see PT2001.A2+
1971.G8 Die guten frauen
1971.H3 Der hausball
Die leiden des jungen Werthers see PT1973+
1971.M2 Das märchen (Tale. Part of Unterhaltungen deutscher ausgewanderten)
1971.M3A-.M3Z School editions. By editor, A-Z
1971.M5 Der mann von fünfzig jahren
1971.N3 Die neue Melusine
1971.N5 Novelle (Das kind mit dem löwen)
1971.R4 Reise der söhne Megaprazons (Fragment)
1971.U5 Unterhaltungen deutscher ausgewanderten
1971.U6 Criticism
1971.W3 Die wahlverwandtschaften (Elective affinities)
1971.W4 Criticism
Wahrheit und dichtung see PT2001.A2+
Werther (Die leiden des jungen Werthers)
Editions
1973 1774-1825 (or 30)
First version. By date

Individual authors or works
1700-ca. 1860/70
Goethe, Johann Wolfgang von, 1749-1832
Works in prose and prose fiction
Works of fiction
Separate works
Werther (Die leiden des jungen Werthers)
Editions
1774-1825 (or 30)
First version. By date -- Continued
1973.A1 Original edition, 1774, and facsimiles
1973.A2 Unauthorized reprints, 1775-1777
Second version
1973.A3 Reproduction of manuscript
1973.A4 Printed edition, 1787
Later editions
1974.A1 Editions. By date
(1974.A2) Editions. By editor
1974.A3A-.A3Z School editions. By editor, A-Z
Translations see PT2026+
1974.A5 Selections, quotations, etc.
Imitations. Parodies
Including verse
German
1975.A1 Contemporary works, 1775-1790
1975.A3 Later works
1975.A5-.A59 English and American
1975.A7-.A79 Other. By language
1977 Illustrations
(1978) Bibliography, catalogs of exhibitions
see Z8350
Criticism
Contemporary works, 1779-1790
1979.A1 Collections
1979.A2-Z Separate
Later works, 1790-
1980 General
1980.Z9 Special topics (not A-Z)
1981.A-.Z7 Special characters, A-Z
Cf. PT2085 Women in Goethe's life
1981.Z8 Wertheriana. Miscellaneous
Wilhelm Meister
1982.A1 Complete editions. By date
1982.A2A-.A2Z Selections, school texts, etc. By editor, A-Z
Translations see PT2026+
Separate parts. By date
1982.A3 Theatralische sendung

Individual authors or works
1700-ca. 1860/70
Goethe, Johann Wolfgang von, 1749-1832
Works in prose and prose fiction
Works of fiction
Separate works
Wilhelm Meister
Separate parts. By date -- Continued
1982.A4 Lehrjahre
1982.A5 Wanderjahre
1982.A7-.Z3 Criticism, interpretation, etc.
Criticism, interpretation, etc. of Goethe's fiction
1984 General
1985 General special
e.g. Technique
1986.A-Z Special topics, A-Z
Other prose works
Autobiographical works see PT2001.A+
Treatises, essays, reviews, etc.
Collections
see PT1970, PT1988+
Special subjects
1988 Literature
For collections only
For individual works, see the subject
1988.A2 Comprehensive collections. By date
1988.A3-Z Special collections
1988.B4 Beiträge zur Jenaische allgemeine literaturzeitung
1988.M2 Maximen und reflexionen
1988.R4 Rezensionen für die Frankfurter gelehrte anzeigen
(1990) Theater and acting
see PT2116+
Art
1992.A1 Collections
1992.A3-Z Separate works
Benvenuto Cellini
see NB623.C332
(1992.K8) Kunst und altertum
see PT2001.G1
1992.P4 Philipp Hackert
1992.P8 Propyläen. Eine periodische schrift
Rameaus neffe see PQ1979.A66
1992.V7 Von deutscher baukunst
1992.W4 Winckelmann und sein jahrhundert

Individual authors or works
1700-ca. 1860/70
Goethe, Johann Wolfgang von, 1749-1832
Works in prose and prose fiction
Other prose works
Treatises, essays, reviews, etc.
Special subjects
Art -- Continued
(1993) Criticism
see PT2203 or the special works
(1995) Science
Collections or separate works
see class Q
1996 Criticism
Cf. PT2206+ Relation to special subjects
1998 Miscellaneous prose works (other than PT1988+)
1998.B4 Beiträge zu Lavaters Physiognomischen fragmenten
1998.B7 Brief des pastors zu * * *.
1998.E7 Ephemerides
1998.L3 Labores juveniles
1998.N3 Nachtrag (biographical sketch of Seckendorff-Aberdar)
1998.N36 Natur (Fragment)
1998.P3 Parodie auf Jacobi's Woldemar
1998.P7 Positiones juris
Autobiographical works
2001.A1 Collections. By date of first volume
Separate works
Annalen see PT2001.H1
Aus meinem leben. Dichtung und wahrheit
2001.A2 Editions. By date
2001.A2A-.A2Z Critical or annotated editions. By editor
2001.A3 Selections, including school editions. By editor
Translations see PT2026+
2001.A9 Biographisches schema
Other works (arranged chronologically)
Schweizerreisen, 1775, 1779, 1797
2001.B1 Briefe aus der Schweiz. 1st and 2d abteilung. By date
2001.B3 Reise in der Schweiz, 1797. (Auf dem nachlass). By date
Italienische reise, 1787-1788
2001.C1 Editions. By date
2001.C3A-.C3Z Selections and school editions. By editor, A-Z
2001.C4 Criticism
2001.D1 Campagne in Frankreich, 1792. By date

Individual authors or works
1700-ca. 1860/70
Goethe, Johann Wolfgang von, 1749-1832
Autobiographical works
Separate works
Other works (arranged chronologically) -- Continued
2001.E1 Belagerung von Mainz, 1793. By date
2001.F1 Sankt Rochus-fest zu Bingen, 1814. By date
2001.F2 Im Rheingau. Herbstage
(Supplement to Sankt-Rochus-fest)
2001.G1 Kunst und altertum am Rhein und Main, 1815. By date
Cf. PT2203 Kunst und altertum...
2001.H1 Tag- und jahreshefte als ergänzung meiner sonstigen bekenntnisse von 1749-1822. By date
2001.H3 Tagebücher
Biographisches schema see PT2001.A9
2003 Criticism, interpretation, etc.
Correspondence
General
2005.A1 Comprehensive collections. By date
Translations see PT2026+
Selections
2005.A3A-.A3Z Miscellaneous. By editor, A-Z
2005.A4A-.A4Z Minor. By editor, A-Z
(2005.A9A-.A9Z) Posthumously published letters
see PT2005.A4A-Z
Special
By period
2006.A1 1766-1788/1800. By editor
2006.A2 1788-1800/1805. By editor
2006.A3 1800/1805-1832. By editor
2006.A5-.Z9 By subject, A-Z
2006.N3 Natural science
Cf. PT2206+ Relation to science
2006.T4 Theater
Cf. PT2116+ Biography
2008.A-Z Special groups. By editor, A-Z
Goethe and the Leipzig friends see PT2006.A1
Goethe and friends in Italy see PT2006.A2
2009.A-Z Special correspondents, A-Z
(2009.A8) Arnim, Bettina von
see PT1808.A4A86
2009.B7 Brentano, Antonia
Arrange by editor

Individual authors or works
1700-ca. 1860/70
Goethe, Johann Wolfgang von, 1749-1832
Correspondence
Special
Special correspondents, A-Z -- Continued

2009.C6 Cotta, Johann Friedrich
Arrange by editor

2009.E4 Eichstädt
Arrange by editor

2009.G3 Goethe, August von
Arrange by editor

2009.G7 Goethe, Johanna (Goethe's wife)
Arrange by editor

2009.G78 Grüner, J.S.
Arrange by editor

2009.H36 Hegel, Georg Wilhelm Friedrich
Arrange by editor

2009.H4 Herder, Johann Gottfried
Arrange by editor

2009.H9 Humboldt, Wilhelm, freiherr von
Arrange by editor

2009.K27 Karl August, grand duke
Arrange by editor

2009.K47 Kestner, August
Arrange by editor

2009.M4 Meyer, Heinrich
Arrange by editor

(2009.M45) Meyer, Nicolaus
see PT2433.M17

2009.O4 O'Donell, Josephine
Arrange by editor

2009.Q36 Quandt, Johann Gottlob von, 1787-1859
Arrange by editor

(2009.S3) Schiller
see PT2471.A2+

2009.S35 Schopenhauer, Arthur, 1788-1860
Arrange by editor

2009.S4 Schultz, Christoph Ludwig Friedrich
Arrange by editor

2009.S63 Soemmerring, Samuel Thomas von, 1755-1830
Arrange by editor

2009.S7 Stein, Charlotte von
Arrange by editor

2009.S8 Stein, Fritz von
Arrange by editor

Individual authors or works
1700-ca. 1860/70
Goethe, Johann Wolfgang von, 1749-1832
Correspondence
Special
Special correspondents, A-Z -- Continued
2009.S84 Šternberg, Kašpar, Graf, 1761-1838
Arrange by editor
2009.S9 Stolberg, Auguste, gräfin zu (afterwards gräfin von Bernstoff)
Arrange by editor
2009.V6 Voigt, Christian Gottlob
Arrange by editor
2009.Z4 Zelter, Karl Friedrich
Arrange by editor
2010 Criticism, interpretation, etc.
2011 Register, indexes, etc.
Conversations
General
2013.A1 Collections. By date
2013.A2A-.A2Z Selections. School editions. By editor, A-Z
Special
2013.A4A-.A4Z By period. By editor, A-Z
2013.A5A-.A5Z By subject, A-Z
Subarrange by editor using successive Cutter numbers
2013.A6-Z With individual persons
2013.E3-.E5 Eckermann
2013.E3 Editions. By date
Translations see PT2026+
2013.E5 Criticism
2013.F2 Falk, Johannes Daniel
2013.M8 Müller, Friedrich von
2017.A-Z Doubtful or spurious works
Including suppressed works
For spurious poems see PT1900
2017.D4 De pulicibus (Juristiche abhandlung über die flöhe)
Prometheus, Deukalion und seine rezensenten see PT2551.W3
2017.U6 Das unglück der Jacobis (Suppressed)
2018 Imitations, paraphrases, adaptations
Cf. PT1901 Imitations, etc. of poems
2020 Translations as subject (Comparative studies, etc.)
e.g. Criticisms of Carlyle's translation of Wilhelm Meiser
Cf. PT1932.A2+ Faust
2022 Illustrations
Class here portfolio, etc., without text, or illustrations with quotations only

Individual authors or works
1700-ca. 1860/70
Goethe, Johann Wolfgang von, 1749-1832
Illustrations -- Continued
Illustrated editions
see PT1891 and separate works, PT1894+
History of Goethe portraits and illustrations see PT2143+

2024 Goethe and music
Texts to which music has been composed and librettos based upon Goethe's works, see ML
Goethe's knowledge of music and references to music in his works see PT2204

Translations
Cf. PT2020 Translations as subject
English
Collected works. By date (date-letters)
2026.A1A70-.A1A99 1770-1799
2026.A1B00-.A1B99 1800-1899
2026.A1C00-.A1C99 1900-1999
2026.A1D00-.A1D99 2000-2099
2026.A2A-.A2Z Selections, anthologies, quotations. By editor, A-Z
Poems
Collections, anthologies, etc.
2026.A3 By date
2026.A3A-.A3Z By translator, A-Z
2026.A4A-.A4Z Special poems. By title, A-Z
e.g.
2026.A4B7-.A4B79 Braut von Korinth
Arrange by translator, using successive cutter numbers
2026.A4E7-.A4E79 Erlkönig
Arrange by translator, using successive cutter numbers
2026.A5 Dramatic works (Collections)
2026.A7-Z Separate poetical and dramatic works
e.g.
For shorter poems see PT2026.A4A+
2026.C5 Clavigo
2026.E2 Egmont
2026.F18 The "Urfaust"
Faust
2026.F2 Anonymous translators. By date
2026.F2A5 Translations of parts 1 and 2, by Anster
2026.F2A51 Translation of part 1, by Anster
2026.F2A52 Translation of part 2, by Anster
2026.F2A6-.F2Z By translator, A-Z

Individual authors or works
1700-ca. 1860/70
Goethe, Johann Wolfgang von, 1749-1832
Translations
English
Separate poetical and dramatic works -- Continued
Goetz von Berlichingen
2026.G4 Anonymous translators. By date
2026.G4A-.G4Z By translator, A-Z
2026.H3 Hermann und Dorothea
2026.I4 Iphigenie auf Tauris
2026.R3 Reineke Fuchs
Stella
2026.S8 Anonymous translators. By date
2026.S8A-.S8Z By translator, A-Z
2026.T7 Torquato Tasso
2026.W3 West-östlichen divan
2026.X2 Xenien
2027 Prose. Prose fiction
2027.A2 Collections
2027.A3-.Z7 Separate works
Autobiography. Aus meinem leben
2027.A8 Anonymous translators. By date
2027.A8A-.A8Z By translator, A-Z
2027.B4 Belagerung von Mainz
2027.B7 Briefe aus der Schweiz
2027.C3 Campagne in Frankreich
2027.C4-.C5 Conversations
2027.C4 General collections
2027.C5 Conversations with Eckermann
2027.G8 Die gute frauen
2027.I7 Italienische reise
2027.K8 Kunst ünd altertum am Rhein und Main
Letters
2027.L4 Collections
2027.L5-.L69 Special correspondents (alphabetically)
Märchen (A tale)
2027.M15 Anonymous translators. By date
2027.M15A-.M15Z By translator, A-Z
2027.M2 Maximen und reflexionen
2027.U6 Unterhaltung deutscher ausgewanderten
Die wahlverwandtschaften
2027.W2 Anonymous translators. By date
2027.W2A-.W2Z By translator, A-Z
Werther
2027.W3 Anonymous translators. By date
2027.W3A-.W3Z By translator, A-Z

Individual authors or works
1700-ca. 1860/70
Goethe, Johann Wolfgang von, 1749-1832
Translations
English
Prose. Prose fiction
Separate works -- Continued

2027.W5 Wilhelm Meister

2029.D6-.D8 Dutch. Flemish

Collections

2029.D6A1 Collected works. By date

2029.D6A2-.D6A29 Selections, anthologies, quotations
Arrange by translator (alphabetically)

2029.D6A3-.D6A39 Poems (Collected)
Arrange by editor or translator

2029.D6A4-.D6A49 Special poems (Alphabetically)

2029.D6A5 Dramatic works (Collected)

2029.D6A7-.D6Z Dramatic and poetical works. Special, A-Z

2029.D69 Prose collections

2029.D7A-.D7Z Fiction. Special works, A-Z

2029.D8A2-.D8A29 Letters (Collections)

2029.D8A3-.D8Z Letters. By correspondent, A-Z

2029.D83 Conversations

2029.D84 Other works, A-Z

French

2029.F4A1 Collected works. By date

2029.F4A2-.F4A29 Selections. Anthologies. Quotations
Arrange by translators (alphabetically)

2029.F4A3-.F4A39 Poems (Collected)
Arrange by editor or translator

2029.F4A4-.F4A49 Special poems (alphabetically)

2029.F4A5-.F4A59 Dramatic works (Collected)

2029.F4A7-.F4Z Dramatic and poetical works. Special, A-Z
Subarrange by translator using consecutive Cutter numbers

2029.F49 Prose collections

2029.F5A-.F5Z Fiction. Special works, A-Z
Subarrange by translators using consecutive Cutter numbers

2029.F6A2-.F6A29 Letters (Collections)

2029.F6A3-.F6Z Letters. By correspondent, A-Z

2029.F63 Conversations

2029.F64A-.F64Z Other works, A-Z

2029.F8 Frisian

Italian

2029.I4A1 Collected works. By date

Individual authors or works
1700-ca. 1860/70
Goethe, Johann Wolfgang von, 1749-1832
Translations
Italian -- Continued

2029.I4A2-.I4A29 Selections. Anthologies. Quotations
Arrange by translators (alphabetically)
2029.I4A3-.I4A39 Poems (Collected)
Arrange by editor or translator
2029.I4A4-.I4A49 Special poems (alphabetically)
2029.I4A5-.I4A59 Dramatic works (Collected)
2029.I4A7-.I4Z Dramatic and poetical works. Special, A-Z
Subarrange by translator using consecutive Cutter numbers
2029.I49 Prose collections
2029.I5A-.I5Z Fiction. Special works, A-Z
Subarrange by translators using consecutive Cutter numbers
2029.I6A2-.I6A29 Letters (Collections)
2029.I6A3-.I6Z Letters. By correspondent, A-Z
2029.I63 Conversations
2029.I64A-.I64Z Other works, A-Z

Portuguese
2029.P4A1 Collected works. By date
2029.P4A2-.P4A29 Selections. Anthologies. Quotations
Arrange by translators (alphabetically)
2029.P4A3-.P4A39 Poems (Collected)
Arrange by editor or translator
2029.P4A4-.P4A49 Special poems (alphabetically)
2029.P4A5-.P4A59 Dramatic works (Collected)
2029.P4A7-.P4Z Dramatic and poetical works. Special, A-Z
Subarrange by translator using consecutive Cutter numbers
2029.P49 Prose collections
2029.P5A-.P5Z Fiction. Special works, A-Z
Subarrange by translators using consecutive Cutter numbers
2029.P6A2-.P6A29 Letters (Collections)
2029.P6A3-.P6Z Letters. By correspondent, A-Z
2029.P63 Conversations
2029.P64A-.P64Z Other works, A-Z

Scandinavian
2029.S2 Danish and Norwegian
2029.S4 Icelandic
2029.S6 Swedish

Spanish
2029.S7A1 Collected works. By date

Individual authors or works
1700-ca. 1860/70
Goethe, Johann Wolfgang von, 1749-1832
Translations
Spanish -- Continued

2029.S7A2-.S7A29 Selections. Anthologies. Quotations
Arrange by translators (alphabetically)

2029.S7A3-.S7A39 Poems (Collected)
Arrange by editor or translator

2029.S7A4-.S7A49 Special poems (alphabetically)

2029.S7A5-.S7A59 Dramatic works (Collected)

2029.S7A7-.S7Z Dramatic and poetical works. Special, A-Z
Subarrange by translator using consecutive Cutter numbers

2029.S79 Prose collections

2029.S8A-.S8Z Fiction. Special works, A-Z
Subarrange by translators using consecutive Cutter numbers

2029.S9A2-.S9A29 Letters (Collections)

2029.S9A3-.S9Z Letters. By correspondent, A-Z

2029.S93 Conversations

2029.S94A-.S94Z Other works, A-Z

2030 Other European languages
Non Slavic
Celtic

2030.C1 Breton (Table PT9)

2030.C2 Cornish (Table PT9)

2030.C3 Gaelic (Table PT9)

2030.C4 Irish (Table PT9)

2030.C5 Manx (Table PT9)

2030.C8 Welsh (Table PT9)

2030.F5 Finnish (Table PT9)

2030.G7 Greek, Modern (Table PT9)

2030.H8 Hungarian (Table PT9)

2030.L2 Latin (Table PT9)
Romance

2030.R37 Catalan (Table PT9)

2030.R8 Romanian (Table PT9)

2030.Y53 Yiddish (Table PT9)

2032 Slavic

2032.B3 Bohemian (Table PT9)

2032.B6 Bulgarian (Table PT9)

2032.C3 Croatian (Table PT9)

2032.L3 Lettish (Table PT9)

2032.L6 Lithuanian (Table PT9)

2032.P3 Polish (Table PT9)

2032.R3 Russian (Table PT9)

Individual authors or works
1700-ca. 1860/70
Goethe, Johann Wolfgang von, 1749-1832
Translations
Other European languages
Slavic -- Continued
2032.R7 Ruthenian (Table PT9)
2032.S6 Slovakian (Table PT9)
2032.W2 Wendic (Table PT9)
2034.A-Z Asian languages, A-Z
Subarrange each by Table PT9
e.g.
2034.A7 Arabic (Table PT9)
2034.A75 Armenian (Table PT9)
2034.H4 Hebrew (Table PT9)
2034.K3 Kazakh (Table PT9)
2034.U73 Urdu (Table PT9)
2035.A-Z Oceanic languages, A-Z
2036.A-Z African languages, A-Z
2037.A-Z American Indian languages, A-Z
2038.A-Z Mixed languages (Pidgin or creole), A-Z
(2038.Y6) Yiddish
see PT2030.Y53
(2039) Artificial languages
see PM
Biography and criticism
(2044) Bibliography
see Z8350
Periodicals and societies
2045 German
2046 Other
2048 Dictionaries, indexes, etc.
Class here general encyclopedic dictionaries only. For dictionaries on special subjects, see the subject
For dictionaries of quotations see PT1892.A2
For dictionaries of characters see PT2183+
For concordances and language dictionaries see PT2239
General treatises. Life and works
2049 English
2050 French
2051 German
2052 Outlines, syllabi, etc.
2053 Other. Danish, Italian, etc.
(2055) Study and teaching
see PT2150
Biography

Individual authors or works
1700-ca. 1860/70
Goethe, Johann Wolfgang von, 1749-1832
Biography and criticism
Biography -- Continued
General see PT2049+
Sources
Cf. PT2005+ Correspondence
Cf. PT2013.A+ Conversations
Autobiography see PT2001.A+
2057 Tagebücher
Cf. PT2001.H3 Autobiographical works
2058 Other general special (not included in any of the following groups)
Special periods
Youth and early education (1749-1775/86)
2060 Comprehensive treatises
2061 Special topics (not A-Z)
1775-1786
2065 General
2066 Special topics (not A-Z)
1786-1816
General see PT2049+
2067 Special topics (not A-Z)
Goethe and Schiller see PT2095+
Goethe's marriage see PT2086
Minna Herzlieb (1807) see PT2085.A5
Marianne von Willemer (1814) see PT2085.A6
Old age and death, 1816-1832
2069 General works
2070 General special
2071 Special topics (not A-Z)
Marriage of August von Goethe and Ottilie von Pogwisch, 1817 see PT2079.A8
Ulrike von Levetzow see PT2085.A7
Birth of Wolfgang von Goethe, 1820 see PT2250.G2
Illness, 1823 see PT2106
Eckermann and Riemer see PT2013.A+
"Ausgabe letzter hand" see PT2155.C6
2073 Death of Goethe. Last days. Funeral and burial place
Eulogies and poems in honor of Goethe see PT2140+
2074 Legends and traditions concerning Goethe's life. Anecdotes

Individual authors or works
1700-ca. 1860/70
Goethe, Johann Wolfgang von, 1749-1832
Biography and criticism
Biography
Legends and traditions concerning Goethe's life.
Anecdotes -- Continued
2074.5 Caricatures and cartoons
Including satirical and comic works
Personal relations
Cf. PT2005+ Letters
Relatives
2075 Family. Ancestry. Home
The Goethe family
General see PT2075
2077 Special
2077.A1 Friedrich Georg Goethe
2077.A3 Johann Kaspar Goethe
2077.A5 His works and letters
2077.A7 Works about him
The Textor family
2077.B1 General
Special
2077.B2 Goethe's maternal grandparents
Katharina Elisabeth (Textor) Goethe
Letters by her
2077.B5 Editions. By date
2077.B6-.B79 Translations. By language (alphabetically)
2077.B9 Works about her
2077.C1 Cornelia Goethe (Frau J.G. Schlosser)
2077.Z5 Other members of the families of Goethe's parents
2079 The Goethe family at Weimar
2079.A2 General
Johanna Christiane Sophia (Vulpius) see PT2086
Christian August Vulpius see PT2549.V8
2079.A6 Alma von Goethe, 1827-1844
2079.A8 August von Goethe, 1787-1830
2079.O8 Ottilie (von Pogwisch) Goethe
2079.U56 Ulrike von Pogwisch, 1798-1875
2079.W3 Walther Wolfgang von Goethe, 1818-1885
Wolfgang Maximilian von Goethe see PT2250.G2
Love and relations to women
2081 General

Individual authors or works
1700-ca. 1860/70
Goethe, Johann Wolfgang von, 1749-1832
Biography and criticism
Biography
Personal relations
Love and relations to women -- Continued

2082 General special
e.g. the "ewig-weibliche" in Goethe's life
Cf. PT1941 Criticism of Faust, Part 2
Cf. PT2184.W7 Female characters in his works

(2083) By period
see PT2060+

(2084) By place
see PT2060+

2085 By name

2085.A1 Gretchen

2085.A15 Anna Katharina Schönkopf

2085.A2 Friederike von Sesenheim (Friederike Elisabeth Brion)

2085.A3 Charlotte Buff
Afterwards Frau Charlotte Kestner
Cf. PT1981.A+ Werther

2085.A35 "Lili." Anna Elisabeth Schönemann
Afterwards Frau Freifrau von Dürckheim

2085.A4 Charlotte von Stein

2085.A43 Corona Schröter

(2085.A45) Christiane Vulpius
see PT2086

2085.A5 Minna Herzlieb
Cf. PT1971.W3 Die wahlverwandtschaften

2085.A6 Marianne von Willemer
Cf. PT1898.W4

2085.A7 Ulrike von Levetzow

2085.A9-Z Other, A-Z

2085.A95 Anna Amalia, Duchess of Saxe-Weimar-Eisenach

2085.B7 Brentano, Maximiliane

2085.E3 Egloffstein, Caroline von

2085.J3 Jagemann, Karoline

2085.K3 Kauffmann, Angelica

2085.L3 LaRoche, Sophie von

2086 Goethe's marriage to Christiane Vulpius

Relations to friends and contemporaries

2088 General

Individual authors or works
1700-ca. 1860/70
Goethe, Johann Wolfgang von, 1749-1832
Biography and criticism
Biography
Personal relations
Relations to friends and contemporaries -- Continued

2089 General special
e.g. Goethe as a friend and in his social intercourse
Cf. PT2105+ Distinguished visitors

(2090) By period
see PT2060+

Individual friends and contemporaries
Goethe and Schiller
Cf. PT321 History of German literature in this period
Cf. PT2471.A2+ Correspondence
Cf. PT2473.A7 English translations

2095 General works

2096 General special. Miscellaneous
Relation to the Romantic school see PT2169.R7

2098 Memorials. Testimonials to their genius
Cf. PT2140+ General
Cf. PT2486.Z3+ Schiller alone

(2099) Monuments, portraits, etc.
see PT2143+

2100.A-Z Other friends and contemporaries, A-Z
Arnim, Bettina (Brentano) von see PT1808.A4

2100.A94 Avenarius, Benedikt Christian, b. 1739

(2100.B3) Beethoven
see ML410.B4

2100.B8 Brentano, Clemens

2100.B9 Byron, George Gordon

2100.C3 Carlyle, Thomas

2100.D5 Diderot, Denis

2100.D53 Diede

Eckermann, Johann Peter
see PT1855.E3; PT2013.E3+

2100.G5 Giovinazzi

2100.G7 Grimm brothers

2100.H4 Herder, Johann Gottfried

2100.H7 Hölderlin, Friedrich

Holtei see PT2101.H7

2100.H8 Horstig, Carl Gottlieb

Individual authors or works
1700-ca. 1860/70
Goethe, Johann Wolfgang von, 1749-1832
Biography and criticism
Biography
Personal relations
Relations to friends and contemporaries
Individual friends and contemporaries
Other friends and contemporaries, A-Z -- Continued

2100.K3 Kant, Immanuel
(2100.K4) Kayser, P.C.
see ML410.K; PT2204
2100.K6 Klopstock, Friedrich Gottlieb
2100.K7 Kotzebue, August von
2100.L4 Lenz, Jacob
2100.L43 Leopold III, Prince of Anhalt-Dessau, 1740-1817
2100.L5 Lessing, Gotthold Ephraim
2100.M35 Manzoni, Alessandro, 1785-1873
2100.M4 Merck, Johann Heinrich
2100.M5 Meyer, Hans Heinrich
2100.M8 Müller, Friedrich von
(2100.N2) Napoleon
see PT2197.N2
2100.R53 Riemer
2100.R8 Runge, Philipp Otto, 1777-1810
2100.S3 Schlegel, August Wilhelm von
2100.S4 Schleiermacher, Friedrich
2100.S6 Soret
2100.S65 Stadelmann
2100.V6 Voigt, Christian Gottlob
2100.W2 Wagner, Heinrich Leopold
2100.W4 Wesley, John
2100.W5 Wieland, Christoph Martin
2100.W55 Winckelmann, Johann Joachim
(2100.Z4) Zelter, Karl Friedrich
see ML410.Z4; PT2204
Relation to actors see PT2120.A1+
2101.A-Z Distinguished visitors, A-Z
2101.A2 General
2101.A3-Z Special, A-Z
2101.H7 Holtei
2101.M5 Mickiewicz
2102 Honors and distinctions
2102.Z9 Works dedicated to Goethe. By author, A-Z

Individual authors or works
1700-ca. 1860/70
Goethe, Johann Wolfgang von, 1749-1832
Biography and criticism
Biography -- Continued
Personality, character, etc.
see PT2049+

(2105)	General
2106	Physical characteristics Cf. PT2143.A2+ Portraits
	Death of Goethe see PT2073
	Mode of life Cf. PT2111+ Character and moral conduct
2108	General
2109	Special Cf. PT2089 Goethe in his social intercourse Cf. PT2200.A6 Alcoholism
	Mode of working see PT2151+
	Character. Moral conduct
2111	General Cf. PT2049+ General works
2112	Special (not A-Z)
	Ethics and religion see PT2193
	Activities
2113	General
2114	Jurist and lawyer
2115	Minister of state
	Goethe and the theater
2116	General (and Weimar hoftheater)
	Stage management
2118.A1	Official documents
2118.A2	Plays produced. Repertoire
2118.A3-Z	Treatises on Goethe's management
	Theories on actors and acting
2119.A1	Treatises by Goethe
2119.A2	Compilations from Goethe's works
2119.A3-Z	Criticism
	Personal relations with actors and actresses
2120.A1	General
2120.A2-Z	Special, A-Z Cf. PN2658.A+ Biographies of actors
2121	Amateur theaters (Weimar, Tiefurt, etc.)
2122	Other special topics (not A-Z)
2125.A-Z	Other activities, A-Z
(2125.A7)	Art amateur and collector see PT2203
2125.A8	Autograph collector

Individual authors or works
1700-ca. 1860/70
Goethe, Johann Wolfgang von, 1749-1832
Biography and criticism
Biography
Activities
Other activities, A-Z -- Continued

2125.C6 Collector (General)
(2125.J6) Journalist
see PT2152
(2125.L5) Literary critic
see PT2190
(2125.S3) Scientist
see PT2206+
(2125.T8) Translator
see PT2190
2127 Goethe as a man of business and affairs
Cf. PT2115 Minister of state
(2129) Relation to publishers
see PT2155
2130 Homes and haunts
For books in which the literary and biographical features predominate
Cf. PT2060+ Special periods
2130.A2 General
2130.A5-Z Special
2130.A7 Alsace-Lorraine
2130.B4 Berlin
2130.D3 Darmstadt
2130.D6 Dornburg
2130.E5 Eisenach
Frankfurt am Main
2130.F8 General
2130.F81 Goethehaus
Cf. PT2145.A2+ Museums
2130.H4 Heidelberg
2130.H45 Hesse
2130.I4 Ilm Valley
2130.I44 Ilmenau
2130.J4 Jena
2130.L4 Leipzig
2130.M27 Mainz (Rhineland-Palatinate, Germany)
2130.N8 Nuremberg
2130.O33 Offenbach am Main
2130.R45 Rhine Valley
2130.S8 Strassburg

Individual authors or works
1700-ca. 1860/70
Goethe, Johann Wolfgang von, 1749-1832
Biography and criticism
Biography
Homes and haunts
Special -- Continued

2130.W3 Weimar
Including both general works and special places
2130.W4 Wetzlar
2130.W6 Wörlitz
2130.Z35 Západočeský kraj, Czechoslovakia
Journeys
2131 General
2132 General special
Special
Cf. PT2065+ Biography, 1775-1786
2133 Germany. By region or place, A-Z
(2135) Other countries, A-Z
Austria and Bohemia see PT2065+
Italy see PT2066
Switzerland see PT2001.B1+
2139 Anniversaries. Celebrations. Festschriften
Arrange by date-letters: .A00-.A99 = 1800-1899; .B00-.B99 = 1900-1999; .C00-.C99 = 2000-2099, e.g. .A32 = 1832; .A82 = 1882; .B32 = 1932
Memorials. Testimonials to his genius
For Goethe and Schiller see PT2098
2140 Poetry and drama
2141 Prose
Iconography
Portraits, medals, etc.
2143.A2 General
2143.A5-Z Special By artist, A-Z
2143.Z5 Silhouettes
Monuments
2144.A2 General
2144.A5-Z By place, A-Z
Museums. Institutions. Exhibitions. Relics
2145.A2 General
2145.A5-Z Special. By name, A-Z
2145.B8 Budapest. Magyar Tudomnyos Akademia. Könyvtr
2145.C37 Casa di Goethe
2145.D8 Düsseldorf. Goethe-Museum
2145.F7 Frankfurt am Main Stadtarchiv
2145.G45 Goethe-Gesellschaft-Hannover

Individual authors or works
1700-ca. 1860/70
Goethe, Johann Wolfgang von, 1749-1832
Biography and criticism
Biography
Museums. Institutions. Exhibitions. Relics
Special. By name, A-Z -- Continued

2145.G5 Goethemuseum, Frankfurt am Main
2145.G6 Goethestiftung
2145.G7 Goethe und Schiller-archiv, Weimar
2145.H37 Harvard College Library
2145.V5 Vienna. Nationalbibliothek
2145.W37 Washington University (Saint Louis). Libraries. Special collections
Weimar. Goethe-National museum see PT2130.W3
2145.Y3-.Y4 Yale University. Speck collection
(2147) Fiction, drama, etc., based upon Goethe's life
see classes PA-PT
(2149) Goethe in France, England, and other countries
see PT2173
Cf. PT1933 Faust on the stage
2150 Study and teaching (Theory and method)
Cf. PT2165+ Criticism and interpretation
Authorship
Cf. PT2187+ Technique
2151 General
2152 General special
2153 Manuscripts. Writing. Signature. Autographs
2153.Z5 Autographs found in books, on portraits, etc.
(2153.Z9) Original manuscripts of particular works and facsimile reproductions
see the special works
2155 Publishing and editing. Relations to publishers
2155.A1 General
2155.A3-Z Special publishers, A-Z
e.g.
2155.C6 Cotta
Correspondence see PT2005+
Sources
2157 General
Cf. PT1894 Separate works
Cf. PT2190.A9 Goethe's knowledge of literature
2158 Special authors or works
(2159) Forerunners. Associates. Followers. Circle. School
Relations to contemporaries
see PT321, PT2088+

Individual authors or works
1700-ca. 1860/70
Goethe, Johann Wolfgang von, 1749-1832
Biography and criticism
Authorship -- Continued
(2160) Influence on literature
see PT2190
2161 Allusions by contemporaries
Cf. PT2169 Collections
2163 Chronology of works
Criticism and interpretation
History of Goethe studies ("Goethe philology")
2165 General (including studies in Germany)
2166 General special
Including influence of Goethe in Germany and elsewhere
Special countries except Germany see PT2173.A+
Influence on literature see PT2190.A9
Influence on science see PT2206+
Influence on art see PT2203
Influence on music
see PT2024 PT2204
2168 Collections of criticism
2168.A2 By Goethe (Comments on his own works)
2168.A3-Z By others, A-Z
2169 Collections of criticism by special groups
Cf. PT361+, PT2088+
2169.A5 Anthroposophic school
2169.R7 Romantic school
2169.Y8 Young Germany (Heine, Börne, etc.)
2171 Other
e.g. Religious points of view
2173.A-Z By region or country, A-Z
Including presentation of Goethe's plays
e.g.
2173.F7 France
Germany see PT2165+
Cf. PT1933 Faust on the stage
2173.G7 Great Britain
(2175) Influence on special authors or persons
see the specific author or person
2177 General works
Cf. PT2045+ Periodicals, societies, collections, dictionaries, etc.
2179 Comparison with other authors, A-Z
(2180) Special forms

Individual authors or works
1700-ca. 1860/70
Goethe, Johann Wolfgang von, 1749-1832
Biography and criticism
Criticism and interpretation
Special forms -- Continued
Lyric works see PT1904+
Epic poems see PT1912
Dramatic works see PT1914
Prose works see PT1984+
Criticism of special works'
see the work
(2182) Philosophy, esthetics, etc.
see PT2193
Characters. Treatment of human life
For studies of a character in a special work, see the work
2183 General works
2184.A-Z Special groups or classes, A-Z
Children see PT2216.C5
2184.W7 Women. "Das Ewig-Weibliche"
Individual characters
see PT1911+
Technique
2187 General
For dramatic technique see PT1964+
For technique in fiction and autobiographical works see PT1984+
Cf. PT2151+ Authorship
2188 General special
Relation to special subjects
(Treatment and knowledge, influence, etc.)
2189 General
2190 Literature
Cf. PT1988 Treatises on literature
2190.A1 General and universal literature
2190.A2 Ancient (Classical)
2190.A3 Oriental
Modern
General see PT2190.A1
2190.A4 German
Volkslied see PT1906
2190.A5 English and American
2190.A6 French
2190.A7A-.Z7Z Other, A-Z
2190.A8-Z Special authors, A-Z
2190.A9 Aristotle

Individual authors or works
1700-ca. 1860/70
Goethe, Johann Wolfgang von, 1749-1832
Biography and criticism
Criticism and interpretation
Relation to special subjects
Literature
Special authors, A-Z -- Continued

2190.B7 Bruno
2190.C3 Calderon
2190.D3 Dante
2190.E9 Euripides
2190.K56 Klopstock, Friedrich Gottlieb
2190.M6 Mori, Ogai
2190.M63 Möser, Justus
2190.P48 Petrarca, Francesco, 1304-1374
2190.P76 Propertius, Sextus
2190.R52 Richter, Johann Paul Friedrich, 1763-1825 (Jean Paul)
2190.R6 Rousseau, Jean Jacques
2190.S4 Shakespeare
2190.S7 Sterne
2190.V7 Voltaire

Theater and acting see PT2119.A1+

2193 Philosophy. Psychology. Ethics. Aesthetics
2194 The supernatural. Folklore. Mythology
2195 Religion. Church. Bible
2196 History. Politics

Goethe as a citizen; Goethe as a patriot
Cf. PT2115 State activities

2197.A-Z Special, A-Z
2197.A2 Absolutism
2197.C6 Constitutional government
2197.C7 Cosmopolitanism
2197.D5 Democracy
2197.E85 Europe
2197.F7 France. French Revolution
2197.F8 Frederick the Great
2197.F9 Freedom of the press
2197.M5 Military history
2197.N2 Napoleon
2197.P3 Patriotism
2197.U6 Unity of Germany
2198 Geography and anthropology

Sociology

2200.A1 General
2200.A3-Z Special, A-Z

Individual authors or works
1700-ca. 1860/70
Goethe, Johann Wolfgang von, 1749-1832
Biography and criticism
Criticism and interpretation
Relation to special subjects
Sociology
Special, A-Z -- Continued

2200.A6 Alcoholism
2200.C7 Crime. Criminals
2200.H65 Homosexuality
2200.J4 Jews
2200.M3 Marriage
2200.P76 Property
2200.S6 Socialization
2200.W6 Work
2201 Law. Goethe's legal knowledge
Cf. PT2114 Goethe as jurist and lawyer
2202 Education
Cf. PT2115 Goethe as a minister of state
2203 Art, architecture, painting, sculpture, etc.
For reproductions of Goethe's drawings and paintings, see Class N
2204 Music
Cf. ML80.A+ Poets and music
(2205) Theater, acting
see PT2119
Science
2206 General
Including natural science
Cf. PT2213+ Nature
2207 General special
2208.A-Z Special topics, A-Z
2208.A2 Aeronautics
2208.A3 Agriculture
2208.A4 Alchemy
2208.A5 Anatomy
2208.A7 Astrology
2208.A8 Astronomy
2208.B5 Biology. Evolution
2208.B7 Botany
2208.C4 Chemistry
2208.C7 Color, Theory of
2208.E6 Electricity
Engineering see PT2211
2208.G4 Geography
2208.G6 Geology

Individual authors or works
1700-ca. 1860/70
Goethe, Johann Wolfgang von, 1749-1832
Biography and criticism
Criticism and interpretation
Relation to special subjects
Science
Special topics, A-Z -- Continued

2208.I6 Insanity
2208.M3 Mathematics
2208.M4 Medicine
2208.M5 Meteorology
2208.M6 Mineralogy
2208.O6 Optics
2208.P5 Physics
2208.P6 Physiognomy
Psychiatry see PT2208.I6
Psychology see PT2193
2208.Z6 Zoology
2211 Technical arts and crafts
Nature
2213 General
2214.A-Z Special, A-Z
2214.B5 Birds
2214.C6 Clouds
2214.F68 Forests and forestry
2214.M6 Mountains
2214.S4 Sea
2214.S6 Spring
2214.S8 Sun
2214.W3 Water
2216.A-Z Other subjects, A-Z
2216.A6 America
2216.A7 Archaeology
2216.C5 Children
2216.C53 Civilization, Western
2216.C56 Clothing and dress
2216.C64 Cookery
2216.C7 Cremation
2216.D3 Dance
2216.D8 Drugs and druggists
2216.D9 Duel
2216.E3 Eating. Food habits
Including eating disorders
2216.E4 Economics
Food habits see PT2216.E3
2216.F7 Freemasons

Individual authors or works
1700-ca. 1860/70
Goethe, Johann Wolfgang von, 1749-1832
Biography and criticism
Criticism and interpretation
Relation to special subjects
Other subjects, A-Z -- Continued

2216.G4 Genealogy
2216.G7 Graphology
2216.G73 Great Britain
2216.J6 Journalism
Languages
2216.L2 General
Special
2216.L3 English
2216.L4 French
2216.L5 German
Cf. PT2225+ Goethe's language and style
2216.M4 Merchants
Occultism see PT2194
2216.O74 Orient
2216.P4 Philistines
Spirits see PT2194
2216.S7 Sports and games
2216.S94 Switzerland
2216.W5 Wine
Textual criticism, commentaries, emendations, etc.
Cf. PT2177 General works
2219 Early works to 1885
2220 Later works, 1885-
Language. Style
For language and style of specific works, see the work
Cf. PT1945+ Language in Faust
Cf. PT1956 Language in Iphigenie auf Tauris
2225 General
Special periods
2226.A2 To 1775/1786
2226.A3 1775/1786-1814
2226.A4 1814-1832
2226.A7-Z Special forms, A-Z
2228 Special topics
Grammar
2231 General
2232 Special
2235 Versification
Cf. PT1948, PT1956, etc. Special works
2236 Prose

Individual authors or works
1700-ca. 1860/70
Goethe, Johann Wolfgang von, 1749-1832
Biography and criticism
Criticism and interpretation
Language. Style -- Continued

2237 Dialect

2239 Dictionaries. Concordances

Cf. PT2048 Biography and criticism

2250.G2 Goethe, Wolfgang Maximilian, freiherr von, 1820-1883 (Table P-PZ40)

2250.G3 Götz, Johann Nikolaus, 1721-1781 (Table P-PZ40)

2250.G5 Goldammer, Leo, b. 1813 (Table P-PZ40)

Gollnow, Ernest see PT2513.S6

2250.G6 Goltz, Bogumil, 1801-1870 (Table P-PZ40)

2250.G7 Gotter, Friedrich Wilhelm, 1746-1797 (Table P-PZ40)

Gotthelf, Jeremias, 1797-1854 see PT1819.B6

2250.G8 Gottschall, Rudolf von, 1823-1909 (Table P-PZ40)

Gottsched, Johann Christoph, 1700-1766

2252.A1 Collected works. By date

2252.A2 Selected works. By date

2252.A4 Poems

2252.A7-.Z3 Separate works

2252.Z4 Journals, letters, etc.

2252.Z49 Prefaces. By date

2252.Z5 Biography and criticism

2253.G1 Gottsched, Luise Adelgunde Viktiora (Kulmus), 1713-1762 (Table P-PZ40)

2253.G2 Goué, August Friedrich von, 1743-1789 (Table P-PZ40)

2253.G3 Grabbe, Christian Dietrich, 1801-1836 (Table P-PZ38 modified)

2253.G3A61-.G3A78 Separate works. By title

2253.G3A61 Aschenbrödel

2253.G3A62 Don Juan und Faust

2253.G3A63 Hannibal

2253.G3A64 Die Hermannsschlacht

2253.G3A65 Herzog Theodor

2253.G3A66 Kaiser Friedrich Barbarossa

2253.G3A67 Kaiser Heinrich der Sechste

2253.G3A68 Marius und Sulla (unfinished)

2253.G3A69 Nannette und Maria

2253.G3A7 Napoleon; oder, Die hundert tage

2253.G3A73 Scherz, satire, ironie

Gradaus see PT2526.S5

2253.G33 Graeber, Theodor (Table P-PZ40)

2253.G35 Gräffer, Franz, 1785-1852 (Table P-PZ40)

2253.G36 Gräter, Friedrich David, 1768-1830 (Table P-PZ40)

Individual authors or works
1700-ca. 1860/70 -- Continued
2253.G37 Grandjean, Moritz Anton, 1821-1891 (Table P-PZ40)
2253.G4 Gregorovius, Ferdinand Adolf, 1821-1891 (Table P-PZ40)
Greif, Martin see PT1869.F45
2253.G8 Griepenkerl, Wolfgang Robert, 1810-1868 (Table P-PZ40)
2253.G9 Gries, Johann Diederich, 1775-1842 (Table P-PZ40)
2253.G92 Griesinger, Theodor, 1809-1884 (Table P-PZ40)
Grillparzer, Franz, 1791-1872
2256.A1 Collected works. By date
(2256.A2) Collected works. By editor, A-Z
2256.A3A-.A3Z Selected works. By editor, A-Z
Including posthumous works
2256.A4 Selections, quotations, etc.
2257 Translations. By language
Separate works see PT2259.A+
2258 Poems
Dramatic works
Collected see PT2256.A1
Separate works
Die ahnfrau
2259.A2 Editions. By date
2259.A3A-.A3Z School editions. By editor, A-Z
2259.A4-.A59 Translations. By language (alphabetically)
2259.A6 Criticism
Die Argonauten see PT2259.G6
2259.B6-.B8 Ein bruderzwist in Habsburg (Table P-PZ43)
2259.E6 Esther (fragment)
2259.E62 Edition completed by Heigel
2259.E64 Edition completed by Krauss
2259.E7 Criticism
Der gastfreund see PT2259.G5
2259.G4-.G7 Das goldene vliess
2259.G4 Complete editions
2259.G5 I. Der gastfreund
2259.G6 II. Die Argonauten
2259.G7 III. Medea
2259.J6-.J8 Die jüdin von Toledo (Table P-PZ43)
2259.K6-.K9 König Ottokars glück und ende
2259.K6 Editions. By date
2259.K7A-.K7Z School editions. By editor, A-Z
Translations
2259.K8 English. By translator
2259.K81-.K89 Other languages (alphabetically)
2259.K9 Criticism
Libussa
2259.L3 Editions. By date

Individual authors or works
1700-ca. 1860/70
Grillparzer, Franz, 1791-1872
Dramatic works
Separate works
Libussa -- Continued
2259.L4A-.L4Z School editions. By editor, A-Z
Medea see PT2259.G7
Des meeres und der liebe wellen
2259.M4 Editions. By date
2259.M5A-.M5Z School editions. By editor, A-Z
2259.M6-.M79 Translations. By language (alphabetically)
2259.M8 Criticism
Melusina
see M, ML
Sappho
2259.S2 Editions. By date
2259.S3A-.S3Z School editions. By editor, A-Z
Translations
2259.S4 English
2259.S41-.S59 Other languages (alphabetically)
2259.S6 Criticism
Der traum, ein leben
2259.T2 Editions. By date
2259.T3A-.T3Z School editions. By editor, A-Z
2259.T4-.T59 Translations. By language (alphabetically)
2259.T6 Criticism
2259.T7 Ein treuer diener seines herrn
2259.W4 Weh dem, der lügt!
2259.Z5A-.Z5Z Minor plays, fragments, projected plays, A-Z
Esther see PT2259.E6
2261 Prose works
2261.A2 Comprehensive collections
2261.A5-Z Separate works
Der arme spielmann
2261.A5 Editions. By date
2261.A6A-.A6Z School editions. By editor, A-Z
2261.A7-.A89 Translations. By language (alphabetically)
2261.A9 Criticism
Das kloster bei Sendomir
2261.K3 Editions. By date
2261.K4A-.K4Z School editions. By editor, A-Z
2261.K5-.K69 Translations. By language (alphabetically)
2261.K7 Criticism
Letters see PT2264.A6+
Autobiography see PT2264.A4
2262 Apocryphal and spurious works

Individual authors or works
1700-ca. 1860/70
Grillparzer, Franz, 1791-1872 -- Continued
2263.A1 Imitations, adaptations, dramatizations
2263.A2 Parodies. Travesties
2263.A3 Translations as subject. Comparative studies, etc.
2263.A5 Illustrations. Collections without text
For illustrated editions, see the other editions
History of Grillparzer portraits and illustrations see PT2268
2263.A9 Music. Texts to which music has been composed
For librettos based upon Grillparzer's works, see ML. For music composed to Grillparzer's works, see M. For Grillparzer's knowledge and treatment of music, see PT2274.M8
Biography and criticism
2264.A1 Periodicals. Societies. Collections
2264.A2 Dictionaries, indexes, etc.
Class here general encyclopedic dictionaries only
For dictionaries on special subjects, see the subject
Concordances and language dictionaries see PT2278
Sources of his biography
2264.A3 General. Collections of autobiographical papers. By date
Special
2264.A4 "Selbstbiographie" (1791-1836). By date
Tagebuchblätter (1808-1855). By date
see DD
(2264.A51) Tagebuch auf der reise nach Italien (1819)
(2264.A52) Tagebuch auf der reise nach Deutschland
see DD
(2264.A53) Tagebuch auf der reise nach Frankreich und England (1836)
see DC
(2264.A54) Tagebuch auf der reise nach Griechenland
see DF
(2264.A55) Erinnerungen aus dem jahr, 1848
see DB
Letters
2264.A6A-.A6Z Collections. By editor, A-Z
2264.A7A-.A7Z Special correspondents, A-Z
Subarrange by editor, using successive cutters
Conversations. "Gespräche"
2264.A8A-.A8Z General. By editor, A-Z
2264.A9A-.A9Z With special persons, A-Z
2265 General works (Literary biography. Life and works)
2266 Special biographical topics

Individual authors or works
1700-ca. 1860/70
Grillparzer, Franz, 1791-1872
Biography and criticism
Special biographical topics -- Continued

2266.A1 Family, name, ancestry, love, marriage, death
2266.A2 Public services
2266.A3 Relations to contemporaries
2266.A4-.Z4 Special, A-Z
2266.Z5 Homes and haunts
2267 Anniversaries. Celebrations. Memorial addresses, poetry, etc.
2268 Iconography. Portraits. Monuments. Museums. Relics
2270 Authorship. Manuscripts. Sources. Allusions. Chronology, etc.
2270.Z5 Influence of special authors, A-Z
Criticism and interpretation
History of the study and appreciation of Grillparzer
2271.A1 General. Theory and method
2271.A2 Contemporary
2271.A3 Later
2271.A4 Representation on the stage
2271.A5-Z Special countries, A-Z
2272 General works
Cf. PT2265 Biography and criticism
Philosophy and esthetics
see PT2270, PT2272
Characters
General see PT2272
Special groups see PT2274.A+
Special characters see PT2259.A+
Plots, scenes, times see PT2272
2274.A-Z Treatment and knowledge of special subjects, A-Z
2274.H5 History, politics, etc.
2274.J4 Jews
2274.L6 Love
2274.M3 Man. Men
2274.M8 Music
2274.N3 Nature
2274.W8 Women
2275 Textual criticism, commentaries, etc.
Language, style, etc.
2276 General works
Cf. PT2272
2277 Versification
2278 Dictionaries, concordances, etc.

PT1-4897

	Individual authors or works
	1700-ca. 1860/70 -- Continued
2281.G15	Grimm, Frau Gisela (von Arnim), 1827-1889 (Table P-PZ40)
2281.G2	Grimm, Herman Friedrich, 1828-1901 (Table P-PZ38 modified)
2281.G2A61-.G2A78	Separate works. By title
2281.G2A62	Armin (Drama)
2281.G2A64	Demetrius (Tragedy)
2281.G2A65	Novellen
2281.G2A7	Traum und erwachen
2281.G2A75	Unüberwindliche mächte
2281.G25	Grimm, Paul (Table P-PZ40)
2281.G4	Grisebach, Eduard Rudolf Autor, 1845-1906 (Table P-PZ38)
	Grönau, Isidore see PT2533.S7
2281.G48	Groller, Balduin, 1848-1916 (Table P-PZ40)
2281.G53	Grosmann, Ernst (Table P-PZ40)
2281.G55	Grosmann, Hans (Table P-PZ40)
2281.G57	Gross von Trockau, Augustina Karolina Johanna, freiin, 1845- (Table P-PZ40)
2281.G6	Grosse, Julius, 1828-1902 (Table P-PZ40)
2281.G614	Grosse, Karl Friedrich August, 1768-1847 (Table P-PZ40)
	Groth, Klaus see PT4848.G7
2281.G64	Grün, Albert, 1822-1904 (Table P-PZ40)
2281.G65	Grün, Albertine Charlotte Louise, 1749-1792 (Table P-PZ38)
	Grün, Anastasius see PT1812.A5
2281.G7	Gubitz, Friedrich Wilhelm, 1786-1870 (Table P-PZ40)
	Günderode, Karoline von, 1780-1806
2281.G8	Collected works. By date Including editions of "Gedichte und phantasien"
2281.G8A5	Poetical fragments
2281.G8A6-.G8A79	Separate works. By title
	Gedichte see PT2281.G8
2281.G8A8-.G8Z	Biography and criticism For the fictitious correspondence by Bettina von Arnim, called Günderode see PT1808.A4A5+
2281.G9	Günther, Johann Christian, 1695-1723 (Table P-PZ38)
2281.G95	Gundling, Julius, 1828-1890 (Table P-PZ40)
	Gutzkow, Karl Ferdinand, 1811-1878
2282.A1	Collected works. By date
2282.A21-.A29	Translations. By language (alphabetically)
2282.A3	Selected works. By editor, A-Z
2282.A4	Dramatic works. By date
2282.A5	Prose works, prose fiction. By date
2282.A6	Poems

Individual authors or works
1700-ca. 1860/70
Gutzkow, Karl Ferdinand, 1811-1878 -- Continued
2282.A7-.Z3 Separate works
2282.A8 Antonio Perez
Aus der knabenzeit see PT2282.Z4A6
Aus der zeit und dem leben see PT2282.Z4A7
2282.B6 Blasedow und seine söhne
2282.B8 Briefe eines narren
2282.C6 Die curstauben
2282.D5 Diakonissin
2282.D6 Dionysius Longinus
2282.D7 Der dreizehnte november
2282.D8 Dschingiskhan
2282.E6 Ella Rose; oder, Die rechte des herzens
2282.F7 Fremdes glück
2282.F8 Fritz Ellrodt
2282.G6 Götter, helden, Don Quixote
2282.H5 Hohenschwangau
2282.K4 Die kleine narrenwelt
2282.K5 Der königsleutenant
2282.K6 König Saul
2282.L4 Lebensbilder
2282.L5 Lenz und söhne; oder, Die komödie der besserungen
2282.L6 Liesli
2282.L7 Lorber und myrte
2282.M2 Ein mädchen aus dem volk
2282.M3 Maha Guru, geschichte eines gottes
2282.N4 Nero
2282.N5 Die neuen Serapionsbruder
2282.O8 Ottfried
2282.P3 Patkul
2282.P4 Die paumgärtner von Hohenschwangau
Philipp und Perez see PT2282.A8
2282.P8 Pugatschew
2282.R5 Richard Savage; oder, Der sohn einer mutter
2282.R6 Der ritter vom geiste
2282.R7 Die rote mütze und der kapuze
Rückblicke auf mein leben see PT2282.Z4R8
2282.S3 Säkularbilder
Die schöneren stunden (Rückblicke) see PT2282.Z4S4
2282.S4 Die schule der reichen
2282.S5 Seraphine
2282.S6 Skizzenbuch
2282.S7 Die söhne Pestalozzis
2282.U2 Der urbild des Tartüffe
Uriel Acosta

Individual authors or works
1700-ca. 1860/70
Gutzkow, Karl Ferdinand, 1811-1878
Separate works
Uriel Acosta -- Continued

2282.U4 Editions. By date
2282.U5A-.U5Z School editions. By editor, A-Z
2282.U6-.U79 Translations
e.g.
2282.U65 English
2282.U8 Criticism
2282.V4 Vergangene tage
Cf. PT2282.W3 Wally
2282.V6 Vom baum der erkenntniss
2282.W2 Der wärwolf
2282.W3 Wally, die zweiflerin
Recast in Vergangene tage, PT2282.V4
2282.W4 Ein weisses blatt
2282.W5 Werner; oder, Herz und welt
2282.W6 Wullenweber
2282.Z2 Der zauberer von Rom
2282.Z3 Zopf und schwert
2282.Z4A-.Z4Z Autobiographical works, A-Z
e.g.
2282.Z4A6 Aus der knabenzeit
2282.Z4A7 Aus der zeit und dem leben
2282.Z4R8 Rückblicke auf mein leben
2282.Z4S4 Die schöneren stunden (Rückblicke)
2282.Z5 Journals, correspondence, etc.
2282.Z6 Biography and criticism
2284.H15 Hacker, Franz Xaver, 1836-1894 (Table P-PZ40)
2284.H2 Hackländer, Friedrich Wilhelm, ritter von 1816-1877 (Table P-PZ40)
2284.H3 Häberlin, Karl Ludwig, 1784-1858 (Table P-PZ40)
Häring, Wilhelm, 1798-1871
2285.A1 Collected works. By date
2285.A2 Translations
2285.A3A-.A3Z Selected works. By editor, A-Z
2285.A4 Dramatic works (Collected)
2285.A5 Prose works (Collected). By date
2285.A6 Poems (Collected)
2285.A7-.Z3 Separate works
2285.A74 Acerbi
Eine aehrenlese vom deutschen grünen hügellande
see DD
2285.A75 Aennchen von Tharau
2285.A78 Alles um ein gericht fische

Individual authors or works
1700-ca. 1860/70
Häring, Wilhelm, 1798-1871
Separate works -- Continued

	Andalusien see DP
2285.B2	Babiolen
	Balladen see PT2285.A78
2285.B4	Begnadigte
2285.C2	Cabanis
2285.C6	Der collaborator Liborius
	Das dampfschiff see DJ
2285.D6	Dorothe
2285.E5	Emmerich
2285.E6	Ein englischer Werther
	Erinnerungen see PT2285.Z4
2285.F2	Der falsche Woldemar
2285.F6	Der fluch der Mauren
2285.F7	Die flucht nach Amerika
2285.F8	Der freyherr
2285.G4	Die geächteten
2285.G6	Der graf in der Wilhelmsstrasse
2285.G7	Die grossmutter
2285.H2	Hans Jürgen und Hans Jochem Cf. PT2285.H5 Die hosen des herrn von Bredow
2285.H25	Hans Preller von Lauffen
2285.H3	Das haus Düsterweg
	Herbstreise durch Skandinavien see DL
2285.H4	Herr von Sacken
2285.H5	Die hosen des herrn von Bredow In two parts: "Hans Jürgen und Hans Jochem"; "Der wärwolf"
2285.I4	Isegrimm
2285.J2	Ja in Neapel
2285.M4	Meerschaumflocken
2285.O3	O'Connor
2285.P7	Der prinz von Pisa
2285.R12	Die rache wartet
2285.R15	Der rechte erbe
	Der Roland von Berlin
2285.R3	Editions. By date
2285.R4-.R59	Translations
2285.R6	Criticism
2285.R65	Rosamunde
2285.R7	Ruhe ist die erste bürgerpflicht

Individual authors or works
1700-ca. 1860/70
Häring, Wilhelm, 1798-1871
Separate works -- Continued

2285.S2 Der salz director
Schattenrisse aus Süd-Deutschland
see DD
2285.S25 Der schatz der Tempelherren
2285.S27 Die schlacht bei Torgau
2285.S3 Schloss Avalon
2285.S6 Die sonette
2285.T7 Die treibjagd
2285.U6 Die unsichtbare geliebte
2285.U7 Urban Grandier
Vaterländische romane
Collection of 8 novels; also published separately
see PT2285.A5
2285.V4 Venus in Rom
2285.W2 Der wärwolf
Cf. PT2285.H5 Die hosen des herrn von Bredow
2285.W6 Walladmor
Wiener bilder
see DB
2285.Z2 Der zauberer Virgilius
2285.Z25 Zwei originale aus unserer zeit
2285.Z3 Zwölf nächte
2285.Z4 Autobiographical works. Letters
2285.Z6 Biography and criticism
2287.H2 Hafner, Philipp, 1731-1764 (Table P-PZ40)
2287.H3 Hagedorn, Friedrich von, 1708-1754 (Table P-PZ40)
2287.H35 Hagen, Ernst August, 1797-1880 (Table P-PZ40)
2287.H37 Hagen, Kaspar, 1820-1885 (Table P-PZ40)
2287.H46 Hahn, Ludwig Philipp, 1746-1814 (Table P-PZ38)
Hahn, R.E. see PT2445.P9
Hahn-Hahn, Ida Marie Luise Sophie Friederike Gustava, gräfin, 1805-1880
2287.H5A1 Collected works. By date
2287.H5A3 Translations
2287.H5A4 Poems (Collected). By date
2287.H5A5-.H5Z3 Separate works
2287.H5A6 Astralion, eine arabeske
2287.H5A7 Aus der gesellschaft
Aus der gesellschaft (Collection, 1844) see PT2287.H5A1
Aus Jerusalem
see BX
2287.H5B6 Der breite weg und der enge strasse

Individual authors or works
1700-ca. 1860/70
Hahn-Hahn, Ida Marie Luise Sophie Friederike Gustava, gräfin, 1805-1880
Separate works -- Continued

2287.H5C4 Cecil
2287.H5C5 Clelia Conti
2287.H5D6 Doralice
2287.H5E2 Die erbin von Cronenstein
(2287.H5E4) Erinnerungen aus und an Frankreich
see DC
2287.H5E6 Die erzählung des hofrats
2287.H5E7 Eudoxia, die kaiserin
2287.H5G3 Die geschichte eines armen fräuleins
2287.H5G5 Die glöcknerstochter
2287.H5G8 Gräfin Faustine
Die heilige Zita see BX4700.A+
Ilda Schönholm see PT2287.H5A7
2287.H5J3 Das jahr der kirche
Jenseits der berge
see D
2287.H5K4 Die kinder auf dem Abendberg
2287.H5L4 Levin
2287.H5M3 Maria Regina
2287.H5N5 Nirwana
Orientalische briefe
see DS
2287.H5P4 Peregrin
2287.H5R3 Der rechte
2287.H5R4 Eine reiche frau
Reisebriefe
see D
2287.H5S5 Sibylle
2287.H5S6 Sigismund Forster
2287.H5U5 Ulrich
2287.H5U6 Unserer lieben frau
2287.H5V4 Venezianische nächte
2287.H5V5 Vergib uns unsere schuld
Vier lebensbilder see BX4651
(2287.H5V7) Von Babylon nach Jerusalem
see BX4705.H2A5
2287.H5W3 Wahl und führung
2287.H5Z2 Zwei frauen
2287.H5Z3 Zwei schwestern
2287.H5Z5 Autobiography. Journals. Letters
2287.H5Z6-.H5Z9 Biography and criticism
Halein, Kathinka (or Tina) see PT2589.Z6

Individual authors or works
1700-ca. 1860/70 -- Continued

2287.H7 Haller, Albrecht von, 1708-1777 (Table P-PZ38 modified)
2287.H7A61-.H7A78 Separate poetical works
2287.H7A77 Versuch schweizerischer gedichte
2287.H7A79-.H7Z Biography and criticism
Haller's biography as an anatomist, physiologist, and botanist see QH31.H3
Halm, Friedrich see PT2438.M3
2287.H9 Hamann, Johann Georg, 1730-1788 (Table P-PZ38)
2289 Hamerling, Robert, 1830-1889 (Table P-PZ39 modified)
2289.A61-.Z48 Separate works. By title
2289.A7 Ahasverus in Rom (Table P-PZ43)
2289.A75 Amor und Psyche (Table P-PZ43)
2289.A8 Aspasia (Table P-PZ43)
2289.B6 Blätter im winde (Table P-PZ43)
Das blumenjahr in bild und lied (Anthology) see PT1171+
2289.D2 Danton und Robespierre (Table P-PZ43)
Hesperische früchte see PQ4205.G5
2289.H6 Homunculus (Table P-PZ43)
2289.K6 Der könig von Sion (Table P-PZ43)
2289.L4 Letzte grüsse aus stiftingshaus (Table P-PZ43)
2289.L6 Lord Luzifer (Table P-PZ43)
2289.S2 Ein sangesgruss vom strande der Adria (Table P-PZ43)
2289.S4 Ein schwanenlied der romantik (Table P-PZ43)
2289.S5 Die sieben todsünden (Table P-PZ43)
2289.S6 Sinnen und minnen (Table P-PZ43)
2289.S8 Stationen meiner lebenspilgerschaft (Table P-PZ43)
2289.T4 Teut (Table P-PZ43)
2289.V4 Venedig (Table P-PZ43)
2289.V5 Venus im exil (Table P-PZ43)
2289.W3 Die waldsängerin (Table P-PZ43)
2289.W4 Was man mich in Venedig erzählt (Table P-PZ43)
2290.H2 Hamm, Wilhelm, ritter von, 1820-1880 (Table P-PZ40)
2290.H3 Hammer, Julius, 1810-1862 (Table P-PZ40)
2290.H4 Hansjakob, Heinrich, 1837-1916 (Table P-PZ38)
2291 Hardenberg, Friedrich Leopold, freiherr von, 1772-1801 ("Novalis") (Table P-PZ39 modified)
2291.A61-.Z48 Separate works. By title
Geistliche lieder
2291.G2 Texts
Translations
2291.G3-.G49 English
2291.G5-.G79 Other languages
2291.H2 Heinrich von Ofterdingen (Table P-PZ43)
2291.H6 Hymnen an die nacht (Table P-PZ43)

Individual authors or works
1700-ca. 1860/70
Hardenberg, Friedrich Leopold, freiherr von, 1772-1801 ("Novalis")
Separate works. By title -- Continued
Die lehrlinge zu Sais
2291.L2 Texts
Translations
2291.L3-.L49 English
2291.L5-.L79 Other languages
2292.H172 Harnisch, Wilhelm, 1787-1864 (Table P-PZ40)
2292.H2 Hartmann, Moritz, 1821-1872 (Table P-PZ40)
Hartner, Emma see PT2542.T9
2292.H4 Haschka, Lorenz Leopold, 1749-1827 (Table P-PZ40)
2292.H6 Hauenschild, Georg von, 1825-1855 (Table P-PZ40)
Hauff, Wilhelm, 1802-1827
2293.A1 Collected works. By date
2293.A6 Selected works. Selections. By date
2293.A61-.Z29 Separate works
2293.B3 Die bettlerin vom Pont des Arts
2293.B5 Das bild des kaisers
2293.B8 Die Bücher und die Lesewelt
Die caravane see PT2293.K6
2293.G4 Die geschichte von Kalif Storch
2293.J8 Jud Süss
2293.J9 Der junge Engländer
Kalif Storch see PT2293.G4
Das kalte herz
2293.K5 Texts. By date
2293.K5A-.K5Z School editions. By editor, A-Z
2293.K6 Die karawane
Kriegs- und volkslieder see PT1155
2293.L4 Die letzten ritter von Marienburg
Lichtenstein
2293.L5 Texts. By date
2293.L5A-.L5Z School editions. By editor, A-Z
Märchen für söhne und töchter gebildeter stände
2293.M2 Collections and selections. By date
Including the Märchen-almanach für söhne ... 1826-1828, in which the tales were first published with a few contributions by others
Special tales
see the titles
2293.M23 Märchen als almanach (Introductory tale of the Almanach)
2293.M3 Der mann im mond
2293.M4 Mittheilungen aus den memoiren des Satan

Individual authors or works
1700-ca. 1860/70
Hauff, Wilhelm, 1802-1827
Separate works
Mittheilungen aus den memoiren des Satan -- Continued

2293.M42 Criticism
2293.O8 Othello
2293.P4 Phantasien im Bremer rathskeller
2293.S2 Die sängerin
2293.S4 Der scheik von Alessandria
Das wirtshaus im Spessart
2293.W4 Texts. By date
2293.W4A-.W4Z School editions. By editor, A-Z
Der zwerg Nase
2293.Z2 Texts. By date
2293.Z2A-.Z2Z School editions. By editor, A-Z
Translations
2293.Z3A-.Z3Z English. By original title, alphabetically
Subarrange by translator
e.g.
2293.Z3M21-.Z3M29 Märchen für söhne und töchter...
2293.Z4A-.Z4Z French. By original title, alphabetically
Subarrange by translator
2293.Z6-.Z69 Other, by language (alphabetically)
e.g.
2293.Z65W5 Irish translation of Das wirthaus im Spessart
Biography and criticism
2293.Z7 Letters. By date
2293.Z8 General works
2293.Z9 Criticism
2294.H4 Hausrath, Adolf, 1837-1909 (Table P-PZ40)
Hebbel, Friedrich, 1813-1863
2295.A1 Collected works. By date
2295.A2A-.A2Z Translations, by language, A-Z
2295.A3 Selected works. By date
Dramatic works see PT2295.A1
2295.A4 Prose works. Prose fiction
2295.A5 Poems
2295.A55A-.A55Z Selections, anthologies. By editor, A-Z
2295.A6-Z Separate works
Agnes Bernauer
2295.A7 Editions. By date
2295.A7A-.A7Z School editions. By editor, A-Z
2295.A9 Criticism
2295.C45 Christus (Fragment)
2295.D2 Demetrius

Individual authors or works
1700-ca. 1860/70
Hebbel, Friedrich, 1813-1863
Separate works -- Continued

2295.D5 Der diamant
Der gehörnte Siegfried see PT2295.N3
2295.G2 Genoveva
2295.G6 Gyges und sein ring
2295.G7 Criticism
2295.H14 Haidvogel und frau
Herodes und Mariamne
2295.H2 Texts. By date
2295.H2A-.H2Z School editions. By editor, A-Z
2295.H3 Criticism
2295.J7 Judith
2295.J8 Julia
Kriemhilds rache see PT2295.N5
2295.M3 Maria Magdalene
2295.M6 Michel Angelo
2295.M7 Moloch
2295.M9 Mutter und kind
Die Nibelungen
2295.N2 Complete editions
Separate parts
2295.N3 Der gehörnte Siegfried (Vorspiel)
2295.N4 Siegfrieds tod
2295.N5 Kriemhilds rache
2295.N7 Criticism
Novellen und erzählungen see PT2295.A4
2295.R9 Der rubin
2295.S3 Schnock; ein niederländsche gemälde
Siegfrieds tod see PT2295.N4
2295.S8 Ein steinwurf
2295.T2 Ein trauerspiel in Sicilien
Biography and criticism
2296.A1 Societies, collections, etc.
2296.A2 Memoirs. Journals. "Tagebücher." By date
2296.A3 Letters
2296.A5-.Z3 Treatises. Life and works
2296.Z5 Criticism
Hebel, Johann Peter, 1760-1826
2298.H3A1 Collected works. By date
Allemannische gedichte
2298.H3A2 In Alemannic dialect. By date
2298.H3A3-.H3A39 In literary German. Alphabetically by translator
Schatzkästlein des Rheinishchen hausfreundes
2298.H3S4 Editions. By date

Individual authors or works
1700-ca. 1860/70
Hebel, Johann Peter, 1760-1826
Schatzkästlein des Rheinishchen hausfreundes -- Continued
2298.H3S42-.H3S49 School editions. By editor
2298.H3Z5-.H3Z99 Biography and criticism
Hedrich, Franz see PT2430.M4
Heiberg, Hermann see PT2617.E25
2298.H7 Heigel, Karl August von, 1835-1905 (Table P-PZ40 modified)
2298.H7A61-.H7Z458 Separate works
2298.H7B25 Bar-Cochba
2298.H7B3 Baronin Müller
2298.H7B7 Brömmels glück und ende
2298.H7D3 Die dame ohne herz
2298.H7E6 Ernste und heitere erzählungen
2298.H7E7 Es regnet
2298.H7E8 Das ewige licht
2298.H7F6 Die flucht nach Italien; humoreske
2298.H7F7 Freunde
2298.H7G4 Das geheimnis des königs
2298.H7G6 Gluck-gluck
2298.H7H3 Heitere erzählungen
2298.H7H4 Der herr stationschef
2298.H7J6 Josephine Bonaparte
2298.H7K3 Der karneval von Venedig
2298.H7M3 Der Maharadschah
2298.H7M4 Marfa
2298.H7N3 Neue erzählungen
2298.H7N4 Die neuen heiligen
2298.H7N5 Novellen
2298.H7N6 Novellen, Neue
2298.H7N7 Novellen, Neueste
2298.H7O4 Ohne gewissen
2298.H7R4 Der reine thor
2298.H7T4 Der theaterteufel
2298.H7V4 Die veranda am Gardasee
2298.H7V6 Volksfreund
2298.H7W3 Walpurg
2298.H7W4 Der weg zum himmel
2298.H7W6 Wo?
2298.H7W7 Wohin?
2298.H7Z3 Die zarin
Heimburg, W. see PT2603.E34
Heine, Heinrich, 1797-1856
Collected works

Individual authors or works
1700-ca. 1860/70
Heine, Heinrich, 1797-1856
Collected works -- Continued
2301.A1 Comprehensive editions. By date
(2301.A2) Critical and annotated editions. By editor
see PT2301.A1
2301.A3 Selected works (Poetry and prose)
For the following works, selected by Heine himself, see separate works: Reisebilder, I-III, PT2309.R25, Der Salon, I-IV, PT2309.S2, "Vermischter schriften," PT2309.V3
2301.A4A-.A4Z Selections, anthologies. By editor, A-Z
(2301.A5) Posthumous works
see PT2301.A3 (Poetry and prose)
see PT2303.A3 (Poetry alone)
see PT2308.A2 (Prose alone)
Poetical works
Original editions (and reprints)
2302.A1 Gedichte, 1822
Tragödien, nebst einem lyrischen intermezzo, 1823 see PT2309.T8
Buch der lieder, 1827 (1837, '39, '41, '44)
2302.A2 Editions 1-5, revised by Heine. By date
2302.A3 Later editions. By date
School editions see PT2303.A4A+
2302.A4 Neue gedichte, 1844, and reprints. By date
Comprehensive editions
2303.A2 Editions. By date
2303.A2A-.A2Z Critical editions. By editor, A-Z
2303.A3 Selections, anthologies, etc.
2303.A4A-.A4Z School editions. By editor, A-Z
Translations see PT2316+
2304.A2 Groups or cycles of poems
2304.A2H4 Hebräische melodien
2304.A2N7 Die Nordsee
2304.A3-Z Special poems, A-Z
2304.G7 Die grenadiere
2304.L6 Die Lorelei
2304.S34 Die schlesischen Weber
2305 Doubtful, spurious poems
2306 Imitations. Adaptations. Parodies
2307 Criticism, interpretation, etc.
Cf. PT2339.A+ Criticism of Heine in general
2308 Prose works
2308.A1 Comprehensive collections

Individual authors or works
1700-ca. 1860/70
Heine, Heinrich, 1797-1856
Collected works
Prose works -- Continued
2308.A2 Selected works. By date
Vermischte schriften, selected by the editor, A. Strodtmann, to be included here. Not to be confused with Heine's work of the same title, PT2309.V3
2308.A3 Novels
2308.A4A-.A4Z Selections, anthologies. By editor, A-Z
2309.A-Z Separate works
2309.A6 Almansor
2309.A8 Atta Troll
Die bäder von Lucca see PT2309.L7
2309.B6 Börne (Ludwig Börne, eine denkschrift)
2309.B7 Briefe aus Berlin, I (No more published)
Appeared in Reisebilder, II, 1827; Omitted in subsequent editions
2309.B8 Briefe über Deutschland (Fragment)
Buch der lieder see PT2302.A2+
Das buch le grand see PT2309.I4
Denunzianten, Über den see PT2309.U4
Deutschland see PT361+
2309.D4 Deutschland, ein wintermärchen, 1844
Cf. PT2302.A4 Neue gedichte, 1844
2309.D7 Der doktor Faust, ein tanzpoem
2309.E5 Elementargeister
Englischer fragmente
see DA
Cf. PT2309.R25 Reisebilder and Nachträge
Faust see PT2309.D7
2309.F5 Florentinische nächte
Die französische bühne
see PN
2309.F8 Französische zustände
Gedichte, 1822, and reprints see PT2302.A1
Geschichte der neueren schönen litteratur in Deutschland
see Die romantische schule, PT361, PT365.H4
Geständnisse see PT2329.A1
2309.G6 Die götter im exil
Die Harzreise
2309.H2 Editions. By date
2309.H2A-.H2Z School editions. By editor, A-Z
Hebräischen melodien see PT2304.A2H4

Individual authors or works
1700-ca. 1860/70
Heine, Heinrich, 1797-1856
Separate works -- Continued

2309.H5 Heimkehr (Poems)
2309.I4 Ideen. Das.buch le grand
2309.L3 "Lebensabriss" (Lettre à Philarète Chasles)
2309.L7 Lucca, Die bäden von
2309.L8 Lucca, Die stadt
Ludwig Börne see PT2309.B6
Lutezia
see DC
2309.L9 Lyrisches intermezzo
Memoiren see PT2329.A1
2309.M4 Memoiren des herrn von Schnabelewopski
Neue gedichte see PT2302.A4
Norderney (Nordsee 3. abt.)
see Reisebilder, II
Die Nordsee see PT2304.A2N7
2309.R2 Der rabbi von Bacharach
Ratcliff see PT2309.W5
2309.R24 Reise von München nach Genus
2309.R25 Reisebilder, I-III and Nachträge
Die romantische schule, 1836 see PT361+
2309.R3 Romanzero (Poems)
2309.S2 Der Salon, I-IV
2309.S3 Der Schwabenspiegel
Shakespeare's Mädchen und frauen see PR2991
2309.T8 Tragödien, nebst einem lyrischen intermezzo
2309.U4 Über den denunzianten
2309.U42 Uber Deutschland
see B2523
Die verbannten Götter see PT2309.G6
2309.V3 Vermischte schriften I-III, 1854
Cf. PT2308.A2
2309.W5 William Ratcliff
Zur geschichte der neueren schönen litteratur in Deutschland see PT361+
Zur geschichte der religion und philosophie in Duetschland
see B2523
(2309.Z9) Prefaces by Heine
see the author prefaced
2312 Doubtful, spurious works
Cf. PT2305 Poems
2313 Imitations, adaptations, parodies
Cf. PT2306 Poems

	Individual authors or works
	1700-ca. 1860/70
	Heine, Heinrich, 1797-1856 -- Continued
2314	Translations (As subject; comparative studies, etc.)
2315	Illustrations to the works
	Musical compositions on his works
	see ML
	Translations
2316	English
2316.A1	Collected works
2316.A3A-.A3Z	Selections, anthologies. By editor, A-Z
2316.A4A-.A4Z	Poems. By translator, A-Z
2316.A5A-.A5Z	Prose works. By translator, A-Z
2316.A7-Z	Separate works, A-Z. Subarrange by translator, A-Z
	e.g.
2316.R4L4	Reisebilder, translated by Leland
2317	French (Table PT1)
2318.A-Z	Other European languages, except Slavic, A-Z
	Subarrange each language by Table PT1a
2318.A6	Albanian (Table PT1a)
	Celtic
2318.C1	Breton (Table PT1a)
2318.C2	Cornish (Table PT1a)
2318.C3	Gaelic (Table PT1a)
2318.C4	Irish (Table PT1a)
2318.C5	Manx (Table PT1a)
2318.C6	Welsh (Table PT1a)
2318.D6	Dutch and Flemish (Table PT1a)
2318.G8	Greek, Modern (Table PT1a)
2318.H8	Hungarian (Table PT1a)
2318.I8	Italian (Table PT1a)
2318.L2	Latin (Table PT1a)
2318.P6	Portuguese (Table PT1a)
2318.R8	Romanian (Table PT1a)
	Scandinavian
2318.S2	Danish (Table PT1a)
2318.S4	Icelandic (Table PT1a)
2318.S5	Norwegian (Table PT1a)
2318.S6	Swedish (Table PT1a)
2318.S8	Spanish (Table PT1a)
2318.Y5	Yiddish (Table PT1a)
2320	Slavic languages
2320.B4	Bohemian (Table PT1a)
2320.B8	Bulgarian (Table PT1a)
2320.C7	Croatian (Table PT1a)
2320.L4	Latvian (Table PT1a)
2320.L5	Lithuanian (Table PT1a)

Individual authors or works
1700-ca. 1860/70
Heine, Heinrich, 1797-1856
Translations
Slavic languages -- Continued
2320.P6 Polish (Table PT1a)
2320.R6 Russian (Table PT1a)
2320.R8 Ruthenian (Table PT1a)
2320.S4 Serbian (Table PT1a)
2320.S5 Slovakian (Table PT1a)
2320.S6 Slovenian (Table PT1a)
2320.W3 Wendic (Table PT1a)
2322 Languages of Asia, Africa, Oceanica, etc.
2322.C5 Chinese (Table PT1a)
2322.H4 Hebrew (Table PT1a)
Yiddish see PT2318.Y5
(2326) Artificial languages
see PM
Biography and criticism
Bibliography see Z8395
2327 Periodicals and societies
2328 General treatises. Life and works
2329 Autobiography
2329.A1 "Lebensabriss," "Geständnisse," "Memoiren" and additions compiled from Heine's works and letters
By editor or translator, A-Z
Letters
2329.A2 Collections. By date
2329.A3A-.A3Z Translations. By language, A-Z
2329.A4A-.A4Z Special correspondents, A-Z
2329.A6 Conversations. By date of publication
2330 Early life and education
2331 Love and marriage. Relations to women
2331.A2 General
2331.A5-Z Special
2331.A5 Mathilde (Mirat) Heine, Heine's wife
2331.K74 Krinitz, Elise, 1830-1896
2332 Later life. Illness and death
2333 Relation to contemporaries, times, etc.
2333.A2 General
2333.A5-Z Special
2333.B7 Brentano, Clemens
2333.B9 Byron, George Gordon
2333.G6 Goethe, Johann Wolfgang von
2333.H53 Heine, Salomon, 1767-1844
2333.H7 Hoffman, E.T.A.
2333.I5 Immermann, Karl Leberecht

Individual authors or works
1700-ca. 1860/70
Heine, Heinrich, 1797-1856
Biography and criticism
Relation to contemporaries, times, etc.
Special -- Continued
2333.M3 Marx, Karl
2333.M8 Musset, Alfred de
2333.V4 Vesque von Püttlingen
Homes and haunts
2334.A2 General
2334.A5-Z Special, A-Z
e.g.
2334.I8 Italy
2335 Anniversaries. Celebrations
2336 Iconography. Portraits. Monuments
2337 Museums. Relics. Exhibitions
Heine in France, England, etc. see PT2339.A+
(2337.9) Heine in poetry, drama, fiction, etc.
see the author
2338 Authorship
Criticism, interpretation, etc.
History of criticism and interpretation
2339.A2 General and in Germany
2339.A5-Z Other countries, A-Z
2339.Z5A-.Z5Z Individual persons, A-Z
2340 General works. Genius, etc.
2341 Philosophy, esthetics, etc.
2342 Special topics (not A-Z)
Treatment and knowledge of special subjects
2343.A2 General
2343.A5-Z Special subjects
2343.A54 Animals
2343.A7 Art
2343.B5 Bible
2343.B67 Boredom
2343.C66 Cookery
2343.D53 Dialectic
2343.D7 Dreams
2343.E53 England
2343.F73 France
2343.G73 Greece
2343.J8 Judaism
2343.L38 Law
2343.L58 Literature
2343.M8 Music
2343.M94 Mythology

Individual authors or works
1700-ca. 1860/70
Heine, Heinrich, 1797-1856
Biography and criticism
Criticism, interpretation, etc.
Treatment and knowledge of special subjects
Special subjects -- Continued

2343.N3 National characteristics
2343.N4 Nature
2343.N45 Near East
2343.P6 Poland
2343.P7 Political questions
2343.R4 Religion
2343.S48 Sex
2343.S72 Spain
2343.W65 Women
2344 Textual criticism
Language. Style
2345.A-.Z3 General
2345.Z6 Versification
2345.Z8 Dictionaries. Concordances
2349.H2 Heinse, Johann Jakob Wilhelm, 1746-1803 (Table P-PZ40)
2349.H35 Helbig, Friedrich, 1832-1896
Hell, Theodor see PT2580.W4
2349.H5 Heller, Robert, 1812-1871 (Table P-PZ40)
Hellmuth, Ernst see PT2506.S3
Helm, Clementina see PT1818.B8
Helmina see PT1837.C2
2349.H55 Hempfing, Karl Friedrich Ernst, 1848- (Table P-PZ40)
2349.H56 Henkel, Frau Friederike, 1826-1895 (Table P-PZ40)
2349.H57 Henrich, Albertine (Röslin), b. 1812? (Table P-PZ40)
2349.H58 Henrici, Christian Friedrich, 1700-1764 (Table P-PZ40)
2349.H6 Hensel, Luise, 1798-1876 (Table P-PZ38)
2349.H65 Hensler, Karl Friedrich, 1761-1825 (Table P-PZ40)
2349.H7 Henzen, Wilhelm, 1850-1910 (Table P-PZ40)
2349.H75 Herbert, Frau Johanna (Leonhardt), 1830-1909 (Table P-PZ40)
Herbert, Lucian see PT2281.G95
2349.H8 Herchenbach, Wilhelm, 1818-1889 (Table P-PZ40)
Cf. PZ31+ Juvenile literature
Herder, Johann Gottfried, 1744-1803
Collected works
2351.A1 Comprehensive editions. By date
2351.A2 Selected works. By date or editor
2351.A25 Poems. By date
2351.A3-Z Selections. Anthologies

Individual authors or works
1700-ca. 1860/70
Herder, Johann Gottfried, 1744-1803 -- Continued
2352.A-Z Separate works
For works on special subjects, see the subject
2352.A4 Adrastea
Briefe see PT2353.A2
2352.B7 Briefe zur beförderung der humanität
2352.B8 Brutus
2352.D4 Denkmal Ulrichs von Hutten
Gedichte see PT2351.A25
Geist der ebräischen poesie see BS1401+
2352.L2 Legenden
2352.L3 Criticism
Stimmer der völker in liedern see PN1345
2352.T3 Terpsichore
Verstand und erfahrung; eine metakritik zur Kritik der reinen vernunft see B2775+
Volkslieder (Compilation) see PN1345
Vom geist der ebräischen poesie see BS1401+
2352.Z15 Zerstreute blätter, 1-6
Translations
English
2352.Z2 Collections
2352.Z21-.Z29 Separate works
French
2352.Z4 Collections
2352.Z41-.Z49 Separate works
2352.Z6-.Z69 Other languages (alphabetically)
e.g.
Spanish
2352.Z67 Collections
2352.Z671-.Z679 Separate works
Biography and criticism
2353.A2 Letters, diaries, etc.
2353.A3-Z General works
2354 Criticism
2355.H2 Herlossohn, Georg Karl Reginald, 1804-1849 (Table P-PZ40)
Hermann, Theodor see PT2445.P3
2355.H25 Hermes, Johann Timotheus, 1738-1821 (Table P-PZ40)
Herrig, Hans see PT2617.E725
2355.H3 Herrmann, Bernhard Anton, 1806-1876 (Table P-PZ40)
2355.H4 Hertz, Wilhelm, 1835-1902 (Table P-PZ40)
2355.H5 Herwegh, Georg, 1817-1875 (Table P-PZ40)
2355.H55 Herzenskron, Hermann Joseph, 1792-1863 (Table P-PZ40)
2355.H57 Herzog, Xaver, 1810-1883 (Table P-PZ40)

Individual authors or works
1700-ca. 1860/70 -- Continued

2355.H6 Hesekiel, George, 1819-1874 (Table P-PZ38)
2355.H65 Hesekiel, Ludovika, 1847-1889 (Table P-PZ40)
2355.H68 Hesslein, Bernhard, 1818-1882 (Table P-PZ40)
(2355.H7) Heun, Karl Gottlob Samuel, 1771-1854
see PT1837.C52
2355.H77 Hevesi, Ludwig, 1843-1910 (Table P-PZ40)
2355.H79 Hey, Wilhelm, 1789-1854 (Table P-PZ40)
Cf. PZ31+ Juvenile literature
2355.H8 Heyden, Friedrich August von, 1789-1851 (Table P-PZ40)
2355.H9 Heyne, Christian Leberecht, 1751-1821 (Table P-PZ40)
Heyse, Paul Johann Ludwig von, 1830-1914
2356.A1 Collected works. By date
2356.A15 Selected works (Drama, poetry, and prose). By date
2356.A2 Dramatic works. By date
2356.A25 Poetical works
Prose works. Novels, Novellen
2356.A3 Comprehensive collections. By date
2356.A33 Selected works. By editor or date
Novellen
2356.A37 Series of works with title Novellen. By date
2356.A37 1855 Novellen, 1855
2356.A37 1858 Neue Novellen, 1858
2356.A37 1859 Vier neue novellen, 1859
2356.A37 1862 Neue novellen, 1862
Gesammelte novellen in versen, 1863 see PT2356.A25
2356.A37 1866 Fünf neue novellen, 1866
2356.A37 1867 Novellen und terzinen, 1867
2356.A37 1871 Neues novellenbuch, 1871
2356.A37 1875 Neue novellen, 1875
2356.A4A-.A4Z Other collections. By title, A-Z
2356.A4B8 Buch der freundschaft
2356.A4B9 Buch der freundschaft. Neue folge
2356.A4D5 Das ding an sich und andere novellen
2356.A4F7 Frau von F. und römische novellen
2356.A4H5 Himmlische und irdische liebe [and other novellen]
2356.A4M2 Melusine und andere novellen
2356.A4M4 Meraner novellen
2356.A4M6 Moralische novellen
2356.A4M8 Neue moralische novellen
2356.A4N4 Ninon und andere novellen
2356.A4N7 Novellen vom Gardasee
2356.A4S5 Der sohn seines vaters und andere novellen
2356.A4T7 Troubadour novellen
2356.A4U6 Unvergessbare worte und andere novellen

Individual authors or works
1700-ca. 1860/70
Heyse, Paul Johann Ludwig von, 1830-1914
Novellen
Other collections. By title, A-Z -- Continued

2356.A4V4 Victoria regia und andere novellen
2356.A4V6 Villa Falconieri und andere novellen
2356.A6-Z Separate works
Arrange texts by date; arrange editions for schools, colleges, etc., by editor, A-Z
2356.A6 Ein abenteuer
2356.A62 Abenteuer eines blaustrümpfchens
2356.A7 Andrea Delfin
2356.A74 Anfang und ende
2356.A76 Annina
2356.A78 L'arrabbiata
2356.A79 Translations
2356.A8 Auf den dächern
2356.B5 Die blinden
Buch der freundschaft see PT2356.A4B8
2356.B9 Der bucklige von Shiras
2356.C2 Ein Canadier
2356.C6 Colberg
2356.D3 David und Jonathan
Das ding an sich und andere novellen see PT2356.A4D5
2356.D6 Don Juans ende
2356.E2 Die einsamen
2356.E6 Er soll dein herr sein
2356.F6 Francesca von Rimini
Frau von F. und römische novellen see PT2356.A4F7
2356.F8 Der friede
Fünf neue novellen see PT2356.A37 1866
2356.G2 Die geburt der Venus
Gedichte see PT2356.A25
2356.G5 Das glück von Rothenburg
2356.H2 Hans Lange
2356.H3 Der heilige
Himmlische und irdische liebe see PT2356.A4H5
2356.H7 Hochzeit auf Capri
2356.I7 Im paradiese
2356.K3 Kinder der welt
2356.K6 König Saul
Kolberg see PT2356.C6
2356.L7 Lottka
2356.L8 Ludwig der Baier
Lyrische dichtungen see PT2356.A25

Individual authors or works
1700-ca. 1860/70
Heyse, Paul Johann Ludwig von, 1830-1914
Separate works -- Continued

2356.M2 Das mädchen von Treppi
2356.M28 Maria Moroni
Maria von Magdala
2356.M3 Editions. By date
2356.M3A-.M3Z School editions. By date
2356.M31A-.M31Z English translations. By translator, A-Z
2356.M32A-.M32Z Other translations. By language, A-Z
Subarrange by translator
2356.M33 Criticism
2356.M4 Marienkind
2356.M42 Marion
2356.M5 Meleager
Melusine und andere novellen see PT2356.A4M2
Meraner novellen see PT2356.A4M4
2356.M63 Merlin
Moralische novellen see PT2356.A4M6
2356.M8 Mutter und tochter
Neue gedichte und jungenlieder see PT2356.A25
Neue novellen see PT2356.A37
2356.N4 Niels mit der offenen hand
Ninon und andere novellen see PT2356.A4N4
Novellen see PT2356.A37+
La rabbiata see PT2356.A78
2356.R8 Der roman der stiftsdame
2356.S2 Die Sabinerinnen
2356.S6 Der sohn seines vaters
Cf. PT2356.A4S5
2356.S7 Der stern von Mantua
2356.T3 Thekla
2356.T4 Die thörichten jungfrauen
Troubadour novellen see PT2356.A4T7
2356.U2 Ueber allen gipfeln
2356.U7 Unter brüdern
Unvergessbare worte und andere novellen see PT2356.A4U6
2356.V2 Vanina Vanini
2356.V25 Der verlorene sohn
2356.V3 Verrathenes glück
2356.V4 Das verschleirte bild zu Sais
2356.V6 Vetter Gabriel
Victoria regia und andere novellen see PT2356.A4V4
Vier neue novellen see PT2356.A37
Villa Falconieri und andere novellen see PT2356.A4V6

Individual authors or works
1700-ca. 1860/70
Heyse, Paul Johann Ludwig von, 1830-1914
Separate works -- Continued

2356.W44 Die Weishut Salomos
2356.Z8 Zwei gefangene
Biography and criticism
2357.A2 Memoirs
2357.A3 Letters
2357.A5-Z General treatises. Life and works
2357.Z5 Criticism
(2358.H2) Hildebrand, E.
see PT2645.O6
2358.H25 Hildebrandt, Johann Andreas Christoph, 1764-1848 (Table P-PZ40)
2358.H3 Hillern, Frau Wilhelmine (Birch) von, 1836-1916 (Table P-PZ40 modified)
2358.H3A61-.H3Z458 Separate works
2358.H3A65 Ein alter streit
2358.H3A66 Am kreuz
2358.H3A7 Ein arzt der seele
2358.H3A73 Die augen der liebe
2358.H3A8 Aus eigener kraft
2358.H3A9 Ein autographensammler
2358.H3D7 Doppelleben
2358.H3F4 Friedhofs-blume
2358.H3G5 Die Geyer-Wally
2358.H3G8 Guten abend!
2358.H3H7 Höher als die kirche
2358.H3R4 's reis am weg
2358.H3S5 Ein sklave der freiheit
2358.H3U6 Und sie kommt doch
2358.H4 Hiltl, Georg, 1826-1878 (Table P-PZ40)
2358.H5 Hippel, Theodor Gottlieb von, 1741-1796 (Table P-PZ40)
Hirsch, Franz Wilhelm see PT2617.I65
Hirsch, Marie see PT2617.I68
Hirschfeld, Hermann see PT2617.I77
2358.H7 Höcker, Gustav, 1832-1911 (Table P-PZ40)
Höcker, Oskar see PT2617.O2
2358.H8 Hoefer, Edmund Franz Andreas 1819-1882 (Table P-PZ40)
2359.H2 Hölderlin, Friedrich, 1770-1843 (Table P-PZ38 modified)
2359.H2A6 Selections
2359.H2A61-.H2A78 Separate works
e.g.
2359.H2A66 Empedokles
2359.H2A67 Criticism
2359.H2A7 Hyperion

Individual authors or works
1700-ca. 1860/70
Hölderlin, Friedrich, 1770-1843 -- Continued

2359.H2A79-.H2Z	Biography and criticism
2359.H4	Hölty, Ludwig Heinrich Christoph, 1748-1776 (Table P-PZ38)
2359.H8	Hoffmann, Bertha Wilhelmine, 1816-1892 (Table P-PZ40)
	Hoffmann, Ernst Theodor Amadeus, 1776-1822
2360.A1	Collected works. By date
2360.A3	Selected works. By date
2360.A6-.Z9	Separate works
2360.A65	Die abentheuer der Sylvesternacht
2360.A7	Der Artushof
2360.A8	Die automate
2360.B3	Der baron von Bagge
2360.B4	Die Bergwerke zu Falun
2360.B7	Die brautwahl
2360.D3	Datura fastuosa
	Des vetters eckfenster see PT2360.V4
2360.D5	Der dichter und der componist
2360.D6	Doge und dogaresse
2360.D7	Don Juan
2360.D8	Die doppeltgänger
2360.E4	Der elementargeist
2360.E6	Die elixiere de teufels
2360.F3	Fantasiestücke in Callot's manier
2360.F4	Der feind
2360.F8	Das fräulein von Scuderi
2360.F9	Das fremde kind
2360.G3	Die geheimnisse
2360.G4	Das gelübde
2360.G5	Die genesung
2360.G6	Der goldene topf
2360.H3	Haimatochare
2360.I4	Ignaz Denner
2360.I7	Die irrungen
2360.J4	Die Jesuiterkirche in G
2360.K3	Der kampf der sänger
2360.K5	Klein-Zaches
2360.K6	Die königsbraut
2360.K7	Kreisleriana
2360.L4	Lebensansichten des katers Murr
2360.M2	Der magnetiseur
2360.M3	Das majorat
2360.M4	Die marquise de la Pivardière
2360.M5	Meister Floh
2360.M6	Meister Johannes Wacht

Individual authors or works
1700-ca. 1860/70
Hoffman, Ernst Theodor Amadeus, 1776-1822
Separate works -- Continued

2360.M7 Meister Martin der küfner und seine gesellen
2360.M8 Menschen und mächte (collection)
2360.N2 Nachricht von den neuesten schicksalen des hundes Berganza
2360.N3 Nachtstücke
2360.N5 Neueste schicksale eines abentheuerlichen mannes
2360.N8 Nussknacker und mausekönig
2360.O3 Das öde haus
2360.P7 Prinzessin Brambilla
2360.R3 Die räuber
2360.R4 Rath Krespel
2360.R5 Ritter Gluck
2360.S2 Das sanctus
2360.S3 Der sandmann
2360.S4 Seltsame leiden eines theater-directors
2360.S5 Die Serapions-brüder (collection)
2360.S6 Signor Formica
2360.S7 Spielerglück
2360.S8 Das steinerne herz
Undine (Opera)
see M
2360.U6 Der unheimliche gast
2360.V4 Des vetters eckfenster
2360.V5 Die vision auf dem schlachtfelde bei Dresden
2360.Z7 Die zusammenhang der dinge
2360.Z9 Die Pagodenburg
2361.A-Z Translations. By language, A-Z
English
2361.E4A14 Unknown translators. By date
2361.E4A3-.E4Z Special translators, A-Z
2361.E5A-.E5Z Special works (by German title)
French
2361.F4A14 Unknown translators. By date
2361.F4A3-.F4Z Special translators, A-Z
2361.F5A-.F5Z Special works (by German title)
2361.Z4 Memoirs, letters, etc. By date
2361.Z5 Biography and criticism
Hoffman, Franz
see PZ7 PZ32 etc.
2362.H3 Hoffmann, Hans Friedrich Karl, 1848-1909 (Table P-PZ40)
School editions of separate works arranged by editor (successive Cutter numbers)
2362.H45 Hoffmann-Donner, Heinrich, 1809-1894 (Table P-PZ40)

Individual authors or works
1700-ca. 1860/70
Hoffmann-Donner, Heinrich, 1809-1894 -- Continued
2362.H45A61-.H45Z458 Separate works. By title
Struwwelpeter see PZ31+
2362.H5 Hoffmann von Fallersleben, August Heinrich, 1798-1874 (Table P-PZ40)
Hohenfurth, Franz von see PT2449.P57
Hohenstein, K. see PT2559.W2
2362.H6 Holbein, Franz Ignaz, edler von Holbeinsberg, 1779-1855 (Table P-PZ40)
2362.H7 Holtei, Karl von, 1798-1880 (Table P-PZ40)
2363.H2 Hopfen, Hans, 1835-1904 (Table P-PZ40)
2363.H24 Horn, Franz Christoph, 1781-1837 (Table P-PZ40)
Horn, W.O. see PT2443.O3
2363.H273 Hosemann, Theodor, 1807-1875 (Table P-PZ40)
2363.H28 Hottinger, Johann Jacob, 1750-1819 (Table P-PZ40)
2363.H3 Houwald, Ernst Christoph, freiherr von, 1778-1845 (Table P-PZ38)
2363.H35 Hrussoczy, Marie, edle von, 1821-1898 (Table P-PZ40)
2363.H4 Huber, Ludwig Ferdinand, 1764-1804 (Table P-PZ40)
Works since 1793 were wholly or in part written by his wife Therese Huber
2363.H5 Huber, Frau Therese (Heyne) Forster, 1764-1829 (Table P-PZ40)
2363.H52 Huber, Stephan (Table P-PZ40)
2363.H55 Hübner, Heinrich, fl. 1851 (Table P-PZ40)
2363.H56 Hübner, Johann, 1668-1731 (Table P-PZ40)
2363.H6 Hülsen, Frau Helene (von Häseler) von, 1829-1892 (Table P-PZ40)
2363.H7 Humbracht, Luise Ernestine Malwina von, 1825-1891 (Table P-PZ40)
2363.H8 Hunold, Christian Friedrich, 1681-1721 (Table P-PZ40)
Iffland, August Wilhelm, 1759-1814
2365.I2 Collected works. By date
2365.I2A2-.I2A29 Translations. By language (alphabetically)
2365.I2A3-.I2Z2 Separate works
2365.I2A4 Die advokaten
2365.I2A5 Albert von Thurneisen
2365.I2A6 Allzuscharf macht schartig
2365.I2A7 Alte zeit und neue zeit
2365.I2A8 Die aussteuer
2365.I2B4 Bewusstseyn!
2365.I2D5 Dienstpflicht
2365.I2E6 Elise von Valberg
2365.I2E8 Das erbtheil des vaters

Individual authors or works
1700-ca. 1860/70
Iffland, August Wilhelm, 1759-1814
Separate works -- Continued
Die erwachsenen töchter see PQ2381.A6+
2365.I2F2 Die familie Lonau
2365.I2F6 Frauenstand
2365.I2F8 Friedrich von Oesterreich
2365.I2G4 Das gewissen
2365.I2G8 Der gutherzige polterer
2365.I2H3 Die hagestolzen
2365.I2H4 Die hausfreunde
2365.I2H5 Hausfrieden
2365.I2H6 Der haustyran
2365.I2H7 Der herbsttag
2365.I2H8 Die höhen
2365.I2J3 Die jäger
2365.I2K6 Die kokarden
2365.I2K7 Der komet
2365.I2K8 Die künstler
2365.I2L3 Liebe um liebe
2365.I2L6 Liussan, fürst von Garisene
2365.I2M8 Die mündel
2365.I2M9 Die müssiggänger
2365.I2O2 Der oheim
2365.I2R4 Die reise nach der stadt
2365.I2R5 Reue versöhnt
Rückwirkung see PQ2381.A6+
2365.I2S3 Scheinverdienst
2365.I2S4 Selbstbeherrschung
2365.I2S7 Der spieler
2365.I2T3 Der taufschein
Über meine theatralische laufbahn see PT2365.I2Z3
2365.I2V2 Vaterfreude
2365.I2V3 Das vaterhaus
2365.I2V4 Verbrechen aus ehrsucht
2365.I2W6 Wohin?
2365.I2Z3 Autobiography. By date
2365.I2Z43 Letters. By date
2365.I2Z5-.I2Z99 Biography and criticism
Immermann, Karl Leberecht, 1796-1840
2365.I4 Collected works. By date
2365.I4A17 Collected poems. By date
2365.I4A19 Collected dramas. By date
2365.I4A5-.I4Z Separate works
Alexis (Trilogy)
2365.I4A6 Complete editions. By date

Individual authors or works
1700-ca. 1860/70
Immermann, Karl Leberecht, 1796-1840
Separate works
Alexis (Trilogy)
Complete editions. By date -- Continued

2365.I4A61 I. Die bojaren
2365.I4A62 II. Das gericht von St. Petersburg
2365.I4A63 III. Eudoxia (Epilogue)
2365.I4A7-.A79 Translations
2365.I4A8-.A89 Criticism
Andreas Hofer see PT2365.I4T6
2365.I4A9 Das auge der liebe
Die bojaren see PT2365.I4A61
2365.I4B78 Die brüder
2365.I4C2 Cardenio und Celinde
2365.I4C3 Der carneval und die somnambule
2365.I4E2 Edwin
2365.I4E3 Die epigonen
Eudoxia see PT2365.I4A63
Das gericht von St. Petersburg see PT2365.I4A62
2365.I4G5 Ghismonda
2365.I4G7 Graf Adam von Schwarzenburg
Der im irrgarten der metrik umhertaumelnde cavalier (an attack on Platen) see PT2448.Z5
2365.I4K3 Kaiser Friedrich der Zweite
2365.I4K6 König Periander und sein haus
Memorabilien see PT2365.I5A1
Merlin
2365.I4M2 Editions. By date
2365.I4M3-.M49 Criticism
2365.I4M5 Miscellen (1830)
2365.I4M6 Ein morgenscherz
2365.I4M8 Münchhausen
Cf. PT2365.I4O2 Oberhof
2365.I4N4 Der neue Pygmalion
2365.I4O2 Der Oberhof
Prose idyl from Münchhausen
(2365.I4O6) Die opfer des schweigens
see PT2365.I4G5
2365.I4P2 Die papierfenster eines eremiten
2365.I4P3 Pater Brey
2365.I4P4 Petrarca
2365.I4P7 Die prinzen von Syrakus
2365.I4R3 Reisenjournal
Die Romanows see PT2365.I4A6+
2365.I4S3 Die schelmische gräfin

Individual authors or works
1700-ca. 1860/70
Immermann, Karl Leberecht, 1796-1840
Separate works -- Continued

2365.I4S4 Die schule der frommen
2365.I4T4 Das thal von Ronceval
2365.I4T6 Das trauerspiel in Tyrol. Andreas Hofer
2365.I4T7 Tristan und Isolde
2365.I4T81-.I4T89 Criticism
2365.I4T9 Tulifäntchen
2365.I4V4 Die verkleidungen
2365.I4V5 Die verschollene
Biography and criticism
2365.I5A1 Memorabilien. By date
2365.I5A2 Letters. By date
2365.I5A3-.I5Z3 General treatises. Life and works
2365.I5Z4-.I5Z9 Criticism
Innocenz see PT2514.S2
Isidorous Orientalis see PT2424.L6
Ivo, Berengarius see PT2531.S7
Jacobi, Friedrich Heinrich, 1743-1819
2368.J2 Collected works. By date
2368.J2A2 Selections, anthologies. By date
Separate works
Cf. B3055+ Philosophical works
2368.J2A5 Eduard Allwills briefsammlung
2368.J2A6 Woldemar
Biography see B3055+
2368.J2A7 Letters. By date
2368.J2A8-.J2Z Literary criticism of Jacobi's works (all or single)
2368.J3 Jacobi, Johann Georg, 1740-1814 (Table P-PZ40)
2368.J35 Jacobson, Eduard, 1833-1897 (Table P-PZ40)
2368.J37 Jacoby, Leopold, 1840-1895 (Table P-PZ40)
2368.J42 Jaenicke, Heinrich Martin, 1818-1872 (Table P-PZ40)
2368.J435 Jagemann, Christian Joseph, 1735-1804 (Table P-PZ40)
2368.J45 Jan, Hermann Ludwig von, 1851- (Table P-PZ40)
2368.J47 Jarke, Frau Franziska Julie (Schlesius), 1815-1896 (Table P-PZ40)
Jean Paul see PT2454+
2368.J5 Jensen, Wilhelm, 1837-1911 (Table P-PZ40)
Jents, Karl see PT2522.S75
Jeremias see PT2514.S2
Jerta see PT1875.F64
2369.J63 Jochmann, Karl Gustav, 1789-1830 (Table P-PZ40)
2370.J3 John, Eugenie, 1825-1887 (Table P-PZ40 modified)
2370.J3A61-.J3Z458 Separate works. By title
2370.J3A8 Amtmanns magd

Individual authors or works
1700-ca. 1860/70
John, Eugenie, 1825-1887
Separate works -- Continued

2370.J3B6 Blaubart
2370.J3E8 Das eulenhaus
2370.J3F8 Die frau mit den karfunkelsteinen
2370.J3G2 Das geheimnis der alten mamsell
2370.J3G5 Goldelse
2370.J3H3 Das haideprinzesschen
2370.J3I2 Im hause des kommerzienrathes
2370.J3I5 Im Schillingshof
2370.J3R4 Reichsgräfin Gisela
2370.J3T5 Thüringer erzählungen
2370.J3Z3 Die zweite frau
2370.J3Z4 Die zwölf apostel
Johnsen, Ludovika (Hesekiel) see PT2355.H65
2370.J4 Jordan, Wilhelm, 1819-1904 (Table P-PZ40)
Juncker, E. see PT2506.S4
Jung-Stilling, Johann Heinrich, 1740-1817
2370.J7 Collected works. By date
2370.J7A15 Collected novels. By date
2370.J7A17 "Erzählungen"
2370.J7A19 Poems
2370.J7A6 Selected works. Selections. By date
2370.J7A7-.J7Z18 Separate works
2370.J7C4 Der christliche menschenfreund
2370.J7C5 Chrysäon; oder, Das goldene zeitalter
2370.J7G3 Die geschichte des herrn von Morgenthau
2370.J7G4 Die geschichte Florentins v. Fahlendorn
2370.J7G7 Der graue mann, eine volksschrift, 1795-1816
Häusliches leben see PT2370.J7Z25
2370.J7H4 Das heimweh
2370.J7H45 Schlüssel zum Heimweh
2370.J7H5 Heinrich Frauenlob
Jünglingsjahre see PT2370.J7Z22
Jugend see PT2370.J7Z21
2370.J7L4 Lebensgeschichte der Theodore von der Linden
Lehrjahre see PT2370.J7Z24
2370.J7S3 Scenen aus dem geisterreiche
Theobald; oder, Der schwärmer
2370.J7T2 Editions. By date
Translations
2370.J7T3 English. By date
2370.J7T5 Criticism
Wanderschaft see PT2370.J7Z23
Autobiography

Individual authors or works
1700-ca. 1860/70
Jung-Stilling, Johann Heinrich, 1740-1817
Autobiography -- Continued

2370.J7Z19 Complete editions
2370.J7Z2 Selections, school editions. By date
2370.J7Z21 Jugend
2370.J7Z22 Jünglingsjahre
2370.J7Z23 Wanderschaft
2370.J7Z24 Lehrjahre
2370.J7Z25 Häusliches leben
2370.J7Z26 Alter
Translations
English
2370.J7Z27 Complete editions or various parts
Special parts
2370.J7Z271 Jugend
2370.J7Z272 Jünglingsjahre
2370.J7Z273 Wanderschaft
2370.J7Z274 Lehrjahre
2370.J7Z275 Häusliches leben
2370.J7Z276 Alter
French
2370.J7Z28 Complete editions or various parts
Special parts
2370.J7Z281 Jugend
2370.J7Z282 Jünglingsjahre
2370.J7Z283 Wanderschaft
2370.J7Z284 Lehrjahre
2370.J7Z285 Häusliches leben
2370.J7Z286 Alter
2370.J7Z29-.J7Z49 Other languages (alphabetically)
Letters
2370.J7Z492 General collections. By date
2370.J7Z493-.J7Z499 By correspondent, A-Z
2370.J7Z5-.J7Z99 Biography and criticism
2370.J9 Junghans, Sophie, 1845-1907 (Table P-PZ40)
2372.K16 Kadelburg, Gustav, 1851- (Table P-PZ40)
Cf. PT1820.B5 Bluenthal, Oskar
Cf. PT2508.S2 Schönthan, Franz von
2372.K2 Kästner, Abraham Gotthelf, 1719-1800 (Table P-PZ40)
2372.K25 Kaffka, Johann Christopf, 1754-1815 (Table P-PZ40)
2372.K28 Kahlert, Karl Friedrich, 1765-1813 (Table P-PZ40)
2372.K3 Kaiser, Friedrich, 1814-1874 (Table P-PZ40)
2372.K36 Kalb, Charlotte von, 1761-1843 (Table P-PZ40)
2372.K4 Kalchberg, Johann Nepomuk, ritter von, 1765-1827 (Table P-PZ40)

	Individual authors or works
	1700-ca. 1860/70 -- Continued
2372.K45	Kalckreuth, Friedrich Ernst Adolf Karl, graf von, 1790-1873 (Table P-PZ40)
2372.K5	Kalisch, David, 1820-1872 (Table P-PZ40)
2372.K55	Kalisch, Ludwig, 1814-1882 (Table P-PZ40)
2372.K6	Kaltenbruner, Karl Adam, 1804-1867 (Table P-PZ40)
	Kampfmuth, Georg see PT2621.E26
2372.K63	Kanne, Friedrich August, 1778-1833 (Table P-PZ40)
2372.K65	Kanne, Johann Arnold, 1773-1824 (Table P-PZ40)
2372.K73	Karcher, Friedrich Albrecht, 1814-1855 (Table P-PZ40)
2372.K75	Karsch (or Karschin), Anna Louise, 1722-1791 (Table P-PZ38)
2372.K8	Kaufmann, Frau Mathilde (Binder), 1835- (Table P-PZ40)
	Keim, Franz see PT2621.E25
	Keiter, Heinrich see PT2621.E26
	Keller, Gottfried, 1819-1890
2374.A1	Collected works. By date
2374.A14	Selected works. By date
2374.A15	Posthumous works. By date
2374.A16	Collected novels
2374.A17	Collected poems
	Translations (Collected or selected)
2374.A2-.A29	English. By translator
2374.A3-.A39	French. By translator
2374.A5-.A59	Other languages
2374.A7-.Z2	Separate works
	Dietegen
2374.D2	Editions. By date
2374.D2A-.D2Z	School editions. By editor, A-Z
2374.D4	Don Correa
2374.D5	Dorotheas blumenkörbchen
	Die drei gerechten kammacher
2374.D7	Editions. By date
2374.D7A-.D7Z	School editions. By veditor, A-Z
2374.E8	Eugenia
	Das fähnlein der sieben aufrechten
2374.F3	Editions. By date
2374.F3A-.F3Z	School editions. By editor, A-Z
2374.F8	Frau Regel Amrain und ihr jüngster
2374.G7	Der grüne Heinrich
2374.H3	Hadlaub
2374.J6	Die Jungfrau als ritter
2374.J7	Die Jungfrau und der teufel
2374.J8	Die Jungfrau und die nonne
	Kleider machen leute
2374.K3	Editions. By date

Individual authors or works
1700-ca. 1860/70
Keller, Gottfried, 1819-1890
Separate works
Kleider machen leute -- Continued

2374.K3A-.K3Z School editions. By editor, A-Z
Der landvogt von Greifensee
2374.L2 Editions. By date
2374.L3 Translations
2374.L4 Criticism
Die leute von Seldwyla
2374.L5 Editions. By date
2374.L6 Translations
2374.L7 Criticism
2374.M3 Martin Salander
2374.M5 Die missbrauchten liebesbriefe
2374.N3 Der narr auf Manegg
2374.P3 Pankraz der schmoller
Romeo und Julia auf dem dorfe
2374.R3 Editions. By date
2374.R3A-.R3Z School editions. By editor, A-Z
2374.S2 Der schlimm-heilige Vitalis
2374.S3 Der schmied seines glückes
Sieben legenden
2374.S5 Editions. By date
2374.S51-.S59 Translations
2374.S6 Criticism
2374.S7 Das sinngedicht
2374.S9 Spiegel, das kätzchen
2374.T3 Das tanzlegenden Ursula
2374.U8 Ursula
2374.V4 Das verlorene lachen
2374.Z2 Züricher novellen
Biography and criticism
2374.Z25 Periodicals and societies
2374.Z28 Anniversaries, exhibitions, etc. By date
2374.Z3-.Z39 Journals, letters
2374.Z4 Biography. Life and works
2374.Z5 Criticism
2376.K15 Keller-Jordan, Frau Henriette, 1835-1909 (Table P-PZ40)
2376.K28 Kerndörffer, Heinrich August, 1769-1846 (Table P-PZ40)
2376.K3 Kerner, Justinus Andreas Christian, 1786-1862 (Table P-PZ40)
2376.K4 Kerner, Theobald, 1817-1907 (Table P-PZ40)
2376.K5 Kessel, Karl von, 1807-1889 (Table P-PZ40)
2376.K6 Kette, Hermann, 1828-1908 (Table P-PZ40)
2376.K65 Kettnacker, Richard, 1843-1897 (Table P-PZ40)

	Individual authors or works
	1700-ca. 1860/70 -- Continued
2376.K7	Keyser, Stefanie, 1847- (Table P-PZ40)
2376.K8	Keyserling, Margarete, gräfin, von, 1846- (Table P-PZ40)
2376.K9	Kiessling, Friedrich Ferdinand, b. 1835 (Table P-PZ40)
2377.K2	Kind, Friedrich, 1768-1843 (Table P-PZ40)
	For Die Freischütz, see ML410.W3K5
	Kindermann, Hans see PT2423.L2
2377.K25	Kindlebn, Christian Wilhelm, 1748-1785 (Table P-PZ40)
2377.K3	Kinkel, Gottfried, 1815-1882 (Table P-PZ38)
2377.K32	Kinkel, Johanna (Mockel), 1810-1858 (Table P-PZ40)
2377.K4	Kirchhoff, Friedrich Christian, 1822-1894 (Table P-PZ40)
2377.K5	Kirschner, Lula, 1854- (Table P-PZ40)
2377.K57	Klein, Anton, edler von, 1748-1810 (Table P-PZ40)
2377.K6	Klein, Julius Leopold, 1810-1876 (Table P-PZ38)
2377.K7	Kleist, Ewald Christian von, 1715-1759 (Table P-PZ40)
2377.K9	Kleist, Franz Alexander von, 1769-1797 (Table P-PZ40)
	Kleist, Heinrich von, 1777-1811
2378.A1	Collected works. By date
2378.A13	Collected minor works. Posthumous works. "Hinterlassene schriften"
2378.A14	Selected works. By date
2378.A15	Collected tales (Novellen)
2378.A17	Collected poems
2378.A19	Collected plays
2378.A2A-.A2Z	Translations. By language, A-Z
	Separate works
2378.A6	Amphitryon
2378.E7	Das erdbeben in Chili
	Die familie Ghonorez see PT2378.F3
2378.F3	Die familie Schroffenstein
	Die feuerprobe see PT2378.K3+
2378.F5	Der Findling
2378.G4	Germania an ihre kinder
2378.H45	Heilige Cäcilie oder, Die Gewalt der Musik
	Die Hermannschlacht
2378.H5	Editions. By date
2378.H5A-.H5Z	Editions. By editor. School editions
2378.H51-.H59	Translations. By language
2378.H6	Criticism
	Das Käthchen von Heilbronn; oder, Die feuerprobe
2378.K3	Editions. By date
2378.K3A-.K3Z	Editions. By editor. School editions
2378.K31-.K39	Translations. By language
2378.K4	Criticism
2378.M3	Die marquise von O.
	Michael Kohlhaas

Individual authors or works
1700-ca. 1860/70
Kleist, Heinrich von, 1777-1811
Separate works
Michael Kohlhaas -- Continued

2378.M6 Editions. By date
2378.M6A-.M6Z Editions. By editor. School editions
2378.M61-.M69 Translations. By language
2378.M7 Criticism
2378.P4 Penthesilea
Phöbus (Periodical) see AP30
Prinz Friedrich von Homburg
2378.P7 Editions. By date
2378.P7A-.P7Z Editions. By editor. School editions
2378.P71-.P79 Translations. By language
2378.P8 Criticism
2378.R6 Robert Guiskard
2378.T6 Todeslitanei
2378.V4 Verlobung in St. Domingo
2378.Z4 Der zerbrochene krug
Biography and criticism
2379.A2 Autobiography, journals, etc.
2379.A3 Letters
2379.A5-.Z4 General treatises. Life and works
2379.Z5 Criticism
2380.K2 Klencke, Hermann, 1813-1881 (Table P-PZ40)
Klescheim, Anton, freiherr von see PF5336+
2380.K3 Kletke, Hermann, 1813-1886 (Table P-PZ40)
2380.K4 Klettenberg, Susanna Katharina von, 1723-1774 (Table P-PZ40)
2380.K6 Klingemann, August, 1777-1831 (Table P-PZ40)
Klinger, Friedrich Maximilian von, 1752-1831
2380.K7 Collected works. By date
2380.K7A6-.K7Z Separate works
2380.K7A7 Aristodemos
2380.K7B4 Betrachtungen und gedanken
2380.K7D2 Damokles
2380.K7D4 Der derwisch
2380.K7E6 Elfride
2380.K7F2 Die falschen spieler
2380.K7F4 Der Faust der Morgenländer; oder, Wanderungen Ben Hafis
Fausts leben, thaten und höllenfahrt
2380.K7F7 Editions. By date
2380.K7F71-.K7F79 Translations
e.g.
2380.K7F72 English

Individual authors or works
1700-ca. 1860/70
Klinger, Friedrich Maximilian von, 1752-1831
Separate works
Fausts leben, thaten und höllenfahrt -- Continued

2380.K7F8	Criticism
2380.K7G4	Geschichte eines Teutschen der neusten zeit
2380.K7G5	Geschichte Giafars des Barmeciden
2380.K7G6	Geschichte Raphaels de Aquillas
2380.K7G7	Geschichte vom goldnen hahn
2380.K7G8	Der günstling
2380.K7K6	Konradin
2380.K7L4	Das leidende weib
2380.K7M4	Medea auf dem Kaukasos
2380.K7M6	Medea in Korinth
2380.K7N4-.K7N5	Die neue Arria
2380.K7O4	Oriantes
2380.K7O6	Orpheus, eine tragisch-komische geschichte
2380.K7O8-.K7O9	Otto
2380.K7P6	Plimplamplasko
2380.K7P7	Prinz Formosos fiedelbogen
2380.K7R4	Reisen vor der sündfluth
2380.K7S2	Sahir, Evas erstgeborner in Paradiese
2380.K7S25	Scenen aus Pyrrhus leben und tod
2380.K7S3	Der schwur gegen die ehe
2380.K7S4-.K7S5	Simsone Grisaldo
2380.K7S6	Stilpo und seine kinder
2380.K7S7-.K7S8	Sturm und drang
2380.K7V4	Der verbannte göttersohn
2380.K7W4-.K7W5	Der weltmann und der dichter
2380.K7Z4-.K7Z5	Die zwillinge
2380.K8A-.K8Z	Biography and criticism
	Klopstock, Friedrich Gottlieb, 1724-1803
2381.A1	Collected works. By date
	Translations see PT2381.Z2+
2381.A3	Selected works. By date
2381.A35	Miscellaneous prose works. By date
	Poems
2381.A4	Collections and selections. By date
2381.A5	Geistliche lieder
2381.A6	Odes. By date
2381.A7	Criticism
2381.A8	Special odes, psalms, etc., A-Z
2381.A9-.Z1	Separate works
2381.D2	David
2381.D5	Die deutsche gelehrtenrepublik

Individual authors or works
1700-ca. 1860/70
Klopstock, Friedrich Gottlieb, 1724-1803
Separate works -- Continued
Grammatische gespräche
see PF

2381.H2 Hermann und die fürsten
2381.H4 Hermanns schlacht
2381.H6 Hermanns tod
2381.M2 Der Messias
Editions, including the older incomplete editions. By date
2381.S2 Salomo
2381.T3 Der tod Adams
Translations
2381.Z2-.Z39 English
2381.Z2 Collected works. By date
2381.Z25 Letters. By date
2381.Z3A-.Z3Z Der Messias. By translator, A-Z
2381.Z35A-.Z35Z Odes. By translator, A-Z
2381.Z4-.Z49 French
e.g.
2381.Z47 Der Messias
2381.Z5-.Z99 Other. By language (alphabetically)
Biography and criticism (including Messias)
Letters
2382.A2 Editions. By editor
Translations see PT2381.Z25
2382.A5-.Z3 General treatises. Life and works
2382.Z5 Criticism
2383.K12 Klopstock, Margareta (Moller), 1728-1758 (Table P-PZ40)
2383.K3 Knebel, Karl Ludwig von, 1744-1834 (Table P-PZ40)
2383.K33 Kneisel, Rudolf, 1832-1899 (Table P-PZ40)
2383.K35 Knigge, Adolf Franz Friedrich Ludwig, freiherr von, 1752-1796 (Table P-PZ40)
2383.K355 Knorr, Josephine, freiin von, 1827-1908 (Table P-PZ40)
2383.K37 Kobbe, Theodor von, 1798-1845 (Table P-PZ40)
2383.K4 Kobell, Franz, ritter von, 1803-1882 (Table P-PZ40)
2383.K43 Koch, Ernst, 1808-1858 (Table P-PZ40)
2383.K45 Koch, Karl Wilhelm, 1785-1860 (Table P-PZ40)
2383.K48 Koch, Wilhelm, 1845-1891 (Table P-PZ40)
2383.K5 Köchy, Karl Georg Heinrich Eduard, 1800-1880 (Table P-PZ40)
2383.K6 Koenig, Ewald August, 1833-1888 (Table P-PZ40)
2383.K7 Koenig, Heinrich Joseph, 1790-1869 (Table P-PZ40)
2383.K8 Koenig, Johann Ulrich von, 1688-1744 (Table P-PZ40)
2383.K92 Köppel, Frau Emmy, 1850- (Table P-PZ40)
2383.K94 Köppen, Friedrich, 1775-1858 (Table P-PZ40)

Individual authors or works
1700-ca. 1860/70 -- Continued

2385.K2 Körner, Theodor, 1791-1813 (Table P-PZ40 modified)
2385.K2A61-.K2Z458 Separate works
2385.K2B7 Die braut
2385.K2G7 Der grüne domino
2385.K2H4 Hedwig
2385.K2K6 Knospen
2385.K2L4 Leyer und schwert
2385.K2R6 Rosamunda
2385.K2T6 Toni
2385.K2V4 Der vetter aus Bremen
2385.K2Z2 Zriny
2385.K24 Kohn, Salomon, 1825-1904 (Table P-PZ40)
2385.K25 Kolisch, Sigmund, 1816-1886 (Table P-PZ40)
2385.K3 Kompert, Leopold, 1822-1886 (Table P-PZ40)
2385.K4 Kopisch, August, 1799-1853 (Table P-PZ40)
2385.K45 Koppel-Ellfeld, Franz, 1838-1920 (Table P-PZ40)
Koromandel, Crescentius see PT2553.W45
2385.K5 Kortum, Karl Arnold, 1745-1824 (Table P-PZ40 modified)
2385.K5A61-.K5Z458 Separate works. By title
2385.K5A7 Adams hochzeitfeier
Die Jobsiade
2385.K5J2 Editions. By date
Translations
2385.K5J3-.K5J39 English
2385.K5J4-.K5J49 French
2385.K5J5-.K5J6 Other
2385.K5J7-.K5J79 Criticism
2385.K5M3 Der märtyrer der mode
2385.K5M4 Die magische laterne
2385.K53 Kortum, Renatus Andreas, 1674-1747 (Table P-PZ40)
2385.K7 Kosegarten, Ludwig Gotthard, 1758-1818 (Table P-PZ40)
Kosmas see PT1833.C4
2385.K77 Kossak, Ernst, 1814-1880 (Table P-PZ40)
2385.K8 Kossak, Karl Ludwig Ernst, 1814-1880 (Table P-PZ40)
Kotzebue, August Friedrich Ferdinand von, 1761-1819
2386.A1 Collected works. By date
2386.A15 Collected and selected prose works, novels, etc. By date
2386.A17 Collected and selected plays. By date
2386.A19 Collected poems
2386.A2-.Z9 Separate works
2386.A2 Die abendstunde
(2386.A25) Der abschied aus Cassel, von F. Germanus (pseud.), see ML
2386.A3 Adelheid von Wulfingen

Individual authors or works
1700-ca. 1860/70
Kotzebue, August Friedrich Ferdinand von, 1761-1819
Separate works -- Continued

(2386.A35) Alfred
see ML
2386.A4 Almanach der chroniken
Almanch dramatischer spiele, 1803-1820 see PT2386.A17
(2386.A45) Die Alpenhütte
see ML
2386.A5 Der alte leibkutscher Peter des Dritten
2386.A55 Die alten liebschaften
(2386.A6) Das arabische pulver
see PT8084.A7
2386.A63 Ariadne auf Naxos
2386.A65 Der arme minnesinger
2386.A67 Der arme poet
2386.A7 Armuth und edelsinn
2386.A8 Ausbruch der verzweiflung
2386.B2 Bäbbel
2386.B25 Die barmherzigen brüder
2386.B3 Bayard
2386.B33 Die beichte
2386.B35 Die beiden Auvergnaten
Die beiden hofmeister see PT2386.B3
2386.B4 Die beiden Klingsberg
2386.B45 Die belagerung von Saragossa; oder, Pachter Feldkümmels hochzeitstag
2386.B47 Bela's flucht
2386.B5 Die bestohlenen
2386.B53 Der besuch
2386.B55 Die biene; oder, Neue kleine schriften. 5 vols.
Cf. "Die grille," continuation of "Die biene"
2386.B57 Blind geladen
(2386.B59) Der blinde gärtner
see ML
2386.B6 Blinde liebe
2386.B7 Die brandschatzung
2386.B75 Braut und bräutigam in einer person
2386.B8 Der brief aus Cadix
(2386.B83) Dei brilleninsel
see ML
2386.B87 Bruder Moritz, der sonderling
2386.B9 Der bruderzwist
2386.C2 Der capitain Belronde
Cf. PQ2381.A6+ Picard

Individual authors or works
1700-ca. 1860/70
Kotzebue, August Friedrich Ferdinand von, 1761-1819
Separate works -- Continued

2386.C3 Carolus Magnus
2386.C35 Chroniken (1816)
2386.C4 Der citherschläger und das gaugericht
2386.C5 Cleopatra
2386.C6 Clios blumenkörbchen
2386.C7 Die Corsen
Des esels schatten see PT2386.E8
Des hasses und die liebe rache see PT2386.H45
2386.D25 Der deserteur
2386.D3 Die deutsche hausfrau
2386.D4 Der deutsche mann und die vornehmen leute
2386.D5 Die deutschen kleinstädter
Cf. PQ2381.A6+ Picard, Petite ville
2386.D6 Doctor Bahrdt mit der eisernen stirn
2386.D7 Don Ranudo de Colibrados
Cf. PT8084.D6 Holberg
2386.D8 Das dorf im gebirge
2386.E15 Die edle lüge
2386.E2 Eduard in Schottland
Cf. PQ2235.D8 Duval, Alexandre
2386.E3 Die eifersüchtige frau
2386.E35 Die englischen waaren
2386.E38 Der entlarvte fromme
2386.E4 Das epigramm
2386.E45 Er und sie; vier romantische gedichte
2386.E5 Der erbschaft
(2386.E55) Der eremit auf Formentera
see ML
(2386.E57) Erinnerungen aus Paris im jahre, 1804
see DC731
(2386.E58) Erinnerungen von einer reise aus Liefland nach
see DG425
2386.E7 Erzählungen (1782)
2386.E8 Des esels schatten
2386.E9 Eulenspiegel
2386.F3 Falsche schaam
Feodora
see ML
2386.F35 Das fest der laune
2386.F4 Die feuerprobe
2386.F45 Der fluch eines Römers
2386.F5 Die flucht
2386.F6 Der flussgott Niemen und Noch Jemand

Individual authors or works
1700-ca. 1860/70
Kotzebue, August Friedrich Ferdinand von, 1761-1819
Separate works -- Continued

(2386.F65) Die französischen kleinstädter
see PQ2381
2386.F7 Die frau von hause
2386.F75 Der freimaurer
Der freimüthige (Periodical) see AP30
2386.F8 Der freimüthige
Für geist und herz (Periodical) see AP30
2386.F9 Der fürstliche wildfang
Der gallatag in Krähwinkel see PT2386.C3
2386.G2 Die gefährliche nachbarschaft
2386.G23 Die gefährliche wette
2386.G27 Der gefangene
2386.G3 Das geheilte herz
Geist aller journale (1809) see AP30
2386.G33 Geprüfte liebe
Unauthorized reprint has title: "Der schutzgeist; eine wahre erzählung." Not to be confused with "Der schutzgeist; dramatische legende," in Almanach, 1816
2386.G35 Der gerade weg der beste
2386.G4 Geschichte kaiser Ludwig des Vierten
2386.G45 Geschichte meines vaters; oder, Wie es zuging, dass ich gebohren wurde
2386.G5 Geschichten für meine söhne
2386.G52 Geschichten für meine tochter
2386.G55 Das gespenst
2386.G57 Der gimpel auf der messe
Cf. PT8084.A+ Holberg
2386.G6 Gisela
2386.G65 Die glücklichen
2386.G68 Graf Benjowsky; oder, Die verschwörung au Kamtschatka
2386.G7 Der graf von Burgund
2386.G73 Der graf von Gleichen
2386.G77 Die grille; oder, Neue kleine schriften
2 vols. Continuation of "Die biene"
2386.G8 Grosse hofversammlung in paris, 1813
2386.G85 Die grossmama
2386.G9 Gustav Wasa
2386.H2 Der häusliche zwist
2386.H25 Der hagestolz und die körbe
2386.H3 Der hahnenschlag

Individual authors or works
1700-ca. 1860/70
Kotzebue, August Friedrich Ferdinand von, 1761-1819
Separate works -- Continued
Hans Max Giesbrecht von der Humpenburg
see ML
2386.H4 Der harem
2386.H45 Des hasses und die liebe rache
2386.H5 Heinrich Reuss von Plauen
Hermann und Thusnelda
see ML
2386.H55 Herr Gottlieb Merks
Die hölzernen säbel
see ML
2386.H6 Die hübsche kleine putzmacherin
2386.H7 Hugo Grotius
2386.H8 Die Hussiten vor Naumburg
2386.H9 Hygea
2386.H95 Der hyperboräische esel
2386.I3 Ich, eine geschichte in fragmenten
2386.I4 Ildegerte, königin von Norwegen
2386.I5 Incognito
2386.I6 Die Indianer in England
2386.I65 Das intermezzo
2386.J7 Johanna von Montfaucon
2386.J8 Die jüngsten kinder meiner laune (Stories, poems, etc., 5 vols., 1793-1797)
Der käficht
see ML
2386.K2 Kaiser Claudius
2386.K3 Der kater und der rosenstock
Der Kiffhäuser berg, see ML
2386.K4 Das kind der liebe
2386.K45 Der kleine declamator
2386.K5 Kleine romane, erzählungen, anekdoten und miscellen, 1805-1809
2386.K6 Die kleine zigeunerin
2386.K7 Die kluge frau im walde
2386.K8 Das köstlichste
2386.K85 Die komödiantin aus liebe
Der kosak und der freiwillige
see ML
2386.K9 Die kreuzfahrer
2386.L2 La Peyrouse
2386.L25 Das landhaus in der heerstrasse
2386.L3 Die leiden der Ortenbergischen familie
2386.L4 Der leineweber

Individual authors or works
1700-ca. 1860/70
Kotzebue, August Friedrich Ferdinand von, 1761-1819
Separate works -- Continued

2386.L5 Leontine
2386.L6 Das liebe dörfchen
2386.L7 Lohn der wahrheit
2386.L8 Der lügenfeind
2386.L9 Das lustspiel am fenster
2386.M2 Mädchenfreundschaft
Magnetisiertes scheidewasser see PT2386.P8
2386.M3 Der mann von vierzig jahren
2386.M35 Marie
2386.M4 Die masken
2386.M5 Max Helfenstein
(2386.M55) Meine flucht nach Paris (1790)
see PT2387.Z4M8
2386.M6 Menschenhass und reue
(2386.M8) Das merkwürdigste jahr meines lebens (1801)
see PT2387.Z4
2386.N3 Der nachtmütze des propheten Elias
2386.N4 Die negersklaven
2386.N5 Die neue frauenschule
2386.N6 Das neue jahrhundert
2386.N8 Noch Jemands reise-abentheuer
2386.O3 Octavia
Opern-almanach, 1815
see ML49.K82
2386.O7 Der opfertod
2386.O8 Die organe des gehirns
2386.P2 Pachter Feldkümmel von Tippelskirchen
2386.P3 Pagenstreiche
2386.P35 Pandorens büchse
2386.P4 Der papagoy
Pervonte
see ML
Peyrouse, La see PT2386.L2
2386.P5 Pfalzgraf Heinrich
2386.P6 Philibert; oder, Die Verhältnisse
2386.P7 Das posthaus in Treuenbrietzen
Die prinzessin von Cacambo
see ML
2386.P8 Pudenda; oder, Archiv der thorheiten unserer zeit
2386.Q3 Die quäker
2386.R2 Der rehbock
2386.R3 Die respectable gesellschaft
2386.R4 Die rosen des herrn von Malesherbes

Individual authors or works
1700-ca. 1860/70
Kotzebue, August Friedrich Ferdinand von, 1761-1819
Separate works -- Continued
Die rosenmädgen (Opera)
see ML
2386.R5 Der rothmantel
2386.R6 Rudolph von Habsburg und König Ottokar von Böhmen
2386.R7 Rübezahl
2386.R8 Die rückkehr der freiwilligen
2386.R85 Der ruf
Die ruinen von Athen
see ML
2386.R9 Der Russe in Deutschland
2386.S14 Der sammtrock
Der schauspieler wider willen see PT2386.S3
2386.S15 Der schelmische freyer
2386.S16 Die schlaue wittwe
2386.S17 Das schmuckkästchen
2386.S175 Die schöne unbekannte
2386.S18 Das schreibepult
Die schule er frauen see PQ1832.E3+
2386.S2 Der schutzgeist
2386.S3 Die seelenwanderung; oder, Der schauspieler wider willen
2386.S4 Die seeschlacht und die meerkatze
Selbstbiographie (1811) see PT2387.Z4
2386.S43 Die selbstmörder
2386.S45 Die seltene krankheit
2386.S47 Der shawl
2386.S5 Die silberne hochzeit
2386.S6 Die sonnenjungfrau
2386.S63 Sorgen ohne noth und noth ohne sorgen
2386.S7 Die Spanier in Peru; oder, Rolla's tod
2386.S8 Die sparbüchse
2386.S83 Der spiegel (Comedy)
Der spiegelritter (Opera)
see ML
2386.S85 Steckbrief der Cassler bürgerschaft hinter Hieronymus Napoleon
2386.S87 Der strandrecht
2386.S9 Die stricknadeln
2386.S93 Der stumme
2386.S95 Sultan Bimbambum
2386.S97 Sultan Wampum
2386.T3 Das taschenbuch

Individual authors or works
1700-ca. 1860/70
Kotzebue, August Friedrich Ferdinand von, 1761-1819
Separate works -- Continued
(2386.T4) Der taubstumme; oder, Der abbé de L'Épée
Translation of Bouilly's L'abbé de L'Épée
see PQ2198.B65
Des teufels lustschloss
see ML
2386.T5 Das thal von Almeria
2386.T6 Die tochter Pharaonis
2386.T7 Der todte neffe
2386.T8 Der trunkenbold
After Holberg's Jeppe paa Bjerget
Cf. PT8084.J4 Holberg's Jeppe paa Bierget
2386.U1 U.a.w.g.; oder Die einladungskarte
2386.U2 Ubaldo
2386.U3 Ueble laune
2386.U4 Die uhr und die mandeltorte
Ungerns erster wohlthäter
see ML
2386.U5 Die unglücklichen
2386.U6 Unser Fritz
2386.U7 Das unsichtbare mädchen
2386.U8 Die unvermählte
2386.U9 Das urtheil des Paris
Die väterliche erwartung
see ML
2386.V2 Der vater von ungefähr
2386.V25 Der verbannte Amor
2386.V27 Die verkleidungen
2386.V3 Die verläumder
2386.V33 Verlegenheit und list
After Contre-temps sur contre-temps, by Pigault-Lebrun, PQ2382.P2
2386.V35 Das verlorne kind
2386.V37 Der verschwiegene wider willen
2386.V4 Die versöhnung
2386.V5 Die verwandtschaften
2386.V6 Der vielwisser
(2386.V9) Vom adel
Fragment of an historical philosophical work, Leipzig, 1792
2386.W3 Der weibliche Jacobiner-clubb
2386.W4 Wer weiss wozu das gut ist
2386.W5 Der wildfang
2386.W55 Der wirrwarr

Individual authors or works
1700-ca. 1860/70
Kotzebue, August Friedrich Ferdinand von, 1761-1819
Separate works -- Continued

2386.W6 Die wittwe und das reitpferd
2386.W8 Die wüste
2386.Z2 Zaide
2386.Z4 Die zerstreuten
2386.Z6 Das zugemauerte fenster
2386.Z7 Die zurückkunft des vaters
2386.Z8 Zwei nichten für eine

Translations

English

2387.A1 Collected works
2387.A13 Selections
2387.A15 Collected plays
2387.A17 Collected prose, novels, tales, etc.
2387.A19 Collected poems
2387.A3A-.A3Z Separate works

Arrange by their original titles as given in PT2386.A2+

2387.A4-.Z3 Translations in other languages, A-Z

e.g.

2387.F8 French
2387.Z4 Autobiography, journals, letters

Erinnerungen aus Paris see DC731

Erinnerungen aus von meine reise aus Liefland nach Rom und Neapel see DG425

2387.Z4M6 Das merkwürdigste jahr meines leben (1801)
2387.Z4M7 English translations. By date
2387.Z4M8 Meine flucht nach Paris im winter, 1790
2387.Z4S4 Selbstbiographie (1811)
2387.Z4S6 Skizze seines lebens und werkens
2387.Z4U4 Über meinen aufenthalt in Wien (1799)
2387.Z5 Biography and criticism
2387.Z6 Criticism
2388.K21 Kram, Joseph, 1852-1874 (Table P-PZ40)
2388.K23 Krane, Anna, freiin von, 1853- (Table P-PZ40)
2388.K27 Kratter, Franz, 1758-1830 (Table P-PZ40)
2388.K3 Kremnitz, Frau Marie Charlotte (von Bardeleben), 1852-1916 (Table P-PZ40)

Cf. PT1858.E4 Elisabeth

(2388.K35) Krez, Konrad

see PT3919.K85

2388.K5 Krug von Nidda, Friedrich, 1776-1843 (Table P-PZ40)
2388.K53 Krüger, Johann Christian, 1723-1750 (Table P-PZ40)
2388.K55 Krummacher, Friedrich Adolf, 1767-1845 (Table P-PZ40)
2388.K6 Kruse, Heinrich, 1815-1902 (Table P-PZ40)

Individual authors or works
1700-ca. 1860/70 -- Continued
2388.K63 Kruse, Laurids, 1778-1839 (Table P-PZ40)
Cf. PT8143.K6 Works in Danish
Kuckuck, Zebedäus, der Jüngere see PT2503.S17
Kueffner, Christopf see PT2388.K83
2388.K67 Kügelgen, Wilhelm Georg Alexander von, 1802-1867 (Table P-PZ40)
2388.K7 Kühne, August, 1829-1883 (Table P-PZ40)
Kürnberger, Ferdinand, 1821-1879
Der Amerika-müde (Novel)
2388.K8A3 Editions. By date
Translations
2388.K8A4-.K8A49 English
2388.K8A5-.K8A59 Other. By language (alphabetically)
2388.K8A7-.K8A79 Criticism
2388.K8A8-.K8Z4 Other works
2388.K8Z8 Letters. By date
2388.K8Z9-.K8Z99 Biography
2388.K83 Kuffner, Christoph, 1780-1846 (Table P-PZ40)
2388.K86 Kuh, Emil, 1828-1876 (Table P-PZ40)
2388.K88 Kuh, Moses Ephraim, 1731-1790 (Table P-PZ40)
2388.K885 Kuhnau, Johann, 1660-1722 (Table P-PZ40)
2388.K89 Kulke, Eduard, 1831-1897 (Table P-PZ40)
2388.K9 Kurz, Hermann, 1813-1873 (Table P-PZ40)
2388.L2 Laddey, Emma (Radtke), 1841-1892
2388.L3 Lafontaine, August Heinrich Julius, 1758-1831 (Table P-PZ40)
Laicus, Philipp see PT2551.W8
2388.L5 Laistner, Ludwig, 1845-1896 (Table P-PZ40)
2388.L6 Lambrecht, Matthias Georg, 1748-1826 (Table P-PZ40)
2389 La Motte-Fouqué, Friedrich Heinrich Karl, freiherr de, 1777-1843 (Table P-PZ39 modified)
2389.A61-.Z48 Separate works. By title
Subarrange each by Table P-PZ43 unless otherwise specified
e.g.
2389.U3-.U5 Undine
2389.U3 Editions. By date
2389.U3A-.U3Z School editions. By editor, A-Z
Translations
2389.U4 English
2389.U41-.U49 Other. By language (alphabetically)
2389.U5 Criticism
2390.L13 La Motte-Fouqué, Karoline Auguste (von Briest), freiin de, 1773-1831 (Table P-PZ40)
2390.L2 Landesmann, Heinrich 1821-1902 (Table P-PZ40)

Individual authors or works
1700-ca. 1860/70 -- Continued
2390.L22 Landsteiner, Karl Boromäus, 1835-1909 (Table P-PZ40)
2390.L25 Lang, Karl, 1766-1822 (Table P-PZ40)
2390.L3 Lang, Ludwig, 1827-1895 (Table P-PZ40)
2390.L35 Lang, Paul, 1846-1898 (Table P-PZ40)
2390.L4 Langbein, August Friedrich Ernst, 1757-1835 (Table P-PZ40)
2390.L5 Lange, Ernst Philipp Karl, 1813-1899 (Table P-PZ40)
2390.L53 Lange, Samuel Gotthold, 1711-1781 (Table P-PZ40)
2390.L55 Langer, Anton, 1824-1879 (Table P-PZ40)
Lanz, Wilhelmine see PT1833.C2
2390.L6 La Roche, Frau Sophie von, 1731-1807 (Table P-PZ40)
2390.L7 L'Arronge, Adolf, 1838-1908 (Table P-PZ40)
2390.L85 Lassalle, Ferdinand Johann Gottlieb, 1825-1864
Class here his only work, Franz von Sickingen (Tragedy)
2390.L85A-.L85Z School editions. By editor, A-Z
2390.L9 Lasswitz, Kurd, 1848-1910 (Table P-PZ40)
Laube, Heinrich, 1806-1884
2391.A1 Collected works. By date
2391.A2 Collected plays. By date
2391.A3 Collected novels and other prose works. By date
2391.A4 Miscellaneous minor works, criticism, etc. By date
Translations
2391.A5-.A59 English. By translator
2391.A6-.A69 French. By translator
2391.A7-.A79 Other languages (alphabetically)
2391.A9-.Z3 Separate works
2391.B3 Die bandomire
2391.B4 Der belgische graf
2391.B5 Die bernsteinhexe
2391.B6 Die Böhminger
2391.B7 Böse zungen
2391.B8 Die bürger (Das junge Europa, III)
2391.C3 Cato von Eisen
2391.D4 Demetrius
2391.D5 Der deutsche krieg
2391.D7 Drei königstädte im norden
2391.E6 Entweder-oder
see DC
Erinnerungen see PT2391.Z4
Französische lustschlösser
see DC148
2391.G5 Das glück
2391.G6 Gottsched und Gellert
2391.G7 Die gräfin Chateaubriant
2391.G8 Graf Essex

	Individual authors or works
	1700-ca. 1860/70
	Laube, Heinrich, 1806-1884
	Separate works -- Continued
2391.H4	Herzog Bernhardt (Der deutsche krieg, III)
2391.J3	Das jagdbrevier
2391.J7	Das junge Europa
2391.J8	Junker Hans (Der deutsche krieg, I)
2391.K3	Die Karlsschüler
2391.K6	Die kleine prinzessin
2391.K7	Die krieger (Das junge Europa, II)
2391.L4	Liebesbriefe
2391.L6	Louison
2391.M6	Monaldeschi
2391.M7	Montrose
2391.N3	Nachsicht für alle
2391.P6	Die poeten (Das junge Europa, I)
2391.P7	Der prätendent
2391.P8	Prinz Friedrich
2391.R4	Reisenovellen
2391.R6	Rokoko
2391.S3	Der schatten Wilhelm (Novelle)
2391.S4	Die schauspielerin
2391.S7	Der statthalter von Bengalen
2391.S8	Struensee
2391.W3	Waldstein (Der deutsche krieg, II)
(2391.Z3)	Other works, classed by subject
2391.Z4	Memoirs, letters
2391.Z5	Biography and criticism
	Lauff, Joseph von see PT2623.A85
2392.L15	Laukhard, Friedrich, 1757 or 8-1822 (Table P-PZ40)
	Laun, Friedrich see PT2514.S2
2392.L2	Lavater, Johann Caspar, 1741-1801 (Table P-PZ40 modified)
2392.L2A3	Aphorisms
2392.L2S2	Schweizerlieder
2392.L2S3	Criticism
2392.L2Z4	Autobiography, memoirs. By date
2392.L2Z5	Letters. By date of publication
2392.L2Z6-.L2Z9	Biography
	Leander, Richard see PT2547.V8
	Leberecht, Peter see PT2536+
2392.L5	Leisewitz, Johann Anton, 1752-1806 (Table P-PZ38)
	Leixner-Grünberg, Otto von see PT2623.E5
	Lenau, Nikolaus, 1802-1850
2393.A1	Collected works. By date
2393.A2	Collected poems. By date. "Gedichte"

	Individual authors or works
	1700-ca. 1860/70
	Lenau, Nikolaus, 1802-1850 -- Continued
	Translations
2393.A3-.A39	English
2393.A4-.A59	Other. By language (alphabetically)
2393.A6-.Z2	Separate works
2393.A7	Die Albigenser (Table P-PZ43)
2393.A8	Anna (Table P-PZ43)
2393.D6	Don Juan (Table P-PZ43)
2393.F2	Faust (Table P-PZ43)
2393.H4	Helena (Table P-PZ43)
2393.J6	Johannes Ziska (Table P-PZ43)
2393.K6	Klara Hebert (Table P-PZ43)
2393.M3	Die marionetten (Table P-PZ43)
2393.M5	Mischka (Table P-PZ43)
2393.S3	Savonarola (Table P-PZ43)
2393.Z3	Letters
	Biography and criticism
2393.Z4	Biography
2393.Z5	Criticism
	Lenz, Hugo see PT2452.R28
	Lenz, Jakob Michael Reinhold, 1751-1792
2394.L3	Collected works. By date
2394.L3A14	Minor collections. By date
2394.L3A15	Collected poems. By date
2394.L3A17	Collected plays. By date
2394.L3A7-.L3Z4	Separate works
2394.L3Z5-.L3Z9	Biography and criticism
2394.L5	Lenz, Ludwig Friedrich, 1717-1780 (Table P-PZ40)
	Lessing, Gotthold Ephraim, 1729-1781
	Collected works
2396.A1	Comprehensive editions. By date
(2396.A11)	Critical and annotated editions. By editor
2396.A12	Selections. Anthologies
	Translations see PT2403+
	Selected works
2396.A15	By date
(2396.A2)	Poetry and drama see PT2396.A1
	Dramatic works
2396.A3	Collections
2396.A4	Comedies
2396.A5	Tragedies
	Translations see PT2403+
	Fragments and projected plays
2396.A55	Collections

Individual authors or works
1700-ca. 1860/70
Lessing, Gotthold Ephraim, 1729-1781
Selected works
Dramatic works
Fragments and projected plays -- Continued
Separate works see PT2398+
Translations by Lessing
see the authors, Voltaire, Plautus, etc.
Cf. PT2396.A9 Collected translations
Prose works
2396.A6 Comprehensive editions. By date
Translations see PT2403+
2396.A7 Selections. By editor, A-Z
Selected works
2396.A72 Miscellaneous
Letters
see PT2407.A2 or special subjects
2396.A75 Contributions to periodicals, journals, etc.
Dramaturgy
see PN
(2396.A77) Philology and archaeology
see D, N, and PA
(2396.A79) Philosophy and theology
see class B
2396.A9 Translations of foreign literature (Collected)
Separate works
see the author (Voltaire, etc.)
2397 Poems
2397.A1 Comprehensive collections. By date
(2397.A2) Critical and annotated editions. By editor
see PT2397.A1
2397.A3 Lieder
First published as "Kleinigkeiten"
2397.A7 Sinngedichte
Translations see PT2403+
2397.A9 Criticism, interpretation (of poems in general)
Separate works
Altdeutscher witz und verstand see PT1105
2398.A6 Die alte jungfer
Alter der oelmalerei
see ND49.L47
Anti-Goeze and Beiträge
see BX
Axiomata (Wider Goeze)
see BX

Individual authors or works
1700-ca. 1860/70
Lessing, Gotthold Ephraim, 1729-1781
Separate works -- Continued

	Beweis des geistes und der kraft see BT
	Beyträge zur historie und aufnahme des theaters see PN1654.B4
	Briefe see PT2407.A2 or subject
	Briefe, die neueste litteratur betreffend see under title, PN504
2398.D3	Damon
	Emilia Galotti
2398.E2	Editions. By date
2398.E3A-.E3Z	School editions. By editor, A-Z
2398.E5	Criticism
2398.E6	Der eremite
2398.E8	Ernst und Falk (Gespräche für freymäuer)
	Die erziehung des menschen-geschlechts see BT127.A2
2398.F2	Fabeln
2398.F3	Faust
	Fragmente des Wolfenbüttelschen ungenannten see BL2773
2398.F7	Der freygeist
	Gedichte see PT2397
	Hamburgishce dramaturgie see PN1664
2398.J7	Die Juden
2398.J8	Der junge gelehrte
2398.J9	Justin Fragment based on Plautus' Pseudolus Cf. PA6568.P8 Pseudolus
	Kleinigkeiten see PT2397.A3
(2398.L3)	Laokoon see N64
	Lieder see PT2397.A3
	Minna von Barnhelm
2398.M2	Editions. By date
2398.M3A-.M3Z	School editions. By editor, A-Z
2398.M4	Criticism
2398.M5	Der misogyn
2398.M6	Miss Sara Sampson
	Nathan der Weise
2399.A1	Editions. By date
(2399.A2)	Critical and annotated editions see PT2398.A1

Individual authors or works
1700-ca. 1860/70
Lessing, Gotthold Ephraim, 1729-1781
Separate works
Nathan der Weise -- Continued
2399.A3 Acting editions. By editor
2399.A4 School editions. By editor
Translations see PT2403+
2399.A5 Continuations, imitations, parodies
Cf. PT2401.A2 General
2399.A6 Poetry (about the play)
Criticism
2399.A7-.Z3 General
2399.Z4 Textual
Special
2399.Z5 Sources
2399.Z6 Stage presentation
Neue hypothese über die Evangelisten
see BS
2400.N6 Noch nähere berichtigung des mährchens von 1000 dukaten
Nöthige antwort auf eine sehr unnöthige frage des ... Goeze
see BX
Eine parabel ... an Goeze
see BX
2400.P4 Philotas
Pope, ein metaphysiker
see PR3620+
2400.S4 Der schatz
(2400.S5) Sinngedichte
see PT2397.A7
Das Testament Johannis see BS2610+
Theatralische bibliothek
see PN
Ein vade mecum für ... Lange
see PA (Horatius)
2400.Z8 Zur geschichte und litteratur. Aus den schätzen der hz. bibliothek zu Wolfenbüttel (known as Wolfenbütteler frägmente)
2401.A1A-.A1Z Doubtful, spurious works, etc., A-Z
2401.A2 Imitations, adaptations, parodies
Cf. PT2399.A5 Nathan der Weise
2401.A3 Translations as subject
2401.A4 Illustrations to Lessing's works
Translations
Under each subdivide by translator (or editor), A-Z

Individual authors or works
1700-ca. 1860/70
Lessing, Gotthold Ephraim, 1729-1781
Translations -- Continued

2403 English
2403.A1 Collected works
2403.A2 Dramatic works
2403.A3 Poems
2403.A4 Prose works
2403.A43 Letters
Separate works
2403.A5 Emilia Galotti
2403.A53 Fables
2403.A55 Faust
(2403.A57) Laokoon
see N64
2403.A6 Minna von Barnhelm
2403.A7 Nathan the wise
2403.A8-Z Other
For works on special subjects, see the subject
2404.A-Z Other languages, A-Z
Subarrange each by Table PT2
e.g.
2404.F8 French (Table PT2)
2404.P7 Portuguese (Table PT2)
Biography and criticism
(2405) Bibliography
see Z8504
2405.5 Periodicals and societies
2406 General treatises. Life and works
Details of his life
2407.A1 Sources
2407.A2 Letters. Collections. By date
For treatises in letter form, see the subject
2407.A3-Z Other special
Cf. PT2418.A+ Criticism
Relation to contemporaries
2409.A1 General
2409.A3-Z Special persons, A-Z
Homes and haunts
2410.A1 General
2410.A3-Z Special, A-Z
2411.A1 Anniversaries, celebrations, etc.
Memorials. Testimonials to his genius
2411.A2 Addresses
2411.A3 Poetry
2411.A4 Iconography. Portraits. Monuments

Individual authors or works
1700-ca. 1860/70
Lessing, Gotthold Ephraim, 1729-1781
Biography and criticism -- Continued

(2411.A5) Fiction, drama, etc., based upon his life
see the author

2412 Authorship

Criticism and interpretation

2413 History of criticism

2413.A2 General and in Germany

2413.A3-Z Other countries, A-Z

2413.9 Study and teaching (Theory and method)

Treatises

2414 General works
Cf. PT2406 General criticism

2415 Philosophy, esthetics, etc.

2416 Dramatic works (Criticism and interpretation)

2417 Lessing and the stage
For Lessing's special plays see PT2398+

2418.A-Z Other special topics, A-Z

2418.A7 Lessing and art

2418.C6 Lessing and classical antiquity

2418.C7 Lessing as a critic

Lessing as a dramatist see PT2416

2418.E97 Lessing and Europe

2418.F67 Lessing and France

2418.F7 Lessing as a Freemason

2418.J4 Lessing and Jews and Judaism

2418.J6 Lessing and journalism
Cf. PT2418.V6 Lessing and the Vossische Zeitung

(2418.M8) Lessing and music
see ML

2418.P3 Lessing as a patriot

Lessing as philosopher see PT2415

2418.P64 Lessing's political and social views

2418.R4 Lessing and religion

Lessing as a theologian see PT2418.R4

2418.V6 Lessing and the Vossische zeitung

2418.W6 Lessing and women

2420 Textual criticism, commentaries, etc.

2421 Language and style
Including grammar (general and special), versification, prose, dictionaries and concordances)

2423.L13 Lessing, Karl Gotthelf, 1740-1812 (Table P-PZ40)

2423.L17 Leuthold, Heinrich, 1827-1879 (Table P-PZ40)

2423.L2 Lewald, August, 1792-1871 (Table P-PZ38)

Individual authors or works
1700-ca. 1860/70 -- Continued
Lewald-Stahr, Fanny, 1811-1889

2423.L3A15	Collected novels
2423.L3A61-.L3Z458	Separate works
2423.L3A7	Adele
2423.L3A8	Auf rother erde
2423.L3B2	Benedikt
2423.L3B6	Benvenuto
2423.L3B8	Bunte bilder
2423.L3C6	Clementine
2423.L3D4	Die dilettanten (Erzählungen, III)
2423.L3D5	Diogena
2423.L3D8	Dünen- und berggeschichten
	England und Schottland see DA
	Erinnerungen aus dem jahr 1848 see PT2423.L3Z41+
2423.L3E8	Die erlöserin
2423.L3E9	Erzählungen
2423.L3F3	Die familie Darner
	Für und wider die frauen see HQ
2423.L3G7	Graf Joachim
2423.L3H4	Helmar
2423.L3I6	Im abendroth
	Italienisches bilderbuch see DG
2423.L3J3	Jasch (Erzählungen, IV)
2423.L3J4	Jenny
2423.L3J6	Josias
2423.L3K3	Die kammerjungfer
2423.L3L4	Eine lebensfrage
2423.L3L5	Liebesbriefe; aus dem leben eines gefangenen
2423.L3M3	Das mädchen von Hela
2423.L3M4	Das mädchen von Oyas (Erzählungen, II)
	Meine lebensgeschichte see PT2423.L3Z45
2423.L3N4	Neue novellen
	Osterbriefe für die frauen see HQ
2423.L3P7	Prinz Louis Ferdinand (Novel)
2423.L3R4	Die reisegefährten
2423.L3S4	Der seehof
	Sommer und winter am Genfersee (Diary) see PT2423.L3Z41+
2423.L3S7	Stella
2423.L3T7	Treue liebe
2423.L3U6	Die unzertrennlichen

Individual authors or works
1700-ca. 1860/70
Lewald-Stahr, Fanny, 1811-1889
Separate works -- Continued

2423.L3V3 Vater and sohn
2423.L3V4 Villa Riunione
Vom Sund zum Posilipp (Letters, 1879-1881) see PT2423.L3Z5
2423.L3V6 Von geschlecht zu geschlecht
2423.L3V7 Vornehme welt (Erzählungen, I)
2423.L3W3 Wandlungen
2423.L3Z3 Zu Weihnachten
Zwölf bilder aus dem leben see PT2423.L3Z41+
2423.L3Z41-.L3Z49 Autobiography, journals, memoirs. By title, e.g.
2423.L3Z44 Gefühltes und gedachtes
2423.L3Z45 Meine lebensgeschichte
2423.L3Z47 Römisches tagebuch
2423.L3Z5 Letters (Collections). By date
Biography and criticism
2423.L4 Lichtenberg, Georg Christoph, 1742-1799 (Table P-PZ40)
2423.L5 Lichtwer, Magnus Gottfried, 1719-1783 (Table P-PZ40)
2423.L54 Lieberkühn, Christian Gottlieb, d. 1761 (Table P-PZ40)
Liliencron, Detlev, freiherr von see PT2623.I5
2423.L7 Lindau, Paul, 1839-1919 (Table P-PZ40)
2424.L2 Lindau, Rudolf, 1829-1910 (Table P-PZ40)
2424.L3 Lindau, Wilhelm Adolf, 1774-1849 (Table P-PZ40)
2424.L35 Lindemayr, Maurus, 1723-1783 (Table P-PZ40)
Linden, Gustav see PT2522.S75
2424.L38 Linderer, Robert, 1824-1886 (Table P-PZ40)
2424.L4 Lindner, Albert, 1831-1888 (Table P-PZ40)
2424.L42 Lindner, F.L. (Friedrich Ludwig) (Table P-PZ40)
Lingen, Ernst see PT2503.S16
2424.L5 Lingg, Hermann ritter von, 1820-1905 (Table P-PZ40)
2424.L52 Linhart, Anton Tomaz, 1756-1795 (Table P-PZ40)
2424.L53 Linz-Godin, Frau Amélie (Speyer), 1824-1904 (Table P-PZ40)
Lips, Fr. Wilh. see PT2443.O3
2424.L55 Liscow, Christian Ludwig, 1701-1760 (Table P-PZ38)
2424.L58 Loden, Adolf, fl. 1840-1841 (Table P-PZ40)
2424.L59 Loeb, Julius, 1822- (Table P-PZ40)
2424.L6 Loeben, Otto, graf von, 1786-1825 (Table P-PZ40)
2424.L62 Loehn-Siegel, Frau Maria Anna, 1830-1902 (Table P-PZ40)
2424.L63 Loën, Johann Michael, freiherr von, 1694-1776 (Table P-PZ40)
2424.L64 Löwen, Johann Friederich, 1727-1771 (Table P-PZ38)

Individual authors or works
1700-ca. 1860/70 -- Continued
2424.L66 Lohmann, Emilie Friederike Sophie, 1783-1830 (Table P-PZ40)
2424.L7 Lohmeyer, Julius, 1835-1903 (Table P-PZ40)
2424.L73 Lorenz, Wilhelmine, 1784-1861 (Table P-PZ40)
Lorm, Hieronymus see PT2390.L2
2424.L77 Lotz, Georg, 1784-1844 (Table P-PZ40)
2424.L8 Lubliner, Hugo, 1846-1911 (Table P-PZ40)
2424.L9 Lubojatzky, Franz, 1807-1887 (Table P-PZ40)
2424.L93 Ludecus, Johanna Caroline Amalia (Kotzebue), 1757-1827 (Table P-PZ40)
2424.L94 Ludwig I, king of Bavaria, 1786-1868 (Table P-PZ40)
2424.L95 Ludwig Salvator, archduke of Austria, 1847-1915 (Table P-PZ40)
Ludwig, Otto, 1813-1865
2426.A1 Collected works. By date
2426.A15 Collected novels. By date
2426.A17 Collected poems. By date
2426.A19 Collected plays. By date
2426.A7-.Z4 Separate works
2426.E2 Der engel von Augsburg (Table P-PZ43)
Der erbförster
2426.E3 Editions. By date
2426.E3A-.E3Z School editions. By editor, A-Z
2426.E4 Criticism
2426.F7 Das fräulein von Scuderi (Table P-PZ43)
Die Heiterethei und ihr widerspiel
2426.H3 Editions. By date
2426.H3A-.H3Z School editions. By editor, A-Z
2426.H4 Criticism
Die Makkabäer
2426.M3 Editions. By date
2426.M4 Criticism
2426.R4 Die rechte des herzens (Table P-PZ43)
2426.T5 Tiberius Gracchus (Table P-PZ43)
2426.T6 Die Torgauer haide (Table P-PZ43)
Zwischen himmel und erde
2426.Z2 Editions. By date
2426.Z2A-.Z2Z School editions. By editor, A-Z
2426.Z3 Criticism
2426.Z5 Biography and criticism
(2427.L3) Lützow, Frau Therese (von Struve) von, 1804-1852 see PT1815.B225
2427.L4 Lyser, Johann Peter Theodore, 1803-1870 (Table P-PZ40)
2428.M15 Mädler, Frau Minna (Witte) von, 1804-1891 (Table P-PZ40)
2428.M2 Mahlmann, August, 1771-1826 (Table P-PZ40)

Individual authors or works
1700-ca. 1860/70 -- Continued

2428.M22 Maltitz, Apollonius, freiherr von, 1795-1870 (Table P-PZ40)
Mandien see PT2440.N5
2428.M23 Manso, Johann Kaspar Friedrich, 1760-1826 (Table P-PZ38)
2428.M3 Marbach, Gotthard Oswald, 1810-1890 (Table P-PZ40)
2428.M33 Marbach, Hans, 1841-1905 (Table P-PZ40)
2428.M4 Marggraff, Hermann, 1809-1864 (Table P-PZ40)
Marlitt, E. see PT2370.J3
2428.M44 Martini, Karl Wilhelm von, 1821-1885 (Table P-PZ38)
2428.M45 Martius, Karl Friedrich Philipp von, 1794-1868 (Table P-PZ40)
2428.M47 Marx, Karl, 1818-1883 (Table P-PZ40)
2428.M5 Marx, Theodor, 19th century (Table P-PZ40)
2428.M6 Matthisson, Friedrich von, 1761-1831 (Table P-PZ40)
2428.M62 Mauvillon, Jakob, 1743-1794 (Table P-PZ40)
2428.M75 Mayer, Karl Friedrich Hartmann, 1786-1870 (Table P-PZ40)
2428.M8 Mayer, Otto, 1846-1924 (Table P-PZ40)
2428.M81 Mayr, Beda, 1742-1794 (Table P-PZ40)
2428.M82 Mayr, Johann Nepomuk Alexius, 1778-1821 (Table P-PZ40)
2430.M2 Meding, Oskar, 1829-1903 (Table P-PZ40)
2430.M3 Meerheimb, Richard Albert von, 1825-1896 (Table P-PZ40)
Meinau, Eulalia see PT2513.S3
2430.M33 Meinert, Joseph Georg, 1775-1844 (Table P-PZ40)
Meinhardt, Adalbert see PT2617.I68
2430.M35 Meinhold, Wilhelm, 1797-1851 (Table P-PZ40 modified)
2430.M35A61-.M35Z458 Separate works. By title
2430.M35M3 Maria Schweidler, die bernsteinhexe
2430.M4 Meissner, Alfred, 1822-1885 (Table P-PZ40)
His later works said to have been written by Franz Hedrich
2430.M45 Meissner, August Gottlieb, 1753-1807 (Table P-PZ40)
2430.M5 Meister, Friedrich, 1841- (Table P-PZ40)
Melena Elpis see PT2515.S4
2430.M53 Meltzer, Adolph Heinrich, 1761-1807 (Table P-PZ40)
Menantes, 1681-1721 see PT2363.H8
2430.M55 Mendelssohn, Moses, 1729-1786 (Table P-PZ40)
Menk-Dittmarsch, F. see PT1846.D15
2430.M6 Menzel, Wolfgang, 1798-1873 (Table P-PZ40)
2430.M7 Merck, Johann Heinrich, 1741-1791 (Table P-PZ38)
Mereau, Frau Sophie (Schubart) see PT1827.B3
2430.M85 Merkel, Garlieb, 1769-1850 (Table P-PZ40)
Meyer, Conrad Ferdinand, 1825-1898
2432.A1 Collected works. By date

Individual authors or works
1700-ca. 1860/70
Meyer, Conrad Ferdinand, 1825-1898 -- Continued
2432.A15 Collected tales (Novellen). By date
2432.A17 Collected poems. By date
2432.A3-.Z29 Separate works
Subarrange school editions by editor
2432.A8 Angela Borgia (Table P-PZ43)
2432.G7 Gustav Adolfs page (Table P-PZ43)
2432.H4 Der heilige (Table P-PZ43)
2432.H7 Der hochzeit des mönchs (Table P-PZ43)
2432.H8 Huttens letzte tage (Table P-PZ43)
2432.J7 Jürg Jenatsch (Table P-PZ43)
2432.Z8 Letters, memoirs, etc. By date
2432.Z8A-.Z8Z Biography. Life and works
2432.Z9 Criticism
2433.M13 Meyer, Friedrich Ludwig Wilhelm, 1759-1840 (Table P-PZ40)
2433.M15 Meyer, Johann Friedrich Ernst, 1791-1851 (Table P-PZ40)
2433.M17 Meyer, Nicolaus, 1775-1855 (Table P-PZ40)
2433.M23 Meyern, Wilhelm Friedrich von, 1762-1829 (Table P-PZ40)
2433.M25 Meyern-Hohenberg, Gustav von, 1826-1878 (Table P-PZ40)
2433.M3 Meyr, Melchior, 1810-1871 (Table P-PZ40)
2433.M4 Meysenbug, Malwida von, 1816-1903 (Table P-PZ40)
2433.M45 Michaelis, Johann Benjamin, 1746-1772 (Table P-PZ38)
2433.M5 Miller, Johann Martin, 1750-1814
Miltenberg see PT2388.L3
2433.M6 Minckwitz, Johannes, 1812-1885 (Table P-PZ40)
2433.M7 Misson, Joseph, 1803-1875 (Table P-PZ40)
2433.M8 Möllhausen, Balduin, 1825-1905 (Table P-PZ40)
2434 Mörike, Eduard Friedrich, 1804-1875 (Table P-PZ39 modified)
2434.A61-.Z48 Separate works. By title
Subarrange each work by Table P-PZ43 unless otherwise specified
Mozart auf der reise nach Prag
2434.M7 Editions. By date
2434.M7A-.M7Z School editions. By editor, A-Z
2435.M2 Möser, Justus, 1720-1794 (Table P-PZ40)
2435.M22 Mohr, Eduard Christian, 1808-1892 (Table P-PZ40)
2435.M221 Mohr, Ludwig, 1833-1900 (Table P-PZ40)
2435.M23 Molitor, Wilhelm, 1819-1880 (Table P-PZ40)
2435.M24 Moltke, Helmuth Karl Bernhard, graf von, 1800-1891 (Table P-PZ40)
"Die beiden freunde," only literary work
2435.M25 Moltke, Max Leopold, 1819-1894 (Table P-PZ40)

Individual authors or works
1700-ca. 1860/70 -- Continued
Montanus, 1806-1876 see PT2592.Z32

2435.M26 Morel, Benedict, in religion Gallus, 1803-1872 (Table P-PZ40)

2435.M3 Moritz, Karl Philipp, 1757-1793 (Table P-PZ40)

Mormann, Bert see PT1818.B26

2435.M4 Mosen, Julius, 1803-1867 (Table P-PZ40)

2435.M5 Mosenthal, Salomon Hermann, ritter von, 1821-1877 (Table P-PZ40)

2435.M6 Moser, Gustav von, 1825-1903 (Table P-PZ40 modified)

Some of his plays written in collaboration with O. Girndt and F. von Schönthan

2435.M6A61-.M6Z458 Separate works. By title

2435.M6B5-.M6S76 School editions

Subarrange by successive cutter numbers

2435.M6B5-.M6B59 Der bibliothekar

2435.M6B53 Ed. by Cooper

2435.M6B54 Ed. by Farr

2435.M6B56 Ed. by Lieder

2435.M6B58 Ed. by Wells

2435.M6S7-.M6S79 Der schimmel

2435.M6S76 Ed. by Stern

2435.M65 Müchler, Karl Friedrich, 1763-1857 (Table P-PZ40)

2435.M7 Mügge, Theodor, 1806-1861 (Table P-PZ40)

Mühlbach, Luise see PT2438.M4

Mühlfeld, Julius see PT2457.R85

Mühlfeld, Louis see PT1818.B26

2436.M2 Müller, Adam Heinrich, ritter von Nitterdorf, 1779-1829 (Table P-PZ40)

2436.M22 Müller, Arthur, 1826-1873 (Table P-PZ40)

2436.M26 Müller, Franz (Table P-PZ40)

2436.M3 Müller, Friedrich, 1749-1825 ("Maler Müller") (Table P-PZ40 modified)

2436.M3A61-.M3Z458 Separate works. By title

2436.M3F6 Faust

2436.M3F8-.M3F89 Criticism

Müller, Friedrich Konrad see PT2436.M8

Müller, Friedrich Max, 1823-1900

Deutsche liebe

His only novel

2436.M45 Editions. By date

2436.M45E5-.M45E9 English translations. By translator

2436.M45Z5-.M45Z59 Other. By language (alphabetically)

2436.M47 Müller, Heinrich (August), 1766-1833 (Table P-PZ40)

Individual authors or works
1700-ca. 1860/70 -- Continued

2436.M48 Müller, Hugo, 1831-1881 (Table P-PZ40)
2436.M49 Müller, Johann Ernst, 1764-1826 (Table P-PZ40)
2436.M5 Müller, Johann Gottwerth, 1743-1828 (Table P-PZ40)
2436.M55 Müller, Johann Heinrich Friedrich, 1738-1815 (Table P-PZ40)
2436.M6 Müller, Karl, 1819-1889 (Table P-PZ40)
2436.M65 Müller, Otto, 1816-1894 (Table P-PZ40)
Müller, Rosalie see PT2458.R84
2436.M7 Müller, Wilhelm, 1794-1827 (Table P-PZ40)
2436.M8 Müller von der Werra, Friedrich Konrad, 1823-1881 (Table P-PZ40)
2436.M9 Müller von Königswinter, Wolfgang, 1816-1873 (Table P-PZ40)
2437 Müllner, Adolph, 1774-1829 (Table P-PZ39)
2438.M3 Münch-Bellinghausen, Eligius Franz Joseph, freiherr von, 1806-1871 (Table P-PZ40)
Münich, Walther von see PT1801.A15
2438.M4 Mundt, Frau Klara (Müller), 1814-1873 (Table P-PZ40)
2438.M42 Mundt, Theodor, 1808-1861 (Table P-PZ38)
2438.M5 Murad, Efendi, 1836-1881 (Table P-PZ40)
2438.M6 Murr, Christoph Gottlieb von, 1733-1811 (Table P-PZ40)
2438.M7 Musäus, Johann Karl August, 1735-1787 (Table P-PZ38)
Mylius, Otfrid see PT2436.M6
2438.M9 Mylius, Wilhelm Christhelf Sigmund, 1754-1827 (Table P-PZ40)
Mystifizinsky, Deutobold Symbolizetti see PT2547.V2+
2440.N16 Nagel, Anton, 1742-1812 (Table P-PZ40)
2440.N2 Nathusius, Frau Maria Karoline Elisabeth Luise (Scheele) von, 1817-1857 (Table P-PZ40)
2440.N22 Naubert, Frau Christiane Benedicte Eugenie (Hebenstreit), 1756-1819 (Table P-PZ40)
2440.N25 Nehracher, Hans Heinrich, 1764-1797 (Table P-PZ40)
Nemmersdorf, Franz see PT2453.R54
2440.N27 Nesmüller, Ferdinand, 1818-1895 (Table P-PZ40)
2440.N28 Nesselrode zu Hugenboett, F.G., freiherr von, fl. 1773 (Table P-PZ40)
2440.N3 Nestroy, Johann Nepomuk, 1801-1862 (Table P-PZ40)
Netz, Paul see PT1819.B25
2440.N33 Neuber, Friederika Karoline (Weissenborn), 1697-1760 (Table P-PZ40)
2440.N34 Neuffer, Ludwig, 1769-1839 (Table P-PZ40)
2440.N35 Neumann, Hermann Kunibert, 1808-1875 (Table P-PZ40)
2440.N36 Neumann, Johanna (Hiepe), 1787-1863 (Table P-PZ40)
2440.N37 Neumann-Strela, Karl, 1838-1921 (Table P-PZ40)
2440.N374 Neumayr, Franz, 1697-1765 (Table P-PZ40)

Individual authors or works

1700-ca. 1860/70 -- Continued

2440.N375 Neumeister, Erdmann, 1671-1756 (Table P-PZ40)

2440.N38 Neumeister, Rudolph, 1822-1909 (Table P-PZ40)

2440.N4 Nicolai, Christoph Friedrich, 1733-1811 (Table P-PZ40)

2440.N42 Nicolay, Ludwig Heinrich von, 1737-1820 (Table P-PZ38)

2440.N45 Niebergall, Ernst Elias, 1815-1843 (Table P-PZ40)

2440.N5 Niedmann, Karl Christian Friedrich, 1802-1830 (Table P-PZ40)

Niemand see PT2440.N5

2440.N6 Niemann, August, 1839-1919 (Table P-PZ40)

2440.N63 Niemann, Johanna, 1844- (Table P-PZ40)

Niembsch edler von Strehlenau, Nikolaus see PT2393.A+

2440.N65 Niemeyer, August Hermann, 1754-1828 (Table P-PZ40)

2440.N67 Nieritz, Karl Gustav, 1795-1876 (Table P-PZ40)

Niese, Charlotte, 1854- see PT2627.I55

2440.N71 Nietschmann, Hermann Otto, 1840-1929 (Table P-PZ40)

2440.N72 Nietzsche, Friedrich Wilhelm, 1844-1900 (Table P-PZ40)

2440.N73 Nissel, Franz, 1831-1893 (Table P-PZ40)

2440.N74 Nissel, Karl, 1817-1900 (Table P-PZ40)

2440.N75 Noë, Heinrich August, 1835-1896 (Table P-PZ40)

2440.N77 Nötel, Louis, 1837-1889 (Table P-PZ40)

Nord, Karl see PT2507.S9

2440.N8 Nordau, Max Simon, 1849-1923 (Table P-PZ40)

2440.N82 Nordmann, Johannes, 1820-1887 (Table P-PZ40)

Nordryck, C. (or Karl Heinrich) see PT1819.B15

Nordstern, Arthur von see PT2440.N86

2440.N86 Nostitz und Jänckendorf, Gottlob Adolf Ernst von, 1765-1836 (Table P-PZ40)

Novalis see PT2291

2440.N9 Nürnberger, Woldemar, 1818-1869 (Table P-PZ40)

Oehlenschläger, Adam Gottlob see PT8145+

2443.O3 Oertel, Wilhelm, 1798-1867 (Table P-PZ40)

Juvenile works see PZ31+

2443.O33 Oertzen, Georg, freiherr von, 1829-1910 (Table P-PZ40)

Oeser, Christian see PT2510.S4

2443.O37 Oeser, Hermann, 1849-1911 (Table P-PZ40)

2443.O4 Oettinger, Eduard Maria, 1808-1872 (Table P-PZ40)

2443.O5 Ohorn, Anton, 1836-1924 (Table P-PZ40)

2443.O55 Oldenburgskiĭ, Petr Georgīevich, prin͡ts, 1812-1881 (Table P-PZ40)

Olinda, Alexander see PT2505.S3

Oscar see PT2377.K2

2443.O8 Otto, Reinhard, 19th cent. (Table P-PZ40)

2443.O9 Overbeck, Christian Adolf, 1755-1821 (Table P-PZ40)

2445.P14 Paalzow, Frau Henriette (Wach) von, 1788-1847 (Table P-PZ40)

Individual authors or works
1700-ca. 1860/70 -- Continued

2445.P16 Pachler, Faust, 1819-1892 (Table P-PZ40)
2445.P18 Pailler, Wilhelm, b. 1838 (Table P-PZ40)
2445.P19 Pall von Pallhausen, Vincenz, 1759-1817 (Table P-PZ40)
2445.P2 Palleske, Emil, 1823-1880 (Table P-PZ40)
Panizza, Oskar see PT2631.A5
2445.P3 Pantenius, Theodor Hermann, 1843-1915 (Table P-PZ40)
Paoli, Betty see PT1889.G2
2445.P315 Pape, Samuel Christian, 1774-1817 (Table P-PZ40)
2445.P32 Pasqué, Ernst Heinrich Anton, 1821-1892 (Table P-PZ40)
2445.P33 Passarge, Ludwig, 1825-1912 (Table P-PZ40)
2445.P35 Passy, Anton, 1788-1847 (Table P-PZ40)
2445.P36 Passy, Joseph, 1786-1820 (Table P-PZ40)
2445.P38 Paul, C.A., 19th cent. (Table P-PZ40)
Paul, Jean see PT2454+
2445.P4 Paulus, Eduard, 1837-1907 (Table P-PZ40)
Pellegrin see PT2389
2445.P43 Pelzeln, Frau Franziska von, 1826-1904 (Table P-PZ40)
2445.P435 Penn, Heinrich Moritz, 1839- (Table P-PZ40)
2445.P437 Perinet, Joachim, 1765-1816 (Table P-PZ40)
2445.P44 Peschkau, Emil, 1856- (Table P-PZ40)
Pestalozzi, Johann Heinrich see LB621+
2445.P445 Petersdorff, Ulrike von, 1843-1902 (Table P-PZ40)
2445.P45 Petersen, Marie, 1816-1859 (Table P-PZ40)
2445.P46 Pezzl, Johann, 1756-1823? (Table P-PZ40)
2445.P47 Pfannenschmidt, Frau Julie (Burow), 1806-1868 (Table P-PZ40)
2445.P48 Pfau, Ludwig, 1821-1894 (Table P-PZ40)
2445.P5 Pfeffel, Gottlieb Konrad, 1736-1809 (Table P-PZ40)
2445.P53 Pfeil, Heinrich 1835-1899 (Table P-PZ40)
2445.P54 Pfeil, Johann Gottlob Benjamin, 1732-1800 (Table P-PZ40)
2445.P55 Pfeil-Burghausz, Richard Friedrich Adelbert, graf von, 1846- (Table P-PZ40)
2445.P57 Pfizer, Gustav, 1807-1890 (Table P-PZ40)
2445.P6 Pflug, Ferdinand, 1823-1888 (Table P-PZ40)
2445.P64 Pfranger, Johann Georg, 1745-1790 (Table P-PZ40)
2445.P67 Philippson, Ludwig, 1811-1889 (Table P-PZ40)
2445.P7 Pichler, Adolf von, 1819-1900 (Table P-PZ40)
2445.P8 Pichler, Frau Karoline (von Greiner), 1769-1843 (Table P-PZ40)
Pierre, Jean see PT2508.S45
2445.P9 Pierson, Frau Karoline Wilhelmine (Leonhardt), 1811-1899 (Table P-PZ40)
2445.P95 Pietsch, Johann Valentin, 1690-1733 (Table P-PZ40)
Platen-Hallermünde, August, graf von, 1796-1835
2447.A1 Collected works. By date

Individual authors or works
1700-ca. 1860/70
Platen-Hallermünde, August, graf von, 1796-1835 -- Continued

2447.A5-Z Separate works
2447.G5 Gaselen
2447.P7 Polenlieder
2447.S5 Sonette
2447.T5 Ter Thurm mit sieben Pforten
Biography and criticism
2448.A2 Memoirs. Journals. By date
2448.A3 Letters. By date of imprint
2448.A5-Z Biography. Life and works
2448.Z5 Criticism
2449.P2 Ploennies, Frau Luise (Leisler) von, 1803-1872 (Table P-PZ40)
2449.P25 Ploetz, Johann, edler von, 1786-1856 (Table P-PZ40)
2449.P3 Plümicke, Carl Martin, 1749-1833 (Table P-PZ40)
2449.P33 Pocci, Franz, graf von, 1807-1876 (Table P-PZ40)
2449.P34 Pöhnl, Hans, 1849-1913 (Table P-PZ40)
2449.P35 Pötzl, Eduard, 1851-1914 (Table P-PZ40)
2449.P38 Pohl, Emil, 1824-1901 (Table P-PZ40)
2449.P4 Polko, Frau Elise (Vogel), 1823-1899 (Table P-PZ40)
2449.P46 Possart, Ernst, ritter von, 1841- (Table P-PZ40)
Postl, Karl see PT2516.S4
2449.P48 Prätzel, Karl Gottlieb, 1785-1861 (Table P-PZ40)
2449.P5 Prantner, Ferdinand, 1817-1871 (Table P-PZ40)
2449.P52 Prechtler, Otto, 1813-1881 (Table P-PZ40)
Preussen, Georg, prinz von see PT1885.G33
2449.P53 Priem, Johann Paul, 1815-1890 (Table P-PZ40)
2449.P54 Proelss, Johannes Moritz, 1853- (Table P-PZ40)
2449.P55 Prokesch von Osten, Anton, graf, 1795-1876 (Table P-PZ40)
2449.P57 Proschko, Franz Isidor, 1816-1891 (Table P-PZ40)
2449.P572 Proschko, Hermine Camilla, 1854- (Table P-PZ40)
2449.P6 Prutz, Robert Eduard, 1816-1872 (Table P-PZ40)
2449.P7 Pückler-Muskau, Hermann Ludwig Heinrich, fürst von, 1785-1871 (Table P-PZ40)
2449.P75 Pustkuchen-Glanzow, Johann Friedrich Wilhelm, 1793-1834 (Table P-PZ40)
2449.P8 Putlitz, Gustav Heinrich Gans, edler herr zu, 1821-1890 (Table P-PZ40)
2449.P85 Puttkamer, Frau Alberta (Weise) von, 1849-1923 (Table P-PZ40)
2449.P88 Pyl, Theodor, 1826-1904 (Table P-PZ40)
2449.P9 Pyra, Immanuel Jakob, 1715-1744 (Table P-PZ40)
2449.P95 Pyrker, Johann Ladislav, 1772-1847 (Table P-PZ40)

Individual authors or works
1700-ca. 1860/70 -- Continued
2451 Raabe, Wilhelm Karl, 1831-1910 (Table P-PZ39 modified)
2451.A6-Z Separate works. By title
Subarrange each work by Table P-PZ43
Subarrange school editions by editor, A-Z
2452.R2 Rabener, Gottlieb Wilhelm, 1714-1771 (Table P-PZ40)
2452.R22 Racovita, Elena (von Dönniges), 1845-1911 (Table P-PZ40)
Raimar, Freimund see PT2459.A+
2452.R25 Raimund, Ferdinand, 1790-1836 (Table P-PZ40)
2452.R28 Rambach, Friedrich Eberhard, 1767-1826 (Table P-PZ40 modified)
2452.R28A61-.R28Z458 Separate works. By title
2452.R28E5 Die eiserne maske, ein schottische geschichte
Last chapter by Johann Ludwig Tieck
2452.R28T5 Thaten un feinheiten renommirter kraft- und-kniffgenies
2452.R3 Ramler, Karl Wilhelm, 1725-1798 (Table P-PZ38)
2452.R35 Rank, Joseph, 1816-1896 (Table P-PZ40)
2452.R38 Rappaport, Moriz, 1808-1880 (Table P-PZ40)
2452.R4 Raspe, Rudolf Erich, 1737-1794 (Table P-PZ38)
For Adventures of Munchausen see PN6193
2452.R43 Rassmann, Christian Friedrich, 1772-1831 (Table P-PZ40)
2452.R46 Ratschky, Joseph Franz, 1757-1810 (Table P-PZ40)
2452.R48 Rau, Heribert, 1813-1876 (Table P-PZ40)
2452.R5 Raupach, Ernst Benjamin Salomon, 1784-1852 (Table P-PZ40)
2452.R53 Rautenstrauch, Johann, 1746-1801 (Table P-PZ40)
2452.R57 Recke, Elisa, baronin von der, 1754-1833 (Table P-PZ38)
2452.R6 Redwitz, Oskar, freiherr von, 1823-1891 (Table P-PZ38)
2452.R7 Rehfues, Philipp Joseph von, 1779-1843 (Table P-PZ40)
2452.R8 Reichard, Heinrich August Ottokar, 1751-1828 (Table P-PZ40)
2452.R85 Reichenbach, Moritz, 1804-1870 (Table P-PZ40)
Reichenbach, Moritz von see PT1818.B7
2452.R9 Reichssiegel, Florian, 1735-1793 (Table P-PZ40)
Reimarus, Hermann Samuel
see B2699.B4; BL180; BL2773
Rein, Ludwig see PT2583.W8
2453.R14 Reinbeck, Georg, 1766-1849 (Table P-PZ40)
2453.R16 Reinbold, Adelheid, 1802-1839 (Table P-PZ40)
2453.R168 Reinhardt, Karl, 1818-1877 (Table P-PZ40)
2453.R17 Reinhardt, Luise, 1807-1878 (Table P-PZ40)
2453.R18 Reinhold, Karl Werner, 1806-1863 (Table P-PZ40)
2453.R2 Reinick, Robert, 1805-1852 (Table P-PZ40)

Individual authors or works
1700-ca. 1860/70 -- Continued
2453.R22 Reinicke, Heinrich, 1756-1788 (Table P-PZ40)
2453.R25 Reinow, M., fl. 1870-1881 (Table P-PZ40)
2453.R3 Reinsberg-Düringsfeld, Isa, freifrau von, 1815-1876 (Table P-PZ40)
2453.R35 Reithard, Johann Jakob, 1805-1857 (Table P-PZ40)
2453.R5 Reitler, Marzellin Adalbert, 1838- (Table P-PZ40)
2453.R52 Reitzenbeck, Heinrich, 1812-1893 (Table P-PZ40)
2453.R54 Reitzenstein, Franziska (von Nyss) freifrau von, 1834-1896 (Table P-PZ40)
2453.R55 Reitzenstein, Karl, freiherr von, fl. 1792 (Table P-PZ40)
Reizenstein
see Reitzenstein
2453.R6 Rellstab, Ludwig, 1799-1860 (Table P-PZ40)
2453.R63 Remagen, H. von (Table P-PZ40)
René, H. see PT2554.W9
Retcliffe, Sir John see PT1889.G6
2453.R7 Reumont, Alfred von, 1808-1887 (Table P-PZ40)
Reuter, Fritz see PT4848.R4+
2453.R75 Reymond, Moritz von, 1833-1921 (Table P-PZ40)
2453.R9 Richter, Eduard J., 1846-1893 (Table P-PZ40)
Richter, Johann Paul Friedrich, 1763-1825
2454.A1 Collected works. By date
2454.A2A-.A2Z Selected works. By editor, A-Z
2454.A3 Selections. Anthologies. Quotations. Thoughts
2454.A7-Z Separate works
2454.A8 Auswahl aus des teufels papieren
2454.B2 Biographische belustigungen
2454.B5 Blumen-, frucht- und dornenstücke; oder, Ehestand ... F. St. Siebenkäs
Des luftschiffers Giannozzo seebuch see PT2454.L8
2454.D6 Dr. Katzenbergers badereise
2454.E94 Exzerpte
2454.F4 Des feldpredigers Schmelzle reise nach Flätz
2454.F5 Flegeljahre
2454.G5 Grönländische prozesse; oder, Satirische skizzen
2454.H2 Das heimliche klaglied der jetzigen männer
2454.H4 Herbst-blumine
2454.H6 Hesperus
2454.J5 Der jubelsenior
2454.K2 Das Kampaner thal; oder, Über die unsterblichkeit der seele
2454.K6 Der komet; oder, Nikolaus Marggraf
2454.L4 Leben des Quintus Fixlein
2454.L5 Leben des vergnügten schulmeisterleins Maria Wuz in Auenthal

Individual authors or works
1700-ca. 1860/70
Richter, Johann Paul Friedrich, 1763-1825
Separate works -- Continued
2454.L6 Leben Fibels
Levana; oder, Erziehungslehre see LB675.R4+
2454.L8 Des luftschiffers Giannozzo seebuch
Maria Wuz see PT2454.L5
2454.P2 Palingenesien
Quintus Fixlein see PT2454.L4
2454.S3 Selina; oder, Ueber die unsterblichkeit der seele
Siebenkäs see PT2454.B5
2454.T3 Titan
2454.T6 Der tod eines engels
2454.U3 Die unsichtbare loge
Vorschule der aesthetik see PN45
2454.W3 Die wunderbare gesellschaft in der neujahrsnacht
2454.Z2 Zerstreute blätter
2454.Z7 Books reviewed by Richter
Special works
see the author
Translations. By language
English
2455.A1 Collected works. By date
2455.A13A-.A13Z Selected works. By editor, A-Z
2455.A15A-.A15Z Selections, quotations, thoughts, etc. By editor, A-Z
2455.A3A-.A3Z Separate works, A-Z
2455.A5-Z Other languages, A-Z
Under each language:
.xA1 Collected works. By date
.xA13 Selected works. By date
.xA15 Selections. By date
.xA3-.xZ Separate works. By title and date
2455.F7A15 Selections in French
Biography and criticism
2456.A1 Periodicals. Societies. Collections
2456.A2 Autobiography. By date
2456.A3 Letters. By date
2456.A4-.Z3 General treatises. Life and works
2456.Z4 Criticism
2456.Z5 Language
2456.Z6 Dictionaries
2457.R15 Richter, Joseph, 1749-1813 (Table P-PZ40)
2457.R18 Richter, Julius Wilhelm Otto, 1839-1921 (Table P-PZ40)
2457.R2 Richthofen, Julie (de Champs), freifrau von, 1785-1840 (Table P-PZ40)
2457.R3 Riehl, Wilhelm Heinrich, 1823-1897 (Table P-PZ40)

Individual authors or works
1700-ca. 1860/70 -- Continued

2457.R33 Riekhoff, Friedrich von, 1809-1881 (Table P-PZ40)
2457.R35 Riemer, Friedrich Wilhelm, 1774-1845 (Table P-PZ40)
2457.R37 Ries, H., fl. 1838 (Table P-PZ40)
2457.R39 Riesch, Franz, graf von, 1794-1833 (Table P-PZ40)
2457.R392 Riese, Wilhelm Friedrich, fl. 1846-1859 (Table P-PZ40)
2457.R4 Ring, Max, 1817-1901 (Table P-PZ40)
2457.R43 Ringseis, Emilie, 1831-1895 (Table P-PZ40)
Riotte, Hermann see PT3919.R62
Ritter, Ernst see PT1819.B33
2457.R5 Rittershaus, Emil, 1834-1897 (Table P-PZ40)
2457.R52 Rittler, Franz, 1782-1837 (Table P-PZ40)
Robert, Ludwig see PT2443.O33
2457.R55 Robert, Ludwig, 1778-1832 (Table P-PZ40)
2457.R56 Roberts, Alexander, baron von 1845-1896 (Table P-PZ40)
2457.R57 Robiano, Louisa Mary (von Köppen) gräfin von, 1821-1886 (Table P-PZ40)
2457.R58 Robinson, Therese Albertine Louise von Jacob, 1797-1870 (Table P-PZ38)
2457.R6 Rochlitz, Friedrich, 1769-1842 (Table P-PZ40)
Cf. ML, Music
Rodenbach, Zoe von see PT2461.S3
2457.R7 Rodenberg, Julius, 1831-1914 (Table P-PZ40)
2457.R73 Roeber, Friedrich, 1819-1901 (Table P-PZ40)
Römer, Dr. see PT1843.D3
2457.R77 Römer, Christian, fl. 1874 (Table P-PZ40)
2457.R78 Römer, Georg Christian, b. 1766 (Table P-PZ40)
2457.R8 Roeper, Gottlieb Friedrich Joachim Peter, 1812-1886 (Table P-PZ40)
2457.R85 Rösler, Robert, 1840-1881 (Table P-PZ40)
Rösler-Mühlbach, Julius see PT2457.R85
2457.R9 Rössler, Robert, 1838-1883 (Table P-PZ40)
2457.R93 Rogge, Friedrich Wilhelm, 1808-1889 (Table P-PZ40)
2457.R95 Rohr, Leopold von, fl. 1816 (Table P-PZ40)
2458.R2 Rollett, Hermann, 1819-1904 (Table P-PZ40)
2458.R3 Roquette, Otto, 1834-1896 (Table P-PZ40)
2458.R35 Rose, Johann Wilhelm, 1742-1801 (Table P-PZ40)
2458.R4 Rosegger, Peter, 1843-1918 (Table P-PZ40)
2458.R5 Rosen, Julius, 1833-1892 (Table P-PZ40)
2458.R53 Rosen, Karl von, 1827-1898 (Table P-PZ40)
Rosenegg, Hermann von Gilm zu see PT1887.G2
2458.R56 Rosenthal, Hermann, 1837-1896 (Table P-PZ40)
2458.R57 Rosenthal-Bonin, Hugo, 1840-1897 (Table P-PZ40)
2458.R7 Roskowska, Maria von, 1828-1889 (Table P-PZ40)

Individual authors or works
1700-ca. 1860/70 -- Continued

2458.R72 Rosner, Ferdinand, pater, 1709-1778 (Table P-PZ40)
For his text of the Oberammergau passion play see PN3241
2458.R73 Rosner, Leopold, 1838-1903 (Table P-PZ40)
2458.R75 Rost, Alexander, 1816-1875 (Table P-PZ40)
2458.R77 Rost, Johann Christoph, 1717-1765 (Table P-PZ40)
Rostowski, K. see PT2559.W2
Rotenkirchen, Bodo von see PT1889.G65
2458.R78 Roth, Daniel, 1801-1859 (Table P-PZ40)
2458.R783 Roth, Karl, 1802-1880 (Table P-PZ40)
2458.R79 Roth, Richard, 1835-1915? (Table P-PZ40)
2458.R8 Rothenburg, Frau Adelheid Katharina Mathilde (von Zastrow) von, 1837-1891 (Table P-PZ40)
2458.R84 Rothpletz, Frau Anna (von Meiss), 1786-1841 (Table P-PZ40)
2458.R93 Rudolphi, Karoline Christiane Louise, d. 1811 (Table P-PZ40)
Rückert, Friedrich, 1788-1866
2459.A1 Collected works. By date
2459.A13 Selected works. By date
2459.A15 Collected poems. By date
2459.A19 Supplementary works. By editor, A-Z
e.g. Rückert's Nachlese
2459.A3-.Z29 Separate works
e.g.
2459.F7 Des fremden kindes heiliger Christ
2459.H8 Die huldigung der künste
2459.L5 Liebesfrühling
2459.W3 Weisheit des brahmanen
Translations
English
2459.Z3 General
2459.Z33-.Z39 Special works. By original title (alphabetically)
e.g.
2459.Z39B7 Weisheit des brahmanen, Tr. by Brooks
2459.Z4-.Z49 French
2459.Z5-.Z59 Other. By language (alphabetically)
(2459.Z7) Rückert's translations of foreign authors or works, A-Z
2459.Z8-.Z9 Biography and criticism
2460.R83 Rüetschi, Henriette Marie Bitzius, 1834-1890 (Table P-PZ40)
2461.R2 Rüffer, Eduard, 1835-1878 (Table P-PZ40)
2461.R4 Rühl, Gustav, 1822-1875 (Table P-PZ40)
2461.R5 Ruess, Wilhelm, 1814-1879 (Table P-PZ40)

Individual authors or works
1700-ca. 1860/70 -- Continued

2461.R55 Rüthling, Johann Friedrich Ferdinand, 1793-1849 (Table P-PZ40)

2461.R7 Ruge, Arnold, 1802-1880 (Table P-PZ40)

Rullman, Wilhelm see PT2635.U685

2461.R75 Rumohr, Karl Friedrich Ludwig Felix von, 1785-1843 (Table P-PZ40)

2461.R76 Ruppius, Otto, 1819-1864 (Table P-PZ40)

2461.R8 Rustige Heinrich Franz Gaudens, 1810-1900 (Table P-PZ40)

2461.S2 Saar, Ferdinand von, 1833-1906 (Table P-PZ40)

2461.S28 Sacher-Masoch, Frau Aurora (Rümelin) von, 1845- (Table P-PZ40)

2461.S3 Sacher-Masoch, Leopold, ritter von, 1835-1895 (Table P-PZ40)

Sachsen, Amalie, prinzessin von see PT1802.A4

2461.S33 Salingré, Hermann, 1833-1879 (Table P-PZ40)

2461.S35 Salis-Seewis, Johann Gaudenz, freiherr von, 1762-1834 (Table P-PZ40)

2461.S4 Sallet, Friedrich von, 1812-1843 (Table P-PZ40)

2461.S43 Sallmayer, Hermann, 1823-1886 (Table P-PZ40)

Salomon, Ludwig see PT2637.A5

Salzbrunn, Alice see PT2526.S43

2461.S49 Salzmann, Christian Gotthilf, 1744-1811 (Table P-PZ40)

Samarow, Gregor see PT2430.M2

San-Marte see PT2513.S65

2461.S53 Sander, Johann Daniel, 1759-1826 (Table P-PZ40)

2461.S6 Saphir Moritz Gottlieb, 1795-1858 (Table P-PZ40)

Sarasin, Paul see PT2637.A7

Satori, J. see PT2440.N36

2461.S62 Sauer, Karl Marquard, 1827-1896 (Table P-PZ40)

2461.S65 Sauerwein, Johann Wilhelm, 1803-1847 (Table P-PZ40)

Cf. PF5441+ Works in Frankfurt dialect

2461.S68 Schacht, Johann August Heinrich, 1817-1863 (Table P-PZ40)

2461.S7 Schack, Adolf Friedrich, graf von, 1815-1894 (Table P-PZ40)

2461.S72 Schad, Johann Baptist, 1758-1834 (Table P-PZ40)

2461.S75 Schaden, Johann Nepomuk Adolf, 1791-1840 (Table P-PZ40)

2461.S77 Schaefer, Jakob, 1838-1905 (Table P-PZ40)

"Bunte schildereien" only work

2461.S8 Schalk, Gustav, 1848-1922? (Table P-PZ40)

2461.S81 Schall, Karl, 1780-1833 (Table P-PZ40)

2461.S82 Schambeck, Johann (Table P-PZ40)

Author of Toussaint (Drama)

Individual authors or works
1700-ca. 1860/70 -- Continued
2461.S83 Schandorph, Sophus Christian Frederik, 1836-1901 (Table P-PZ40)
Schanz, Frida see PT2639.O9
2461.S84 Schanz, Julius (or "Uli"), 1828-1902 (Table P-PZ40)
2461.S842 Schanz, Frau Pauline (Leich), b. 1828 (Table P-PZ40)
Schartenmeyer, Philipp Ulrich see PT2547.V2+
2461.S847 Schasler, Franz (Table P-PZ40)
2461.S85 Schaufert, Hippolyt August, 1835-1872 (Table P-PZ40)
2461.S86 Schaumberger, Heinrich, 1843-1874 (Table P-PZ40)
Scheer, Hans see PT2463.S6
2461.S9 Schefer, Leopold, 1784-1862 (Table P-PZ40)
Scheffel, Joseph Viktor von, 1826-1886
2462.A1 Collected works. By date
2462.A17 Collected poems. By date
Including "Gedichte aus dem nachlass"
2462.A3-.Z29 Separate works
2462.A3 Aus heimat und fremde
2462.B2 Bergpsalmen
2462.B7 Der brautwillkomm auf der Wartburg
2462.E3 Ekkehard
School editions. By editor, A-Z
2462.E6 Episteln
2462.F2 Frau Aventiure
2462.F6 Fünf dichtungen
2462.G3 Gaudeamus
2462.H4 Der Heini von Steier
2462.H6 Hugideo
2462.J3 Juniperus
Reisebilder see D919
2462.S5 Die Schweden in Rippoldsau
Der Trompeter von Säkkingen
2462.T3 Editions. By date
2462.T3A-.T3Z School editions. By editor, A-Z
2462.T5 Parodies, travesties, etc.
2462.T7 Criticism
2462.W2 Waldeinsamkeit
Translations
2462.Z3-.Z39 English. By original title and translator
2462.Z4-.Z49 French
2462.Z5-.Z59 Other. By language (alphabetically)
Biography and criticism
2462.Z8A1-.Z8A2 Periodicals. Yearbooks. Societies
2462.Z8A3 Letters. Collections, by date
2462.Z8A5-.Z8Z8 General works. Life and letters
2462.Z9A-.Z9Z Criticism

Individual authors or works
1700-ca. 1860/70 -- Continued
2463.S2 Scheibe, Theodor, 1820-1881 (Table P-PZ40)
Scheliha, Doris (gräfin von Matuschka) see PT2638.E5
2463.S3 Schelling, Karoline (Michaelis), 1763-1809 (Table P-PZ38)
2463.S35 Schenk, Eduard von, 1788-1841 (Table P-PZ40)
2463.S4 Schenkendorf, Max von, 1783-1817 (Table P-PZ38)
2463.S5 Scherenberg, Christian Friedrich, 1798-1881 (Table P-PZ38)
2463.S53 Scherer, Georg, 1828-1909 (Table P-PZ40)
2463.S57 Scherl, Friedrich, d. 1881 (Table P-PZ40)
Schernberk, Theodoricus, der Journeys see PT2510.S4
2463.S6 Scherr, Johannes, 1817-1886 (Table P-PZ40)
Schier, Benjamin see PT2638.I38
2463.S7 Schiessler, Sebastian Willibald, 1791-1867 (Table P-PZ40)
2463.S8 Schiff, Hermann, 1801-1867 (Table P-PZ40)
2463.S9 Schikaneder, Emanuel, 1751-1812 (Table P-PZ40)
2463.S97 Schildbach, Johann Gottlieb, fl. 1801 (Table P-PZ40)
Schiller, Johann Christoph Friedrich von, 1759-1805
2465 Collected works. By date (date-letters) of first volume
2465.A00-.A99 1800-1899
2465.B00-.B99 1900-1999
2465.C00-.C99 2000-2099
(2465.Z5) Critical and annotated editions. By editor
Translations see PT2473+
2465.Z6 Selected works. By date or editor
2465.Z7 Supplementary works. Fragments. Posthumous works. By date
2465.Z8A-.Z8Z Selections. Quotations. Birthday books, etc. By editor, A-Z
Poetical works
Comprehensive collections
2466.A1 Editions. By date
2466.A2 Critical and annotated editions. By editor
Translations see PT2473+
Selections. Anthologies
General
2466.A3 Anonymous. By date
2466.A4 Editions. By editor
2466.A5 School editions. By editor
2466.A6-.A79 Special forms (alphabetically)
2466.A62 Ballads
2466.A65 Epigrams
Special poetical works
Das lied von der glocke
2466.A8 Editions. By date

Individual authors or works
1700-ca. 1860/70
Schiller, Johann Christoph Friedrich von, 1759-1805
Poetical works
Special poetical works
Das lied von der glocke -- Continued

(2466.A81) Editions, by editor
see PT2466.A8

2466.A82A-.A82Z School editions. By editor, A-Z

2466.A83 Selections

2466.A84 Criticism

2466.A9-Z Other works (including special poems)

Anthologie auf das jahr 1782
A compilation edited by Schiller, containing contributions by him
see PT1169

2466.B8 Die Bürgschaft

2466.D4 Deutsche grösse

2466.G3 Der gang nach dem eisenhammer

2466.G7 Graf von Habsburg

2466.H3 Der handschuh

2466.I4 Die ideale

2466.K2 Der kampf mid dem drachen

2466.K8 Die Künstler

2466.L5 Lied an die freude

Musenalmanach see PT1169

2466.O8 Orpheus

2466.R5 Ritter Toggenburg

2466.S6 Der spaziergang

2466.T3 Der taucher

(2466.X2) Xenien
see Goethe, PT1898.X2

2467.A1A-.A1Z Spurious poems. By editor, A-Z
Cf. PT2472.A1 Doubtful works
Cf. PT2472.A2 General

2467.A2A-.A2Z Imitations, parodies, etc. By editor, A-Z

(2467.A3) Musical compositions written for Schiller's works
see class M

2467.A4 Illustrations
Cf. PT2472.A7 General

2467.A5-.Z3 Criticism, interpretation, etc.

2467.Z5 Special topics. By author, A-Z

Dramatic works

2468.A1 Comprehensive collections. By date

(2468.A2) Editions. By editor, A-Z
see PT2468.A1

Individual authors or works
1700-ca. 1860/70
Schiller, Johann Christoph Friedrich von, 1759-1805
Dramatic works -- Continued

(2468.A3) Selected plays
see PT2465.Z6

(2468.A4) Fragments, posthumous works
see PT2465.Z7

(2468.A5) Selections, quotations, etc.
see PT2465.Z8

Translations see PT2473+

2468.A7-Z Separate works

Die braut von Messina

2468.B3 Editions. By date

2468.B4A-.B4Z School editions. By editor, A-Z

2468.B6 Criticism

Demetrius (fragment)

2468.D2 Editions. By date

2468.D4 Criticism

Don Carlos

2468.D6 Editions. By date

2468.D7A-.D7Z School editions. By editor, A-Z

2468.D8 Briefe über Don Carlos, by Schiller

2468.D9 Criticism

Fiesko see PT2468.V4

2468.H8 Die huldigung der künste

2468.I3 Ich habe mich rasieren lassen

Iphigenie in Aulis see PA3976.A+

Die jungfrau von Orleans

2468.J6 Editions. By date

2468.J7A-.J7Z School editions. By editor, A-Z

2468.J9 Criticism

Kabale und liebe

2468.K2 Editions. By date

2468.K3A-.K3Z School editions. By editor, A-Z

2468.K5 Criticism

Macbeth see PR2782.A+

Maria Stuart

2468.M4 Editions. By date

2468.M5A-.M5Z School editions. By editor, A-Z

2468.M7 Criticism

Der menschenfeind see PT2468.V6

Der neffe als onkel

Translation of "Encore de Ménechmes," by Picard
Cf. PQ2381.A6+ Picard

2468.N3 Editions. By date

2468.N4A-.N4Z School editions. By editor, A-Z

Individual authors or works
1700-ca. 1860/70
Schiller, Johann Christoph Friedrich von, 1759-1805
Dramatic works
Separate works
Der neffe als onkel -- Continued
2468.N6 Criticism
Der parasit
Translation of "Médiocre et rampant," by Picard
Cf. PQ2381.A6+ Picard
2468.P2 Editions. By date
2468.P3A-.P3Z School editions. By editor, A-Z
2468.P5 Criticism
Phädra see PQ1898
Die Phönizierinnen see PA3976.A+
Die räuber
2468.R2 Editions. By date
2468.R4 Acting editions. By date
Cf. PT2468.R2 Older editions
2468.R5 Criticism
Semele
2468.S3 Editions. By date
2468.S4A-.S4Z School editions. By editor, A-Z
2468.S6 Criticism
Tell (Wilhelm Tell)
2468.T2 Editions. By date
2468.T3A-.T3Z School editions. By editor, A-Z
2468.T5 Criticism
2468.T6-.T9 Turandot prinzessin von China, ein tragikomisches märchen nach Gozzi
Cf. PQ4703 Gozzi, Carlo
2468.V4 Die verschwörung des Fiesko zu Genua
2468.V6 Die versöhnte menschenfeind (Fragment)
Wallenstein
2468.W1 Comprehensive editions. By date
2468.W2 Acting editions. By date
2468.W3A-.W3Z School editions. By editor, A-Z
Special parts
Arrange editions by date. Arrange school editions by editor, A-Z
2468.W4 Wallensteins lager
2468.W5 Die Piccolomini
2468.W6 Wallensteins tod
2468.W8 Criticism
Wilhelm Tell see PT2468.T2+
Prose works
2469.A1 Collections and selections

Individual authors or works
1700-ca. 1860/70
Schiller, Johann Christoph Friedrich von, 1759-1805
Prose works -- Continued
Translations see PT2473+
Fiction
Collections see PT2469.A1
Separate works
Arrange editions by date. Arrange school editions by editor, A-Z

2469.G2 Der geisterseher
2469.G21 Continuations
2469.G6 Eine grosmüthige handlung aus der neuesten geschichte
2469.S7 Der spaziergang unter den linden
2469.V2 Der verbrecher aus verlorener ehre

Historical works
see B, D, or F

Philosophical works
see B, BH, BJ, M, N, or PN

Correspondence
2471.A1 Collections and selections. By date
Cf. PT2471.A3A+ Goethe and Schiller
2471.A15Z-.A15Z School editions. By editor, A-Z
2471.A17 Letter to Schiller (Collected)
2471.A19 Correspondence with Charlotte (von Lengefeld) Schiller. By date

Correspondence with Goethe
2471.A2 Editions. By date
2471.A3A-.A3Z School editions. By editor, A-Z
2471.A5A-.A5Z Correspondence with others, A-Z
Translations see PT2473+

2471.7 Works reviewed by Schiller
2471.7.A2 Collections and selections. By date
(2471.7.A5-Z) Individual works
see the author

2472.A1 Doubtful, spurious works, etc.
Cf. PT2467.A1A+ Poems
2472.A2 Imitations, adaptations, parodies
Cf. PT2467.A2A+ Poems

Translations (as subject; comparative studies, etc.)
2472.A3 General
Special works (alphabetically)
2472.A4 Poems (General and special)
2472.A6 Wallenstein

Individual authors or works
1700-ca. 1860/70
Schiller, Johann Christoph Friedrich von, 1759-1805 -- Continued

2472.A7 Illustrations
Class here portfolios, etc., without text, or illustrations with quotations. For illustrated works, see the work
Cf. PT2467.A4 Poetical works
History of Schiller portraits and illustrations see PT2487

(2472.A9) Music
For text to which music has been composed and librettos based upon Schiller's works, see ML
For music composed to Schiller's works, see M
Schiller's knowledge of music see PT2496.M8

Translations
English
2473.A1A-.A1Z Collected works. By editor or translator, A-Z
2473.A13A-.A13Z Selections, anthologies. By editor, A-Z
Poems (including selections)
2473.A2 Anonymous. By date
2473.A2A-.A2Z By translator, A-Z
Special poems
Das lied von der glocke (Song of the bell)
2473.A3 Anonymous translations. By date
2473.A3A-.A3Z By translator, A-Z
2473.A33A-.A33Z Other poems. By title, A-Z and translator
Dramatic works
2473.A4 Collections. By translator or editor, A-Z
Separate works see PT2473.A8+
Prose and prose fiction
2473.A5A-P%2473.A5Z Collections. By translator or editor, A-Z
Separate works see PT2473.A8+
Correspondence
2473.A6 General collections
2473.A7 Correspondence with Goethe
2473.A71-.A79 Correspondence with other persons (alphabetically)
2473.A8-Z Separate works. By original titles and translator
2473.D5 Don Carlos
2473.G4 Der geisterseher
2473.J7 Die jungfrau von Orleans
2473.K3 Kabale und liebe
2473.M3 Maria Stuart
2473.N3 Der neffe als onkel
2473.R3 Die räuber
2473.T3 Tell (Wilhelm Tell)
2473.V2 Der verbrecher der verlorner ehre

	Individual authors or works
	1700-ca. 1860/70
	Schiller, Johann Christoph Friedrich von, 1759-1805
	Translations
	English
	Separate works. By original titles and translator -- Continued
2473.V4	Die verschwörung des Fiesko
2473.W3	Wallenstein
2473.W4	Wallensteins lager
2473.W5	Die Piccolomini
2473.W6	Wallensteins tod
(2473.X2)	Xenien see PT2026.X2
	Other languages
2474.D6	Dutch. Flemish (Table PT8)
2474.F4	French (Table PT8)
2474.F8	Frisian (Table PT8)
2474.I4	Italian (Table PT8)
2474.P2	Portuguese (Table PT8)
	Scandinavian
2474.S2	Danish, Norwegian (Table PT8)
2474.S4	Icelandic (Table PT8)
2474.S6	Swedish (Table PT8)
2474.S8	Spanish (Table PT8)
2475	Other European (except Slavic)
2475.C2	Catalan (Table PT8)
	Celtic
2475.C3	Breton (Table PT8)
2475.C4	Cornish (Table PT8)
2475.C5	Gaelic (Table PT8)
2475.C6	Irish (Table PT8)
2475.C7	Manx (Table PT8)
2475.C8	Welsh (Table PT8)
2475.F5	Finnish (Table PT8)
2475.G7	Greek (Table PT8)
2475.G8	Greek, Modern (Table PT8)
2475.H8	Hungarian (Table PT8)
2475.L3	Latin (Table PT8)
2475.P7	Provençal (Table PT8)
2475.R6	Romansh (Table PT8)
2475.R8	Rumanian (Table PT8)
2475.Y53	Yiddish (Table PT8)
2476	Slavic
2476.B4	Bohemian (Table PT8)
2476.B8	Bulgarian (Table PT8)
2476.C4	Croatian (Table PT8)

Individual authors or works
1700-ca. 1860/70
Schiller, Johann Christoph Friedrich von, 1759-1805
Translations
Other languages
Slavic -- Continued
2476.L4 Lettish (Table PT8)
2476.L6 Lithuanian (Table PT8)
2476.P6 Polish (Table PT8)
2476.R7 Russian (Table PT8)
2476.R8 Ruthenian (Table PT8)
2476.S3 Serbian (Table PT8)
2476.S6 Slovakian (Table PT8)
2476.S8 Slovenian (Table PT8)
2476.W4 Wendic (Table PT8)
2477 Asiatic
2477.H4 Hebrew (Table PT8)
For Yiddish see PT2475.Y53
2481.A-Z Other, A-Z
For artificial languages see PM8001+
(2481.Y5) Yiddish
see PT2475.Y53
Biography and criticism
2482.A1 Periodicals. Societies. Collections
(2482.A2) Bibliography
see Z8793
2482.A4 Dictionaries, indexes, etc.
Class here general works only
For dictionaries of contemporaries see PT2484.A2+
For concordances and language dictionaries see PT2499.Z9
2482.A5-.Z7 General treatises. Life and works
2482.Z9 Anecdotes
Biographical details
Sources
2483.A2 Journals, calendar, etc.
Letters see PT2471.A1+
2483.A3 Family. Ancestry. Name. Descendants. Heraldry, etc.
2483.A4 Early life. Education. Karlsschule
Love. Marriage
2483.A5 General
Charlotte (von Lengefeld) von Schiller
2483.A6 Letters. By date of publication
Cf. PT2471.A19
2483.A7 Biography
2483.A8 Later life
2483.A9 Death and burial. Schiller's skull

Individual authors or works
1700-ca. 1860/70
Schiller, Johann Christoph Friedrich von, 1759-1805
Biography and criticism -- Continued
Relations to contemporaries
2484.A2 General
2484.A6-Z Special persons
Goethe see PT2095+
Correspondence with Goethe see PT2471.A2+
Translations see PT2473.A7
2484.H6 Hölderlin, Friedrich
2484.K2 Kalb, Charlotte von
2484.K6 Körner, Theodor
2484.S4 The Schlegels
2485 Homes and haunts
2486 Anniversaries. Celebrations. Festschriften
Arrange by date letters
2486.A55 1855
2486.A59 1859
2486.B05 1905
2486.B55 1955
2486.B59 1959
Memorials. Testimonials to his genius (other than centennial)
For Schiller and Goethe see PT2098
2486.Z3 Poetry
2486.Z5 Prose. Addresses, essays, lectures, etc.
(2486.Z7) Fiction based upon Schiller's life
see the author
(2486.Z9) Drama based upon Schiller's life
see the author
2487 Iconography. Museums. Exhibitions
For Schiller and Goethe see PT2143+
2487.A1 Portraits, medals, etc.
2487.A2 Monuments
Museums, endowments, relics, exhibitions
2487.A3 General
2487.A5A-.A5Z Special. By place, A-Z
Schiller in France, Great Britain, etc. see PT2491.A+
2488 Study and teaching
Cf. PT2490+
2489 Authorship
2489.A1 Manuscripts. Autographs
Facsimiles. By date of publication
Treatises. By author, A-Z
For special works, see the work
2489.A2 Sources

Individual authors or works
1700-ca. 1860/70
Schiller, Johann Christoph Friedrich von, 1759-1805
Biography and criticism
Authorship -- Continued
2489.A3 Forerunners
2489.A5-Z Associates. Followers. Circle. School
Cf. PT321 Goethe and Schiller
2489.Z5 Allusions
2489.Z7 Chronology of works
Criticism and interpretation
History of the study and appreciation of Schiller
Collections of criticism
2490.A3 Contemporary
2490.A4 Later
2490.A5-Z General and in Germany
Cf. PT2472.A3+ Translations (as subject)
2491.A-Z Other countries, A-Z
e.g.
2491.F7 France
2491.G7 Great Britain
2491.R8 Russia
2491.U6 United States
2492 General works. Treatises, etc.
2493 Characters
Including special groups, women, etc.
For individual characters see PT2466+
2494 Technique. Dramatic art
2495 Schiller and the stage
2495.A2 General works
Representation on the stage
2495.A3 General
2495.A5-Z Special. By place, A-Z
2495.B4 Berlin
2496.A-Z Relation to special subjects, A-Z
Including treatment and knowledge of the subject, influence, etc.
2496.A56 Anthropology
2496.A6 Art. Painting, etc.
2496.C45 China
2496.C66 Cookery
2496.E8 Esthetics
2496.E9 Ethics
2496.E94 Europe
2496.H5 History
2496.I5 Individualism
2496.J6 Journalism

Individual authors or works
1700-ca. 1860/70
Schiller, Johann Christoph Friedrich von, 1759-1805
Biography and criticism
Criticism and interpretation
Relation to special subjects, A-Z -- Continued

2496.L3 Law
2496.L4 Liberty
2496.L5 Literature
2496.L68 Love
2496.M8 Music
2496.N24 Nationalism
2496.N3 Nature
2496.P4 Philosophy
2496.P6 Political thought
2496.P7 Psychology
2496.P82 Publishers and publishing
2496.R4 Religion
2496.S3 Science
2496.S6 Social sciences
2496.S64 Spain
2498 Textual criticism, commentaries, etc.
For interpretation of a special work, see the work
Language. Style
2499.A1-.Z3 General works
2499.Z5 Grammar
2499.Z7 Dialect
2499.Z8 Versification
2499.Z9 Dictionaries. Concordances
2503.S12 Schiller, Josef, 1846-1897 (Table P-PZ40)
2503.S15 Schilling, August, ritter von Henrichau, 1815-1886 (Table P-PZ40)
2503.S16 Schilling, Elisabeth, 1832-1907 (Table P-PZ40)
2503.S17 Schilling, Gustav, 1766-1839 (Table P-PZ40)
2503.S2 Schink, Johann Friedrich, 1755-1835 (Table P-PZ38)
2503.S25 Schirmer, Adolf, 1821-1886 (Table P-PZ40)
2503.S28 Schlägel, Max von, 1840-1891 (Table P-PZ40)
2503.S3 Schlegel, August Wilhelm von, 1767-1845 (Table P-PZ38)
Schlegel, Caroline (Michaelis) see PT2463.S3
2503.S55 Schlegel, Dorothea von, 1764-1839 (Table P-PZ38)
Schlegel, Friedrich von, 1772-1829
2503.S6A16 Collected essays. By date
2503.S6A6 Selected works. By date
2503.S6L7 Lucinde, ein roman
Letters
2503.S6Z2 General collections. By date
2503.S6Z21-.S6Z29 By correspondent (alphabetically)

Individual authors or works
1700-ca. 1860/70
Schlegel, Friedrich von, 1772-1829
Letters -- Continued

2503.S6Z3 Translations into English of collected and selected works. By date

2503.S7 Biography and criticism
Cf. B3086.S5+ Philosophy

2503.S75 Schlegel, Johann Adolf, 1721-1793 (Table P-PZ40)

2503.S8 Schlegel, Johann Elias, 1719-1749 (Table P-PZ40)

Schlegel, Karoline (Michaelis) see PT2463.S3

2503.S85 Schleich, Martin E., 1827-1881 (Table P-PZ40)

2503.S87 Schleiermacher, Friedrich, 1768-1834 (Table P-PZ40)
Class here literary works only
For other works see BX4827.S3

2504.S2 Schleifer, Matthias Leopold, 1771-1842 (Table P-PZ40)

2504.S25 Schlenkert, Friedrich Christian, 1757-1826 (Table P-PZ40)

2504.S3 Schlesinger, Sigmund, 1832-1918 (Table P-PZ40)

2504.S4 Schleyer, Johann Martin, 1831-1911 (Table P-PZ40)

2504.S5 Schlichtkrull, Aline von, 1832-1863 (Table P-PZ40)

2504.S6 Schlieben, Erwin, 1831-1884 (Table P-PZ40)

2504.S7 Schlögl, Friedrich, 1821-1892 (Table P-PZ40)

2504.S8 Schloenbach, Arnold, 1807-1866 (Table P-PZ40)

2504.S88 Schmid, Christoph von, 1768-1854 (Table P-PZ40)
Juvenile literature see PZ31+

2504.S9 Schmid, Ferdinand von, 1823-1888 (Table P-PZ40)

2505.S2 Schmid, Hermann Theodor von, 1815-1880 (Table P-PZ40)

2505.S3 Schmidt, Alexander, 1838-1909 (Table P-PZ40)

2505.S4 Schmidt, Auguste, 1833-1902 (Table P-PZ40)

2505.S6 Schmidt, Elise, b. 1824 (Table P-PZ40)

2505.S7 Schmidt, Ferdinand, 1816-1890 (Table P-PZ40)

2505.S8 Schmidt, Friedrich Ludwig, 1772-1841 (Table P-PZ40)

2505.S85 Schmidt, Friedrich Wilhelm August, 1764-1838 (Table P-PZ40)

2505.S88 Schmidt, Klamer Eberhard Karl, 1746-1824 (Table P-PZ40)

2505.S9 Schmidt, Maximilian, 1832-1919 (Table P-PZ40)

2506.S2 Schmidt-Cabanis, Richard, 1838-1903 (Table P-PZ40)

2506.S3 Schmidt-Weissenfels, Eduard, 1833-1893 (Table P-PZ40)

2506.S4 Schmieden, Frau Else (Kobert), 1841-1896 (Table P-PZ40)

2506.S5 Schmieder, Heinrich Gottlieb, 1763-1828 (Table P-PZ40)

2506.S6 Schmitt, Karl, 1828-1855 (Table P-PZ40)

Schmitthenner, Adolf see PT2638.M76

2506.S8 Schmolck, Benjamin, 1672-1737 (Table P-PZ40)

2506.S85 Schnabel, Johann Gottfried 1692-ca. 1750 (Table P-PZ38 modified)

Individual authors or works
1700-ca. 1860/70
Schnabel, Johann Gottfried 1692-ca. 1750 -- Continued

2506.S85A61-.S85A78 Separate works. By title
2506.S85A7 Die insel Felsenburg
2506.S9 Schneckenburger, Max, 1819-1849 (Table P-PZ38)
2507.S2 Schneeberger, Franz Julius, 1827-1892 (Table P-PZ40)
2507.S3 Schneegans, Ludwig, 1842-1922 (Table P-PZ40)
2507.S4 Schneider, Christian Jakob von, 1772-1829 (Table P-PZ40)
(2507.S45) Schneider, Heinrich Emil
see PT3919.S44
2507.S5 Schneider, Louis, 1805-1878 (Table P-PZ40)
2507.S54 Schneider-Clauss, Wilhelm, 1862-1949 (Table P-PZ40)
2507.S6 Schneller, Christian, 1831-1908 (Table P-PZ40)
2507.S7 Schnitter, Wilhelm, 1802-1887 (Table P-PZ40)
2507.S8 Schönaich, Christoph Otto, freiherr von, 1725-1807 (Table P-PZ40 modified)
2507.S8A61-.S8Z458 Separate works. By title
2507.S8H3 Heinrich der Vogler
Hermann
2507.S8H6 Texts. By date
Translations
2507.S8H7 English. By date
2507.S8H8-.S8H89 Other. By language (alphabetically)
2507.S8H9 Criticism
2507.S8M2 Mariamne
2507.S8M7 Montezum
2507.S8O3 Oden
2507.S8S5 Der sieg des Mischmasches
2507.S8T4 Thusnelde
2507.S8Z12 Zarine
2507.S8Z14 Zayde
Schönaich-Carolath, Emil, prinz von see PT2638.O32
2507.S9 Schöne, Karl Christian Ludwig, 1779-1852 (Table P-PZ40)
2508.S2 Schönthan, Franz, edler von Pernwald, 1849-1913 (Table P-PZ40)
Some of his plays in collaboration with Paul von Schönthan, G. von Moser, Rudolf Presber, or G. Kadelburg
2508.S22 Schönthan, Paul, edler von Pernwald, 1853-1905 (Table P-PZ40)
2508.S4 Schöpf, Johann, 1811-1895 (Table P-PZ40)
2508.S45 Schöpfel, Johann Wolfgang Andreas, b. 1752. (Table P-PZ40)
2508.S48 Scholtz, Johann David, b. 1785 (Table P-PZ40)
2508.S5 Scholz, Bernhard, 1831-1871 (Table P-PZ40)
2508.S56 Schopenhauer, Adele, 1797-1849 (Table P-PZ40)

Individual authors or works
1700-ca. 1860/70 -- Continued

2508.S6 Schopenhauer, Frau Johanna Henriette (Trosiener), 1766-1838 (Table P-PZ40)
2508.S7 Schoppe, Frau Amalie Emma Sophie Katharina (Weise), 1791-1858 (Table P-PZ40)
2508.S75 Schott, Arthur, 1814-1875 (Table P-PZ40)
Poems only
Schoultz de Torma see PT2513.S4
2509.S2 Schrader, August, 1815-1878 (Table P-PZ40)
2509.S3 Schram, Karl, 1827-1905 (Table P-PZ40)
Schrattenthal, Karl see PT2647.E527
2509.S4 Schreiber, Aloys Wilhelm, 1761-1841 (Table P-PZ40)
2509.S5 Schreiber, Christian, 1781-1857 (Table P-PZ40)
2509.S6 Schreyer, Otto, 1831-1914 (Table P-PZ40)
2509.S7 Schreyvogel, Joseph, 1768-1832 (Table P-PZ40)
2509.S8 Shröckinger, Karl, 1798-1819 (Table P-PZ40)
2510.S2 Schröder, Friedrich Ludwig, 1744-1816 (Table P-PZ40)
Schröder, Wilhelm see PT4848.S4
2510.S4 Schröer, Tobias Gottfried, 1791-1850 (Table P-PZ40)
2510.S5 Schubart, Christian Friedrich Daniel, 1739-1791 (Table P-PZ40)
2510.S6 Schubert, Friedrich Karl, 1832-1892 (Table P-PZ40)
2510.S7 Schubert, Gotthilf Heinrich von, 1780-1860 (Table P-PZ40)
2511 Schücking, Levin, 1814-1883 (Table P-PZ39)
2512.S22 Schücking, Frau Louise (von Gall), 1815-1855 (Table P-PZ40)
2512.S226 Schüller, Eduard, fl. 1866 (Table P-PZ40)
2512.S3 Schütz, Friedrich, 1845-1908 (Table P-PZ40)
2512.S4 Schütz, Friedrich Wilhelm von, 1757-1821 (Table P-PZ40)
2512.S5 Schütz, Wilhelm von, 1776-1847 (Table P-PZ40)
2512.S6 Schütze, Johann Friedrich, 1758-1810 (Table P-PZ40)
2512.S7 Schütze, Stephan, 1771-1839 (Table P-PZ40)
Schuhmann, Sophie (Junghans) see PT2370.J9
2512.S9 Schultes, Karl, 1822-1904 (Table P-PZ40)
2513.S2 Schults, Adolf, 1820-1858 (Table P-PZ40)
2513.S3 Schultz, Friedrich, 1766-1845 (Table P-PZ40)
2513.S4 Schultz, Georg Julius, 1808-1875 (Table P-PZ40)
2513.S5 Schultz, Karl Gustav Theodor, 1835-1900 (Table P-PZ40)
2513.S55 Schultz, Marie (Table P-PZ40)
2513.S6 Schultze, Ernst Wilhelm, 1837-1910 (Table P-PZ40)
Schultze, Victor see PT2638.U55
Scultzky, Otto see PT2638.U56
2513.S65 Schulz, Albert, 1802-1893 (Table P-PZ38)
2513.S7 Schulz, Eduard, 1813-1842 (Table P-PZ40)
2513.S8 Schulz, Joachim Christoph Friedrich, 1762-1798 (Table P-PZ40)

Individual authors or works

1700-ca. 1860/70 -- Continued

2513.S9 Schulze, Ernst Konrad Friedrich, 1789-1817 (Table P-PZ40)

2514.S2 Schulze, Friedrich August, 1770-1849 (Table P-PZ40)

Schulze-Smidt, Frau Bernhardine see PT2638.U78

2514.S4 Schumacher, August, 1790-1864 (Table P-PZ40)

2514.S44 Schumacher, Franz Alois, 1703-1784 (Table P-PZ40)

2514.S5 Schumacher, Wilhelm, 1800-1837 (Table P-PZ40)

2514.S6 Schumann, August, 1773-1826 (Table P-PZ40)

2514.S63 Schummel, Johann Gottlieb, 1748-1813 (Table P-PZ40)

2514.S65 Schupp, Ambros, 1840-1914 (Table P-PZ40)

2514.S7 Schwab, Gustav Benjamin, 1792-1850 (Table P-PZ40)

2514.S8 Schwaiger, Michael Josef, 1841-1887 (Table P-PZ40)

2514.S9 Schwaldopler, Johann, 1777-1808 (Table P-PZ40)

2515.S2 Schwan, Christian Friedrich, 1733-1815 (Table P-PZ40)

Schwartz, August see PT2515.S5

2515.S4 Schwartz, Marie Esperance (Brandt) von, 1818-1899 (Table P-PZ40)

2515.S5 Schwartzkopff, August Heinrich Theodor, 1818-1886 (Table P-PZ40)

2515.S6 Schwarz, Bernhard, 1844-1901 (Table P-PZ40)

2515.S7 Schwarzenau, Marie von, 1815-1880 (Table P-PZ40)

2515.S9 Schwebel, Oskar, 1845-1891 (Table P-PZ40)

2516.S2 Schweichel, Robert, 1821-1907 (Table P-PZ40)

2516.S25 Schweighofer, Felix, 1842-1912 (Table P-PZ40)

2516.S3 Schweitzer, Jean Baptista von, 1833-1875 (Table P-PZ40)

2516.S35 Schwerin, Josephine Elisabeth Felicitas, gräfin von, 1836- (Table P-PZ40)

2516.S4 Sealsfield, Charles, 1793-1864 (Table P-PZ40)

See, Gustav vom see PT2532.S4

Seeburg, Franz von see PT2284.H15

2516.S65 Seeger, Ludwig Wilhelm Friedrich, 1810-1864 (Table P-PZ40)

2516.S67 Sehring, Wilhelm, 1816-1900 (Table P-PZ40)

2516.S7 Seidel, Heinrich, 1842-1906 (Table P-PZ40)

2516.S75 Seidel, Samuel, 1698-1755 (Table P-PZ40)

2516.S8 Seidl, Franz Xaver, 1845-1892 (Table P-PZ40)

2516.S9 Seidl, Johann Gabriel, 1804-1875 (Table P-PZ40)

Author of poems in Lower Austrian dialect

2517.S2 Seifart, Karl, 1821-1885 (Table P-PZ40)

2517.S22 Seis, Eduard, 1842-1905 (Table P-PZ40)

Selmar see PT1827.B63

Selmar (Swedish literature) see PT8831.B4

2517.S23 Semmig, Herman (Table P-PZ40)

2517.S25 Sessa, Karl Boromäus Alexander, 1786-1813 (Table P-PZ40)

Individual authors or works
1700-ca. 1860/70 -- Continued
2517.S3 Seume, Johann Gottfried, 1763-1810 (Table P-PZ40)
Severus see PT2461.R5
2517.S315 Seybold, David Christoph, 1747-1804 (Table P-PZ40)
2517.S4 Silberstein, August, 1827-1900 (Table P-PZ40)
Silva, Carmen see PT1858.E4
Simon, Frau Emma (Couvely) see PT2639.I64
2517.S55 Sinclair, Isaak von, 1775-1815 (Table P-PZ40)
Sirano, Paul see PT2513.S5
2517.S7 Smets, Wilhelm, 1796-1848 (Table P-PZ40)
2517.S8 Smidt, Heinrich, 1798-1867 (Table P-PZ40)
2517.S83 Smith, John Frederick, 1804?-1890 (Table P-PZ40)
2517.S9 Soden, Julius, graf von, 1754-1831 (Table P-PZ40)
2518.S2 Söndermann, Adolf, 1834-1892 (Table P-PZ40)
Solitaire, M. see PT2440.N9
2518.S3 Sondershausen, Karl, 1792-1882 (Table P-PZ40)
Sonnabend, Tobias see PT2423.L2
2518.S4 Sostmann, Wilhelmine (Blumenhagen), 1788-1864 (Table P-PZ40)
Soyaux, Frau Frida (Schanz) see PT2639.O9
Spättgen, Doris, freiin von see PT2638.E5
Specht, Karl August see PT2639.P32
Spielhagen, Friedrich, 1829-1911
2519.A1 Collected works. By date
Translations see PT2519.Z3+
Selected works
2519.A13 General. Miscellaneous
2519.A15 Novels and stories
2519.A16 Short novels, stories, etc. (Kleine romane, novellen)
2519.A17 Poems
2519.A19 Plays
2519.A2-.Z2 Separate works
2519.A3 Allzeit voran!
2519.A4 An der heilquelle
2519.A6 Angela
2519.A7 Auf der düne
2519.A9 Aus meinem skizzenbuche
2519.B7 Breite schultern
2519.C6 Clara Vere
2519.D4 Deutsche pioniere
2519.D6 Die dorfkokette (Dorfcoquette)
2519.D7 Drei erzählungen
2519.D8 Durch nacht zum licht
2519.F2 Faustulus
Finder und erfinder see PT2520.A2
2519.F7 Frei geboren

Individual authors or works
1700-ca. 1860/70
Spielhagen, Friedrich, 1829-1911
Separate works -- Continued

2519.G4 Gerettet
2519.H2 Hammer und amboss
2519.H3 Hans und Grete (Novelle)
2519.H4 Hans und Grete (Schauspiel)
2519.H6 Herrin
2519.I4 In der zwölften stunde
2519.I6 In eiserner zeit
2519.I8 In reih' und glied
Kleine romane see PT2519.A16
2519.L5 Liebe für liebe
2519.M4 Mesmerismus
2519.N4 Ein neuer Pharao
2519.N6 Noblesse oblige
2519.O6 Opfer
2519.P4 Die philosophin
2519.P6 Platt land
2519.P7 Problematische naturen
2519.Q4 Quisisana
2519.R6 Röschen vom hofe
2519.S2 Die schönen Amerikanerinnen
Cf. PT2519.U8 Unter tannen
2519.S3 Selbstgerecht
2519.S4 Das skelett im hause (Novelle)
2519.S5 Das skelett im hause (Lustspiel)
2519.S55 Skizzen, geschichten und gedichte
2519.S6 Sonntagskind
2519.S7 Stumme des himmels
2519.S8 Sturmflut
2519.S95 Susi, ein hofgeschichte
2519.U3 Uhlenhans
2519.U6 Ultimo
2519.U8 Unter tannen
Comprises two novels: Die schönen Amerikanerinnen; Der vergnügungskommissar
2519.V4 Der vergnügungskommissar
Cf. PT2519.U8 Unter tannen
2519.V6 Die von Hohenstein
Von Neapel bis Syrakus
see DG
2519.W2 Was die schwalbe sang
2519.W4 Was will das werden?
2519.Z2 Zum zeitvertreib
2519.Z3-.Z69 Translations

Individual authors or works
1700-ca. 1860/70
Spielhagen, Friedrich, 1829-1911 -- Continued
2520 Biography and criticism
2520.A2 Autobiography. Finder und erfinder
(Erinnerungen aus meinem leben)
2520.A3 Journals. Letters
2520.A5-Z Treatises. Life and works
Spiess, Christian Heinrich see PT2514.S2
2521.S3 Spiess, Christian Heinrich, 1755-1799 (Table P-PZ40)
Spiller von Hauenschild, Richard Georg see PT2292.H6
Spindler, Alexander see PT1819.B25
Spindler, Karl, 1796-1855
2521.S5 Collected works. By date
2521.S5A6 Selected works. By date
2521.S5A7-.S5Z4 Separate works
2521.S5A8 Aus dem leben eines glücklichen
2521.S5B6 Boa constrictor
2521.S5J3 Der Jesuit
2521.S5J4 English translations
2521.S5J8 Der Jude
2521.S5L2 Lenzblüthen
2521.S5T4 Der Teufelimbade
2521.S5W2 Walpurgisnächte
2521.S6 Biography and criticism
2521.S7 Spitta, Karl Johann Philipp, 1801-1859 (Table P-PZ40)
Spitteler, Carl see PT2639.P6
2521.S93 Spitzer, Daniel, 1835-1893 (Table P-PZ40)
2521.S975 Sprickman, Anton Mathias, 1749-1833 (Table P-PZ40)
2521.S98 Spyri, Frau Johanna (Heusser), 1827-1901 (Table P-PZ40)
Juvenile works see PZ31+
Stade, J.F.A. see PT1801.A6
2522.S2 Stadion, Emerich, graf von, 1838-1901 (Table P-PZ40)
2522.S25 Stägemann, Friedrich August von, 1763-1840 (Table P-PZ40)
Stahl, Arthur see PT1823.B6
2522.S3 Stahr, Adolf Wilhelm Theodor, 1805-1876 (Table P-PZ40)
2522.S4 Starklof, Ludwig, 1789-1850 (Table P-PZ40)
2522.S5 Stavenow, Bernhard, 1848-1890 (Table P-PZ40)
2522.S6 Steffens, Henrich, 1773-1845 (Table P-PZ38)
2522.S7 Steigentesch, August, freiherr von, 1774-1826 (Table P-PZ40)
Stein, Armin see PT2440.N71
Stein, Bernhard see PT2372.K28

Individual authors or works
1700-ca. 1860/70 -- Continued

2522.S73 Stein, Charlotte Albertine Ernestine von, 1742-1827 (Table P-PZ40)
For correspondence with Goethe see PT2009.S7
For her biography see PT2085.A4
2522.S75 Stein, Karl, 1773-1855 (Table P-PZ40)
2522.S77 Stein, Max, fl. ca. 1860 (Table P-PZ40)
Stein, Paul see PT2349.H57
2522.S8 Steinbeck, Johann, 1846-1889 (Table P-PZ40)
2522.S9 Steinhausen, Heinrich, 1836-1917 (Table P-PZ40)
2523.S2 Steinmann, Friedrich Arnold, 1801-1875 (Table P-PZ40)
Steinmann, J. see PT2526.S3
2523.S3 Stelzhamer, Franz, 1802-1874 (Table P-PZ40)
For his Austrian dialect poems, see PF
2523.S4 Stelzig, Ignaz Alfons, 1823-1865 (Table P-PZ40)
Stendro, Julius see PT2507.S4
2523.S5 Stengel, Franziska von, 1801-1843 (Table P-PZ40)
2523.S6 Stephanie, Christian Gottlob, 1733-1798 (Table P-PZ40)
2523.S7 Stephanie, Gottlieb, 1741-1800 (Table P-PZ40)
2523.S8 Stern, Adolf, 1835-1907 (Table P-PZ40)
Stern, Julius see PT2532.S5
2524.S2 Stern, Max Emanuel, 1811-1873 (Table P-PZ40)
Sternberg, Alexander von see PT2545.U4
2524.S3 Stettenheim, Julius, 1831-1916 (Table P-PZ40)
2524.S4 Steub, Ludwig, 1812-1888 (Table P-PZ40)
2524.S5 Stieglitz, Frau Charlotte Sophie (Willhöft), 1806-1834 (Table P-PZ40)
2524.S6 Stieglitz, Heinrich Wilhelm August, 1801-1849 (Table P-PZ40)
2524.S7 Stieler, Karl, 1842-1885 (Table P-PZ40)
2524.S8 Stifft, Andreas, freiherr von, 1819-1877 (Table P-PZ40)
Stifter, Adalbert, 1805-1868
2525.A1 Collected works. By date
2525.A15 Collected fiction. By date
2525.A16 Collected essays. By date
2525.A1995-.A59 Translations (Collected or selected)
2525.A1995 Polyglot. By date
2525.A2-.A29 English. By translator, if given, or date
2525.A3-.A39 French. By translator, if given, or date
2525.A5-.A59 Other. By language
2525.A6 Selected works. Selections. By date
2525.A61-.Z2 Separate works. By title
Subarrange each work by Table P-PZ43
2525.Z4 Biography and criticism
2525.Z5 Criticism
Stille, Karl see PT1843.D4

Individual authors or works
1700-ca. 1860/70 -- Continued
Stilling, Heinrich see PT2370.J7+
2526.S3 Stinde, Julius Ernst Wilhelm, 1841-1905 (Table P-PZ40 modified)
2526.S3A61-.S3Z458 Separate works. By title
For comedies in Low German see PT4848.S8
Ännchen von Tharau
see class M
2526.S3A63 Alltagsmärchen
Die blumenhändlerin von St. Pauli see PT4848.S8B5
Buchholz series
2526.S3B13 Bucholzens in Italien
Die familie Buchholz (4 parts)
2526.S3B14 Complete editions
Including pts. 1-2 and 1-3
2526.S3B15 Frau Wilhelmine (part 3)
2526.S3B16 Wilhelmine Buchholz' memoiren (part 4)
2526.S3B17 Frau Buchholz im Orient
2526.S3B18 Hotel Buchholz
2526.S3B19 Bei Buchholzens
Translations
2526.S3B2-.S3B29 English
2526.S3B2 Buchholzens in Italien
Die familie Buchholz
2526.S3B21 Complete
2526.S3B22 Frau Wilhelmine
2526.S3B23 Wilhelmine Buchholz' memoiren
2526.S3B24 Frau Buchholz im Orient
2526.S3B25 Hotel Buchholz
2526.S3B26 Bei Buchholzens
2526.S3B3-.S3B99 Other languages, alphabetically
Das decameron der verkannten see PT2526.S3W3
2526.S3D8 Die dumme frau
2526.S3E6 Emma, das geheimnisvolle hausmädchen
Die familie Karstens see PT4848.S8
2526.S3F6 Die flaschenbrüder
2526.S3G4 Geschichten von drüben
Eine Hamburger köchin see PT4848.S8
Hamburger leiden see PT4848.S8
2526.S3H4 Heinz Treulieb und allerlei anderes
2526.S3H8 Humoresken
Ihre familie see PT4848.S8
2526.S3I6 In eiserne faust
Das letzte kapitel see PT4848.S8
2526.S3L6 Der liedermacher
2526.S3M2 Martinhagen

Individual authors or works
1700-ca. 1860/70
Stinde, Julius Ernst Wilhelm, 1841-1905
Separate works -- Continued
Die nachtigal aus dem Bäckergang see PT4848.S8
2526.S3O7 Die opfer der wissenschaft
2526.S3P3 Die perlenschnur und anderes
2526.S3P4 Pienchens brautfahrt
2526.S3P7 Prinz Unart
2526.S3P8 Prinzess Tausendschön
Tante Lotte see PT4848.S8
2526.S3T6 Das torfmoor
Ut'n knick see PT4848.S8
2526.S3W2 Waldnovellen
2526.S3W3 Die wandertruppe; oder, Das dekameron der verkannten
2526.S3Z3 Zigeunerkönigs sohn und andere noveletten
2526.S4 Stocker, Franz August, 1833-1892 (Table P-PZ40)
2526.S43 Stockhausen, Anna (Oschatz) freifrau von, 1849- (Table P-PZ40)
2526.S44 Stockhausen, Fanny, 1846-1916 (Table P-PZ40)
2526.S45 Stockmans, Gertrud von, 1848-1889 (Table P-PZ40)
2526.S5 Stöber, Daniel Ehrenfried, 1779-1835 (Table P-PZ40)
2526.S6 Stökl, Frau Helene (Boeckel), 1845-1929 (Table P-PZ40)
2527.S2 Stolberg, Christian, graf zu, 1748-1821 (Table P-PZ40)
2527.S4 Stolberg, Friedrich Leopold, graf zu, 1750-1819 (Table P-PZ40)
2527.S6 Stolle, Ferdinand, 1806-1872 (Table P-PZ40)
Stolterfoth, Adelheid von see PT2592.Z8
2527.S62 Stoltze, Friedrich, 1816-1891 (Table P-PZ40)
2527.S63 Stolze, Franz, 1836-1910 (Table P-PZ40)
Storch, Arthur see PT2507.S2
2527.S8 Storch, Ludwig, 1803-1881 (Table P-PZ40)
Storm, Theodor, 1817-1888
2528.A1 Collected works. By date
2528.A12 Selected works
Miscellaneous collections entitled "novellen," "neue novellen," etc.
For series of novels and tales with distinct titles see PT2528.A4+
Drei märchen see PT2528.G2
2528.A13 Drei novellen
2528.A15 Novellen, 1868
Von jenseit des meeres; In St. Jurgen; Eine malerarbeit
2528.A17 Novellen und gedenkblätter, 1874
2528.A19 Neue novellen, 1878

Individual authors or works
1700-ca. 1860/70
Storm, Theodor, 1817-1888
Miscellaneous collections entitled "novellen," "neue novellen," etc. -- Continued

2528.A2 Drei neue novellen, 1880
Eekenhof; Im brauerhaus; Zur "wald und wasserfreude"

2528.A21 Novellen, 1882
Die söhne des senators; Der Herr Etatsrat

2528.A23 Zwei novellen, 1883
Schweigen; Hans und Heinz Kirch

2528.A25 Collected poems. By date

2528.A3 Translations

2528.A4-.Z3 Separate works
Arrange school editions by editor, A-Z

2528.A42 Abseits

2528.A45 Der amtschirurgus-heimkehr

2528.A47 Angelika

2528.A5 Aquis submersus

2528.A6 Auf dem staatshof

2528.A7 Auf der universität
2d edition called "Lenore"

2528.B3 Bei kleinen leuten

2528.B4 Beim Vetter Christian

2528.B5 Ein bekenntnis

2528.B7 Bötjer Basch

2528.B8 Bulemanns haus

2528.C3 Carsten Curator

2528.D6 Ein doppelgänger

2528.D7 Draussen im heidedorf

Drei märchen see PT2528.G2

Drei neue novellen see PT2528.A2

Drei novellen see PT2528.A13

2528.D8 Drüben am markt

2528.E4 Eekenhof

2528.E6 Es waren zwei königskinder

2528.F4 Ein fest auf Haderslevhuus

2528.F5 Der finger

2528.G2 Geschichten aus der tonne

2528.G7 Ein grünes blatt

2528.H2 Eine halligfahrt

2528.H3 Hans und Heinz Kirch

2528.H4 Heimkehr

2528.H5 Der Herr Etatsrat

2528.H6 Hinzelmeier

2528.I12 Im brauerhause

2528.I14 Im nachbarhause links

Individual authors or works
1700-ca. 1860/70
Storm, Theodor, 1817-1888
Separate works -- Continued

2528.I16 Im saal
2528.I18 Im schloss
2528.I2 Im sonnenschein
Immensee
2528.I3 Editions. By date
2528.I3A-.I3Z Editions. By editor. School texts
2528.I4A-.I4Z Translations. By language, A-Z
e.g.
2528.I4E5 English
2528.I5 Criticism
2528.I6 In der sommermondnacht
2528.I7 In St. Jürgen
School texts. By editor, A-Z
2528.J6 John Riew'
Karsten Kuratorn see PT2528.C3
2528.K6 Der kleine Häwelmann
2528.L4 Lena Wies
Lenore see PT2528.A7
2528.M2 Eine malerarbeit
2528.M3 Marthe und ihre uhr
Neue novellen see PT2528.A19
Novellen see PT2528.A13
2528.P3 Pole Poppenspäler
School texts. By editor, A-Z
2528.P6 Posthuma
2528.P7 Psyche
2528.R4 Regentrude
2528.R5 Renate
2528.S2 Der schimmelreiter
2528.S35 Schweigen
2528.S4 Die söhne des senators
2528.S6 Sommer-geschichten und lieder
2528.S8 Späte rosen
2528.S85 Die stadt
2528.S9 Ein stiller musikant
2528.U6 Unter dem tannenbaum
2528.V3 Veronika
2528.V4 Viola tricolor
2528.V5 Von heute und ehedem
2528.V6 Von jenseit des meeres
2528.V7 Von kindern und katzen
2528.V8 Vor zeiten
2528.W2 Waldwinkel

Individual authors or works
1700-ca. 1860/70
Storm, Theodor, 1817-1888
Separate works -- Continued

2528.W4 Wenn die äpfel reif sind
2528.Z12 Zerstreute kapitel
2528.Z13 Zur chronik von Grieshuus
2528.Z15 Zur "wald- und wasserfreude"
2528.Z17 Zwei kuchenesser der alten zeit
Zwei novellen see PT2528.A23
2528.Z19 Zwei Weihnachtsidyllen
Abseits; Unter dem tannenbaum
2528.Z4 Letters. Memoirs
2528.Z5 Biography. Life and works
2528.Z6 Criticism
2531.S2 Strachwitz, Moritz, graf von, 1822-1847 (Table P-PZ40)
2531.S25 Stranitzky, Joseph Anton, 1676-1726 (Table P-PZ40)
2531.S3 Strauss, David Friedrich, 1808-1874 (Table P-PZ38 modified)
Cf. BX4827.S8 Religious biography
(2531.S3A61-.S3A78) Separate works
see the subject
2531.S4 Strauss and Torney, Viktor Friedrich von, 1809-1899 (Table P-PZ40)
2531.S5 Streckfuss, Adolf, 1823-1895 (Table P-PZ40)
2531.S6 Streckfuss, Adolf Friedrich Karl, 1778-1844 (Table P-PZ40)
Streff, E. see PT2440.N45
2531.S65 Strehle, Ferdinand, 1834-1910 (Table P-PZ40)
"Olympia," only work
2531.S7 Streiter, Joseph, 1804-1873 (Table P-PZ40)
2532.S2 Strodtmann, Adolf, 1829-1879 (Table P-PZ40)
2532.S3 Strubberg, Friedrich Armand, 1808-1889 (Table P-PZ40)
2532.S4 Struensee, Gustav Karl Otto von, 1803-1875 (Table P-PZ40)
2532.S44 Studer, Franz Ludwig, 1804-1873 (Table P-PZ40)
2532.S5 Sturm, Julius, 1816-1896 (Table P-PZ40)
2532.S53 Sturm, Marcelin, 1760-1812 (Table P-PZ40)
2532.S55 Sturz, Helferich, Peter, 1736-1779 (Table P-PZ40)
2532.S6 Stutz, Jakob, 1801-1877 (Table P-PZ40)
Süd, A.V.T. see PT2542.T7
2533.S15 Sutro-Schücking, Kathinka, b. 1835 (Table P-PZ40)
2533.S2 Suttner, Arthur Gundaccar, freiherr von, 1850-1902 (Table P-PZ40)
2533.S3 Suttner, Bertha Felicie Sophie (Kinsky), freifrau von, 1843-1914 (Table P-PZ40)
2533.S4 Swiedack, Karl, 1815-1888 (Table P-PZ40)
2533.S5 Swoboda, Heinrich, 1837-1910 (Table P-PZ40)

Individual authors or works
1700-ca. 1860/70 -- Continued
2533.S6 Sydow, Friedrich von, 1780-1845 (Table P-PZ40)
2533.S7 Sydow, Wilhelmine (von Criegern) von, 1789-1867 (Table P-PZ40)
Sylva, Carmen see PT1858.E4
Talvi, 1797-1870 see PT2457.R58
Talvj, 1797-1870 see PT2457.R58
2534.T14 Tanera, Karl, 1844-1904 (Table P-PZ40)
2534.T17 Tannenhofer, Karl, 1839-1893 (Table P-PZ40)
2534.T2 Tarnow, Fanny (Franziska), 1779-1862 (Table P-PZ40)
2534.T25 Tarnowski, Ladislaus, 1811-1847 (Table P-PZ40)
2534.T3 Tauber, Josef Samuel, 1822-1879 (Table P-PZ40)
2534.T35 Taubert, Emil, 1844-1895 (Table P-PZ40)
2534.T37 Taurinius, Zacharias (Table P-PZ40)
Taylor, George see PT2294.H4
Telmann, Konrad see PT2642.H4
2534.T5 Temme, Jodocus Donatus Hubertus, 1798-1881 (Table P-PZ40)
2534.T53 Tempeltey, Eduard, 1832-1919 (Table P-PZ40)
(2534.T58) Tersteegen, Gerhard
see BV484
2534.T7 Thalboth, Heinrich, 1841-1896 (Table P-PZ40)
2534.T8 Thilo, Friedrich Gottlieb ("Theophilus"), 1749-1825 (Table P-PZ40)
2534.T85 Thoma, Hans, 1839-1924 (Table P-PZ40)
2534.T88 Thon, Eleonore, 1753-1807 (Table P-PZ40)
2534.T9 Thümmel, Moritz August von, 1738-1817 (Table P-PZ40)
2534.T95 Thumb-Neuburg, Karl Konrad, freiherr von, 1785-1831 (Table P-PZ40)
Tian see PT2281.G8+
Tibiscanus, Elias see PT2510.S4
Tieck, Johann Ludwig, 1773-1853
2536.A1 Collected works. By date
Selected works
2536.A15 Miscellaneous. By date
2536.A2 Dramatic works
2536.A3 Poems
Prose
2536.A4 Novels
(2536.A43) Dramaturgische blätter
see PN
(2536.A45) Kritische schriften
see PN
2536.A5 Selections. Anthologies
2537.A-Z Separate works, A-Z
2537.A12 Abdallah

Individual authors or works
1700-ca. 1860/70
Tieck, Johann Ludwig, 1773-1853
Separate works, A-Z -- Continued

2537.A15 Abraham Tonelli
2537.A2 Der abschied
2537.A25 Adalbert und Emma
2537.A3 Dle ahnenprobe
2537.A4 Alla-Moddin
2537.A5 Almansur
Published as part of a story called "Nesseln," by Falkenhain, i. e., August Ferdinand Bernhardi
Das alte buch und die reise ins blaue hinein see PT2537.R4
2537.A6 Der alte vom berge
2537.A7 Anti-Faust; oder, Geschichte eines dummen teufels
2537.A8 Der aufruhr in den Cevennen
Der autor see PT2537.N4
2537.B4 Die beiden merkwürdigsten tage aus Siegmunds leben
Blaubart (Ritter Blaubart) see PT2537.R6
Blaubart (Die sieben weiber des Blaubart) see PT2537.S6
2537.B6 Der blonde Eckbert
2537.B7 Die brüder
Carl von Berneck see PT2537.K4
Denkwürdige geschichtschronik der schildbürger see PT2537.S4
Des lebensüberfluss see PT2537.L4
2537.D5 Dichterleben
Don Quixote see PQ6331
2537.D7 Das Donauweib
2537.E4 Eigensinn und laune
Die eiserne maske see PT2452.R28E5
2537.E6 Die elfen
Epicoene see PR2612
Evremont (Novel) see PT1818.B42E8
Felsenburg see PT2537.I5
2537.F3 Fermer der geniale
2537.F4 Das fest zu Kenelworth
2537.F5 Fortunat
2537.F6 Franz Sternbalds wanderungen
2537.F7 Der fremde
2537.F8 Die freunde
2537.F9 Der fünfzehnte November
2537.G2 Der geheimnissvolle
2537.G3 Der gelehrte
2537.G4 Die gelehrte gesellschaft

Individual authors or works
1700-ca. 1860/70
Tieck, Johann Ludwig, 1773-1853
Separate works, A-Z -- Continued

2537.G5 Die gemälde
2537.G6 Genoveva
Geschichte des herrn William Lovell see PT2537.W4
Eine geschichte ohne abentheuerlichkeiten see PT2537.P3
Die geschichte von den Heymonskindern see PT2537.H6
Geschichtschronik der schildbürger see PT2537.S4
2537.G7 Die gesellschaft auf dem lande
2537.G8 Der gestiefelte kater
2537.G85 Der getreue Eckart und der Tannenhäuser
2537.G9 Glück giebt verstand
Golo und Geneveva
see ML
2537.G95 Der griechische kaiser
2537.H2 Hanswurst als emigrant
2537.H4 Herzensergiessungen eines kunstliebenden klosterbruders. (By Tieck and Wackenroder)
2537.H5 Der hexen-sabbath
2537.H6 Heymonskinder
2537.I5 Die insel Felsenburg
2537.J2 Der jahrmarkt
2537.J7 Das jüngste gericht
2537.J8 Der junge tischlermeister
2537.K3 Kaiser Octavianus
2537.K4 Karl von Berneck
2537.K6 Die Klausenburg
Leben und thaten des kleinen Thomas, genannt Däumchen see PT2537.L4
Leben und tod der heiligen Genoveva see PT2537.G6
Leben und tod des kleinen Rothkäppchens see PT2537.R8
2537.L4 Des lebens überfluss
2537.L5 Liebeswerben
2537.L6 Liebeszauber
2537.M2 Die männliche mutter
Märchen und zaubergeschichten see PT2537.P5
2537.M3 Magelone
2537.M4 Melusina
2537.M5 Melusine (fragment)
Merkwürdige lebensgeschichte seiner Majestät Abraham Tonelli see PT2537.A15
2537.M6 Der mondsüchtige

Individual authors or works
1700-ca. 1860/70
Tieck, Johann Ludwig, 1773-1853
Separate works, A-Z -- Continued

2537.M8 Musikalische leiden und freuden
2537.N2 Der naturfreund
2537.N4 Der neue Hercules am scheidewege, eine parodie in versen
Published also as "Der autor, eine fastnachtsschwank"
Octavianus see PT2537.K3
2537.P2 Paramythien
2537.P3 Peter Lebrecht, eine geschichte ohne abentheuerlichkeiten
Phantasien über die Kunst, by Wackenroder und Tieck see N7445.4
2537.P4 Phantasus
2537.P5 Pietro von Abano; oder, Petrus Apone (Märchen und zaubergeschichte)
2537.P6 Der pokal ("The cup")
2537.P7 Prinz Zerbino
2537.P8 Ein prolog
2537.P9 Der psycholog
2537.R2 Die rechtsgelehrten (nach dem französischen)
2537.R3 Das reh (Feenmärchen)
2537.R4 Die reise ins blaue hinein
2537.R5 Die reisenden
2537.R6 Ritter Blaubart
2537.R7 Der roman in briefen
2537.R8 Rothkäppchen
2537.R9 Der Runenberg
St. Evremont see PT1818.B42E8
2537.S3 Schicksal; erzählung nach dem französischen
2537.S4 Die schildbürger
2537.S5 Ein schurke über den andern; oder, Die fuchsprelle
Sehr wunderbare historie von der Melusina see PT2537.M4
2537.S6 Die sieben weiber des Blaubart
2537.S7 Die sommernacht
2537.S8 Eine sommerreise
Sternbalds wanderungen see PT2537.F6
Strausfedern. Eine sammlung kleine romane und erzählungen (by various authors; vols. 4-8, by Tieck) see PT1315
Der sturm
see Shakespeare's "The Tempest" in German PR2782.T4
2537.T2 Ein tagebuch

Individual authors or works
1700-ca. 1860/70
Tieck, Johann Ludwig, 1773-1853
Separate works, A-Z -- Continued
Thaten und feinheiten renommirter kraft- und kniffgenies see PT2452.R28T5
2537.T4 Die theegesellschaft
Thomas, genannt Däumchen see PT2537.L4
2537.T6 Der tod des dichters
Tonelli see PT2537.A15
2537.U6 Ulrich der empfindsame
Das ungeheuer und der verzauberte wald see ML
2537.V3 Die verkehrte welt
2537.V4 Die verlobung
2537.V5 Die versöhnung
2537.V6 Vittoria Accorombona
2537.V7 Die vogelscheuche
2537.V8 Volksmärchen
Three volumes published by Tieck containing the following works which are also listed as separates: Ritter Blaubart; Der blonde Eckbert; Die geschichte von den Heymonskindern; Der gestiefelte kater; Wundersame liebesgeschichte der schönen Magelone; Ein prolog; Karl von Berneck; Denkwürdige geschichtschronik der schildbürger
2537.W3 Waldeinsamkeit
2537.W4 William Lovell
Based upon Le paysan perverti, by Restif de la Bretonne
Cf. PQ2025.P4 Restif de la Bretonne, Le paysan perverti
2537.W5 Criticism
2537.W6 Wunderlichkeiten
Wundersame liebesgeschichte der schönen Magelone see PT2537.M3
2537.W8 Die wundersüchtigen
2537.Z3 Das zauberschloss
Translations
English
2538.A1 Collected works. By date
2538.A13 Selected works. By editor
2538.A3A-.A3Z Separate works. By original titles
Subarrange by translators
2538.A5-Z Other languages, A-Z
e.g.
French
2538.F7A1 Collected works

Individual authors or works
1700-ca. 1860/70
Tieck, Johann Ludwig, 1773-1853
Translations
Other languages, A-Z
French -- Continued

2538.F7A13	Selected works
2538.F7A3-.F7Z	Separate works. By original titles Subarrange by translator
	Biography and criticism
2539.A2	Journals, memoirs, etc.
2539.A4-.A59	Letters
2539.A42-.A59	By correspondent
2539.A43	Brockhaus
2539.A45	Goethe, Johann Wolfgang von
2539.A47	Raumer, Friedrich von
2539.A49	The Schlegels
2539.A5	Solger, Karl Wilhelm Ferdinand
2539.A6-Z	General treatises. Life and works
2540	Criticism
(2542.T13)	Tieck, Sophie see PT1818.B42
2542.T2	Tiedge, Christoph August, 1752-1841 (Table P-PZ40)
2542.T22	Tietz, Friedrich, 1803-1879 (Table P-PZ40)
2542.T24	Töpfer, Karl Friedrich Gustav, 1792-1871 (Table P-PZ40)
2542.T25	Törring-Gutenzell, Joseph August, graf von, 1753-1826 (Table P-PZ40)
	Toucement, Jean Chretien see PT2542.T65
2542.T3	Träger, Albert, 1830-1912 (Table P-PZ40)
2542.T5	Trautmann, Franz, 1813-1887 (Table P-PZ40)
2542.T52	Trautzschen, Hans Karl Heinrich von, 1730-1812 (Table P-PZ40)
2542.T525	Trebitz, Johann Christian Karl, 1818-1884 (Table P-PZ40)
2542.T53	Treitschke, Friedrich, 1776-1842 (Table P-PZ40)
2542.T55	Treller, Franz, 1843-1908 (Table P-PZ40)
2542.T65	Trömer, Johann Christian, 1698?-1756 (Table P-PZ40)
2542.T68	Trojan, Johannes, 1837-1915 (Table P-PZ40)
	Tromlitz, August von see PT2580.W8
2542.T7	Tschabuschnigg, Adolf, ritter von, 1809-1877 (Table P-PZ40)
2542.T75	Tschischwitz, Benno, 1828-1890 (Table P-PZ40)
2542.T8	Türcke, Albert, 1824-1886 (Table P-PZ40)
2542.T9	Twardowska, Emma Eva Henriette von, 1845-1889 (Table P-PZ40)
2542.U52	Uechtritz, Friedrich von, 1800-1875 (Table P-PZ38)
2542.U55	Uexküll, Julie Charlotte, freifräulein von, fl. 1860 (Table P-PZ40)

	Individual authors or works
	1700-ca. 1860/70 -- Continued
2542.U8	Uhl, Friedrich, 1825-1906 (Table P-PZ40)
	Uhland, Ludwig, 1787-1862
2543.A1	Collected works. By date
	Cf. PD27 Uhland's schriften zur geschichte der dichtung und sage
	Poems
2543.A2	Comprehensive editions. By date
2543.A3	Selections or school editions. By editor
2543.A33	Special groups
	e.g. Balladen und romanzen; Vaterländische gedichte
2543.A35A-.A35Z	Special poems, A-Z
2543.A38	Dramatic works, and fragments. By date
	Special dramas
2543.A4	Ernst, Herzog von Schwaben
2543.A6	Ludwig der Baier
2543.A8-.Z19	Translations. By language and date
	English
2543.E5	Collections and selections
	Poems
2543.E6	Collections and selections
2543.E61	Special poems
	Plays
2543.E62	Collections and selections
2543.E63	Special plays
	Biography and criticism
2543.Z2	Letters
2543.Z3	Biography by Frau Emilie (Vischer) Uhland
2543.Z4	Biography and criticism by others
2543.Z5	Criticism
2545.U15	Uhlemann, Maximilian Adolph, fl. 1860 (Table P-PZ40)
2545.U18	Uhlich, Adam Gottfried, 1720-1756 (Table P-PZ38)
2545.U19	Uhlich, Leberecht, 1799-1872 (Table P-PZ40)
2545.U2	Unger, Frau Friederike Helene (von Rotherburg), 1751-1813 (Table P-PZ40)
2545.U4	Ungern-Sternberg, Alexander, freiherr von, 1806-1868 (Table P-PZ40)
2545.U5	Unzer, Johann Christoph, 1747-1809 (Table P-PZ40)
2545.U55	Unzer-Ziegler, Johanne Charlotte, 1725-1782 (Table P-PZ40)
2545.U6	Uschner, Karl Richard Waldemar, b. 1834 (Table P-PZ40)
2545.U8	Usteri, Johann Martin, 1763-1827 (Table P-PZ40)
2545.U9	Uz, Johann Peter, 1720-1796 (Table P-PZ40)
2546.V15	Vacano, Emil Mario, 1840-1892 (Table P-PZ40)
	Valmy, Alfred de see PT2526.S3

Individual authors or works
1700-ca. 1860/70 -- Continued

2546.V18 Varnbüler, Theodor Lorenz Friedrich von, 1821-1892 (Table P-PZ40)
2546.V2 Varnhagen von Ense, Karl August Ludwig Philipp, 1785-1858 (Table P-PZ40)
2546.V22 Varnhagen von Ense, Rahel Antonie Friederike (Levin), 1771-1833 (Table P-PZ38)
Varnhagen von Ense, Rosa Maria see PT1810.A8
Veit, Dorothea (Mendelssohn) see PT2503.S55
2546.V3 Veith, Johann Emanuel, 1787-1876 (Table P-PZ40)
2546.V4 Velde, Karl Franz van der, 1779-1824 (Table P-PZ40)
Vely, Emma see PT2639.I64
Verden, C. see PT2546.V7
Vetter, Daniel see PT2526.S5
2546.V5 Vezin, Hermann, 1829-1910 (Table P-PZ40)
Villinger, Hermine see PT2645.I6
2546.V7 Vincenti, Karl Ferdinand, ritter von, 1835-1917 (Table P-PZ40)
2546.V8 Vincke, Gisbert, freiherr von, 1813-1892 (Table P-PZ40)
Vischer, Friedrich Theodor von, 1807-1887
2547.V2 Collected works. By date
2547.V2A3 Selections. By date
Separate works
2547.V2A4 Allotria
2547.V2A5 Altes und neues
2547.V2A52 Neue folge
2547.V2A7 Auch einer
Faust; der tragödie dritten Theil see PT1921
2547.V2K7 Kritische gänge
2547.V2K72 Neue folge
2547.V2L8 Lyrische gänge
Vorträge
see BH193, (Esthetics) and PR2897, (Shakespeare)
2547.V2Z5-.V2Z99 Biography and criticism
2547.V3 Vogel, Jakob, 1816-1899 (Table P-PZ40)
2547.V35 Vogel, Wilhelm, 1772-1843 (Table P-PZ40)
2547.V4 Vogl, Johann Nepomuk, 1802-1866 (Table P-PZ40)
Voigt, Frau Johanna (Ambrosius) see PT2645.O47
Voigtel, Valeska see PT1823.B6
Volger, Adolf see PT2645.O57
Volger, Eduard see PT2645.O58
Volger, Franz see PT2645.O59
Volger, Fritz see PT2645.O6
Volger, Paul see PT2645.O62
2547.V8 Volkmann, Richard von, 1830-1889 (Table P-PZ40)
2547.V9 Vollmar, Agnes, 1836-1910

Individual authors or works
1700-ca. 1860/70 -- Continued
Voss, Ernestine see PT2549.V5
2549.V2 Voss, Johann Heinrich, 1751-1826 (Table P-PZ40)
2549.V4 Voss, Julius von, 1768-1832 (Table P-PZ40)
2549.V5 Voss, Marie Christine Ernestine, 1756-1834 (Table P-PZ40)
Voss, Richard see PT2645.O88
2549.V8 Vulpius, Christian August, 1762-1827 (Table P-PZ40)
2551.W2 Wachenhusen, Hans, 1823-1898 (Table P-PZ40)
2551.W25 Wackenroder, Wilhelm Heinrich, 1773-1798 (Table P-PZ38)
2551.W28 Wagner, Christian, 1835-1918 (Table P-PZ40)
2551.W29 Wagner, Ernst, 1769-1812 (Table P-PZ40)
2551.W3 Wagner, Heinrich Leopold, 1747-1779 (Table P-PZ38)
Wagner, Richard, 1813-1883
2551.W35 Literary works
2551.W36 Criticism of literary works
2551.W37 Wagner, Wilhelm, fl. (Table P-PZ40)
2551.W39 Wahr, Franz (Table P-PZ40)
2551.W4 Waiblinger, Wilhelm Friedrich, 1804-1830 (Table P-PZ40)
Wald, E. von see PT2589.Z2
Wald, Richard E. see PT2526.S3
Wald-Zedtwitz see PT2589.Z2
Waldau, Max see PT2292.H6
Walden, H. see PT1887.G8
Waldmüller, Robert see PT1849.D3
Waldow, Ernst von see PT1820.B3
2551.W5 Waldstein, Max, 1836- (Table P-PZ40)
Wall, Anton see PT2355.H9
2551.W55 Wallenrodt, Johanne Isabelle Eleonore (freiin von Koppy) von, 1740-1819 (Table P-PZ40)
Waller, Kurt see PT2423.L2
2551.W6 Wallnau, Eugenie, fl. 1838 (Table P-PZ40)
2551.W7 Wangenheim, Franz Theodor, 1805-1849 (Table P-PZ40)
2551.W75 Warburg, Frau Emilie Erhardine (freiin von der Goltz) von, 1833-1907 (Table P-PZ40)
Warso, A. see PT2515.S5
2551.W79 Wartenburg, Karl, 1826-1889 (Table P-PZ40)
2551.W8 Wasserburg, Philipp, 1827-1897 (Table P-PZ40)
2551.W84 Wassermann, Moses, 1811-1892 (Table P-PZ40)
2553.W18 Weber, Beda, 1798-1858
2553.W2 Weber, Friedrich Wilhelm, 1813-1894 (Table P-PZ40)
Weber, Karl Julius, 1767-1832
2553.W3D3 Demokritos (best-known work)
2553.W3D4 Selections
2553.W3D5-.W3D59 Translations. By language

Individual authors or works
1700-ca. 1860/70
Weber, Karl Julius, 1767-1832
Demokritos (best-known work) -- Continued
2553.W3D6-.W3D69 Criticism. By author
2553.W35 Weber, Robert, 1824-1896 (Table P-PZ40)
2553.W4 Weddigen, Otto, 1851- (Table P-PZ40)
2553.W45 Wedekind, Christoph Friedrich, 18th cent. (Table P-PZ40)
2553.W47 Weerth, Georg, 1822-1856 (Table P-PZ40)
2553.W5 Wehl, Feodor von, 1821-1890 (Table P-PZ40)
2553.W54 Weickum, Karl, 1815-1896 (Table P-PZ40)
2553.W56 Weidmann, Paul, 1748-1801 (Table P-PZ40)
2553.W58 Weil, Josef, ritter von Weilen, 1828-1889 (Table P-PZ40)
2553.W6 Weil, Julius, 1847- (Table P-PZ40)
Weilen, Josef, ritter von Weilen see PT2553.W58
2553.W7 Weill, Alexandre, 1811-1899 (Table P-PZ40)
Cf. PQ2479.W4 French literature
2553.W75 Weise, Clara (Stock), 1823-1890 (Table P-PZ40)
2553.W77 Weiser, Karl, 1848-1913 (Table P-PZ40)
2553.W8 Weisflog, Karl, 1770-1828 (Table P-PZ40)
Weiss, Karl Franz Joseph see PT2647.E527
2554.W2 Weisse, Christian Felix, 1726-1804 (Table P-PZ40)
2554.W3 Weisser, Friedrich Christoph, 1761-1836 (Table P-PZ40)
Weitbrecht, Karl see PT2647.E56
Weitbrecht, Richard see PT2647.E562
2554.W46 Weitzmann, Karl Borromäus, 1767-1828 (Table P-PZ40)
2554.W52 Wekhrlin, Wilhelm Ludwig, 1739-1792 (Table P-PZ40)
2554.W6 Wellmer, Arnold, 1835-1915 (Table P-PZ40)
2554.W7 Welten, Oskar, 1844-1894 (Table P-PZ40)
Werder, C. see PT2559.W2
2554.W8 Werg, August, b. 1794 (Table P-PZ40)
Werner, E. see PT1831.B2
Werner, Franz von see PT2438.M5
2554.W9 Werner, Hedwig, 1849- (Table P-PZ38)
2555 Werner, Zacharias, 1768-1823 (Table P-PZ39 modified)
2555.A61-.Z48 Separate works. By title
2555.A8 Attila, könig der Hunner (Table P-PZ43)
2555.C8 Cunegunde die heilige (Table P-PZ43)
2555.K7 Das Kreuz an der Ostsee (Table P-PZ43)
Die kreuzesbrüder see PT2555.S8
Martin Luther; oder, Die weihe der kraft
2555.M3 Editions. By date
2555.M4A-.M4Z Translations. By language, A-Z
2555.M5 Criticism
2555.M8 Die mutter der Makkabäer (Table P-PZ43)
2555.S6-.S9 Die söhne des thales
2555.S7 Part 1. Die templar auf Cypern

Individual authors or works
1700-ca. 1860/70
Werner, Zacharias, 1768-1823
Separate works. By title
Die söhne des thales -- Continued
2555.S8 Part 2. Die Kreuzesbrüder
2555.S9 Criticism
Die templer auf Cypern see PT2555.S7
2555.V5 Der vierundzwanzigste Februar (Table P-PZ43)
2555.W2 Wanda, königin der Sarmaten (Table P-PZ43)
Weihe der kraft see PT2555.M3+
2555.W4 Die weihe der unkraft, ein ergänzungsblatt zur deutschen haustafel (Table P-PZ43)
2557.W2 Werther, Julius von, 1838-1910 (Table P-PZ40)
2557.W3 Werther, Karl Ludwig, 1809-1861 (Table P-PZ40)
2557.W4 Werthes, Friedrich August Clemens, 1748-1817 (Table P-PZ40)
2557.W6 Wesendonck, Frau Mathilde (Luckemeyer), 1828-1902 (Table P-PZ40)
2557.W65 Wessenberg, Ignaz Heinrich Karl, Freiherr von, 1774-1860 (Table P-PZ40)
West, C.A. see PT2509.S7
West, Karl August see PT2509.S7
West, Thomas see PT2509.S7
2557.W8 Wetzel, Friedrich Gottlob, 1779-1819 (Table P-PZ40)
2557.W9 Wezel, Johann Karl, 1747-1819 (Table P-PZ40)
Wichert, Ernst, 1831-1902
2558.A1 Collected works. By date
Selected works
2558.A12 General. Novels and plays
Special
Novels and tales
2558.A13 Comprehensive editions
2558.A14 Selections
2558.A15 "Kleine romane"
2558.A16 "Novellen"
2558.A18 Dramatic works
2558.A19 Poems
2558.A2-.Z29 Separate works. By title
Subarrange each work by Table P-PZ43
2558.Z8-.Z9 Biography and criticism
2559.W2 Wichmann von Sebog und Glenz, Paul Victor, 1829-1907 (Table P-PZ40)
2559.W25 Wichtrich, Gerhard, fl. 1870 (Table P-PZ40)
2559.W3 Wickede, Julius von, 1819-1896 (Table P-PZ40)
2559.W4 Wickenburg, Albrecht Capello, graf von, 1838-1911 (Table P-PZ40)

Individual authors or works
1700-ca. 1860/70 -- Continued
2559.W5 Wickenburg-Almásy, Wilhelmine, gräfin von, 1845-1890 (Table P-PZ40)
2559.W88 Widmann, Adolf, 1818-1878 (Table P-PZ40)
2559.W9 Widmann, Joseph Victor, 1842-1911 (Table P-PZ40)
2559.W95 Widmer, Leonhard, 1808-1868 (Table P-PZ38)
Wieland, Christoph Martin, 1733-1813
2562.A1 Collected works. By date
2562.A2A-.A2Z Selections, anthologies, quotations. By editor, A-Z
Selected works
2562.A3 Miscellaneous (Prose and verse). By date
2562.A5 Poetical works
2562.A6 Prose works
Letters see PT2570.A2+
2563.A-Z Separate works
2563.A2 Die Abderiten
Die abenteuer des Don Sylvio see PT2563.D7
Abraham see PT2563.G3
2563.A4 Agathodämon
2563.A5 Agathon
Alceste, ein singspiel
see ML
Amadis, Der neue see PT2563.N4
2563.A7 Araspes und Panthea
2563.A8 Aristipp
Auserlesene gedichte see PT2562.A5
Briefe see PT2570.A2+
2563.C6 Clelia und Sinibald
2563.C7 Combabus
2563.C8 Comische erzählungen
2563.C9 Cyrus
2563.D3 Danischmend
Dialogen (im Elysium) see PT2563.G5
Dialogen des Diogenes see PT2563.D5
2563.D5 Diogenes von Sinope
2563.D7 Don Sylvio von Rosalva
Elysium, Gespräche im see PT2563.G5
2563.E8 Euthanasia
Gedichte see PT2562.A5
Geheime geschichte des philosophen Peregrinus see PT2563.P4
2563.G3 Der gepryfte Abraham
Geschichte der Abderiten see PT2563.A2
Geschichte des Agathon see PT2563.A5
2563.G4 Geschichte des prinzen Biribinkers
Story in Don Sylvio, published separately

Individual authors or works
1700-ca. 1860/70
Wieland, Christoph Martin, 1733-1813
Separate works -- Continued
Geschichte des weisen Danischmend see PT2563.D3
2563.G5 Gespräche im Elysium
2563.G6 Göttergespräche
2563.G7 Neue Göttergespräche
2563.G8 Der goldne spiegel; oder, Die könige von Scheschian
2563.G9 Die grazien
2563.H3 Hann und Gulpenheh
2563.H4 Hermann
2563.H5 Das hexameron von Rosenhayn
2563.H8 Hymnen
2563.I8 Idris und Zenide
Die könige von Scheschian see PT2563.G8
Kombabus see PT2563.C7
2563.K7 Krates und Hipparchia
2563.L3 Lady Johanna Gray
2563.M4 Menander und Glycerion
2563.M6 Der mönch und die nonne auf dem Mittelstein
2563.M7 Musarion; oder, Die philosophie der grazien
2563.N3 Die natur der dinge
2563.N4 Der neue Amadis
Neue göttergespräche see PT2563.G7
Neueste gedichte see PT2562.A5
2563.O2 Oberon
2563.P4 Peregrinus Proteus
Pervonte see PT2563.W8
Die prüfung Abrahams see PT2563.G3
Rosamund (Rosemunde), ein singspiel see ML
2563.S3 Schach Lolo
Der sieg der natur über die Schwärmerey see PT2563.D7
Sixt und Clärchen see PT2563.M6
Sokrates Mainomenos see PT2563.D5
2563.S6 Das sommermährchen
2563.S8 Sympathien
2563.W3 Die wasserkufe
2563.W5 Das wintermährchen
2563.W8 Die wünsche; oder, Pervonte
2567.A1 Doubtful and spurious works
2567.A2 Imitations, adaptations, parodies
Translations (as subject; comparative studies, etc.)
2567.A3 General
2567.A4A-.A4Z Special works, A-Z

Individual authors or works
1700-ca. 1860/70
Wieland, Christoph Martin, 1733-1813 -- Continued
2567.A7 Illustrations
Illustrated editions see PT2562.A1
2567.A9 Music. Texts to which music has been composed
For the music itself, see Class M
2568 Translations
English
2568.A1 Collected works
2568.A13 Selected works
2568.A15 Selections. Quotations
2568.A17 Poetic works
2568.A19 Prose
2568.A3A-.A3Z Separate works. By original title, A-Z
Subdivide by translator (alphabetically)
Cf. PT2563.A+ Separate works
2568.A5-Z Other translations. By language, A-Z
Under each language:

.xA1-.xA19	*Collections*
.xA1	*General*
.xA13	*Selected works*
.xA15	*Selections. Quotations*
.xA17	*Poetic works*
.xA19	*Prose*
.xA2-.xZ	*Separate works. By original title, A-Z* *Subarrange by successive Cutter numbers for translators*

Biography and criticism
2569 General works
Letters
2570.A2 General
2570.A3A-.A3Z Special. By correspondents, A-Z
2570.A4-.Z5 Biographical details
2570.Z7 Anniversaries, celebrations, memorial addresses, etc. By date
2570.Z9 Iconography. Portraits. Monuments. Museums
2571 Criticism
2573 Language. Grammar. Versification
2577.W2 Wieland, Ludwig, 1777-1819 (Table P-PZ40)
2577.W4 Wienbarg, Ludolf Christian, 1802-1872 (Table P-PZ40)
2577.W5 Wiese, Sigismund, 1800-1864 (Table P-PZ40)
2577.W53 Wiest, F. (Franz), 1814-1847 (Table P-PZ40)
Wilbrandt, Adolf von, 1837-1911
2578.A1 Collected works. By date

Individual authors or works
1700-ca. 1860/70
Wilbrandt, Adolf von, 1837-1911 -- Continued
Selected works
2578.A12 General (Novels and plays)
Special
Novels and tales
2578.A13 Comprehensive collections
2578.A14 Selected novels
2578.A15 "Novellen"
2578.A16 "Neue novellen"
2578.A17 Ein neues novellenbuch
Novellen aus der Heimat see PT2578.N8
2578.A18 Dramatic works
2578.A19 Poems
2578.A41-.Z3 Separate works
Arrange school editions of texts by editor, A-Z
2578.A5 Adams söhne
2578.A7 Arria und Messalina
2578.D5 Der dornenweg
2578.E4 Erika
2578.F4 Feuerblumen
2578.F6 Franz
2578.F7 Fridolins heimliche ehe
2578.G3 Geister und menschen
2578.G4 Gespräche und monologe
2578.G5 Giordano Bruno
2578.G6 Die glückliche frau
2578.G7 Gracchus der volkstribun
2578.G8 Der graf von Hammerstein
2578.G9 Grosse zeiten
2578.H3 Hairan
2578.H5 Hermann Ifinger
2578.H6 Hiddensee
2578.H7 Hildegard Mahlmann
2578.I7 Irma
2578.J7 Jugendliebe
2578.K6 König Teja
2578.K7 Kriemhild
2578.M3 Die Maler
2578.M4 Meister Amor
2578.M5 Der meister von Palmyra
2578.N3 Natalie
2578.N4 Nero
2578.N8 Novellen aus der heimat
2578.O6 Die Osterinsel
2578.R7 Robert Kerr

Individual authors or works
1700-ca. 1860/70
Wilbrandt, Adolf von, 1837-1911
Separate works -- Continued

2578.R8 Die Rothenburger
2578.S3 Der sänger
2578.S4 Schleichendes gift
2578.T6 Timandra
2578.T7 Die tochter
2578.U8 Das urteil des Paris
2578.V3 Vater Robinson
2578.V4 Vater und sohn, und andere geschichten
2578.V5 Die vermählten
2578.V6 Villa Maria
2578.Z4 Letters
2578.Z5 Biography and criticism
Wildenbruch, Ernst von see PT2647.I43
2580.W2 Wildermuth, Frau Ottilie (Rooschutz), 1817-1877 (Table P-PZ40)
Wilhelmi, Alexander see PT2587.Z4
2580.W24 Wilhelmi, Heinrich Friedrich, 1786-1860 (Table P-PZ40)
2580.W26 Willamov, Johann Gottlieb, 1736-1777 (Table P-PZ40)
2580.W265 Willemer, Marianne von, 1784-1860 (Table P-PZ40)
"Suleika" of Goethe's "West-östlicher divan"
Cf. PT1898.W4 West-östlicher divan
2580.W27 Willenbücher, Frau Elisabeth Karoline (Thie), 1844- (Table P-PZ40)
2580.W3 Willkomm, Ernst, 1810-1886 (Table P-PZ40)
2580.W32 Willmar, Wilhelmine, 1779-1822 (Table P-PZ40)
2580.W35 Winckelmann, Johann Joachim, 1717-1768 (Table P-PZ40)
2580.W4 Winkler, Karl Gottfried Theodor, 1775-1856 (Table P-PZ40)
2580.W5 Winterfeld, Adolf Wilhelm Ernst von, 1824-1888 (Table P-PZ40)
2580.W6 Witschel, Johann Heinrich Wilhelm, 1769-1847 (Table P-PZ40)
2580.W65 Witte, Johann Heinrich Friedrich Karl, 1800-1883 (Table P-PZ40)
The education of Karl Witte see LB675.A+
Witte, Minna see PT2428.M15
2580.W7 Wittenberg, Albrecht, 1728-1807 (Table P-PZ40)
2580.W73 Wittmann, Karl Friedrich, 1839-1903 (Table P-PZ40)
2580.W78 Witzleben, Ferdinand, freiherr von, 1833-1894 (Table P-PZ40)
2580.W8 Witzleben, Karl August Friedrich von, 1773-1839 (Table P-PZ40)
Wörishöffer, Sophie (Andresen) see PT2647.O236
2580.W88 Wohlmuth, Alois, 1849- (Table P-PZ40)

Individual authors or works
1700-ca. 1860/70 -- Continued

2580.W95 Wolf, Ferdinand Joseph, 1796-1866 (Table P-PZ40)
2583.W2 Wolff, Julius, 1834-1910 (Table P-PZ40 modified)
2583.W2A61-.W2Z458 Separate works. By title
2583.W2A7 Assalide
2583.W2A8 Aus dem felde
2583.W2D7 Drohende wolken
2583.W2F3 Der fahrende schüler
2583.W2F6 Der fliegende Holländer
2583.W2H5 Die Hohkönigsburg
2583.W2J8 Die junggesellensteur
2583.W2K3 Kambyses
2583.W2L3 Der landsknecht von Cochem
2583.W2L8 Lurlei
2583.W2P2 Die Pappenheimer
2583.W2R2 Der rattenfänger von Hameln
2583.W2R3 Der raubgraf
2583.W2R4 Das recht der hagestolze
2583.W2R5 Renata
2583.W2S2 Der Sachsenspiegel
2583.W2S4 Das schwarze weib
2583.W2S5 Singuf; Rattenfängerlieder
2583.W2S8 Der sülfmeister
2583.W2T3 Tannhäuser. Ein minnesang
2583.W2T5 Till Eulenspiegel redivivus
2583.W2W5 Der wilde jäger
2583.W2W6 Das wildfangrecht
2583.W2Z2 Zweifel der liebe
2583.W3 Wolff, Oskar Ludwig Bernhard, 1799-1851 (Table P-PZ40)
2583.W32 Wolff, Pius Alexander, 1782-1828 (Table P-PZ40)
2583.W35 Wolfhagen, Friederike, 1813-1878 (Table P-PZ40)
Wolfram, Leo see PT2449.P5
2583.W36 Wollenweber, Ludwig August, 1807-1888 (Table P-PZ40)
Woltersberg, C.H. see PT1819.B15
2583.W4 Woltmann, Karl Ludwig von, 1770-1817 (Table P-PZ40)
2583.W42 Woltmann, Frau Karoline (Stosch) von, 1782-1847 (Table P-PZ40)
2583.W5 Wolzogen, Karoline (von Lengefeld) von, 1763-1847 (Table P-PZ40)
2583.W8 Würkert, Ludwig Friedrich, 1800-1876 (Table P-PZ40)
Württemberg, Alexander, graf von see PT1801.A7
2583.W85 Wurzbach, Constantin, ritter von Tannenberg, 1818-1893 (Table P-PZ40)

Individual authors or works
1700-ca. 1860/70 -- Continued

2583.W9 Wyss, Johann David, 1743-1818 (Table P-PZ40)
Author of Der schweizerische Robinson ("The Swiss Family Robinson") which was first published by his son, Johann Rudolf Wyss
2583.W92 Wyss, Johann Rudolf, 1781-1830 (Table P-PZ40)
2587.Y7 Young, Frau Betty, 1832-1887 (Table P-PZ40)
2587.Z15 Zabel, Eugen, 1851-1924 (Table P-PZ40)
2587.Z17 Zabuesnig, Johann Christoph von, 1747-1827 (Table P-PZ40)
2587.Z2 Zachariä, Friedrich Wilhelm, 1726-1777 (Table P-PZ40 modified)
2587.Z2A61-.Z2Z458 Separate works. By title
2587.Z2C6 Cortes
2587.Z2L3 Lagosiade
2587.Z2M8 Murner in der Hölle
2587.Z2P3 Der Phaeton
Die pilgrime auf Golgatha
see ML
2587.Z2R4 Der renommist
2587.Z2S4 Die schöpfung der Hölle
2587.Z2T2 Die tageszeiten
2587.Z2T3 Tayti
2587.Z2T4 Der tempel des friedens
2587.Z2V5 Die vier stufen des weiblichen alters
Zapf, Philipp see PT3919.Z27
Zapp, Arthur see PT2653.A76
2587.Z3 Zappert, Bruno, 1845-1892 (Table P-PZ40)
2587.Z4 Zechmeister, Alexander Victor, 1817-1877 (Table P-PZ40)
2587.Z6 Zedelius, Fräulein Theodore, 1834-1905 (Table P-PZ40)
2587.Z7 Zedlitz, Joseph Christian, freiherr von, 1790-1862 (Table P-PZ40)
2589.Z2 Zedtwitz, Ewald von, 1840-1896 (Table P-PZ40)
2589.Z25 Zeise, Heinrich, 1822-1914 (Table P-PZ40)
2589.Z3 Zelion, Emma von, 1840- (Table P-PZ40)
2589.Z35 Zeller, Frau Luise (Pichler), 1823-1889 (Table P-PZ40)
Zianitzka, K. Th. see PT2589.Z7
2589.Z38 Ziegler, Friedrich Wilhelm, 1759-1827 (Table P-PZ40)
2589.Z4 Ziemssen, Ludwig, 1823-1895 (Table P-PZ40)
2589.Z48 Zimmermann, Heinrich Karl Sigismund, edler von, 1847-1911 (Table P-PZ40)
Zimmermann, Moritz B. see PT1818.B26
2589.Z49 Zingeler, Karl Theodor, 1845-1923 (Table P-PZ40)
2589.Z5 Zingerle, Ignaz Vincenz, edler von Summersberg, 1825-1892 (Table P-PZ40)

Individual authors or works
1700-ca. 1860/70 -- Continued
2589.Z55 Zinzendorf, Nicolaus Ludwig, Graf von, 1700-1760 (Table P-PZ40)
Zitelmann, Ernst see PT2653.I7
Zitelmann, Ernst Otto Konrad see PT2642.E3
Zitelmann, Katharina see PT2653.I8
2589.Z6 Zitelmann, Otto Konrad, 1814-1889 (Table P-PZ40)
2589.Z7 Zitz, Frau Kathinka (Halein), 1801-1877 (Table P-PZ40)
Zöge von Manteuffel, Ursula see PT2653.O42
2589.Z75 Zoller, Franz Carl, 1748-1829 (Table P-PZ40)
2589.Z8 Zollikofer, Hektor, 1799-1853 (Table P-PZ40)
2589.Z9 Zschokke, Emil, 1808-1889 (Table P-PZ40)
Zschokke, Heinrich, 1771-1848
2591.A1 Collected works. By date
2591.A15 Collected novels and tales
2591.A3-.Z29 Separate works. By title
Subarrange school editions by editor, A-Z
2591.A3 Abällino der grosse bandit. ("The bravo of Venice.")
2591.A4 Das abenteuer des neujahrsnacht
2591.A5 Addrich im moos
2591.A6 Aehrenlese
2591.A7 Alamontade der galeerensklave
2591.B3 Der baierischen geschichten
2591.B6 Das blaue wunder
2591.B8 Die branntweinpest
2591.F4 Feldblumen
2591.F7 Der freihof von Aarau
2591.G3 Galeerensklave
2591.G6 Das goldmacherdorf
2591.J6 Jonathan Frock
2591.L6 Das loch im aermel
2591.M4 Meister Jordan ("Labour stands on golden feet.")
2591.P7 Die prinzessin von Wolfenbüttel
2591.R6 Die rose von Disentis
Eine selbstschau see PT2591.Z8
2591.T6 Der tote Gast
Veronica see PT2591.F7
2591.W6 Das wirtshaus zu Cransac
2591.Z2 Der zerbrochene krug
Translations
2591.Z3-.Z39 English
Alphabetically by original title. Subdivide by translator, e.g.
2591.Z32L4 Abällino, tr. by Lewis
2591.Z4-.Z49 French

Individual authors or works
1700-ca. 1860/70
Zschokke, Heinrich, 1771-1848
Translations -- Continued
2591.Z5-.Z69 Other languages (alphabetically)
e.g.
2591.Z6L6 Spanish tr. of Das loch in aermel
2591.Z7 Adaptations, imitations, dramatizations
Biography and criticism
2591.Z8 Autobiography. By date
2591.Z8A5-.Z8Z Translations. By language, A-Z
e.g.
2591.Z8E5 English
2591.Z9 General treatises. Life and works
2592.Z3 Zuccalmaglio, Anton Wilhelm Florentin von, 1803-1869 (Table P-PZ40)
2592.Z32 Zuccalmaglio, V. J. von (Vincenz Jacob), 1806-1876 (Table P-PZ40)
Zündt, Ernst Anton Joseph see PT3919.Z8
2592.Z5 Zwicky, Leberecht, 1820-1906 (Table P-PZ40)
2592.Z8 Zwierlein, Adelheid (von Stolterfoth) baronin von, 1800-1875 (Table P-PZ40)
1860/70-1960
Except PT2616 and PT2638, the author number is to be taken from that part of the name beginning with the second letter. Under PT2616, a special scheme is provided. Under PT2638, names beginning with "Sch," the author number is taken from that part of the name beginning with the fourth letter
Subarrange each author by Table P-PZ40 unless otherwise specified
2600 Anonymous works (Table P-PZ28)
2601 A - Az
2601.C53 Achleitner, Arthur, 1858- (Table P-PZ40)
2601.D64 Adlersfeld, Frau Eufemia (Ballestrem di Castellengo), 1854- (Table P-PZ40)
2601.K7 Akunian, Frau Ilse (Lévien), 1852-1908 (Table P-PZ40)
Al-Raschid Bey, Frau Helene see PT2603.O32
2601.L14 Albers, Paul, 1852- (Table P-PZ40)
Alberti, Conrad see PT2639.I92
2601.L4 Alexandrowitsch, Leon (Table P-PZ40)
2601.L78 Altenberg, Peter, 1859-1919 (Table P-PZ40)
Ambrosius, Johanna see PT2645.O47
Andreas, Alexander, 1836-1898 see PT2603.A265
2601.N37 Andreas, Fred, 1898- (Table P-PZ40)
2601.N4 Andreas-Salomé, Lou, 1861-1937 (Table P-PZ40)
2601.N437 Andresen, Stine, 1849-1927 (Table P-PZ40)

Individual authors or works
1860/70-1960
A - Az -- Continued

2601.R55 Arnold, Franz, 1878- (Table P-PZ40)
2601.S2 Asch, Shalom, 1880- (Table P-PZ40)
Aspern, Elisabeth von see PT2639.T865
Aspern-Buchmeier, Elisabeth von see PT2639.T865
2601.U18 Aubertin, Victor, 1870- (Table P-PZ40)
Auer, Grethe, b. l871 see PT2613.U76
2601.U293 Auerbach, Walter, 1909- (Table P-PZ40)
2601.U3 Auernheimer, Raoul, 1876- (Table P-PZ40)
2601.V5 Avenarius, Ferdinand, 1856-1923 (Table P-PZ40)
2603 B - Bz
2603.A2 Bachwitz, Hans, 1882- (Table P-PZ40)
2603.A265 Badendick, Alexander, 1836-1898 (Table P-PZ40)
2603.A286 Baeran, Alois, 1872-1936 (Table P-PZ40)
2603.A33 Bahr, Hermann, 1863- (Table P-PZ40)
2603.A53 Barlach, Ernst, 1870-1938 (Table P-PZ40)
Barthel, Kurt see PT2621.U112
2603.A578 Barthel, Max, 1893- (Table P-PZ40)
2603.A63 Bartsch, Rudolf Hans, 1873- (Table P-PZ40)
2603.A73 Baudissin, Wolf Ernst Hugo Emil, graf von, 1867-1926 (Table P-PZ40)
2603.A778 Bauer, Michael, 1871-1929 (Table P-PZ40)
2603.A81 Baum, Oskar, 1883- (Table P-PZ40)
2603.A815 Baum, Vicki, 1888- (Table P-PZ40)
2603.A82 Baumbach, Rudolf, 1840-1905 (Table P-PZ40)
2603.A886 Bayer, Haus, 1914- (Table P-PZ40)
2603.A9 Bayer, Robert von, 1835-1902 (Table P-PZ40)
2603.E15 Becner, Johannes, 1891-1958 (Table P-PZ40)
2603.E33 Beheim-Schwarzbach, Martin, 1900- (Table P-PZ40)
2603.E34 Behrens, Bertha, 1850-1912 (Table P-PZ40)
Bell, Anthea see PT2603.E422
2603.E422 Bemmann, Hans (Table P-PZ40)
2603.E46 Benn, Gottfried, 1886- (Table P-PZ40)
2603.E55 Beradt, Martin, 1881- (Table P-PZ40)
2603.E58 Berend, Alice, 1878- (Table P-PZ40)
2603.E59 Bergengruen, Werner, 1892 (Table P-PZ40)
2603.E7 Bernhard, Marie, 1852- (Table P-PZ40)
2603.E715 Bernoulli, Carl Albrecht, 1868-1937 (Table P-PZ40)
2603.E72 Bernstein, Elsa (Porges), 1866- (Table P-PZ40)
2603.E73 Bernstein, Max, 1854- (Table P-PZ40)
2603.E755 Berstl, Julius, 1883- (Table P-PZ40)
2603.E79 Bethge, Friedrich, 1891-1963 (Table P-PZ40)
2603.E8 Bethge, Hans, 1876- (Table P-PZ40)
2603.E85 Betsch, Roland, 1888- (Table P-PZ40)
2603.E94 Beyerlein, Franz Adam, 1871- (Table P-PZ40)

Individual authors or works
1860/70-1960
B - Bz -- Continued

2603.I23 Biedermann, Felix, 1870- (Table P-PZ40)
2603.I25 Bierbaum, Otto Julius, 1865-1910 (Table P-PZ40)
2603.I45 Billinger, Richard, 1893- (Table P-PZ40)
2603.I59 Binding, Rudolf Georg, 1867- (Table P-PZ40)
2603.I75 Birkner, Friede, 1891- (Table P-PZ40)
2603.L13 Blaich, Hans Erich, 1873-1945 (Table P-PZ40)
2603.L27 Blasius (Table P-PZ40)
2603.L33 Bleibtreu, Karl, 1859- (Table P-PZ40)
2603.L6 Bloem, Walter, 1868- (Table P-PZ40)
2603.L62 Bloem, Walter Julius, 1898- (Table P-PZ40)
2603.L75 Blunck, Hans Friedrich, 1888- (Table P-PZ40)
2603.O25 Bodemer, Horst, 1875- (Table P-PZ40)
2603.O32 Böhlau, Helene, 1859- (Table P-PZ40)
2603.O36 Böhme, Frau Margarete, 1869- (Table P-PZ40)
2603.O394 Böll, Heinrich, 1917- (Table P-PZ40)
2603.O395 Bölsche, Wilhelm, 1861- (Table P-PZ40)
2603.O42 Bötticher, Georg, 1849-1918 (Table P-PZ40)
2603.O44 Bötticher, Hans, 1883-1934 (Table P-PZ40)
2603.O614 Bondy, Fritz, 1888- (Table P-PZ40)
2603.O65 Bonsels, Waldemar, 1881- (Table P-PZ40)
2603.O68 Borchardt, Georg Hermann, 1871- (Table P-PZ40)
2603.O92 Boy-Ed, Frau Ida, 1852-1928 (Table P-PZ40)
2603.R15 Brachvogel, Frau Carry (Hellmann), 1864- (Table P-PZ40)
2603.R34 Braun, Felix, 1885- (Table P-PZ40)
2603.R357 Braun, Isabella, 1851-1886 (Table P-PZ40)
2603.R36 Braun, Lily (von Kretschman) von Gizycki, 1865-1916 (Table P-PZ40)
2603.R39 Brausewetter, Artur Friedrich Leon, 1864- (Table P-PZ40)
2603.R415 Brehm, Bruno, 1892- (Table P-PZ40)
2603.R657 Broch, Hermann, 1886-1951 (Table P-PZ40)
2603.R68 Brod, Max, 1884- (Table P-PZ40)
2603.R72 Bröger, Karl, 1886- (Table P-PZ40)
Bruckner, Ferdinand, 1891-1958 see PT2642.A3
2603.R85 Brust, Alfred, 1891- (Table P-PZ40)
2603.U15 Buber, Martin, 1878- (Table P-PZ40)
2603.U16 Buchbinder, Bernhard, 1854- (Table P-PZ40)
2603.U51 Bulcke, Carl, 1876- (Table P-PZ40)
Bülow, Frida Sophie Luise, freifraulein von see PT1828.B75
Burckhardt, Felix see PT2603.L27
2603.U67 Burggraf, Waldfried, 1895- (Table P-PZ40)

Individual authors or works
1860/70-1960
B - Bz -- Continued

2603.U8 Busch, Wilhelm, 1832-1908 (Table P-PZ40)
Cf. NC1509.B8 Caricature
Cf. PN6195 Wit and humor
2603.U86 Busse, Carl, 1872-1918 (Table P-PZ40)
2603.U865 Busse, Hermann Eris, 1891- (Table P-PZ40)
2603.U9 Butenschön, Frau Helene, 1874- (Table P-PZ40)
2605 C - Cz
2605.A65 Carossa, Hans, 1878- (Table P-PZ40)
2605.H2 Chamberlain, Houston Stewart, 1855-1927 (Table P-PZ40)
2605.H5 Chlumberg, Hans, d. 1930 (Table P-PZ40)
2605.H54 Chodziesner, Gertrud, 1894-1943? (Table P-PZ40)
2605.L25 Clark-Schwarzenbach, Annemarie, 1908-1942 (Table P-PZ40)
2605.L394 Clement, Bertha, 1852-1930 (Table P-PZ40)
2605.O32 Cohn, Frau Clara (Viebig), 1860- (Table P-PZ40)
2605.O328 Cohn, Moritz, 1844- (Table P-PZ40)
2605.O4 Colerus, Egmont, 1888- (Table P-PZ40)
2605.O5 Conradi, Hermann, 1862-1890 (Table P-PZ40)
Correi, El- see PT2642.H63
Coryllis, Peter see PT2601.U293
2605.O94 Courths, Frau Hedwig (Mahler), 1867- (Table P-PZ40)
2605.S7 Csokor, Franz Theodor, 1885- (Table P-PZ40)
2607 D - Dz
2607.A25 Däubler, Theodor, 1876- (Table P-PZ40)
2607.A83 Dauthendey, Max, 1867-1918 (Table P-PZ40)
2607.A92 Davis, Gustav, 1856- (Table P-PZ40)
2607.E32 Dehmel, Richard, 1863-1920 (Table P-PZ40)
Delle Grazie, Eugenie see PT2613.R41
2607.E47 Delmont, Joseph, 1873- (Table P-PZ40)
2607.H65 Dhorn, Anton (Table P-PZ40)
2607.I37 Diederichs, Frau Helene (Voigt), 1875- (Table P-PZ40)
2607.I44 Diers, Frau Marie (Binde), 1867- (Table P-PZ40)
2607.I4645 Dietz, Rudolf, 1863-1942 (Table P-PZ40)
2607.I47 Dill, Liesbet, 1877- (Table P-PZ40)
2607.I6 Ditzen, Rudolf, 1893-1947 (Table P-PZ40)
2607.O35 Döblin, Alfred, 1878- (Table P-PZ40)
2607.O37 Dörfler, Peter, 1878- (Table P-PZ40)
2607.O42 Döring, Konrad (Table P-PZ40)
Doermann, Felix see PT2603.I23
2607.O493 Dohm, Hedwig, 1833-1919 (Table P-PZ40)
2607.O53 Dominik, Hans Joachim, 1872- (Table P-PZ40)
2607.R66 Dreyer, Max, 1862- (Table P-PZ40)
2607.R75 Droonberg, Emil, 1864- (Table P-PZ40)

Individual authors or works
1860/70-1960
D - Dz -- Continued

2607.U36 Dülberg, Franz, 1873- (Table P-PZ40)
2607.U493 Dürrenmatt, Friedrich (Table P-PZ40)
2607.U77 Duncker, Dora, 1855-1916 (Table P-PZ40)
2607.W5 Dwinger, Edwin, Erich, 1898- (Table P-PZ40)
2609 E - Ez
2609.B2 Ebbinghaus, Jörgen, 1896- (Table P-PZ40)
2609.B42 Ebermann, Leo, fl. 1897 (Table P-PZ40)
2609.B43 Ebermayer, Erich, 1900- (Table P-PZ40)
Ebers, Georg Moritz see PT1851.E6
2609.C48 Eckart, Dietrich, 1868-1923 (Table P-PZ40)
2609.C63 Eckstein-Deiner, Bertha, 1874-1948 (Table P-PZ40)
2609.D7 Edschmid, Kasimir, 1890- (Table P-PZ40)
2609.G6 Egidy, Emmy von, 1872- (Table P-PZ40)
2609.H72 Ehrenfels, Alma Johanna, freifrau von, 1889- (Table P-PZ40)
2609.H78 Ehrler, Hans Heinrich, 1872- (Table P-PZ40)
2609.I29 Eider, K. von der, 1867-1941 (Table P-PZ40)
2609.I3 Eidlitz, Walther, 1892- (Table P-PZ40)
2609.I7 Eisenlohr, Friedrich, fl. 1920- (Table P-PZ40)
2609.L87 Elster, Otto, 1852-1922 (Table P-PZ40)
2609.L94 Elzer, Frau Margarete, 1889- (Table P-PZ40)
2609.N43 Engel, Alexander, 1869- (Table P-PZ40)
2609.N45 Engel, Georg Julius Leopold, 1866-1931 (Table P-PZ40)
2609.N484 Engel, Theodor, 1842-1933 (Table P-PZ40)
2609.N76 Enking, Ottomar, 1867- (Table P-PZ40)
Epp, Jovita, 1909- see PT2609.P37
2609.P37 Epp de Hary, Leonor, 1909- (Table P-PZ40)
Ernst, Otto see PT2638.M5
2609.R73 Ernst, Paul, 1866-1933 (Table P-PZ40)
2609.R86 Ertl, Emil, 1860- (Table P-PZ40)
2609.S52 Eschstruth, Nataly von, 1860- (Table P-PZ40)
2609.S81 Essig, Hermann, 1878-1918 (Table P-PZ40)
2609.U43 Eulenberg, Herbert, 1876- (Table P-PZ40)
2609.W45 Ewers, Hanns Heinz, 1871- (Table P-PZ40)
2609.Y7 Eyth, Max von, 1836-1906 (Table P-PZ40)
2611 F - Fz
2611.A29 Fabrizius, Peter (Table P-PZ40)
Fabry, Joseph B. see PT2611.A29
2611.A52 Falk, Minna, 1874- (Table P-PZ40)
2611.A57 Falke, Gustav, 1853-1916 (Table P-PZ40)
Fallada, Hans, 1893-1947 see PT2607.I6
2611.E24 Federer, Heinrich, 1866-1928 (Table P-PZ40)
2611.E62 Fellinger, Richard Joseph, 1872 (Table P-PZ40)
2611.E83 Fercher von Steinwand, 1828-1902 (Table P-PZ40)

Individual authors or works
1860/70-1960
F - Fz -- Continued

2611.E8375	Ferrari, A., fl. 1869-1870 (Table P-PZ40)
2611.E85	Feuchtwanger, Lion, 1884- (Table P-PZ40)
2611.I33	Fillak, Anton, 1895-1977 (Table P-PZ40)
2611.I39	Finckh, Ludwig, 1876- (Table P-PZ40)
2611.I66	Fischer, Hans, 1869- (Table P-PZ40)
2611.L14	Flaischlen, Cäsar, 1864-1920 (Table P-PZ40)
2611.L2	Flake, Otto, 1882- (Table P-PZ40)
2611.L46	Fleisser, Marieluise, 1901- (Table P-PZ40)
2611.L72	Florenz, Karl, 1865-1939 (Table P-PZ40)
	Fock, Gorch, 1880-1916 see PT2621.I6
2611.O52	Forbes-Mosse, Frau Irene (Flemming), 1864- (Table P-PZ40)
2611.R186	Franck, Hans, 1879- (Table P-PZ40)
2611.R23	Frank, Bruno, 1887- (Table P-PZ40)
2611.R255	Frank, Josef Maria, 1895- (Table P-PZ40)
2611.R26	Frank, Leonhard, 1882- (Table P-PZ40)
2611.R27	Frank, Paul, 1885- (Table P-PZ40)
	Frank, Ulrich, 1850-1924 see PT2647.O63
2611.R3	Franzos, Karl Emil, 1848-1904 (Table P-PZ40)
	Frapan, Ilse see PT2601.K7
2611.R38	Freissler, Ernst Wolfgang, 1884- (Table P-PZ40)
2611.R39	Freksa, Friedrich, 1882- (Table P-PZ40)
2611.R42	Frenssen, Gustav, 1863- (Table P-PZ40)
2611.R485	Frey, Alexander Moriz, 1881- (Table P-PZ40)
2611.R657	Friedlaender, Salomo, 1871-1946 (Table P-PZ40)
2611.R67	Friedmann, Armin, 1863- (Table P-PZ40)
2611.R7	Friedmann-Frederich, Fritz, 1883- (Table P-PZ40)
2611.R87	Fröschel, Georg, 1891- (Table P-PZ40)
2611.U44	Fünfgeld, Frau Margarete Marie (von Oertzen), 1868- (Table P-PZ40)
2611.U72	Fulda, Ludwig, 1862- (Table P-PZ40)
2613	G - Gz
2613.A14	Gabelentz, Georg von der, 1868- (Table P-PZ40)
2613.A31	Gagern, Friedrich, freiherr von, 1882- (Table P-PZ40)
	Galahad, Sir, 1874-1948 see PT2609.C63
2613.A51	Ganghofer, Ludwig Albert, 1855-1920 (Table P-PZ40)
2613.E26	Geibel, Peter, 1841-1901 (Table P-PZ40)
2613.E28	Geiger, Albert, 1866-1915 (Table P-PZ40)
2613.E33	Geissler, Horst Wolfram, 1893- (Table P-PZ40)
2613.E34	Geissler, Max, 1868- (Table P-PZ40)
2613.E456	Gensichen, Otto Franz, 1847- (Table P-PZ40)
2613.E47	George, Stefan Anton, 1868-1933 (Table P-PZ40)
2613.E495	Ger, A., 1857-1922 (Table P-PZ40)
2613.E53	Gerhard, Frau Adele, 1868- (Table P-PZ40)

Individual authors or works
1860/70-1960
G - Gz -- Continued

2613.E75 Gersdorff, Ada von, 1854- (Table P-PZ40)
2613.E95 Geyer, Siegfried (Table P-PZ40)
2613.F4 Gfeller, Simon, 1868-1943 (Table P-PZ40)
2613.I78 Ginzkey, Franz Karl, 1871- (Table P-PZ40)
2613.L3 Glaeser, Ernst, 1902- (Table P-PZ40)
2613.L8 Gluth, Oskar, 1887- (Table P-PZ40)
2613.M4 Gmelin, Otto, 1886- (Table P-PZ40)
2613.O37 Gött, Emil, 1864-1908 (Table P-PZ40)
2613.O38 Götz, Kurt, 1888- (Table P-PZ40)
2613.O39 Goetz, Wolfgang, 1885- (Table P-PZ40)
2613.O56 Goldschmidt, Lothar, 1862- (Table P-PZ40)
2613.R14 Grabein, Paul, 1869- (Table P-PZ40)
2613.R27 Graf, Oskar Maria, 1894- (Table P-PZ40)
2613.R41 Grazie, Marie Eugenie delle, 1864-1931 (Table P-PZ40)
2613.R42 Greber, Julius, 1868-1914 (Table P-PZ40)
2613.R46 Greinz, Rudolf Heinrich, 1866- (Table P-PZ40)
2613.R464 Grelling, Richard, 1853-1929 (Table P-PZ40)
2613.R5 Griese, Friedrich, 1890- (Table P-PZ40)
2613.R52 Grimm, Hans, 1875- (Table P-PZ40)
2613.R846 Grünn, Karl, 1855-1930 (Table P-PZ40)
2613.U33 Guenther, Johannes von, 1886- (Table P-PZ40)
2613.U45 Guggenheim, Werner Johannes, 1895- (Table P-PZ40)
2613.U5 Gumppenberg, Hanns, freiherr von, 1866- (Table P-PZ40)
2613.U76 Güterbock, Grethe Auer, b. 1871 (Table P-PZ40)
2613.Y7 Gysae, Otto, 1877- (Table P-PZ40)
2615 H - Hauptmann
2615.A16 Haas, Rudolf, 1877- (Table P-PZ40)
2615.A215 Habernig, Christine (Thonhausen), 1915-1973 (Table P-PZ40)
2615.A26 Haebler, Hans von, 1870- (Table P-PZ40)
2615.A263 Hähnel, Franziskus, 1864- (Table P-PZ40)
2615.A2634 Haemmerling, Konrad, 1888-1957 (Table P-PZ40)
2615.A265 Haensel, Carl, 1889- (Table P-PZ40)
2615.A34 Halbe, Max, 1865- (Table P-PZ40)
2615.A36 Halberthal, Awrum, 1881- (Table P-PZ40)
2615.A539 Hampel, Fritz, 1895-1932 (Table P-PZ40)
2615.A55 Handel-Mazzetti, Enrica Ludovica Maria, freiin von, 1871- (Table P-PZ40)
2615.A576 Hansson, Laura Mohr, 1854-1928 (Table P-PZ40)
2615.A58 Hansson, Ola, 1860-1929 (Table P-PZ40)
Hansson-Marholm, Laura, 1854-1928 see PT2615.A576
2615.A59 Hanstein, Adalbert von, 1861-1904 (Table P-PZ40)
2615.A6 Hanstein, Otfrid von, 1869- (Table P-PZ40)

Individual authors or works
1860/70-1960
H - Hauptmann -- Continued
2615.A62 Harbou, Thea von, 1888- (Table P-PZ40)
2615.A628 Harden, Maximilian, 1861-1927 (Table P-PZ40)
2615.A637 Hardt, Ernst, 1876- (Table P-PZ40)
2615.A65 Harich, Walther, 1888- (Table P-PZ40)
2615.A67 Harlan, Walter, 1867-1931 (Table P-PZ40)
2615.A75 Hart, Julius, 1859-1930 (Table P-PZ40)
2615.A76 Hartleben, Otto Erich, 1864-1905 (Table P-PZ40)
2615.A8 Hasenclever, Walter, 1890- (Table P-PZ40)
2615.A96 Hauptmann, Carl Ferdinand Maximilian, 1858-1921 (Table P-PZ40)
Hauptmann, Gerhart Johann Robert, 1862-
2616.A1 Collected works. By date
2616.A15 Collected fiction. By date
2616.A17 Collected poems. By date
2616.A19 Collected plays. By date
2616.A3-.Z29 Separate works
2616.A6 Anna, ein ländliches liebesgedicht
2616.A65 Der apostel
2616.A7 Der arme Heinrich
2616.A8 Atlantis
2616.A85 Die Atriden-Tetralogie
2616.B3 Bahnwärter Thiel; Der apostel
2616.B4 Der baum von Gallowayshire
2616.B5 Der biberpelz
2616.B55 Die blaue blume
2616.B6 Der bogen des Odysseus
2616.B8 Buch der leidenschaft
2616.C6 College Crampton
2616.D3 Der dämon
2616.D6 Dorothea Angermann
2616.E5 Einsame menschen
2616.E6 Elga
2616.E8 Eulenspiegel
2616.F2 Familiendramen (4 plays)
2616.F3 Fasching
2616.F4 Festspiel in deutschen reimen
2616.F5 Florian Geyer
2616.F7 Das friedensfest
2616.F8 Fuhrmann Henschel
2616.G3 Gabriel Schillings flucht
2616.G55 Die goldene harfe
Griechischer frühling see DF726
2616.G6 Griselda
2616.H3 Hamlet in Wittenberg

Individual authors or works
1860/70-1960
Hauptmann, Gerhart Johann Robert, 1862-
Separate works -- Continued

2616.H4 Hanneles himmelfahrt
2616.H5 Hexenritt, ein satyrspiel
2616.H6 Das hirtenlied
2616.H7 Die hochzeit auf Buchenhorst
2616.I3 Im wirbel der berufung
2616.I4 Indipohdi
2616.I5 Die insel der grossen mutter
2616.I6 Iphigenie in Delphi
2616.J7 Die jungfern vom Bischofsberg
2616.K3 Kaiser Karls geisel
2616.K45 Der Ketzer von Soana
Kollege Crampton see PT2616.C6
(2616.L4) Lohengrin
see PZ34.1
2616.M3 Märchendramen (5 plays)
2616.M4 Das meerwunder
2616.M5 Michael Kramer
2616.N3 Der narr in Christo, Emanuel Quint
(2616.P3) Parsival
see PZ34.1
2616.P4 Peter Brauer
2616.P5 Phantom
2616.P7 Promethidenloos
2616.R3 Die ratten
2616.R6 Rose Bernd
2616.R7 Der rote hahn
2616.S4 Schluck und Jau
2616.S6 Sonette
2616.S65 Die spitzhacke
2616.S7 Spuk: Die schwarze maske, schauspiel; Hexenritt, einsatyrspiel (2 one-act plays)
Till Eulenspiegel see PT2616.E8
2616.U5 Um volk und geist, ansprachen
2616.U6 Und Pippa tanzt
2616.V35 Veland
Die versunkene glocke
2616.V4 Texts. By date
2616.V4A-.V4Z Edition. By editor
2616.V6 Vor sonnenaufgang
2616.V7 Vor sonnenuntergang
Wanda (Der dämon) see PT2616.D3
2616.W4 Die weber
2616.W45 Der weisse heiland

Individual authors or works
1860/70-1960
Hauptmann, Gerhart Johann Robert, 1862-
Separate works -- Continued

2616.W5 Winterballade
Translations
2616.Z3-.Z39 English (Table PT3)
2616.Z4-.Z49 French (Table PT3)
2616.Z6-.Z69 Other languages (alphabetically)
2616.Z8 Journals. Memoirs. Letters. By date
2616.Z9 Biography and criticism
2617 Hauptmann - Hz
2617.A14 Hauptmann, Hans, 1865- (Table P-PZ40)
2617.A46 Hausmann, Manfred, 1898- (Table P-PZ40)
2617.A77 Havemann, Julius, 1866- (Table P-PZ40)
2617.E22 Heer, Jakob Christoph, 1859-1925 (Table P-PZ40)
2617.E24 Hegeler, Wilhelm, 1870- (Table P-PZ40)
2617.E25 Heiberg, Hermann, 1840-1910 (Table P-PZ40 modified)
2617.E25A61-.E25Z458 Separate works
2617.E25A7 Apotheker Heinrich
2617.E25A8 Aus den papieren der herzogin von Seeland
2617.E25D2 Dr. Gaarz' patienten
2617.E25D8 Dunst aus der tiefe
2617.E25F3 Die familie von Stiegritz
2617.E25F4 Fast um eine nichts
2617.E25G6 Die goldene schlange
2617.E25H4 Heimat
2617.E25L2 Der landvogt von Pelworm
2617.E25L8 Liebeswerben und andere geschichten
2617.E25M4 Merkur und Amor
2617.E25R6 Die Rixdorfs
2617.E25S3 Schulter an schulter
2617.E25S4 Die schwarze marit
2617.E25S6 Die spinne
2617.E25S7 Streifzüge ins leben
(2617.E27) Heijermans, Herman, 1864-1924
see PT5841
2617.E32 Heimann, Moritz, 1868-1925 (Table P-PZ40)
Held, Franz see PT2617.E822
2617.E59 Henckell, Karl Friedrich, 1864- (Table P-PZ40)
2617.E6 Henschke, Alfred, 1891-1928 (Table P-PZ40)
Hermann, Georg see PT2603.O68
2617.E725 Herrig, Hans, 1845-1892 (Table P-PZ40 modified)
2617.E725A61-.E725Z458 Separate works. By title

Individual authors or works
1860/70-1960
Hauptmann - Hz
Herrig, Hans, 1845-1892
Separate works. By title -- Continued

2617.E725L6-.E725L9 Luther
2617.E725L6 Texts. By date
2617.E725L7-.E725L79 Translations. By language (alphabetically)
2617.E725L7 English translations. By date
2617.E725L8-.E725L9 Criticism
2617.E734 Herrmann, Gerhart, 1901- (Table P-PZ40)
2617.E75 Herschel, Max, 1840-1921 (Table P-PZ40)
2617.E78 Herwig, Franz, 1880- (Table P-PZ40)
2617.E822 Herzfeld, Franz, 1862-1908 (Table P-PZ40)
2617.E825 Herzl, Theodor, 1860-1904 (Table P-PZ40)
2617.E83 Herzog, Rudolf, 1869- (Table P-PZ40)
2617.E85 Hesse, Hermann, 1877- (Table P-PZ40)
2617.E855 Hessel, Franz, 1880- (Table P-PZ40)
2617.E86 Hesselbacher, Karl, 1871- (Table P-PZ40)
2617.E88 Heubner, Rudolf, 1867- (Table P-PZ40)
2617.E92 Heyck, Hans, 1891- (Table P-PZ40)
2617.E94 Heyking, Elisabeth (von Flemming) baronin von, 1861-1925 (Table P-PZ40)
2617.E95 Heymann, Robert, 1879- (Table P-PZ40)
Hildebrand, E. see PT2645.O6
2617.I374 Hille, Peter, 1854-1904 (Table P-PZ40)
2617.I65 Hirsch, Franz Wilhelm, 1844-1920 (Table P-PZ40)
2617.I68 Hirsch, Marie, 1848-1911 (Table P-PZ40)
2617.I76 Hirschfeld, Georg, 1873- (Table P-PZ40)
2617.I77 Hirschfeld, Hermann, 1842- (Table P-PZ40)
2617.I78 Hirschfeld, Ludwig, 1882- (Table P-PZ40)
2617.O15 Hochdorf, Max, 1880- (Table P-PZ40)
2617.O18 Hochstetter, Gustav, 1873- (Table P-PZ40)
2617.O19 Hoechstetter, Sophie, 1873- (Table P-PZ40)
2617.O2 Höcker, Oskar, 1840-1894 (Table P-PZ40)
2617.O22 Höcker, Paul Oskar, 1865- (Table P-PZ40)
Höffer, W. see PT2647.O236
2617.O24 Höffner, Johannes, 1868- (Table P-PZ40)
2617.O245 Höffner, Frau Klara (Gutsche), 1875- (Table P-PZ40)
2617.O2647 Hönig, Franz, 1867-1927 (Table P-PZ40)
2617.O316 Hofer, Fridolin, 1861-1920 (Table P-PZ40)
Hoffman, Bertha Wilhelmine see PT2359.H8
2617.O452 Hoffmann von Wangenheim, Pauline, 1856- (Table P-PZ40)

Individual authors or works
1860/70-1960
Hauptmann - Hz -- Continued

2617.O47 Hofmannsthal, Hugo Hofmann, edler von, 1874-1929 (Table P-PZ40)
2617.O53 Hohlbaum, Robert, 1886- (Table P-PZ40)
2617.O58 Holitscher, Arthur, 1869- (Table P-PZ40)
2617.O61 Hollaender, Felix, 1868- (Table P-PZ40)
2617.O64 Hollander, Walther Georg Heinrich von, 1892- (Table P-PZ40)
2617.O66 Holm, Korfiz, 1872- (Table P-PZ40)
Holmsen, Bjarne Peter (pseudonym of Arno Holz and Johannes Schlaf) see PT2617.O72
2617.O72 Holz, Arno, 1863-1929 (Table P-PZ40)
2617.O74 Holzamer, Wilhelm, 1870-1907 (Table P-PZ40)
Horst, Sophie von der see PT2647.O236
2617.O87 Hostasch, Josef, 1864- (Table P-PZ40)
2617.O918 Hotz, Georg, b. 1862 (Table P-PZ40)
2617.U26 Huch, Friedrich Georg Edmund, 1873-1913 (Table P-PZ40)
2617.U28 Huch, Frau Ricarda Octavia, 1864- (Table P-PZ40)
2617.U29 Huch, Rudolf, 1862- (Table P-PZ40)
2617.U42 Hülsen, Hans von, 1890- (Table P-PZ40)
2617.U57 Huggenberger, Alfred, 1867- (Table P-PZ40)
2617.U66 Huna, Ludwig, 1872- (Table P-PZ40)
2617.Y2 Hyan, Hans, 1868- (Table P-PZ40)
2618 I - Iz
2618.L3 Ilgenstein, Heinrich, 1875- (Table P-PZ40)
2618.M6 Impekoven, Anton, 1881- (Table P-PZ40)
2618.S4 Isemann, Bernd, 1881- (Table P-PZ40)
2619 J - Jz
2619.A2 Jacob, Heinrich Eduard, 1889- (Table P-PZ40)
2619.A36 Jacoby, Carl M., 1871- (Table P-PZ40)
2619.A37 Jacoby, Wilhelm, 1855- (Table P-PZ40)
2619.A38 Jacques, Norbert, 1880- (Table P-PZ40)
2619.A63 Jakob, der Zweite (Table P-PZ40)
2619.A68 Janitschek, Frau Maria (Tölk), 1860-1927 (Table P-PZ40)
2619.E26 Jegerlehner, Johann, 1871- (Table P-PZ40)
2619.E36 Jellinek, Oskar, 1886- (Table P-PZ40)
2619.E8 Jerusalem, Frau Else (Kotnyi), 1877- (Table P-PZ40)
For her works in Spanish see PQ7797.J35
2619.E82 Jerusalem, Julie (Table P-PZ40)
2619.O6 Johst, Hanns, 1890- (Table P-PZ40)
2619.O85 Josky, Felix, 1875- (Table P-PZ40)
2619.U5 Jungnickel, Max, 1890- (Table P-PZ40)
2621 K - Kz
2621.A23 Kästner, Erich, 1899- (Table P-PZ40)

Individual authors or works
1860/70-1960
K - Kz -- Continued

2621.A26 Kafka, Franz, 1883-1924 (Table P-PZ40)
Kahlenberg, Hans von see PT2621.E79
2621.A33 Kaiser, Georg, 1878- (Table P-PZ40)
Kampfmuth, Georg see PT2621.E26
2621.A55 Kantor-Berg, Friedrich, 1908- (Table P-PZ40)
2621.A58 Kappus, Franz Xaver, 1883- (Table P-PZ40)
2621.A595 Karger, Robert, 1874-1946 (Table P-PZ40)
2621.A64 Karlweis, Marta, 1889- (Table P-PZ40)
2621.A66 Karrillon, Adam, 1853-1938 (Table P-PZ40)
2621.A95 Kaus, Frau Gina, 1894- (Table P-PZ40)
2621.E25 Keim, Franz, 1840-1918 (Table P-PZ40)
2621.E26 Keiter, Heinrich, 1853-1898 (Table P-PZ40)
2621.E27 Keiter, Frau Therese (Kellner), 1859- (Table P-PZ40)
2621.E38 Keller, Paul, 1873- (Table P-PZ40)
2621.E51 Kellermann, Bernhard, 1879- (Table P-PZ40)
2621.E58 Kempner-Hochstädt, Max, 1863- (Table P-PZ40)
2621.E75 Kesser, Hermann, 1880- (Table P-PZ40)
2621.E79 Kessler, Frau Helene (von Monbart), 1870- (Table P-PZ40)
2621.E83 Kesten, Hermann, 1900- (Table P-PZ40)
2621.E93 Keyserling, Eduard Heinrich Nikolaus, graf von, 1855-1918 (Table P-PZ40)
2621.I6 Kinau, Johann, 1880-1916 (Table P-PZ40)
2621.I7 Kirchbach, Wolfgang, 1857-1906 (Table P-PZ40)
2621.I89 Kiss, Edmund, 1886- (Table P-PZ40)
Klabund see PT2617.E6
2621.L34 Klein, Ernst, 1876- (Table P-PZ40)
2621.L683 Klitzing, Wilhelm von (Table P-PZ40)
2621.L7 Kloerss, Frau Sophie (Kessler), 1866- (Table P-PZ40)
2621.N36 Kneip, Jakob, 1881- (Table P-PZ40)
Knight, Max see PT2611.A29
Knobelsdorff-Brenkenhoff, Frau von see PT2609.S52
2621.O2362 Koch, Wilhelm, 1845- (Table P-PZ40)
2621.O35 Kölwel, Gottfried, 1889- (Table P-PZ40)
2621.O48 Koerber, Adolf-Victor von, b. 1891 (Table P-PZ40)
2621.O58 Kohlenegg, Viktor von, 1872- (Table P-PZ40)
2621.O6 Kohlrausch, Robert, 1850- (Table P-PZ40)
Kohn, S. (Salomon), 1825-1904 see PT2621.O637
2621.O637 Kohn, Salomon, 1825-1904 (Table P-PZ40)
2621.O68 Kolbenheyer, Erwin Guido, 1878- (Table P-PZ40)
Kolmar, Gertrud see PT2605.H54
2621.O83 Kosel, Herrmann Clemens, 1867- (Table P-PZ40)
2621.O846 Kostic, Laza, 1841-1910 (Table P-PZ40)
2621.R13 Kraatz, Curt, 1857- (Table P-PZ40)

Individual authors or works
1860/70-1960
K - Kz -- Continued

2621.R15 Kraft, Zdenko von, 1886- (Table P-PZ40)
2621.R18 Kralik, Richard, ritter von Meyrswalden, 1852- (Table P-PZ40)
2621.R219 Kranewitter, Franz, 1860-1938 (Table P-PZ40)
2621.R2928 Krauss, Hans Nikolaus, 1861-1906 (Table P-PZ40)
2621.R537 Krempl, Josef (Table P-PZ40)
2621.R55 Kretzer, Max, 1854- (Table P-PZ40)
2621.R56 Kreutzer, Guido, 1886- (Table P-PZ40)
2621.R67 Kröger, Timm, 1844-1918 (Table P-PZ40)
2621.R75 Kronberg, Max (Table P-PZ40)
2621.R82 Krüger, Hermann, Anders, 1871- (Table P-PZ40)
2621.U112 Kuba, 1914-1967 (Table P-PZ40)
2621.U16 Küchler, Kurt, 1883- (Table P-PZ40)
2621.U37 Külpe, Frau Frances (James), 1862- (Table P-PZ40)
2621.U55 Kuhnert, Adolfo Artur, 1905- (Table P-PZ40)
2621.U86 Kurz, Hermann, 1880- (Table P-PZ40)
2621.U88 Kurz, Isolde, 1853- (Table P-PZ40)
2621.U89 Kurz, Karl Friedrich, 1878- (Table P-PZ40)
2621.Y7 Kyser, Hans, 1882- (Table P-PZ40)

2623 L - Lz

2623.A27 Lambrecht, Nanny, 1868- (Table P-PZ40)
2623.A35 Land, Hans, 1861- (Table P-PZ40)
2623.A4 Landsberger, Artur Hermann, 1876- (Table P-PZ40)
2623.A49 Lang, Willie, 1883- (Table P-PZ40)
2623.A53 Langenscheidt, Paul, 1860- (Table P-PZ40)
2623.A66 Langmann, Philipp, 1862- (Table P-PZ40)
2623.A76 Lasker-Schüler, Else, 1869-1945 (Table P-PZ40)
Lasswitz, Kurd, 1848-1910 see PT2390.L9
2623.A81 Latzko, Adolf Andreas, 1876- (Table P-PZ40)
2623.A83 Lauckner, Rolf, 1887- (Table P-PZ40)
2623.A85 Lauff, Joseph von, 1855- (Table P-PZ40)
Lavant, Christine, 1915-1973 see PT2615.A215
2623.E22 Lederer, Joe, 1907- (Table P-PZ40)
2623.E24 Lee, Heinrich, 1862- (Table P-PZ40)
2623.E26 Le Fort, Gertrud, freiin von, 1876- (Table P-PZ40)
2623.E324 Lehmann, Marcus, 1831-1890 (Table P-PZ40)
2623.E45 Leip, Hans, 1893- (Table P-PZ40)
2623.E492 Leitner, Franz Johann, 1849-1922 (Table P-PZ40)
2623.E5 Leixner-Grünberg, Otto von, 1847-1907 (Table P-PZ40)
2623.E6 Leonhard, Rudolf, 1889- (Table P-PZ40)
2623.E656 Lepp, Adolf, 1847-1906 (Table P-PZ40)
2623.E74 Lernet-Holenia, Alexander Maria, 1897- (Table P-PZ40)
2623.E83 Leutelt, Gustav, 1860-1947 (Table P-PZ40)
2623.E84 Leutz, Ilse, 1896- (Table P-PZ40)

Individual authors or works
1860/70-1960
L - Lz -- Continued
Lévien, Ilse see PT2601.K7
2623.E86 Levy, Hermann, 1881- (Table P-PZ40)
2623.I41 Lienhard, Friedrich, 1865-1929 (Table P-PZ40)
2623.I43 Liepmann, Heinz, 1905- (Table P-PZ40)
2623.I5 Lileincron, Detlev, freiherr von, 1844-1909 (Table P-PZ40)
2623.I53 Lilienfein, Heinrich, 1879- (Table P-PZ40)
2623.I635 Linke, Oskar, 1854-1928 (Table P-PZ40)
2623.O36 Löns, Hermann, 1866-1914 (Table P-PZ40)
2623.O698 Lorenz, Heinz, 1866-1966 (Table P-PZ40)
2623.O85 Lothar, Rudolph, 1865- (Table P-PZ40)
2623.U23 Lucka, Emil, 1877- (Table P-PZ40)
2623.U31 Ludwig, Emil, 1881- (Table P-PZ40)
2623.U32 Ludwig, Max, 1873- (Table P-PZ40)
2623.U93 Lux, Joseph August, 1871- (Table P-PZ40)
2625 M - Mz
2625.A22 Mackay, John Henry, 1864- (Table P-PZ40)
2625.A32 Mahn, Frau Anny (Wothe), 1858-1919 (Table P-PZ40)
2625.A33 Mahner-Mons, Hans (Table P-PZ40)
2625.A39 Maltzahn, Elisabeth, freiin von, 1868- (Table P-PZ40)
2625.A43 Mann, Heinrich, 1871- (Table P-PZ40)
2625.A435 Mann, Klaus, 1906- (Table P-PZ40)
2625.A44 Mann, Thomas, 1875-1955 (Table P-PZ40)
Marholm, Laura, 1854-1928 see PT2615.A576
Marholm, Leonard, 1854-1928 see PT2615.A576
Marriot, Emil see PT2625.A74
2625.A74 Mataja, Emilie, 1855- (Table P-PZ40)
2625.A75 Matthaei, Clara, 1884-1934 (Table P-PZ40)
2625.A786 Matthis, Albert, 1874-1930 (Table P-PZ40)
2625.A84 Mauser, Frau Lydia (Table P-PZ40)
2625.A843 Mauthner, Fritz, 1849-1923 (Table P-PZ40)
2625.A848 May, Karl Friedrich, 1842-1912 (Table P-PZ40)
2625.A92 Mayer, Theodor Heinrich, 1884- (Table P-PZ40)
2625.E22 Megede, Johannes Richard zur, 1864-1906 (Table P-PZ40)
2625.E24 Mehring, Walter, 1896- (Table P-PZ40)
2625.E248 Meier, Emerenz, 1874-1928 (Table P-PZ40)
2625.E25 Meier-Graefe, Julius, 1867- (Table P-PZ40)
2625.E38 Mell, Max, 1882- (Table P-PZ40)
2625.E4 Mendelssohn, Peter, 1908- (Table P-PZ40)
2625.E9 Meyer-Förster, Wilhelm, 1862-1934 (Table P-PZ40)
2625.E95 Meyrink, Gustav, 1868-1932 (Table P-PZ40)
2625.I25 Michaelson, Margarete, 1873- (Table P-PZ40)
2625.I31 Michel, Robert, 1876- (Table P-PZ40)

	Individual authors or works
	1860/70-1960
	M - Mz -- Continued
2625.I4	Miegel, Agnes, 1879- (Table P-PZ40)
	Mihaly, Jo, 1902- see PT2639.T259
2625.I79	Misch, Robert, 1860- (Table P-PZ40)
2625.O22	Möller, Alfred, 1877- (Table P-PZ40)
2625.O27	Moersberger, Frau Rose (Schliewen) (Table P-PZ40)
2625.O29	Moeschlin, Felix, 1882- (Table P-PZ40)
	Mohr, Laura, 1854-1928 see PT2615.A576
2625.O35	Mohr, Max, 1891- (Table P-PZ40)
2625.O42	Molo, Walter, ritter von, 1880- (Table P-PZ40)
2625.O5	Mombert, Alfred, 1872- (Table P-PZ40)
	Monbart, Helene von see PT2621.E79
	Moreck, Curt, 1888-1957 see PT2615.A2634
2625.O64	Morgenstern, Christian, 1871-1914 (Table P-PZ40)
	Mostar, Herrman, 1901-1973 see PT2617.E734
2625.U22	Mühlenfels, Frau Hedwig von, 1874-1923 (Table P-PZ40)
2625.U37	Müller, Fritz, 1875- (Table P-PZ40)
2625.U43	Müller, Hans, 1882- (Table P-PZ40)
2625.U55	Müller-Guttenbrunn, Adam, 1852-1923 (Table P-PZ40)
2625.U6	Müller-Schlösser, Hans, 1884- (Table P-PZ40)
2625.U68	Münch, Paul Georg, 1877- (Table P-PZ40)
2625.U7	Münch-Born, Philipp, b. 1870 (Table P-PZ40)
2625.U71	Münchhausen, Börries, freiherr von, 1874- (Table P-PZ40)
2625.U76	Münzer, Kurt, 1879- (Table P-PZ40)
	Mynona see PT2611.R657
2627	N - Nz
2627.A27	Nadel, Arno, 1878- (Table P-PZ40)
2627.E14	Neal, Max, 1865- (Table P-PZ40)
2627.E73	Neumann, Alfred, 1895- (Table P-PZ40)
2627.E78	Neumann, Robert, 1897- (Table P-PZ40)
	Ney, Elisabeth see PT2639.T865
2627.I55	Niese, Charlotte, 1854- (Table P-PZ40)
2627.O23	Noder, Anton, 1864- (Table P-PZ40)
2629	O - Oz
2629.E67	Oestéren, Friedrich Werner van, 1874- (Table P-PZ40)
2629.L3	Olden, Balder, 1882- (Table P-PZ40)
2629.L5	Oliven, Fritz, 1874- (Table P-PZ40)
2629.M7	Ompteda, Georg, freiherr von, 1863-1931 (Table P-PZ40)
2629.R75	Ortner, Hermann Heinz, 1895- (Table P-PZ40)
2629.S32	Oschwald-Ringier, Fanny, 1840-1918 (Table P-PZ40)
	Oswald, E. see PT2638.U78
2629.T7	Ott, Arnold, 1840-1910 (Table P-PZ40)
2629.T835	Otto-Walster, August, 1834-1898 (Table P-PZ40)

Individual authors or works
1860/70-1960
O - Oz -- Continued
Owlglass, Dr., 1873-1945 see PT2603.L13
2631 P - Pz
2631.A19 Paganin, Valentino, 1802- (Table P-PZ40)
2631.A5 Panizza, Oskar, 1853-1921 (Table P-PZ40)
2631.A52 Pannwitz, Rudolf, 1881- (Table P-PZ40)
2631.A545 Pappenheim, Bertha, 1859-1936 (Table P-PZ40)
2631.A55 Paquet, Alfons Hermann, 1881- (Table P-PZ40)
2631.A73 Paudler, Amand, 1844- (Table P-PZ40)
2631.A74 Paul, Adolf Georg, 1863- (Table P-PZ40)
2631.E43 Perfall, Anton, freiherr von, 1853-1912 (Table P-PZ40)
2631.E44 Perfall, Karl Theodor Gabriel Christoph, freiherr von, 1851- (Table P-PZ40)
2631.E5 Perutz, Leo, 1884- (Table P-PZ40)
2631.H55 Philippi, Felix, 1851-1921 (Table P-PZ40)
2631.I763 Piringer, Otto, 1874-1950 (Table P-PZ40)
2631.L35 Platen, Leontine (von Winterfeld) von, 1883- (Table P-PZ40)
2631.O44 Polenz, Wilhelm von, 1861-1903 (Table P-PZ40)
2631.O48 Polgar, Alfred, 1875- (Table P-PZ40)
2631.O64 Ponten, Josef, 1883- (Table P-PZ40)
2631.O642 Popp, August, 1873-1943 (Table P-PZ40)
Possendorf, Hans see PT2625.A33
2631.R25 Preczang, Ernst, 1870- (Table P-PZ40)
2631.R33 Prellwitz, Gertrud, 1869- (Table P-PZ40)
2631.R35 Presber, Rudolf, 1868-1935 (Table P-PZ40)
2631.R38 Presser, Eduard, 1842-1911 (Table P-PZ40)
2631.R46 Preuschen, Hermione, baronin von, 1854-1918 (Table P-PZ40)
2631.U83 Puttkamer, Marie Madeleine (Günther), freifrau von, 1881- (Table P-PZ40)
2633 Q - Qz
2633.U55 Quindt, William (Table P-PZ40)
2635 R - Rz
2635.A247 Radeschin, Hubert Wenzel Franz Hieronymus von, b. 1829 (Table P-PZ40)
2635.A27 Radványi, Netty Reiling, 1900- (Table P-PZ40)
2635.A36 Raff, Helene, 1865- (Table P-PZ40)
2635.A397 Raimond, Golo, 1825-1882 (Table P-PZ40)
2635.A78 Ratzka-Wendler, Frau Clara, 1872- (Table P-PZ40)
2635.E2 Reck-Malleczewen, Fritz Percy, 1884- (Table P-PZ40)
2635.E25 Redern, Hedwig von, 1866- (Table P-PZ40)
2635.E3 Rehfisch, Hans J., 1891- (Table P-PZ40)
2635.E68 Remarque, Erich Maria, 1898- (Table P-PZ40)
2635.E73 Renker, Gustav Friedrich, 1889- (Table P-PZ40)

Individual authors or works
1860/70-1960
R - Rz -- Continued
Renn, Ludwig, 1889- see PT2645.I445
2635.E85 Reuter, Gabriele, 1859- (Table P-PZ40)
2635.E89 Reventlow, Franziska, gräfin zu, 1871-1918 (Table P-PZ40)
2635.I26 Richter, Hans, 1889- (Table P-PZ40)
2635.I28 Richter, Hermann, 1887- (Table P-PZ40)
2635.I33 Richthofen, Hartmann, freiherr von, 1878- (Table P-PZ40)
2635.I416 Rieger, Sebastian, 1867-1953 (Table P-PZ40)
2635.I63 Rikart, Heinö (Table P-PZ40)
2635.I65 Rilke, Rainer Maria, 1875-1926 (Table P-PZ40)
Ringelnatz, Joachim, 1883-1934 see PT2603.O44
Riotte, Hermann see PT3919.R62
2635.I85 Rittner, Thaddäus, 1873-1921 (Table P-PZ40)
2635.O24 Roda Roda, Alexander Friedrich Ladislaus, 1872- (Table P-PZ40)
2635.O42 Rössler, Carl, 1864- (Table P-PZ40)
2635.O428 Röttger, Karl, 1877- (Table P-PZ40)
2635.O6 Roniger, Emil, 1883- (Table P-PZ40)
2635.O7 Rosenhayn, Paul, 1877-1929 (Table P-PZ40)
Rosmer, Ernst see PT2603.E72
2635.O77 Rosner, Karl Peter, 1873- (Table P-PZ40)
2635.O84 Roth, Joseph, 1894- (Table P-PZ40)
2635.U42 Rüdiger, Frau Minna (Waack), 1841-1920 (Table P-PZ40)
2635.U685 Rullmann, Wilhelm, b. 1841 (Table P-PZ40)
2635.U7 Rump, Johann, 1871- (Table P-PZ40)
2635.U73 Runkel, Ferdinand, 1867- (Table P-PZ40)
2635.U8 Rust, Albert Otto, 1890- (Table P-PZ40)
2637 S - Scg
Sagitta see PT2625.A22
2637.A44 Salburg, Edith, gräfin, 1868- (Table P-PZ40)
2637.A5 Salomon, Ludwig, 1844-1911 (Table P-PZ40)
2637.A52 Salten, Felix, 1869- (Table P-PZ40)
2637.A55 Salus, Hugo, 1866- (Table P-PZ40)
2637.A63 Sandt, Emil, 1864- (Table P-PZ40)
2637.A7 Sarasin, Paul, 1856-1929 (Table P-PZ40)
2637.A82 Saudek, Robert, 1880- (Table P-PZ40)
Scarpi, N.O., 1888- see PT2603.O614
2638 Scha - Schz
For names beginning with "Sch," the author number is taken from that part of the name beginning with the fourth letter
2638.A22 Schabelsky, Elsa von, 1860- (Table P-PZ40)
2638.A358 Schäfer, Georg, 1840-1914 (Table P-PZ40)

Individual authors or works
1860/70-1960
Scha - Schz -- Continued

2638.A4 Schäfer, Walter Erich, 1901- (Table P-PZ40)
2638.A42 Schäfer, Wilhelm, 1868- (Table P-PZ40)
2638.A45 Schaeffer, Albrecht, 1885- (Table P-PZ40)
2638.A53 Schätzler-Perasini, Gebhard, 1866- (Table P-PZ40)
2638.A56 Schaffner, Jakob, 1875- (Table P-PZ40)
Schanz, Frida see PT2639.O9
2638.A72 Scharrelmann, Wilhelm, 1875- (Table P-PZ40)
2638.A86 Schaukal, Richard, 1874- (Table P-PZ40)
2638.A867 Schaumberg, Georg, 1855- (Table P-PZ40)
2638.A868 Schaumberger, Julius, 1858-1924 (Table P-PZ40)
2638.A87 Schaumburg, Paul Erich Bruno Richard, 1884- (Table P-PZ40)
2638.E4 Scheerbart, Paul, 1863-1915 (Table P-PZ40)
2638.E45 Scheff, Werner, 1888- (Table P-PZ40)
2638.E472 Scheffer, Thassilo Fritz H. von, 1873- (Table P-PZ40)
2638.E5 Scheliha, Doris (gräfin von Matuschka), 1847-1925 (Table P-PZ40)
2638.E6 Schendell, Werner, 1891- (Table P-PZ40)
2638.I22 Schickele, René, 1883- (Table P-PZ40)
2638.I38 Schier, Benjamin, 1847-1910 (Table P-PZ40)
2638.I87 Schirokauer, Alfred, 1880- (Table P-PZ40)
2638.L2 Schlaf, Johannes, 1862- (Table P-PZ40)
2638.L255 Schlapp, George (Table P-PZ40)
2638.L32 Schleicher, Hans (Table P-PZ40)
Schlicht, freiherr von see PT2603.A73
2638.M48 Schmidt, Nikolaus (Table P-PZ40)
2638.M5 Schmidt, Otto Ernst, 1862-1926 (Table P-PZ40)
2638.M62 Schmidtbonn, Wilhelm August, 1876- (Table P-PZ40)
2638.M76 Schmitthenner, Adolf, 1854-1907 (Table P-PZ40)
2638.M85 Schmitz, Oscar A.H., 1873- (Table P-PZ40)
2638.N5 Schnitzler, Arthur, 1862-1931 (Table P-PZ40)
2638.N67 Schnurre, Wolfdietrich, 1920- (Table P-PZ40)
2638.O32 Schönaich-Carolath, Emil Rudolf Osman, prinz von, 1852-1908 (Table P-PZ40)
2638.O44 Schoenfeld, Hans, b. 1883 (Table P-PZ40)
2638.O58 Schönherr, Karl, 1869- (Table P-PZ40)
2638.O65 Schöttler, Horst, 1874- (Table P-PZ40)
2638.O73 Scholz, Wilhelm von, 1874- (Table P-PZ40)
Schrattenthal, Karl see PT2647.E527
2638.R38 Schreckenbach, Paul, 1866-1922 (Table P-PZ40)
2638.R6 Schricker, Rudolf Hans (Table P-PZ40)
2638.R8 Schröer, Gustav Wilhelm, 1876- (Table P-PZ40)
2638.U44 Schulenburg, Werner von der, 1881- (Table P-PZ40)
2638.U444 Schuler, Alfred, 1865-1923 (Table P-PZ40)

Individual authors or works
1860/70-1960
Scha - Schz -- Continued

2638.U55 Schultze, Victor, 1851- (Table P-PZ40)
2638.U56 Schultzky, Otto, 1848- (Table P-PZ40)
2638.U73 Schulze, Paul, 1873- (Table P-PZ40)
2638.U78 Schulze-Smidt, Frau Bernhardine, 1846-1920 (Table P-PZ40)
2638.U82 Schumacher, Heinrich Vollrat, 1861-1919 (Table P-PZ40)
2638.W23 Schwanzara, Josef Rudolf Leo, 1878- (Table P-PZ40)
Schwarzenbach, Annemarie, 1908-1942 see PT2605.L25
2638.W3 Schwarzkopf, Gustav, 1853- (Table P-PZ40)
2638.W85 Schweriner, Oskar T., 1873- (Table P-PZ40)
2639 Se - Su
2639.E28 Seeliger, Ewald Gerhard Hartmann, 1877- (Table P-PZ40)
Seghers, Anna, 1900- see PT2635.A27
2639.E4 Seidel, Frau Ina (Seidel), 1885- (Table P-PZ40)
2639.E44 Seidel, Willy, 1887-1934 (Table P-PZ40)
2639.E738 Senn, Jakob, 1824-1879 (Table P-PZ40)
2639.E98 Seyth, Adyr, b. 1862 (Table P-PZ40)
2639.I37 Siegfried, Walther, 1858- (Table P-PZ40)
2639.I55 Silberer, Geza, 1876- (Table P-PZ40)
2639.I64 Simon, Frau Emma (Couvely), 1848- (Table P-PZ40)
2639.I685 Sinoja, J.E. de (Table P-PZ40)
2639.I92 Sittenfeld, Konrad, 1862- (Table P-PZ40)
2639.K6 Skowronnek, Richard, 1862- (Table P-PZ40)
Slang, 1895-1932 see PT2615.A539
Sonka see PT2639.O66
Sonneck, Oscar George Theodore see PT3919.S73
2639.O66 Sonnenschein, Hugo, 1890- (Table P-PZ40)
2639.O9 Soyaux, Frau Frida (Schanz), 1859- (Table P-PZ40)
2639.O95 Soyka, Otto, 1882- (Table P-PZ40)
Spättgen, Doris, freiin von see PT2638.E5
2639.P32 Specht, Karl August, 1845-1909 (Table P-PZ40)
2639.P36 Speckmann, Diedrich, 1872- (Table P-PZ40)
2639.P52 Speyer, Wilhelm, 1887- (Table P-PZ40)
2639.P6 Spitteler, Carl, 1845-1924 (Table P-PZ40)
2639.T21 Stamm, Karl, 1890-1919 (Table P-PZ40)
2639.T259 Steckel, Elfriede (Table P-PZ40)
2639.T28 Steffen, Albert, 1884- (Table P-PZ40)
2639.T31 Stegemann, Hermann, 1870- (Table P-PZ40)
2639.T34 Stehr, Hermann, 1864- (Table P-PZ40)
2639.T355 Stein, Heinrich, freiherr von, 1857-1887 (Table P-PZ40)
2639.T36 Stein, Leo Walther, 1858- (Table P-PZ40)
2639.T4 Steiner, Rudolf, 1861-1925 (Table P-PZ40)
Steinwand, Fercher von, 1828-1902 see PT2611.E83

Individual authors or works
1860/70-1960
Se - Su -- Continued

2639.T481 Stern, Maurice Reinhold von, 1860- (Table P-PZ40)
2639.T484 Sterneder, Hans, 1889- (Table P-PZ40)
2639.T5 Sternheim, Carl, 1878- (Table P-PZ40)
2639.T55 Stilgebauer, Edward, 1868- (Table P-PZ40)
2639.T57 Stobitzer, Heinrich, 1856- (Table P-PZ40)
2639.T72 Stratz, Rudolf, 1864- (Table P-PZ40)
2639.T75 Strauss, Emil, 1866- (Table P-PZ40)
2639.T78 Strauss und Torney, Lulu von, 1873- (Table P-PZ40)
2639.T84 Strobl, Karl Hans, 1877- (Table P-PZ40)
2639.T865 Strong, Pitt (Table P-PZ40)
2639.T87 Strübe, Hermann, 1879- (Table P-PZ40)
2639.T95 Sturm, Hans, 1874-1933 (Table P-PZ40)
2639.T98 Stutzer, Therese, 1841-1916 (Table P-PZ40)

Sudermann, Hermann, 1857-1928

2640.A1 Collected works. By date
2640.A15 Collected novels
2640.A16 Collected essays, Miscellanies, etc.
2640.A19 Collected plays
2640.A3-.Z29 Separate works
2640.B4 Der bettler von Syrakus
Das bilderbuch meiner jugend see PT2640.Z8A3
2640.B6 Das blumenboot
2640.D4 Die denkmalsweihe
2640.D6 Die drei reiherfedern
2640.E4 Die ehre
2640.E6 Die entgötterte welt (3 dramas)
Die freundin; Die gutgeschnittene ecke; Das höhere leben
See also the separate items
2640.E7 Es lebe das leben
2640.E8 Es war
2640.F4 Die ferne prinzessin
Cf. PT2640.R6 Rosen
2640.F55 Die frau des Steffen Tromholt
2640.F6 Frau Sorge
2640.F64 Die freundin
Cf. PT2640.E6 Die entgötterte welt
2640.F7 Fritzchen
Cf. PT2640.M6 Morituri
2640.G4 Geschwister, zwei novellen
Die geschichte der stillen mühle; Der wunsch
2640.G5 Das glück im winkel
2640.G7 Der gute ruf

Individual authors or works
1860/70-1960
Sudermann, Hermann, 1857-1928
Separate works -- Continued

2640.G8 Die gutgeschnittene ecke
Cf. PT2640.E6 Die entgötterte welt
2640.H3 Der hasenfellhändler
2640.H35 Heilige zeit; szenische bilder
2640.H4 Heimat
2640.H5 Das höhere leben
Cf. PT2640.E6 Die entgötterte welt
2640.H6 Das hohe lied (Novel)
2640.I3 Im paradies der heimat
2640.I4 Im zwielicht
2640.I6 Die indische lilie
2640.I9 Iolanthes hochzeit
2640.J5 Johannes
2640.J6 Johannisfeuer
2640.J7 Jons und Erdme
Cf. PT2640.L5 Litauische geschichten
2640.K3 Der katzensteg
2640.L5 Litauische geschichten (4 stories)
2640.L6 Die lobgesänge des Claudian
2640.M6 Morituri: Teja; Fritzchen; Das ewig-männliche (Three one-act plays)
2640.N6 Notruf
2640.O6 Opfer
2640.P8 Purzelchen
2640.R3 Die Raschhoffs
2640.R4 Die reise nach Tilsit
Cf. PT2640.L5 Litauische geschichten
2640.R6 Rosen: Die ferne prinzessin; Margot; Die lichtbänder; Der letzte besuch (4 one-act plays)
2640.S4 Die schmetterlingsschlacht
2640.S5 Sodoms ende
2640.S6 Stein unter steinen
2640.S7 Strandkinder
2640.S8 Der sturmgeselle Sokrates
2640.T4 Teja
Cf. PT2640.M6 Morituri
2640.T6 Der tolle professor
2640.W5 Wie die träumenden
2640.W8 Der wunsch
Cf. PT2640.G4 Geschwister

Translations
English
2640.Z3 Collected works. By date

Individual authors or works
1860/70-1960
Sudermann, Hermann, 1857-1928
Translations
English -- Continued
2640.Z3A-.Z3Z Separate works. By original title, A-Z
French
2640.Z4 Collected works. By date
2640.Z4A-.Z4Z Separate works. By original title, A-Z
2640.Z6-.Z69 Other languages (alphabetically)
2640.Z7-.Z79 Adaptations, imitations, etc. By title
2640.Z8 Autobiography. Journals. Letters
2640.Z8A3 Das bilderbuch meiner jugend
2640.Z8A33 English translation
2640.Z8A5 Letters. By date
2640.Z8A6-Z Criticism and interpretation
2641 Sudermann - Sz
2641.U73 Supper, Frau Auguste, 1867- (Table P-PZ40)
2641.Z5 Szimits, Johann, 1852-1910 (Table P-PZ40)
2642 T - Tz
2642.A3 Tagger, Theodor, 1891- (Table P-PZ40)
2642.E3 Telmann, Konrad, 1854-1897 (Table P-PZ40)
2642.E853 Teuchert, Anton Wilhelm, ca. 1862-ca. 1916 (Table P-PZ40)
2642.H4 Thiess, Frank, 1890- (Table P-PZ40)
2642.H58 Thoma, Ludwig, 1867-1921 (Table P-PZ40)
2642.H63 Thomass-Correï, Ella, 1887- (Table P-PZ40)
2642.I15 Tiaden, Heinrich, 1873- (Table P-PZ40)
2642.O65 Toller, Ernst, 1893- (Table P-PZ40)
Torberg, Friedrich, 1908- see PT2621.A55
2642.O78 Toto Ignoto (Table P-PZ40)
2642.O9 Tovote, Heinz, 1864- (Table P-PZ40)
2642.R23 Tralow, Johannes, 1888- (Table P-PZ40)
(2642.R33) Traven, B.
see PT3919.T7
2642.R34 Trebitsch, Arthur, 1880-1927 (Table P-PZ40)
2642.R36 Trebitsch, Siegfried, 1868- (Table P-PZ40)
2642.R42 Trenck, Siegfried von der, 1882- (Table P-PZ40)
Troll, Thaddäus, 1914- see PT2603.A886
2643 U - Uz
2643.L5 Ulitz, Arnold, 1888- (Table P-PZ40)
2643.N37 Unger, Hellmuth, 1891- (Table P-PZ40)
2643.N7 Unruh, Fritz von, 1885- (Table P-PZ40)
2643.R3 Urbanitzky, Grete von, 1893- (Table P-PZ40)
2643.R89 Ury, Else, 1877-1943 (Table P-PZ40)
2643.Z3 Uzarski, Adolf, 1885- (Table P-PZ40)
2645 V - Vz

Individual authors or works
1860/70-1960
V - Vz -- Continued

2645.A13 Vacano, Stefan, 1874- (Table P-PZ40)
Vely, Emma see PT2639.I64
2645.E7 Vesper, Will, 1882- (Table P-PZ40)
Viebig, Clara see PT2605.O32
2645.I423 Viera-Segerer, Josef Sebastian, 1890- (Table P-PZ40)
2645.I445 Vieth von Golssenau, Arnold Friedrich, 1889- (Table P-PZ40)
2645.I6 Villinger, Hermine, 1849-1917 (Table P-PZ40)
2645.O24 Vögtlin, Adolf, 1861- (Table P-PZ40)
2645.O47 Voigt, Frau Johanna (Ambrosius), 1854- (Table P-PZ40)
2645.O57 Volger, Adolf, 1843- (Table P-PZ40)
2645.O58 Volger, Eduard, 1847- (Table P-PZ40)
2645.O59 Volger, Franz, 1848-1917 (Table P-PZ40)
2645.O6 Volger, Fritz, 1841-1893 (Table P-PZ40)
2645.O62 Volger, Paul, 1856- (Table P-PZ40)
2645.O88 Voss, Richard, 1851-1918 (Table P-PZ40)
2645.R5 Vring, Georg von der, 1889- (Table P-PZ40)
2647 W - Wz
2647.A23 Wäckerle, Hyazinth, 1836-1896 (Table P-PZ40)
2647.A345 Wagner, Ernst, 1874-1938 (Wagner, Ernst, Hauptlehrer) (Table P-PZ40)
2647.A36 Wagner, Hermann, 1880- (Table P-PZ40)
Waldeck, Heinrich Suso, 1873-1943 see PT2631.O642
2647.A6344 Walloth, Wilhelm, 1856- (Table P-PZ40)
2647.A67 Walter, Robert, 1883- (Table P-PZ40)
2647.A8 Warncke, Paul, 1866-1933 (Table P-PZ40)
2647.A92 Wassermann, Jakob, 1873-1934 (Table P-PZ40)
2647.A96 Watzlik, Hans, 1879- (Table P-PZ40)
2647.E14 Weber, Alexander Otto, 1868- (Table P-PZ40)
2647.E26 Wedekind, Frank, 1864-1918 (Table P-PZ40)
2647.E32 Wegner, Armin Tarik, 1886- (Table P-PZ40)
2647.E37 Weigand, Wilhelm, 1862- (Table P-PZ40)
2647.E52 Weiss, Ernst, 1882-1940 (Table P-PZ40)
2647.E527 Weiss, Karl Franz Joseph, 1846- (Table P-PZ40)
2647.E56 Weitbrecht, Karl, 1847-1904 (Table P-PZ40)
2647.E562 Weitbrecht, Richard, 1851-1911 (Table P-PZ40)
2647.E77 Werfel, Franz V., 1890- (Table P-PZ40)
2647.E82 Wertheimer, Paul, 1874- (Table P-PZ40)
2647.E87 Westkirch, Luise, 1858- (Table P-PZ40)
2647.I12 Wibbelt, Augustin, 1962-1947 (Table P-PZ40)
2647.I25 Wiechert, Ernst Emil, 1887- (Table P-PZ40)
2647.I27 Wiegand, Johannes, 1874- (Table P-PZ40)
2647.I43 Wildenbruch, Ernst von, 1845-1909 (Table P-PZ40)
2647.I45 Wildgans, Anton, 1881-1932 (Table P-PZ40)

Individual authors or works
1860/70-1960
W - Wz -- Continued
2647.I54 Wille, Bruno, 1860- (Table P-PZ40)
2647.I63 Winckler, Josef, 1881- (Table P-PZ40)
2647.I67 Winsloe, Christa (Table P-PZ40)
Das mädchen Manuela; der roman von Mädchen in uniform, 1933
2647.O23 Wöhrle, Oskar, 1890- (Table P-PZ40)
2647.O236 Wörishöffer, Sophia (Andresen), 1838-1890 (Table P-PZ40)
2647.O25 Wohl, Ludwig von, 1903- (Table P-PZ40)
2647.O3 Wohlbrück, Olga, 1869- (Table P-PZ40)
2647.O58 Wolff, Ludwig, 1876- (Table P-PZ40)
2647.O63 Wolff, Ulla (Hirschfeld), 1840-1924 (Table P-PZ40)
2647.O7 Wolfskehl, Karl, 1869-1948 (Table P-PZ40)
2647.O83 Wolzogen, Hans von, 1848-1938 (Table P-PZ40)
2647.O84 Wolzogen und Neuhaus, Ernst Ludwig, freiherr von, 1855- (Table P-PZ40)
2647.O89 Worms, Carl, 1857- (Table P-PZ40)
2647.U44 Wundt, Theodor Karl Wilhelm von, 1858-1929 (Table P-PZ40)
2649 X - Xz
2651 Y - Yz
2653 Z - Zz
2653.A42 Zahn, Ernst, 1867- (Table P-PZ40)
2653.A76 Zapp, Arthur, 1852-1925 (Table P-PZ40)
2653.I34 Ziebland, Georg Friedrich, 1800-1873 (Table P-PZ40)
2653.I7 Zitelmann, Ernst, 1852-1923 (Table P-PZ40)
Zitelmann, Ernst Otto Konrad see PT2642.E3
2653.I8 Zitelmann, Katharina, 1844-1923? (Table P-PZ40)
2653.O2 Zobeltitz, Fedor Karl Maria Hermann August von, 1857-1934 (Table P-PZ40)
2653.O24 Zobeltitz, Hanns von, 1853-1918 (Table P-PZ40)
2653.O25 Zobeltitz, Hans Caspar Anton Konstantin von, 1883- (Table P-PZ40)
2653.O42 Zöge von Manteuffel, Ursula, "Frau von Trebra-Lindenau," 1850-1910 (Table P-PZ40)
2653.U33 Zuckmayer, Karl, 1896- (Table P-PZ40)
2653.W4 Zweig, Arnold, 1887- (Table P-PZ40)
2653.W42 Zweig, Stefan, 1881- (Table P-PZ40)

Individual authors or works -- Continued
1961-2000
The author number is determined by the letter following the letter or letters for which each class number stands
Subarrange each author by Table P-PZ40 unless otherwise specified
Here are usually to be classified authors beginning to publish about 1950, flourishing after 1960

2660	Anonymous works (Table P-PZ28)
2661	A
	Akos, Mohar see PT2661.P47
2661.L42	Alexander, Elizabeth, 1923- (Table P-PZ40)
2661.P47	Apatride, Jean (Table P-PZ40)
	Arras, S. see PT2678.I472
2661.U78	Aust, Stefan (Table P-PZ40)
2662	B
2662.E694	Berndt, Karl Heinz, 1923- (Table P-PZ40)
2662.O77	Bosetzky, Horst (Table P-PZ40)
2663	C
	Subarrange each author by Table P-PZ40 unless otherwise specified
2664	D
2664.I358	Diehl, Wolfgang (Table P-PZ40)
2664.O58	Dora (Table P-PZ40)
2665	E
	Subarrange each author by Table P-PZ40 unless otherwise specified
2666	F
2666.O26	Foelske, Walter (Table P-PZ40)
	Fragner-Unterpertinger, Johannes see PT2676.E717
2667	G
	Subarrange each author by Table P-PZ40 unless otherwise specified
	Guben, Berndt, 1923- see PT2662.E694
2667.U3	Gunther, Heinz, 1921- (Table P-PZ40)
2668	H
2668.A7396	Hartmann, Sven (Table P-PZ40)
	Huby, Felix see PT2668.U553
2668.U553	Hungerbühler, Eberhard (Table P-PZ40)
2669	I
	Subarrange each author by Table P-PZ40 unless otherwise specified
2670	J
	Subarrange each author by Table P-PZ40 unless otherwise specified
2670.A87	Jaschke, Gerhard

Individual authors or works
1961-2000 -- Continued

2671 K
Subarrange each author by Table P-PZ40 unless otherwise specified
Knobel, Betty see PT2685.E463
Konzalik, Heinz see PT2667.U3
-ky see PT2662.O77

2672 L
2672.O34 Loewig, Roger (Table P-PZ40)

2673 M
Subarrange each author by Table P-PZ40 unless otherwise specified

2674 N
2674.E789 Newhausler, Anton, 1919- (Table P-PZ40)

2675 O
Subarrange each author by Table P-PZ40 unless otherwise specified

2676 P
Subarrange each author by Table P-PZ40 unless otherwise specified
2676.E717 Perting, Hans (Table P-PZ40)
Preisendorfer, Bruno, 1957- see PT2678.I25

2677 Q
Subarrange each author by Table P-PZ40 unless otherwise specified

2678 R
2678.A72 Rappl, Erich, 1925- (Table P-PZ40)
2678.I25 Richard, Bruno, 1957- (Table P-PZ40)
2678.I472 Riesen, Armin (Table P-PZ40)
Rinseis, Franz, 1919- see PT2674.E789

2679 Sa - Scg
Subarrange each author by Table P-PZ40 unless otherwise specified

2680 Sch
For names beginning with "Sch," the author number is taken from that part of the name beginning with the fourth letter
Subarrange each author by Table P-PZ40 unless otherwise specified

2681 Sci - Sz
2681.T4348 Steinwachs, Ginka (Table P-PZ40)

2682 T
Subarrange each author by Table P-PZ40 unless otherwise specified

2683 U
Subarrange each author by Table P-PZ40 unless otherwise specified

Individual authors or works
1961-2000 -- Continued
2684 V
Subarrange each author by Table P-PZ40 unless otherwise specified
2685 W
Subarrange each author by Table P-PZ40 unless otherwise specified
Wafner, 1925- see PT2678.A72
2685.E339 Wedel, Walter
2685.E463 Wehrli-Knobel, Betty (Table P-PZ40)
2686 X
Subarrange each author by Table P-PZ40 unless otherwise specified
2687 Y
Subarrange each author by Table P-PZ40 unless otherwise specified
2688 Z
Subarrange each author by Table P-PZ40 unless otherwise specified
2001-
The author number is determined by the second letter of the name unless otherwise specified
Subarrange each author by Table P-PZ40 unless otherwise specified
2700 Anonymous works (Table Table P-PZ8)
2701 A
2702 B
2703 C
2704 D
2705 E
2706 F
2707 G
2708 H
2709 I
2710 J
2711 K
2712 L
2713 M
2714 N
2715 O
2716 P
2717 Q
2718 R
2719 Sa - Scg

Individual authors or works
2001- -- Continued
2720 Sch
For names beginning whith "Sch," the author number is takenfrom theat part of the name beginning with the fourth letter
2721 Sci - Sz
2722 T
2723 U
2724 V
2725 W
2726 X
2727 Y
2728 Z
Provincial, local, colonial, etc.
Subarrange individual places by Table P-PZ26 unless otherwise specified
Class here literary history, biography, criticism and collections of the literature of provinces, regions, islands and places belonging to Germany
Countries with German literature outside of Germany: Austria, Switzerland, German colonies and German literature outside of Europe
For works, biography and criticism of individual authors, except North American see PT1501+
3701-3746 Germany (Democratic Republic, 1949-1990) (Table P-PZ22 modified)
Local see PT3801+
Individual authors see PT2600+
By region, state, province, etc.
3801 A - Al
Subarrange each place by Table P-PZ26
Alsace and Lorraine
For French literature see PQ3803.A+
Literary history
3802.A1-.A5 Periodicals
History
3802.A6-Z General
3802.1 General special
3802.2 Biography
3802.3 Poetry
3802.4 Other
Collections
3802.5 General
3802.6 Poetry
3802.7 Drama
3802.75 Other

Provincial, local, colonial, etc.
By region, state, province, etc.
Alsace and Lorraine -- Continued

3802.8.A-Z Local, A-Z
Subarrange each place by Table P-PZ26
3802.9 Translations
(3802.95) Individual authors
see PF5248; PT1501+
Altenburg see PT3805.T4+
3803.A4-.A42 Anhalt (Duchy) (Table P-PZ26)
3803.B3-.B32 Baden (Table P-PZ26)
3803.B4-.B42 Bavaria (Table P-PZ26)
3803.B56-.B562 Bergisches Land (Table P-PZ26)
3803.B6-.B62 Brandenburg (Table P-PZ26)
3803.B8-.B82 Bremen (Table P-PZ26)
3803.B9-.B92 Brunswick (Table P-PZ26)
Coburg-Gotha see PT3805.T4+
3803.D35-.D352 Darmstadt-Dieburg (Table P-PZ26)
Elsass-Lothringen see PT3802+
3803.E7-.E72 Ermland (Table P-PZ26)
3803.F7-.F72 Franconia (Table P-PZ26)
3803.F75-.F752 Friesland (Table P-PZ26)
3803.H3-.H32 Halle (Bezirk) (Table P-PZ26)
Hamburg see PT3807.H3+
3803.H33-.H332 Hanover (Table P-PZ26)
3803.H4-.H42 Hesse (Table P-PZ26)
Including Hesse-Darmstadt and Hesse-Nassau, being for the greater part the former electorate Hesse-Cassel
3803.H6-.H62 Hohenlohe (Table P-PZ26)
Holstein see PT3803.S7+
3803.H63-.H632 Holzminden (Landkreis) (Table P-PZ26)
3803.K53-.K532 Klettgau Valley (Germany and Switzerland) (Table P-PZ26)
3803.L25-.L252 Lahn Valley (Table P-PZ26)
3803.L28-.L282 Leipzig (Bezirk) (Table P-PZ26)
3803.L3-.L32 Lippe (Table P-PZ26)
3803.L6-.L62 Low German regions (German literature) (Table P-PZ26)
3803.L8-.L82 Lübeck (Table P-PZ26)
3803.M3-.M32 Mecklenburg (Table P-PZ26)
Including Mecklenburg-Schwerin and Mecklenburg-Strelitz
Meinigen see PT3805.T4+
Nassau (Duchy) see PT3803.H4+
3803.O3-.O32 Oldenburg (Table P-PZ26)
3803.O77-.O772 Ostfriesland (Table P-PZ26)
3803.P2-.P22 Palatinate (Table P-PZ26)
Cf. PT3803.R5+ Rhine River and Valley
3803.P5-.P52 Pomerania (Table P-PZ26)
3803.P6-.P62 Posen (Table P-PZ26)

Provincial, local, colonial, etc.
By region, state, province, etc. -- Continued
Prussia (Kingdom)
see German literature in general and the special provinces
3803.P8-.P82 Prussia (Province), East and West Prussia (Table P-PZ26)
Reuss see PT3805.T4+
3803.R5-.R52 Rhine River and Valley, including Rhine province (Table P-PZ26)
Cf. PT3803.P2+ Palatinate
3803.R8-.R82 Ruhr Valley (Table P-PZ26)
3803.S13-.S132 Saar Valley (Table P-PZ26)
3803.S2-.S22 Saxony (Kingdom) (Table P-PZ26)
3803.S4-.S42 Saxony (Province) (Table P-PZ26)
3803.S6-.S62 Schaumburg-Lippe (Table P-PZ26)
3803.S7-.S72 Schleswig-Holstein-Lauenburg (Table P-PZ26)
Schwarzburg see PT3805.T4+
3803.S8-.S82 Silesia (Table P-PZ26)
Swabia
Literary history
3804.A1-.A5 Periodicals
History
3804.A6-Z General
3804.1 General special
3804.2 Biography
3804.3 Poetry
3804.4 Other
Collections
3804.5 General
3804.6 Poetry
3804.7 Drama
3804.75 Other
3804.8.A-Z Local, A-Z
Subarrange each place by Table P-PZ26
3804.9 Translations
(3804.95) Individual authors
see PF5288; PT1501+
3805.T4-.T42 Thuringia (Table P-PZ26)
Including Saxe-Weimar-Eisenach, Saxe-Altenburg, Saxe-Coburg-Gotha, Saxe-Meiningen and the principalities of Schwarzburg-Rudolstadt, Schwarzburg-Sondershausen and Reuss (older and younger lines)
3805.W2-.W22 Waldeck and Pyrmont (Principality) (Table P-PZ26)
3805.W4-.W42 Westphalia (Province) (Table P-PZ26)
Württemberg see PT3804+
3805.W8-.W82 Wuppertal (Table P-PZ26)

Provincial, local, colonial, etc. -- Continued
3807.A-Z By place, A-Z
Subarrange each place by Table P-PZ26
e.g.
Berlin
3807.B3 History
3807.B4 Collections
3807.C6-.C62 Cologne (Table P-PZ26)
Göttingen
3807.G7 History
3807.G8 Collections
Hamburg
3807.H3 History
3807.H4 Collections
3807.M8-.M82 Munich (Table P-PZ26)
German literature outside of Germany
General
3808 History
3809 Collections
Special
Europe
3810-3828 Austria (Table PT5)
3830-3837.5 Czechoslovakia. Bohemia (Table PT4)
3840-3847.5 Hungary (Table PT4)
3850-3857.5 Soviet Union. Russia (Table PT4)
3860-3878 Switzerland (Table PT5)
Cf. PN849.S9+ Literature of Switzerland
3895.A-Z Other European, A-Z
German literature outside of Europe
America
3900-3921 General. North America. United States (Table PT5 modified)
For Pennsylvania-German dialect see PF5931+
3919 Individual authors
3919.A1-.A46 Anonymous works
3919.A47-Z Authors
3919.A75 Asmus, Georg, 1830-1896? (Table P-PZ40)
3919.B48 Benignus, Wilhelm, 1861- (Table P-PZ40)
3919.B79 Bromm, Emma (Table P-PZ40)
3919.C32 Carus, Paul, 1852-1919 (Table P-PZ40)
3919.G75 Grimm, Albert Friedrich Wilhelm, 1864- (Table P-PZ40)
3919.G82 Grumbine, Ezra Light, 1845- (Table P-PZ40)
For poems in Pennsylvania-German dialect see PF5931+
3919.H363 Harders, Gustav (Table P-PZ40)
3919.H49 Heinzen, Karl Peter, 1809-1880 (Table P-PZ40)

Provincial, local, colonial, etc.
German literature outside of Germany
Special
German literature outside of Europe
America
General. North America. United States
Individual authors
Authors -- Continued

3919.I4 Ilgen, Pedro, 1869- (Table P-PZ40)
3919.K85 Krez, Konrad, 1828-1897 (Table P-PZ40)
3919.L85 Ludvigh, Samuel Gottlieb, 1801-1869 (Table P-PZ40)
3919.M15 Mack, Valentine (Table P-PZ40)
3919.N5 Nieberg-Wagner, Frau Mathilde, 1839- (Table P-PZ40)
3919.N52 Nies, Konrad, 1861-1921 (Table P-PZ40)
3919.R25 Rattermann, Heinrich Armin, 1832-1923 (Table P-PZ40)
3919.R35 Reitzel, Robert, 1849-1898 (Table P-PZ40)
3919.R62 Riotte, Hermann, 1846-1916 (Table P-PZ40)
3919.R79 Rothensteiner, John Ernest, 1860- (Table P-PZ40)
3919.R89 Ruppins, Otto (Table P-PZ40)
3919.S44 Schneider, Heinrich Emil, 1839-1928 (Table P-PZ40)
3919.S67 Solger, Reinhold, 1820-1866 (Table P-PZ40)
3919.S73 Sonneck, Oscar George Theodore, 1873-1928 (Table P-PZ40)
3919.T7 Traven, B. (Table P-PZ40)
3919.V5 Viereck, George Sylvester, 1884- (Table P-PZ40)
3919.W85 Wollenweber, Louis August, 1807-1888 (Table P-PZ40)
3919.Z27 Zapf, Philipp, 1825-1872 (Table P-PZ40)
3919.Z8 Zündt, Ernst Anton Joseph, 1819-1897 (Table P-PZ40)

Juvenile literature
3920 History and criticism
(3921) Literature
see PZ31+
3930-3948 Central and South America. West Indies (Table PT5)
3951 Africa
Individual authors see PT1501+
3961 Asia
Individual authors see PT1501+
3971 Oceania
Individual authors see PT1501+

Low German literature
History and criticism
4801 Periodicals. Societies. Collections
4802 Encyclopedias. Dictionaries
4803 Study and teaching
History
4805 General
General special
4807 Relations to history, civilization, etc.
4808 Relations to other literatures
4809 Translations
4810.A-Z Treatment of special subjects, A-Z
4811.A-Z Treatment of special classes, A-Z
Special periods
4813 Early. Medieval
4814 Modern
4815 Biography (Collective)
Poetry
4817 General
Early, Medieval see PT4813
4818 Modern
4819 20th century
4820 Special. Epic, lyric, etc.
4821 Drama
4823 Prose. Prose fiction
Other forms
4827 Wit and humor
4828 Miscellaneous
Folk literature
see GR1+
(4829) Treatises
(4830) Collections of texts
Collections
4831 General
4832 Minor. Selections
Poetry
4834 General
4835 Special forms. Ballads, folk songs, etc.
4836 Translations
Drama
4837 General
4838 Special
Prose
4839 General
4840 Fiction
4841 Oratory. Sermons, etc.
4842 Letters

Low German literature
Collections
Prose -- Continued
4844 Wit and humor
4845 Miscellaneous
Individual authors and works
4846 To 1600
e.g.
4846.A5 Alexander the Great (Romance)
4846.D3 Dance of death
4846.E3 Eberhard, of Gandersheim, fl. 1204-1216
Author of Die Gandersheimer reimchronik
4846.I6 Immessen, Arnold, 15th cent.
4846.I6S8 Der sündenfall
4846.R35 Redentiner osterspiel
4846.R4 Reinke de Vos
4846.R5 Criticism
4847 17th-18th centuries
e.g.
4847.K6 Klinggedichte (ca. 1650)
4847.L3 Lauremberg, Johann, 1590-1658 (Table P-PZ40)
4848 19th century
4848.A24 A. W. (Alwine Wuthenow), 1820-1908 (Table P-PZ40)
4848.F4 Fehrs, Johann Hinrich, 1838-1916 (Table P-PZ40)
4848.F73 Freudenthal, Friedrich, 1849-1929 (Table P-PZ40)
4848.G7 Groth, Klaus, 1819-1899 (Table P-PZ40)
4848.J33 Jahn, Moritz, 1884-1979 (Table P-PZ40)
Reuter, Fritz, 1810-1874
4848.R4 Collected works. By date
4848.R4A2 Selected works. By date
4848.R4A3 Selections. By date
4848.R4A5-.R4Z7 Separate works
Including High German versions
4848.R4D5 Dörchläuchting
Olle kamellen, pt. 6
4848.R4H3 Hanne Nüte un de lütte pudel
4848.R4K4 Kein hüsung (Verse)
4848.R4L3 Läuschen un rimels
4848.R4L5 Neue folge
4848.R4M4 De meckelnbörgschen Montecchi un Capuletti; oder, De reis' nah Konstantinopel
Olle kamellen, pt. 7
4848.R4O5 Olle kamellen (7 parts)
4848.R4P6 Polterabendgedichte
High German and Low German poems
4848.R4R4 De reis' nah Belligen
De reis' nah Konstantinopel see PT4848.R4M4

Low German literature
Individual authors and works
19th century
Reuter, Fritz, 1810-1874
Separate works -- Continued

4848.R4S3 Schurr-Murr

4848.R4T6 Twei lustige geschichten
Olle kamellen, pt. 1; (1) Woans ik tau 'ne fru kamm; (2) Ut de Franzoesentid

4848.R4U3 Ut de Franzosentid
Olle kamellen, pt. 1

4848.R4U5 Ut mine festungstid
Olle kamellen, pt. 2

4848.R4U8 Ut mine stromtid
Olle kamellen, pts. 3-5

4848.R4W7 Woans ik tau 'ne fru kamm
Olle kamellen, pt. 1

4848.R4Z8 Memoirs. Letters. By date
Zwei lustige geschichten see PT4848.R4T6

4848.R5A-.R5Z3 Biography and criticism

4848.R5Z5 Grammar

4848.R5Z7 Glossaries

4848.R5Z9 Illustrations to Reuter's works

4848.R6A-.R6Z Translations, by language, A-Z

4848.R8 Rocco, Wilhelm, 1819-1897 (Table P-PZ40)

4848.S4 Schröder, Wilhelm, 1808-1878 (Table P-PZ40)

4848.S8 Stinde, Julius Ernst Wilhelm, 1841-1905
Class here comedies in Low German

4848.S8B5 Die blumenhändlerin von St. Pauli

Wuthenow, Alwine, 1820-1908 see PT4848.A24

4849 20th century

4849.H34 Harhues, Dieter (Table P-PZ40)

4849.S8 Stavenhagen, Fritz, 1876-1906 (Table P-PZ38)

4849.T3 Tarnow, Rudolf (Table P-PZ40)

4849.3 21st century
Subarrange each author by Table P-PZ40 unless otherwise specified

Local and foreign
For individual authors, except United States see PT4846+

Germany

4851 By region, province, etc.

4855.A-Z By city, A-Z
e.g.

4855.B7 Bremen

4855.H3 Hamburg

4855.L8 Lübeck

Low German literature
Local and foreign -- Continued
4859.A-Z Other European countries, A-Z
America
4860-4867.5 General. North America. United States (Table PT4)
Local
4868.A-Z By region or state, A-Z
4868.5.A-Z By city, A-Z
4869.A-Z Individual authors, A-Z
4870 Canada. British America
4875 Spanish America
4877 Brazil
Other countries
4880 Africa
4885 Asia
4887 Australia. New Zealand
4890 Oceania
4896-4897 Translations from Low German into other languages (Table P-PZ30)

Dutch literature
Including Flemish literature before 1830
Literary history and criticism
5001 Periodicals. Serials
(5003) Yearbooks
see PT5001
5005 Societies
5007 Congresses
5009 Museums. Exhibitions
Subarrange by author
5019 Encyclopedias. Dictionaries
5021 Theory and principles of the study of Dutch literature
5025 History of literary history
5029 Philosophy. Psychology. Aesthetics
Includes national characteristics in literature
Study and teaching
5040 General
5041 General special
5042.A-Z By region or country, A-Z
5043.A-Z By school, A-Z
Biography of teachers, critics, and historians
5043.5 Collective
5044.A-Z Individual, A-Z
Subarrange each by Table P-PZ50
Criticism
5050 Treatises. Theory
5052 History
5053 Special topics (not A-Z)
5054 Collections of essays in criticism
History of Dutch literature
General works
5060 Dutch
5061 English
5062 French
5063 German
5064.A-Z Other languages, A-Z
5069 Outlines, syllabi, etc.
Miscellaneous special aspects
5073 Relation to history, civilization, etc.
Relation to other literatures
5075 General works
5076.A-Z Special, A-Z
5080 Translation of other literatures into Dutch (as subject)
5081 Translation of Dutch literature (as subject)
Treatment of special subjects
5085.A-Z Special topics, A-Z
5085.C67 Cosmology

Literary history and criticism
History of Dutch literature
Treatment of special subjects
Special topics, A-Z -- Continued
5085.F3 Farm life
5085.F34 Fasts and feasts
5085.H47 Heroes
5085.H6 Homosexuality
5085.M55 Mirrors
5085.N3 Nature
5085.P53 Plagiarism
5085.R4 Religion
5085.W37 War
5090.A-Z Special countries and races, A-Z
5093.A-Z Special classes, A-Z
5093.A5 Aliens
5093.N6 Notaries
5093.W6 Women
5095.A-Z Special characters, persons, etc., A-Z
Biography. Memoirs, letters, etc.
5100 Biography (Collective)
5102 Memoirs. Letters
5103 Relations to women, love, marriage, etc.
5104 Iconography: Portraits, monuments, etc.
5105 Literary landmarks. Homes and haunts of authors
5110 Women authors. Literary relations of women
5112.A-Z Other classes of authors, A-Z
5112.J4 Jewish
Special periods
Medieval to 1500/1550
5121 General works
5123.A-Z Special topics, A-Z
5123.C36 Charlemagne, Emperor, 742-814
(5125) Historical literature
see class D
(5129) Religious literature
see class B
(5130) Proverbs
see PN6430+
Poetry
5131 General
5132 Epic
Includes prose romances
5133 Lyric. Minnesingers
5134 Other
5135 Drama
5137 Prose

Literary history and criticism
History of Dutch literature
Special periods -- Continued
16th-17th centuries
5141 General works
5145.A-Z Special topics, A-Z
5145.A46 Almanacs
5145.A47 America
5145.C5 Chambers of rhetoric
5145.E4 Emblems
5145.F35 Family
Literary style see PT5145.S79
5145.L57 Literature and society
5145.N54 Nil Volentibus Arduum (Society)
5145.P67 Pornography
5145.P76 Prostitution
5145.S79 Style, Literary
5145.W58 Wit and humor
5145.W66 Women
Special periods
5150 Reformation period, 1500-1550
5155 Classical period, 1580-1670. The Augustan age
18th century
5160 General works
5165.A-Z Special topics, A-Z
5165.R3 Realism
5165.R7 Romanticism
19th century
5170 General works
5175.A-Z Special topics, A-Z
5175.C37 Catholics
5175.C5 Chambers of rhetoric
5175.D43 Decadence
5175.H47 Heroes
5175.J4 Jews
5175.N35 Naturalism
5175.R4 Religion
5175.S6 Social problems
20th century
5180 General works
5185.A-Z Special topics, A-Z
5185.A8 Authorship
5185.B47 Bergen (Netherlands)
5185.C5 Characters
5185.E4 Emblem books
5185.F44 Feminism
5185.I53 Indonesia

Literary history and criticism
History of Dutch literature
Special periods
20th century
Special topics, A-Z -- Continued

5185.N36 National socialism
5185.P37 Patronage
5185.S63 Soccer
5185.S68 South Africa

21st century

5190 General works
5195.A-Z Special topics, A-Z

Special forms
Poetry

5201 General works
5205.A-Z Special topics, A-Z

Special periods

(5210) Medieval

see PT5131+

16th-17th centuries

5215 General works
5217.A-Z Special topics, A-Z
5217.C49 Christian poetry
5217.C68 Country life
5217.P35 Pamphlets
5217.R38 Refrain
5217.S66 Sonnets

18th century

5220 General works
5222.A-Z Special topics, A-Z

19th century

5225 General works
5227.A-Z Special topics, A-Z

20th century

5230 General works
5232.A-Z Special topics, A-Z

21st century

5233 General works
5234.A-Z Special topics, A-Z

Special forms

5235 Epic poetry
5237 Lyric poetry
5239 Popular poetry. Ballads, songs, etc.
5241.A-Z Other special, A-Z
5241.D5 Didactic
5241.E4 Elegiac
5241.H5 Heroid

Literary history and criticism
Special forms
Poetry
Special forms
Other special, A-Z -- Continued
5241.P3 Pastoral
5241.S4 Sea songs
5243.A-Z Special subjects, A-Z
5243.L6 Love
5243.N3 Nature
5243.R4 Religion
Drama
History of the Dutch stage see PN2710+
5250 General works
5255.A-Z Special topics, A-Z
Special periods
(5260-5262) Medieval
see PT5135
16th-17th centuries
5265 General works
5267.A-Z Special topics, A-Z
5267.F37 Fate
5267.P65 Politics
5267.W66 Women
18th century
5270 General works
5272.A-Z Special topics, A-Z
19th century
5275 General works
5277.A-Z Special topics, A-Z
20th century
5280 General works
5282.A-Z Special topics, A-Z
21st century
5283 General works
5284.A-Z Special topics, A-Z
Special forms
5285 Tragedy
5287 Comedy
5289 Vaudeville. Farce
5293 Folk drama
5295.A-Z Other special, A-Z
Prose
5300 General works
Special periods
(5305) Medieval
see PT5137

Literary history and criticism
Special forms
Prose
Special periods -- Continued
5307 16th-17th centuries
5309 18th century
5311 19th century
5313 20th century
5315 21st century
Special forms
Prose fiction
5320 General works
Special topics
5325 Romanticism
5327 Realism
5330.A-Z Other, A-Z
5330.B55 Bildungsromans
Special periods
Medieval see PT5137
5333 16th-17th centuries
5334 18th century
5335 19th century
5336 20th century
5337 21st century
5340 Oratory
5342 Letters
5344 Essays
5346 Wit and humor
5348 Miscellaneous
Folk literature
For general works on and collections of folk literature, see GR
History
(5351) Periodicals. Societies. Collections
(5352) General works
Collections (of texts exclusively)
(5355) General
Chapbooks
5357 General works
Collections
5358 Reprints
5359 Originals
Includes collections of separate chapbooks bound together
5361 Special chapbooks
Class here originals and reprints
(5365) Poetry, ballads, folk songs, etc.
see PT5480

Folk literature
Collections (of texts exclusively) -- Continued
(5367) Folk drama
see PT5508+
Legends
(5370) General
(5372.A-Z) Local, A-Z
(5375) Fairy tales
(5385) Individual tales
(5395.A-Z) Translations. By language, A-Z
5398 Juvenile literature (General)
For special genres, see the genre
Collections of Dutch literature
General
5400 Collections before 1801
5401 Collections, 1801-
5404 Selections, anthologies, etc.
5409.A-Z Special topics (Prose and verse), A-Z
5409.A5 Amsterdam
5409.A54 Animals
5409.A74 Arnhem, Netherlands
5409.C5 Christmas
5409.E2 Easter
5409.F5 Floods
5409.G64 God
5409.I53 Indonesia
5409.N47 Netherlands
5409.N65 Nonsense literature
5409.R34 Railroads
5409.S86 Suriname
5409.W5 Windmills
5409.W66 Women
5409.Y68 Youth
Translations into foreign languages
5410 Polyglot
5411 English
5412 French
5413 German
5414.A-Z Other. By language, A-Z
Special periods
Medieval (to ca. 1550)
5420 General
Poetry
5425 General
5428 Epic
5431 Lyric
5435.A-Z Other, A-Z

Collections of Dutch literature
Special periods
Medieval (to ca. 1550) -- Continued
Drama
5440 General
5443.A-Z Individual plays, A-Z
5443.A2 Abel spel vanden winter ende vanden somer (Table P-PZ43)
5443.E4 Elckerlije (Everyman) (Table P-PZ43)
5443.E8 Esmoreit (Table P-PZ43)
5443.L3 Lanseloet van Denemarken (Table P-PZ43)
5443.M3 Mariken van Nimmegen (Table P-PZ43)
5443.S4 Sevenste bliscap van Maria (Table P-PZ43)
5444 Prose
5445.A-Z Translations. By language, A-Z
5450 16th-18th centuries
5455 19th century
5460 20th century
5465 21st century
Special forms
Poetry
5470 Collections before 1801
5471 Collections, 1801-
5473 Selections, anthologies, etc.
5474 Selections from women authors
Translations into foreign languages
5475.A2 Polyglot
5475.A5-Z By language, A-Z
Special periods
Medieval see PT5425+
5477 16th-18th centuries
5478 19th-20th centuries
5479 21st century
Special forms and subjects
5480 Ballads, songs, lyrics
5482 Erotic poetry
5484 Historical, political, patriotic poetry
Religious poetry
5486 General works
Hymns
see class B
5488.A-Z Other, A-Z
5488.A2 Achterberg, Gerrit
5488.A5 Animals
5488.C5 Children
5488.C55 Christmas
5488.D4 Death

Collections of Dutch literature
Special forms
Poetry
Special forms and subjects
Other, A-Z -- Continued

5488.D65 Don Quixote
5488.D86 Dutch language
5488.G45 German occupation, 1940-1945
5488.H5 History
5488.L6 Love
5488.M35 Marriage
5488.M4 Medicine
5488.M57 Months
5488.M6 Mothers
5488.M87 Music
5488.N33 Nature
5488.N37 Netherlands
5488.N4 New Year
5488.P4 Peace
5488.P63 Poets
5488.R68 Rotterdam
5488.S3 Satire
5488.S35 Sea songs
5488.S4 Sentimentalism
5488.S6 Sonnets
5488.T48 Textile industry
5488.W3 West Friesland
5488.W45 Wine
5488.W5 Wit and humor
5488.W65 Women
5488.W67 World War I

Drama
5490 Collections before 1801
5491 Collections, 1801-
5493 Selections, anthologies, etc.
5495 Translations. By language, A-Z
Special periods
Medieval see PT5440+
5497 16th-18th centuries
5498 19th-20th centuries
5499 21st century
Special forms
5501 Tragedies
5502 Comedies
5505 Farces (Kluchten), vaudevilles, etc.
Folk drama
5508 General

Collections of Dutch literature
Special forms
Drama
Special forms
Folk drama -- Continued
5509.A-Z Special plays, A-Z
5515.A-Z Other special, A-Z
Prose
5517 General
5518 Selections
5519.A-Z Special classes of authors, A-Z
5519.T73 Travelers
Fiction
5520 General
5523 Selections
5525.A-Z Translations. By language, A-Z
Special periods
Medieval see PT5444
5528 16th-18th centuries
5530 19th-20th centuries
5531 21st century
5532.A-Z Special forms and topics, A-Z
5532.C5 Christmas
5532.D4 Detective and mystery stories
5532.E2 Easter stories
5532.E7 Erotic stories
5532.F35 Fantastic fiction
5532.I53 Indonesia
5532.J47 Jews
5532.N37 Nature stories
5532.N47 Netherlands
5532.S3 Science fiction
5532.S4 Sea stories
5532.T44 Theater
5535 Oratory
5537 Letters
5539 Essays
5539.H7 Hollandsche spectator
5541 Wit and humor
5543 Fables
(5545) Proverbs
see PN6430+
5547 Miscellaneous
Individual authors or works

Individual authors or works -- Continued
Medieval authors, medieval works
Subarrange one number authors by Table P-PZ37 unless otherwise specified
Subarrange Cutter number authors by Table P-PZ40 unless otherwise specified
Subarrange individual works by Table P-PZ43 unless otherwise specified
For medieval plays see PT5443.A+

5555 A - Flo
Baertmaker, Jannede see PT5587.S6
5555.B4 Beatrijs (Table P-PZ43)
5555.B5 Boec van den houte (Table P-PZ43)
5555.B6 Boethius. De consolations philosophiae (Medieval Dutch versions) (Table P-PZ43)
5555.B7 Brendan, Saint. Legend (Medieval Dutch version) (Table P-PZ43)
5555.C3 Catonis disticha (Medieval Dutch version) (Table P-PZ43)
5555.D5 Diederic van Assenede, 13th cent. (Table P-PZ40)
5555.E94 Everaert,Cornelis, ca. 1480-1556 (Table P-PZ40)
5555.F44 Ferguut (Table P-PZ43)
5555.F47 Flandrijs (Table P-PZ43)
5559 Flo - He
5559.F5 Florigout (Table P-PZ43)
Floris ende Blancefloer see PT5555.D5
5559.G34 Gelre, ca. 1345-1414 (Table P-PZ40)
5559.G5 Gloriant (Table P-PZ43)
5559.H2 Haagsch liederenhandschrift (Table P-PZ43)
Cf. PT1419.H2 German songs of the ms.
5559.H3 Hadewijch, Beguine, 13th cent. (Table P-PZ40)
5559.H4 Heer Halewijn (Table P-PZ43)
5560 Hein van Aken, fl. 1280-1325 (Table P-PZ37)
5561 He - Jan
5561.H3 Heinric en Margriete van Limbroch (Table P-PZ43)
Hendrik van Veldeke see PT1540+
5561.J5 Jan Praet, 14th cent. (Table P-PZ40)
5564 Jan van Boendale, called de Clerc, d. 1365 (Table P-PZ37)
5566 Jan van Heelu, fl. 1288 (Table P-PZ37)
5567 Jan - Lan
5567.K3 Karel ende Elegast (Table P-PZ43)
5568 Lancelot, Roman van (Table P-PZ37)
5569 Lan - Mae
Lanseloet van Denemarken see PT5443.L3
5569.L6 Lodewijk, van Velthem, ca. 1270-ca. 1326 (Table P-PZ40)

Individual authors or works
Medieval authors, medieval works
Lan - Mae -- Continued

5569.M3	Madelghijs (Table P-PZ43)
	Cf. PQ1496.M35+ Maugis d'Aigremont (Chanson de geste)
5570-5571	Maerlant, Jacob van, 1235?-1300 (Table P-PZ36)
5575	Mae - Par
5575.O37	Oestvoren, Jacob van (Table P-PZ40)
5576	Partonopeus de Blois (Dutch) (Table P-PZ37)
5577	Par - Pot
5577.P45	Penninc, 13th cent. (Table P-PZ40)
5578	Potter, Dirc, d. 1428 (Table P-PZ37)
5579	Pot - Rei
	Praet, Jan, 14th cent. see PT5561.J5
5579.Q3	Quatre fils Aimon (Dutch) (Table P-PZ43)
	Reinaert de Vos
	Texts
5583.A1	By date
5583.A2A-.A2Z	By editor, A-Z
5584	Translations
5585	History and criticism
5587	Rei - St
5587.R44	Remen, Marigen (Table P-PZ40)
	Renaut de Montauban (Chanson de geste) see PT5579.Q3
5587.R45	Ridderboek
5587.R46	Rijssele, Colijn van, ca. 1430-1503 (Table P-PZ40)
5587.R48	Roman van den riddere metter mouwen (Table P-PZ43)
5587.R5	Roovere, Anthonis de, d. 1482 (Table P-PZ40)
5587.S5	Seven Sages (Dutch) (Table P-PZ43)
5587.S6	Smeken, Jan, d. 1517 (Table P-PZ40)
5587.S74	Speculum Virginum (Medieval Dutch version) (Table P-PZ43)
5588	Stoke, Melis, ca. 1235-1305 (Table P-PZ37)
5589	St - Wee
5589.T8	Tundal's vision (Dutch) (Table P-PZ43)
5589.V28	Van den derden Eduwaert (Table P-PZ43)
5589.V3	Van den levene Ons Heren (Table P-PZ43)
5592	Weert, Jan de, d. 1362? (Table P-PZ37)
5595	Wee - Z
5595.W39	Willem, H., ca. 1250 (Table P-PZ40)
5595.W5	Willem, van Hildegaersberch, ca. 1350-1408 (Table P-PZ40)

Individual authors or works -- Continued
16th-18th centuries
Subarrange Cutter number authors by Table P-PZ40 unless otherwise indicated
Subarrange one number authors by Table P-PZ39 unless otherwise indicated

5600 Anonymous works (Table P-PZ28 modified)
5600.A1A-.A1Z Works without any indication of author, either by symbol or initial. By title, A-Z
5600.A1E7 Esopus in Europa
5601 A - Ans
5601.A7 Alphen, Hieronymus van, 1746-1803 (Table P-PZ40)
5602 Anslo, Reyer (or Reinier), 1626-1669 (Table P-PZ39)
5603 Ans - Ant
5604 Antonides van der Goes, Johannes, 1647-1684 (Table P-PZ39)
5605 Ant - Bij
5605.A84 Asselijn, Thomas, 1620-1701 (Table P-PZ40)
5606 Bijns, Anna, 1494-1575 (Table P-PZ39)
5607 Bij - Bra
Bilderdijk, Willem see PT5810+
5607.B5 Bolswert, Boëce van, ca. 1580-1633 (Table P-PZ40)
5608 Brandt, Geeraert, 1626-1685 (Table P-PZ39)
5609 Bra - Bre
5610 Bredero, Gerbrand Adriaenszoon, 1585-1618 (Table P-PZ39)
5611 Bre - Cat
5611.B8 Brune, Johan de, 1589-1658 (Table P-PZ40)
Cats, Jacob, 1577-1660
5620 Collected works. By date
5621 Selected works
5622 Selections. Anthologies
5623.A-Z Translations. By language, A-Z
Separate works
Emblemata
5625 Texts. By date
5626 Translations. By language and translator
5627 Criticism
5630.A-Z Other works, A-Z
5635 Memoirs, letters, etc
5636 Biography
5637 Criticism
5639 Cats - Coor
5640 Coornhert, Dirk Volkertszoon, 1522-1590 (Table P-PZ39)
5641 Coor - Cos
5642 Coster, Samuel, 1579-1665 (Table P-PZ39)
5643 Cos - Dec

Individual authors or works
16th-18th centuries
Cos - Dec -- Continued

5643.D3 Dale, Jan van den, fl. 1494-1528 (Table P-PZ40)
5644 Decker, Jeremias de, ca. 1609-1666 (Table P-PZ39)
5645 Dec - Dek
(5646) Deken, Agatha
see PT5738
5647 Dek - Eff
5647.D72 Droste, Coenraet, 1642-1734 (Table P-PZ40)
5647.D77 Duijkerius, Johannes, 1661 or 2-1702 (Table P-PZ40)
5647.D83 Duym, Jacob (Table P-PZ40)
5648 Effen, Justus van, 1684-1735 (Table P-PZ39)
For Hollandsche spectator see PT5539.H7
5649 Eff - Fei
5649.E47 Elstland, Lourens van, ca.1643-1698 (Table P-PZ 40)
5650 Feith, Rhijnvis, 1753-1824 (Table P-PZ39)
5651 Fei - Ghi
5651.F6 Focquenbroch, Willem Godschalk van, 1640-1670 (Table P-PZ40)
5652 Ghistele, Cornelis van, 16th cent. (Table P-PZ39)
5653 Ghi - Har
Goes, Johannes Antonides van der see PT5604
5653.G66 Goossens, Gerard, ca. 1545-1603 (Table P-PZ40)
5653.G68 Goudanus (Table P-PZ40)
5653.G76 Grotius, Hugo, 1583-1645 (Table P-PZ40)
Cf. K457.G7 Law (General)
5653.H7 Harduijn, Justus de, 1582-1641 (Table P-PZ40)
5654 Haren, Willem van and Onno Zwier van Haren
5655.H2 Haren, Onno Zwier van, 1711-1779 (Table P-PZ40)
5655.H3 Haren, Willem van, 1710-1768 (Table P-PZ40)
5655.H4-.H9 Haren - Heems
5656 Heemskerk, Johan van, 1597-1656 (Table P-PZ39)
5657 Heems - Hein
5658 Heinsius, Nicolaas, 1656?-1718 (Table P-PZ39)
5659 Hein - Hoof
5659.H84 Hogendorp, Gijsbrecht van, 1589-1639 (Table P-PZ40)
5660 Hooft, Pieter Corneliszoon, 1581-1647 (Table P-PZ39)
5661 Hoof - Hou
5661.H3 Hoogstraten, Jan van, 1662-1756 (Table P-PZ40)
5661.H6 Hout, Jan van, 1542-1609 (Table P-PZ40)
5662 Houwaert, Jan Baptista, 1533-1599 (Table P-PZ39)
5663 Hou - Huy
5664 Huygens, Constantijn, heer van Zuilichem, 1596-1687 (Table P-PZ39)
5665 Huy - Lan
5665.J27 Jansz., Lauris (Table P-PZ40)

Individual authors or works
16th-18th centuries
Huy - Lan -- Continued

5665.J3 Japiks, G. (Table P-PZ40)
5665.K38 Kersteman, Franciscus Lievens, 1728-1793? (Table P-PZ40)
5665.K4 Kersteman, Petrus Lievens (Table P-PZ40)
5665.K5 Kinker, Johannes, 1764-1845 (Table P-PZ40)
5665.K65 Koning, Harmanus, ca. 1735-ca. 1803 (Table P-PZ40)
5665.K78 Krul, Jan Hermansz., 1602-1646 (Table P-PZ40)
5666 Langendijk, Pieter, 1683-1756 (Table P-PZ39)
5667 Lan - Loo
5667.L39 Leenheer, Jan de, 1642-1691 (Table P-PZ40)
5668 Loosjes, Adriaan Pieterszoon, 1761-1818 (Table P-PZ39)
5669 Loo - Lui
5670 Luiken, Jan, 1649-1712 (Table P-PZ39)
5671 Lui - Mar
5671.M3 Mander, Carel van, 1548-1606 (Table P-PZ40)
5672 Marnix, Philippe de, seigneur de Saint-Aldegonde, 1538-1598 (Table P-PZ39)
5673 Mar - Nie
5673.M6 Moonen, Arnold, 1644-1711 (Table P-PZ40)
5674 Nieuwland, Pieter, 1764-1794 (Table P-PZ39)
5675 Ni - Oud
5675.N49 Nomez, Johannes, 1738-1803 (Table P-PZ40)
5675.N5 Noot, Jan van der, 1539 or 40-ca. 1595 (Table P-PZ40)
5676 Oudaan, Joachim, 1628-1692 (Table P-PZ39)
5677 Oud - Poo
5677.O4 Overdorp, Elisabeth Maria (Post), 1755-1812 (Table P-PZ40)
5677.P15 Paape, G. (Gerrit), 1752-1803 (Table P-PZ40)
5677.P45 Perponcher Sedlnitzky, Willem Emmery de, 1741-1819 (Table P-PZ40)
5678 Poot, Hubert Korneliszoon, 1689-1733 (Table P-PZ39)
5679 Poo - Smi
Post, Elisabeth Maria, 1755-1812 see PT5677.O4
5679.R4 Revius, Jacobus, 1586-1658 (Table P-PZ40)
5679.R58 Rodenburgh, Theodore, 1574-1644 (Table P-PZ40)
5679.S37 Schagen, Pieter Jansz, 1578-1636 (Table P-PZ40)
5679.S46 Schonck, E. J. B. (Evert Jan B.), 1745-1821 (Table P-PZ40)
5679.S48 Schurman, Anna Maria van, 1607-1678 (Table P-PZ40)
5679.S57 Six van Chandelier, J. (Jan), 1620-1695 (Table P-PZ40)
5679.S8 Smeeks, Hendrik, d. 1721 (Table P-PZ40)
5680 Smits, Dirk, 1702-1752 (Table P-PZ39)
5681 Smi - Spi

Individual authors or works
16th-18th centuries -- Continued
5682 Spieghel, Hendrick Laurenszoon, 1549-1612 (Table P-PZ39)
5683 Spi - Sta
Subarrange each by Table P-PZ40
5684 Starter, Jan Janszoon, b. 1594 (Table P-PZ39)
5685 Sta - Stee
5686 Steendam, Jacob, b. 1616 (Table P-PZ39)
5687 Stee - Vis
5687.S55 Steven, Andries, ca. 1676-1747 (Table P-PZ40)
5687.S79 Swaanenburg, Willem van, 1679-1728 (Table P-PZ40)
5687.V37 Venne, Adriaen Pietersz, van de, 1589-1662 (Table P-PZ40)
Visscher family
5688 General works
5690 Visscher, Roemer, 1547-1620 (Table P-PZ39)
5692 Visscher, Anna Roemers, 1583-1651 (Table P-PZ39)
5694 Visscher, Maria Tesselschade, 1594-1649 (Table P-PZ39)
5696 Vis - Vol
5696.V49 Visvliet, Jacob, 17th/18th cent. (Table P-PZ40)
5696.V53 Vlaming, Pieter, 1686-1733 (Table P-PZ40)
5697 Vollenhove, Joannes, 1632-1708 (Table P-PZ39)
5698 Vol - Von
Vondel, Joost van den, 1587-1679
5700 Collected works. By date
5701.A-Z Selected works. By editor, A-Z
5703 Selections. Anthologies
5705.A-Z Translations. By language, A-Z
5707 Dictionaries, concordances, etc.
Drama
5710 Collected works
5711 Translations
Separate works
Lucifer
5715 Texts
5716.A-Z Translations. By language, A-Z
5717 Criticism
5718.A-Z Others, A-Z
e.g.
5718.G9 Gysbrecht van Aemstel
5718.M2 Maria Stuart
5718.P2 Palamedes
Lyrics
5720 Collected works
5721.A-Z Translations. By language, A-Z

Individual authors or works
16th-18th centuries
Vondel, Joost van den, 1587-1679
Lyrics -- Continued

5722.A-Z Separate works, A-Z
5725.A-Z Other works, A-Z
5730 Memoirs, letters, etc.
5731 Biography
5732 Criticism
5735 Von - Vos
5736 Vos, Jan, 1620-1667 (Table P-PZ39)
5737 Vos - Wol
5737.V75 Vries, S. de (Simon), b. 1630 (Table P-PZ40)
5737.W43 Wellekens, Jan Baptista, 1658-1726 (Table P-PZ40)
5737.W45 Westerop, R. (Table P-PZ40)
5737.W48 Weyerman, Jacob Campo, 1677-1747 (Table P-PZ40)
5737.W62 Willink, Daniel, 1676-1722 (Table P-PZ40)
5737.W624 Winter, Nicolaas, Simon van, 1718-1795 (Table P-PZ40)
5737.W66 Witte, Jacob Eduard de, 1763-1853 (Table P-PZ40)
5737.W67 Witte Acoleyen (Society) (Table P-PZ40)
5738 Wolff, Elisabeth (Bekker), 1738-1804, and Agatha Deken, 1741-1804 (Table P-PZ39)
5739 Wol - Z
5739.Z45 Zevecote, Jacob van, ca. 1590-1642 (Table P-PZ40)

1800-1960

Subarrange Cutter number authors by Table P-PZ40 unless otherwise indicated

Subarrange one number authors by Table P-PZ39 unless otherwise indicated

5800 Anonymous works (Table P-PZ28)
5801 A - Alb
5801.A6 Aafjes, Bertus, 1914- (Table P-PZ40)
5801.A63 Achterberg, Gerrit, 1905- (Table P-PZ40)
5802 Alberdingk Thijm, Josephus Albertus, 1820-1889 (Table P-PZ39)
5804 Alberdingk Thijm, Karel Joan Lodewijk, 1864-1952 (Table P-PZ39)
5805 Alb - Ant
5805.A6 Ammers-Küller, Jo van, 1884- (Table P-PZ40)
5806 Antal-Opzoomer, Adèle Sophia Cornelia von, 1857-1925 (Table P-PZ39)
5807 Ant - Bee
5807.B717 Barnard, W., 1920- (Table P-PZ40)
5808 Beets, Nicolaas, 1814-1903 (Table P-PZ39)
5809 Bee - Bil
Belcampo, 1902- see PT5868.S32
5809.B62 Bergh, Herman van den, 1897- (Table P-PZ40)

Individual authors or works
1800-1960 -- Continued
Bilderdijk, Willem, 1756-1831
5810 Works. By date
5811 Dictionaries, concordances, etc.
5812 Biography and criticism
5813 Bil - Bog
5813.B5 Blijstra, Reinder, 1901-1975 (Table P-PZ40)
5813.B53 Bloem, Jakobus Cornelis, 1887- (Table P-PZ40)
5813.B545 Boekeren, Rinse Koopmans van, 1832-1896 (Table P-PZ40)
5815 Bogaers, Adrianus, 1795-1870 (Table P-PZ39)
5816 Bog - Bor
5816.B585 Bomans, Godfriend Jan Arnold, 1913- (Table P-PZ40)
5816.B7 Bordewijk, Ferdinand, 1884- (Table P-PZ40)
5817 Borel, Henri, 1869-1933 (Table P-PZ39)
5818 Bor - Bos
5819 Bosboom-Toussaint, Anna Louisa Geertruida, 1812-1886 (Table P-PZ39)
5820 Bos - Bri
Brabander, Gerard den see PT5844.J57
Brandt, Willem see PT5850.K46
5820.B5 Boudier-Bakker, Ina, 1875- (Table P-PZ40)
5820.B55 Boutens, Pieter Cornelis, 1870-1943 (Table P-PZ40)
5820.B65 Braak, Menno ter, 1902-1940 (Table P-PZ40)
5821 Brink, Jan ten, 1834-1901 (Table P-PZ39)
5822 Bri - Cos
5822.B38 Brinkel, B.G.F., 1927- (Table P-PZ40)
5822.B67 Brugman, Til, 1888-1958 (Table P-PZ40)
5822.B7 Bruijn, Cornelis Pieter, 1883- (Table P-PZ40)
5822.B74 Bruin, Hein de, 1899-1947 (Table P-PZ40)
5822.B768 Bruning, Henri, 1900- (Table P-PZ40)
Busken Huet, Conrad, 1826-1886 see PT5844.H77
5822.C32 Campert, Jan, 1902-1943 (Table P-PZ40)
5822.C323 Campert, Remco, 1929- (Table P-PZ40)
Charles, J.B., 1910- see PT5860.N22
5822.C43 Christemeijer, Jan Bastijaan, 1794-1872 (Table P-PZ40)
5822.C515 Coenen, Frans, 1866-1936 (Table P-PZ40)
5822.C6 Coolen, Antoon, 1897- (Table P-PZ40)
Corsari, Willy, 1897- see PT5830.D66
5823 Costa, Izaäc da, 1798-1860 (Table P-PZ39)
5824 Cos - Cou
5825 Couperus, Louis Marie Anne,1863-1923 (Table P-PZ39)
5826 Cou - Cre
5827 Cremer, Jacobus Jan, 1827-1880 (Table P-PZ39)
5828 Cre - Dek
Daalberg, Bruno see PT5879

Individual authors or works
1800-1960
Cre - Dek -- Continued

5828.D6 Daum, Paul Adriaan, 1849-1898 (Table P-PZ40)
5828.D7 Debrot, Cola, 1902- (Table P-PZ40)
5829 Dekker, Eduard Douwes, 1820-1887 (Table P-PZ39)
5830 Dek - Eed
5830.D4 Dekker, Maurits Rudolph Jöel, 1896- (Table P-PZ40)
Dendermande, Max see PT5840.H42
5830.D434 Dermoût, Maria, 1888- (Table P-PZ40)
Deyssel, L. van see PT5804
Doolaard, A. den, 1901- see PT5868.S8
5830.D66 Douwes-Schmidt, Wilhelmina Angela, 1900- (Table P-PZ40)
5830.D68 Droogleever Fortuyn-Leenmans, Margaretha, 1909- (Table P-PZ40)
5830.D74 Dubois, Pierre Hubert, 1917- (Table P-PZ40)
5831 Eeden, Frederik Willem van, 1860-1932 (Table P-PZ39)
5832 Eed - Em
5832.E5 Eggink, Clara, 1906- (Table P-PZ40)
5833 Emants, Marcellus, 1848-1923 (Table P-PZ39)
5834 Em - Gen
5834.E54 Engelman, Jan, 1900- (Table P-PZ40)
5834.E83 Eyck, Pieter Nicolaas van, 1887-1954 (Table P-PZ40)
5834.E9 Eysselsteijn, Ben van, 1898- (Table P-PZ40)
5834.F3 Fabricius, Jan, 1871- (Table P-PZ40)
5834.F32 Fabricius, Johan Wigmore, 1899 (Table P-PZ40)
Falkland, Samuel see PT5841
5834.F48 Feylbrief, J.K., 1876-1951 (Table P-PZ40)
5834.F75 Franquinet, Robert, 1915- (Table P-PZ40)
5835 Genestet, Petrus Augustus de, 1829-1861 (Table P-PZ39)
5836 Gen - Gor
5836.G35 Gerhardt, Ida Gardina Margaretha, 1905 (Table P-PZ40)
5836.G37 Gerretson, Frederik Carel, 1884-1958 (Table P-PZ40)
Geuring, E.W., 1832-1896 see PT5813.B545
5837 Gorter, Herman, 1864-1927 (Table P-PZ39)
5838 Gor - Has
Gossaert, Geerten, 1884-1958 see PT5836.G37
5838.G63 Graaff, Chris de, 1890-1955 (Table P-PZ40)
Graft, Guillaume van der see PT5807.B717
5838.G7 Greshoff, Jan, 1888- (Table P-PZ40)
5838.G738 Groeningen, August P. van, 1866-1894 (Table P-PZ40)
5838.G74 Grönloh, J.H.F., 1881-1961 (Table P-PZ40)
5838.G78 Groot, Jan Hendrik de, 1901- (Table P-PZ40)
5838.H4 Haan, Jacob Israël de, 1881-1924 (Table P-PZ40)
5838.H44 Haas-Okken, Titia K.E. de (Table P-PZ40)
Hage, Jan van den see PT5861

Individual authors or works
1800-1960
Gor - Has -- Continued
5838.H65 Hartog, Jan de, 1914- (Table P-PZ40)
5838.H92 Hasebroek, Elisabeth Johanna, 1811-1887 (Table P-PZ40)
5839 Hasebroek, Johannes Petrus, 1812-1896 (Table P-PZ39)
5840 Has - Hei
5840.H2 Haspels, George Frans, 1864-1916 (Table P-PZ40)
5840.H3 Hattum, Jac van, 1900- (Table P-PZ40)
5840.H4 Haverschmidt, François, 1835-1894 (Table P-PZ40)
5840.H42 Hazelhoff, Henk, 1919- (Table P-PZ40)
5840.H43 Heeroma, Klaas Hanzen, 1909- (Table P-PZ40)
5841 Heijermans, Herman, 1864-1924 (Table P-PZ39)
5842 Hei - Hel
5843 Helmers, Jan Frederik, 1767-1813 (Table P-PZ39)
5844 Helm - Kate
Helman, Albert, 1903- see PT5854.L5
5844.H526 Hermans, Willem Frederik, 1921- (Table P-PZ40)
5844.H537 Heusden, E.G. van (Table P-PZ40)
5844.H538 Heyermans, Herman, 1824-1910 (Table P-PZ40)
Hildebrand see PT5808
5844.H6 Hoop, Adriaan van der, 1802-1841 (Table P-PZ40)
5844.H62 Hoornik, Eduard, 1910- (Table P-PZ40)
(5844.H75) Huël, Frits
see PT5844.H78
5844.H77 Huet, Coenraad Busken, 1826-1886 (Table P-PZ40)
5844.H78 Huffnagel, Godfried Eliza, 1892 (Table P-PZ40)
Jacobse, Muus see PT5840.H43
5844.J34 Jansen, P.G. (Table P-PZ40)
5844.J57 Jofriet, J.G., 1900- (Table P-PZ40)
Jonathan see PT5839
5845 Kate, Jan Jakob Lodewijk ten, 1819-1888 (Table P-PZ39)
5846 Kate - Kel
5846.K9 Kelk, Cornelis Jan, 1901-5847 (Table P-PZ40)
5847 Keller, Gerard, 1829-1899 (Table P-PZ39)
5848 Kel - Klo
5848.K36 Kemp, Pierre, 1886- (Table P-PZ40)
5848.K444 Keuning, Jan, 1850-1926 (Table P-PZ40)
5848.K446 Keuning, Willem Eduard, 1887-1939 (Table P-PZ40)
5848.K54 Klant, Johannes Jacobus, 1915- (Table P-PZ40)
Klikspaan see PT5850.K5
5849 Kloos, Willem Johannes Theodorus, 1859-1938 (Table P-PZ39)
5850 Klo - Lap
5850.K46 Klooster, W.S.B., 1905- (Table P-PZ40)
5850.K5 Kneppelhout, Johannes, 1814-1885 (Table P-PZ40)

Individual authors or works
1800-1960
Klo - Lap
5850.K65 Koenen, Marie, 1879- (Table P-PZ40)
5850.K7 Koetsveld, Cornelis Elisa van, 1807-1893 (Table P-PZ40)
5850.K77 Kossmann, Alfred, 1922- (Table P-PZ40)
5850.K859 Krüseman, Mina, 1839-1922 (Table P-PZ40)
Langen, Ferdinand see PT5862.P415
5851 Lapidoth-Swarth, Stephanie Hélène, 1859-5852 (Table P-PZ39)
5852 Lap - Len
5852.L64 Leeuw, Aart van der, 1876-1931 (Table P-PZ40)
5852.L66 Lehmann, L. Th., 1920- (Table P-PZ40)
5852.L8 Lennart, Clare, 1904- (Table P-PZ40)
5853 Lennep, Jakob van, 1802-1868 (Table P-PZ39)
5854 Len - Log
5854.L4 Leopold, Jan Hendrik, 1865-1925 (Table P-PZ40)
5854.L5 Lichtveld, Lou, 1903- (Table P-PZ40)
5854.L55 Linde, Gerrit van de, 1808-1858 (Table P-PZ40)
5854.L6 Lindo, Mark Prager, 1819-1877 (Table P-PZ40)
5854.L77 Lodeizen, Hans, 1924-1950 (Table P-PZ40)
Loenen, Gabrielle van see PT5868.S19
5855 Loghem, Martinus Gesinus Lambert van, 1849-1934 (Table P-PZ39)
5856 Log - Mau
5856.L7 Looy, Jacobus van, 1855-1930 (Table P-PZ40)
Lucebert see PT5870.S79
Maartens, Maarten see PR5299.S44
5856.M62 Marja, A., 1917-1964 (Table P-PZ40)
5856.M63 Markus, Lion, 1867-1926 (Table P-PZ40)
5856.M64 Marsman, Hendrik, 1899-1940 (Table P-PZ40)
5857 Maurik, Justus van, 1846-1904 (Table P-PZ39)
5858 Mau - Mes
Mauritz see PT5828.D6
Mauritz see PT5867
5858.M47 Meijer, Hendrik Arnold, 1810-1854 (Table P-PZ40)
Mendes, Joost see PT5866.Q39
5858.M5 Mens, Jans, 1897- (Table P-PZ40)
Mérode, Willem de see PT5848.K446
5859 Messchert, Willem, 1790-1844 (Table P-PZ39)
5860 Mes - Olt
5860.M43 Meulen, J. van der (Table P-PZ40)
5860.M7 Moens, Petronella, 1762-1843 (Table P-PZ40)
5860.M72 Moerkerken, Pieter Hendrik van, 1877-1951 (Table P-PZ40)
5860.M74 Mok, Maurits, 1907- (Table P-PZ40)

Individual authors or works
1800-1960
Mes - Olt -- Continued
5860.M752 Mondrian, Piet, 1872-1944 (Table P-PZ40)
Cf. ND653.M76 Painting
Mooij, Arend Theodoor, 1917-1964 see PT5856.M62
5860.M76 Morrien, Adriaan, 1912- (Table P-PZ40)
5860.M85 Mulisch, Harry, 1927- (Table P-PZ40)
Multatuli see PT5829
Naeff, Top see PT5866.R65
5860.N22 Nagel, Willem Hendrik (Table P-PZ40)
Nescio, 1881-1961 see PT5838.G74
5860.N42 Netscher, Frans, 1864-1923 (Table P-PZ40)
5860.N487 Nievelt, Carel van (Table P-PZ40)
5860.N495 Nijhoff, Antoinette Hendrika (Wind), 1897- (Table P-PZ40)
5860.N5 Nijhoff, Martinus, 1894-1953 (Table P-PZ40)
5860.N6 Nouhuys, Willem Gerard van, 1854-1914 (Table P-PZ40)
5861 Oltmans, Jan Frederik, 1806-1854 (Table P-PZ39)
5862 Olt - Per
O'Mill, John see PT5860.M43
Oudshoorn, J. van see PT5834.F48
5862.P3 Paap, Willem Anthony, 1856-1923 (Table P-PZ40)
5862.P415 Pannekoek, E., 1918- (Table P-PZ40)
5862.P43 Pauwels, François Désiré, 1888- (Table P-PZ40)
5863 Perk, Jacques Fabrice Herman, 1859-1881 (Table P-PZ39)
5864 Per - Pot
5864.P3 Perron, Edgar du, 1899-1940 (Table P-PZ40)
5864.P37 Philips, Marianne, 1886-1951 (Table P-PZ40)
Plas, Michel van der see PT5822.B38
5865 Potgieter, Everhardus Johannes, 1808-1875 (Table P-PZ39)
5866 Pot - Roc
5866.Q39 Querido, Emanuel, 1871-1943 (Table P-PZ40)
5866.Q4 Querido, Israël, 1874-1932 (Table P-PZ40)
5866.R5 Rees, Willem Adriaan van, 1820-1898 (Table P-PZ40)
5866.R545 Rensburg, J.K., 1870-1943 (Table P-PZ40)
5866.R65 Rhijn-Naeff, Antoinette van, 1878-1953 (Table P-PZ40)
5866.R713 Riemsnijder, Hendrik (Table P-PZ40)
5867 Rochemont, Johannes Izaak de (Table P-PZ39)
5868 Roc - Sta
5868.R26 Roelofsz, Charles, 1897- (Table P-PZ40)
5868.R27 Roest Crollius, B., 1912- (Table P-PZ40)
5868.R48 Roland Holst, Adrianus, 1888- (Table P-PZ40)
5868.R5 Roland Holst, Henriette (van der Schalk), 1869-1952 (Table P-PZ40)
Saks, J. see PT5880.W486

Individual authors or works
1800-1960
Roc - Sta -- Continued
5868.S18 Schagen, Johan Christiaan Jacob van, 1891- (Table P-PZ40)
5868.S19 Schaik-Willing, Jeanne Gabrielle van, 1895- (Table P-PZ40)
5868.S236 Scheltema, Carel Steven Adama van, 1877-1924 (Table P-PZ40)
5868.S24 Schendel, Arthur van, 1874-1946 (Table P-PZ40)
5868.S3 Schimmel, Hendrik Jan, 1823-1906 (Table P-PZ40)
5868.S32 Schöfeld Wichers, Herman (Table P-PZ40)
5868.S39 Schuur, Koos, 1915- (Table P-PZ40)
Schuurstra, Hajo, 1832-1896 see PT5813.B545
Schwartz, Jozua Marius Willem van der Poorten see PR5299.S44
5868.S56 Slauerhoff, Jan Jacob, 1898-1936 (Table P-PZ40)
5868.S634 Smit, Wisse Alfred Pierre, 1903- (Table P-PZ40)
5868.S8 Spoelstra, Cornelis, 1901- (Table P-PZ40)
5869 Staring, Antoni Christiaan Winand, 1767-1840 (Table P-PZ39)
5870 Sta - Tol
Steen, Eric van der see PT5880.Z54
5870.S75 Stuiveling, Garmt, 1907- (Table P-PZ40)
5870.S77 Suchtelen, Nicolaas Johannes van, 1878- (Table P-PZ40)
5870.S79 Swaanswijk, Lubertus Jacobus, 1924- (Table P-PZ40)
Swarth, Hélène, 1859-1941 see PT5851
Thijssen, Adam, 1832-1896 see PT5813.B545
Tinarlo, Frans, 1832-1896 see PT5813.B545
5873 Tollens, Hendrik, 1780-1856 (Table P-PZ39)
5874 Tol - Ver
Vasalis, M see PT5830.D68
5874.V27 Veen, Adriaan van der, 1916- (Table P-PZ40)
5874.V385 Ver Huell, Alexander, 1822-1897 (Table P-PZ40)
For works limited to biography see N6953.A+
5874.V6 Vermaat, Wilhelmina, 1873- (Table P-PZ40)
5875 Verwey, Albert, 1865-1937 (Table P-PZ39)
5876 Ver - Vos
5876.V43 Vestdijk, Simon, 1898- (Table P-PZ40)
5876.V463 Vinkenoog, Simon, 1928- (Table P-PZ40)
5876.V48 Visser, Ab, 1913- (Table P-PZ40)
5877 Vosmaer, Carel, 1826-1888 (Table P-PZ39)
5878 Vos - Wac
5878.V58 Vries, Hendrik de, 1896- (Table P-PZ40)
5878.V75 Vriesland, Victor Emanuel van, 1892- (Table P-PZ40)
5878.V8 Vroman, Leo, 1915- (Table P-PZ40)

Individual authors or works
1800-1960
Vos - Wac -- Continued

5878.V85 Vrught, Johanna P., 1906- (Table P-PZ40)
5879 Wacker van Zon, Petrus de, 1758-1818 (Table P-PZ39)
5880 Wac - Z
Wallis, A.S.C. see PT5806
Werfhorst, Aar van de see PT5844.J34
5880.W4 Wermeskerken, Henri van, 1882- (Table P-PZ40)
5880.W45 Werumeus Buning, Johan Willem Frederik, 1891- (Table P-PZ40)
5880.W486 Wiedijk, Pieter, 1867-1938 (Table P-PZ40)
Wiegman, J.L.N., 1832-1896 see PT5813.B545
Wilma see PT5874.V6
5880.W68 Woude, Johan van der, 1906- (Table P-PZ40)
5880.Z47 Zernike, Elizabeth, 1891- (Table P-PZ40)
5880.Z54 Zijlstra, D., 1907- (Table P-PZ40)
5881-5881.36 1961-2000 (Table P-PZ29 modified)
Here are usually to be classified authors beginning to publish about 1950, flourishing after 1960
5881.1 A
Andreus, Hans, 1926-1977 see PT5881.36.A55
5881.1.R6 Armando, 1929- (Table P-PZ40)
5881.14 D
Dijkman, Bart see PT5881.18.A74
Dodeweerd, Herman Dirk van, 1929- see PT5881.1.R6
5881.17 G
5881.17.R595 Groot, Boudewijn de, 1944- (Table P-PZ40)
Groot, Frank de, 1944- see PT5881.17.R595
5881.18 H
5881.18.A74 Harthoorn, W. L. (Table P-PZ 40)
5881.25 O
5881.25.P85 Opsomer, D. (Table P-PZ40)
5881.26 P
5881.26.I7 Piraña, Julien (Table P-PZ40)
5881.29 S
Sing, Eugene Wilfried Wong Loi see PT5881.33.O39
5881.32 V
Viresman, D. see PT5881.25.P85
5881.33 W
Wielemaker, Kees see PT5881.26.I7
5881.33.O39 Wols, Frits (Table P-PZ40)
5881.36 Z
5881.36.A55 Zant, Johan Wilhelm van der, 1926-1977 (Table P-PZ40)
5882-5882.36 2001- (Table P-PZ29 modified)
5882.21 K
Klundert, Raymond van de, 1964- see PT5882.21.L88

Individual authors or works
2001-
K -- Continued
5882.21.L88 Kluun, 1964- (Table P-PZ40)
Dutch literature: Provincial, local, foreign
For works and biography and criticism of individual authors, except North American see PT5555+

Provincial, local, etc.
5901.A-Z By region, A-Z
Subarrange individual places by Table P-PZ26
5902.A-Z By province, A-Z
Subarrange individual places by Table P-PZ26
5903.A-Z By place, A-Z
Subarrange individual places by Table P-PZ26
Dutch literature in Belgium (Before 1830)
For Flemish literature since 1830 see PT6000+
5905 General
5906.A-Z By province, A-Z
Subarrange individual places by Table P-PZ26
5907.A-Z By place, A-Z
Subarrange individual places by Table P-PZ26
Dutch literature outside of the Netherlands
5910 General
5911-5929 Dutch East Indies
5911 General works
5912 General special
5914 Biography (Collective)
Special periods
5916 To 1800
5917 19th-20th centuries
5918 21st century
Special forms
5919 Poetry
5920 Drama
5921 Prose fiction
5922 Other
Collections
5923 General
5924 Poetry
5925 Drama
5926 Prose fiction
5927 Other special forms
5928.A-Z Local, A-Z
Subarrange individual places by Table P-PZ26
(5929) Individual authors
5931-5949 Dutch West Indies
5931 General works

Dutch literature: Provincial, local, foreign
Dutch literature outside of the Netherlands
Dutch West Indies -- Continued

5932 General special
5934 Biography (Collective)
Special periods
5936 To 1800
5937 19th-20th centuries
5938 21st century
Special forms
5939 Poetry
5940 Drama
5941 Prose fiction
5942 Other
Collections
5943 General
5944 Poetry
5945 Drama
5946 Prose fiction
5947 Other special forms
5948.A-Z Local, A-Z
Subarrange individual places by Table P-PZ26
(5949) Individual authors
North America, except Dutch West Indies
5951 General works
5952 General special
5954 Biography (Collective)
Special periods
5956 To 1800
5957 19th-20th centuries
5958 21st century
Special forms
5959 Poetry
5960 Drama
5961 Prose fiction
5962 Other
Collections
5963 General
5964 Poetry
5965 Drama
5966 Prose fiction
5967 Other special forms
Local
United States
5968 General works
5969.A-.W By state, A-W
Subarrange individual states by Table P-PZ26

Dutch literature: Provincial, local, foreign
Dutch literature outside of the Netherlands
North America, except Dutch West Indies
Local -- Continued

5972.A-Z Other countries, A-Z
Subarrange individual places by Table P-PZ26

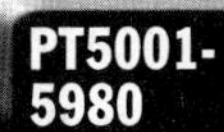

5975.A-Z Individual authors, A-Z
Subarrange each author by Table P-PZ40

5980.A-Z Other countries, A-Z
Subarrange individual places by Table P-PZ26

Flemish literature since 1830
For literature before 1830, see Dutch literature
For surveys of Belgium literature as a whole see PQ3810+
Literary history and criticism
6000 Periodicals. Serials
(6003) Yearbooks
see PT6000
6005 Societies
6007 Congresses
6010 Museums
6019 Encyclopedias. Dictionaries
6021 Theory and principles of the study of Flemish literature
6027.A-Z Biography of historians and critics, A-Z
6029 Philosophy. Psychology. Aesthetics
Includes national characteristics in literature
6040 Study and teaching
6050 Criticism
History of Flemish literature
6060 General works
6069 Outlines, syllabi, etc.
Miscellaneous special aspects
6075 Relation to other literature
6081.A-Z Treatment of special subjects, A-Z
6081.A58 Antwerp
6081.A73 Ardennes
6081.A97 Authorship
6081.M87 Music
6081.T4 Teachers
6081.Y6 Youth
6100 Biography. Memoirs. Letters
6110 Women authors
Special periods
6120 19th century
6130 20th century
6133 21st century
Special forms
6140 Poetry
6150 Drama
For history of the Belgian stage see PN2700+
Prose
6160 General works
6170 Fiction
Other forms
6180 Oratory
6185 Letters
6190 Essays
6195 Wit and humor

Literary history and criticism
History of Flemish literature
Special forms
Prose
Other forms -- Continued
6199 Miscellaneous
Folk literature
For general works on and collections of folk literature, see GR
(6200) History and criticism
Collections (of texts exclusively)
(6215) General
6217 Chapbooks
(6219) Poetry, ballads, songs
see PT6330+
Prose tales. Legends
(6221) General works
(6223.A-Z) Special localities, A-Z
(6224) Fairy tales
(6225.A-Z) Special characters, persons, etc., A-Z
(6228.A-Z) Individual tales, A-Z
(6230.A-Z) Translations. By language, A-Z
6250 Juvenile literature (General)
For special genres, see the genre
Collections of Flemish literature
6300 General
6315 Minor
6320.A-Z Translations. By language, A-Z
Special forms
Poetry
6330 General
6335 Minor
6340.A-Z Translations. By language, A-Z
Special forms and subjects
6342 Ballads, songs, lyrics
6344 Historical, political, patriotic poetry
6346 Religious poetry
6348.A-Z Other, A-Z
6348.B77 Brussels
6348.F45 Flanders
6348.L7 Love poetry
6348.L9 Lys Valley
Drama
6350 General
6355 Minor
6360.A-Z Translations. By language, A-Z
Prose
6365 General

Collections of Flemish literature
Special forms
Prose -- Continued
6367 Minor. Selections
Fiction
6370 General
6375 Minor
6380.A-Z Translations. By language, A-Z
6382.A-Z Special subjects, A-Z
Other special forms
6385 Oratory
6388 Letters
6391 Essays
6394 Wit and humor
6397 Miscellaneous
Individual authors or works
Subarrange Cutter number authors by Table P-PZ40 unless otherwise indicated
Subarrange one number authors by Table P-PZ39 unless otherwise indicated
1830-1960
6400 Anonymous works (Table P-PZ28)
6401 A - Beer
6401.A8 Aken, Piet van, 1920- (Table P-PZ40)
6404 Beers, Jan van, 1821-1888 (Table P-PZ39)
6405 Beer - Berg
Bellefroid, Marthe see PT6430.G75
6405.B6 Belser, Reimond Karel Maria de (Table P-PZ40)
6406 Bergmann, Anton (Table P-PZ39)
6407 Berg - Buy
6407.B18 Berkhof, Aster, 1920- (Table P-PZ40)
6407.B54 Bo, Leonard Lodewijk de, 1826-1885 (Table P-PZ40)
6407.B557 Bom, Emmanuel de, 1868-1953 (Table P-PZ40)
6407.B57 Boon, Louis Paul, 1909- (Table P-PZ40)
6407.B66 Brabant, Luc van, 1909- (Table P-PZ40)
6407.B776 Brulez, Raymond, 1895- (Table P-PZ40)
6407.B9 Burssens, Gaston, 1896-1965 (Table P-PZ40)
6408 Buysse, Cyriël, 1859-1932 (Table P-PZ39)
6408.5 Buysse - Clercq
6408.5.B3 Buysse, Émile (Table P-PZ40)
6408.5.C3 Cauwelaért, August van, 1885-1945 (Table P-PZ40)
6408.5.C46 Ceuppens, Henri Paul René, 1923- (Table P-PZ40)
6409 Clercq, René de, 1877-1932 (Table P-PZ39)
6410 Cl - Con
6410.C5 Claes, Ernest, 1885- (Table P-PZ40)
6410.C553 Claus, Hugo, 1929- (Table P-PZ40)
Conscience, Hendrik, 1812-1883

Individual authors or works
1830-1960
Conscience, Hendrik, 1812-1883i -- Continued
6411.A1 Collected works. By date
6411.A5-Z Separate works
6412 Biography and criticism
6416 Con - Cou
6416.C47 Coole, Marcle, 1913- (Table P-PZ40)
6416.C58 Coupé, C.P., 1918- (Table P-PZ40)
6417 Courtmans-Berchmans, Johanna Desideria, 1811-1890 (Table P-PZ39)

6418 Cou- Dro
Daisne, Johan see PT6458.T35
6418.D23 Dautzenberg, Jon Michiel, 1808-1869 (Table P-PZ40)
6418.D33 Decorte, Bert, 1915- (Table P-PZ40)
6418.D338 Delcroix, Désiré (or Desideer), 1823-1887 (Table P-PZ40)
6418.D34 Demedts, André, 1906- (Table P-PZ40)
6418.D343 Demedts, Gabriëlle, 1909- (Table P-PZ40)
6418.D42 Dewatchter, Richard, 1897- (Table P-PZ40)
6423 Droogenbroeck, Jan Amand van, 1835-1902 (Table P-PZ39)
6424 Dro - Duy
Du Parc, Jean see PT6442.P82
6425 Duyse, Prudens van, 1804-1859 (Table P-PZ39)
6426 Duy - Gey
Elsschot, Willem, 1882-1960 see PT6442.R5
Ferguut, Jan see PT6423
6427 Geyter, Jan de, 1830-1915 (Table P-PZ39)
6428 Gey - Gez
6429 Gezelle, Guido, 1830-1899 (Table P-PZ39)
6430 Gez - Hie
6430.G35 Gheldere, Karl de, 1839-1913 (Table P-PZ40)
Gijsen, Marnix see PT6430.G67
6430.G5 Gilliams, Maurice, 1900- (Table P-PZ40)
6430.G67 Goris, Jan Albert, 1899- (Table P-PZ40)
6430.G75 Gronon, Rose, 1901-1979 (Table P-PZ40)
6430.G8 Gyselen, Blanka, 1909- (Table P-PZ40)
Hegeling, W. see PT6442.P82
6430.H4 Hemeldonck, Emiel van, 1897- (Table P-PZ40)
Hensen, Herwig see PT6440.M45
6431 Hiel, Emanuel, 1834-1899 (Table P-PZ39)
6432 Hie - Ker
6432.J3 Janssen, Jos, 1888- (Table P-PZ40)
6432.J75 Jonckheere, Karel, 1906- (Table P-PZ40)
6432.J79 Joostens, Renaat Antoon, 1902- (Table P-PZ40)
6433 Kerckhoven, Peter Frans van, 1818-1857 (Table P-PZ39)

	Individual authors or works
	1830-1960 -- Continued
6434	Ker - Led
6434.K85	Kuypers, Julien, 1892- (Table P-PZ40)
6434.L43	Lampo, Hubert, 1920- (Table P-PZ40)
6434.L5	Langendonck, Prosper van, 1862-1920 (Table P-PZ40)
6434.L6	Lateur, Frank, 1871-1969 (Table P-PZ40)
6434.L7	Labeau, Paul, 1908- (Table P-PZ40)
6435	Ledeganck, Karel Lodewijk, 1805-1847 (Table P-PZ39)
6436	Led - Lov
6437	Loveling, Rosalie, 1834-1875 (Table P-PZ39)
6439	Loveling, Virginie, 1836-1923 (Table P-PZ39)
6440	Lov - Mont
6440.M323	Martens, Gaston Marie, 1883- (Table P-PZ40)
6440.M33	Matthijs, Marcel, 1899-1964 (Table P-PZ40)
	Michiels, Ivo, 1923- see PT6408.5.C46
6440.M45	Mielants, Florent Constant Albert, 1917- (Table P-PZ40)
6440.M54	Minne, Richard, 1891- (Table P-PZ40)
6440.M7	Moens, Wies, 1898- (Table P-PZ40)
6441	Mont, Karel Maria Polydoor de, 1857-1931 (Table P-PZ39)
6442	Mont - Rij
6442.M9	Mussche Achilles Jozef, 1896- (Table P-PZ40)
6442.N2	Nahon, Alice, 1896-1933 (Table P-PZ40)
6442.N5	Nijlen, Jan van, 1879- (Table P-PZ40)
6442.O4	Oever, Karel van den, 1879-1926 (Table P-PZ40)
6442.O8	Ostayen, Paul van, 1896-1928 (Table P-PZ40)
6442.P436	Persijn, Jules, 1878-1933 (Table P-PZ40)
6442.P44	Pillecyn, Filip de, 1891- (Table P-PZ40)
6442.P82	Putnam, Willem, 1900-1954 (Table P-PZ40)
6442.R5	Ridder, Alfons de, 1882-1960 (Table P-PZ40)
6443	Rijswijck, Theodoor van, 1811-1849 (Table P-PZ39)
6444	Rij - Roo
6444.R6	Rodenbach, Albrecht, 1856-1800 (Table P-PZ40)
6444.R66	Roelants, Maurice, 1895- (Table P-PZ40)
6445	Rooses, Max, 1839-1914 (Table P-PZ39)
6446	Roo - Sle
	Ruyslinck, Ward see PT6405.B6
6447	Sleeckz, Jan Lambrecht Domien, 1818-1901 (Table P-PZ39)
6448	Sle - Sni
6449	Snieders, August, 1825-1904 (Table P-PZ39)
6451	Snieders, Jan Renier, 1812-1888 (Table P-PZ39)
6452	Sni - Sti
6453	Stijns, Reimond, 1850-1905 (Table P-PZ39)
6454	Sti - Str
	Streuvels, Stijn see PT6434.L6
6456	Str - Tei

Individual authors or works
1830-1960
Str - Tei -- Continued
6456.T8 Teirlinck, Herman, 1879- (Table P-PZ40)
6457 Teirlinck, Isidoor, 1851-1934 (Table P-PZ39)
6458 Tei - Vuy
6458.T35 Thiery, Herman (Table P-PZ40)
6458.T37 Thiry, Antoon Frans, 1888-1954 (Table P-PZ40)
6458.T39 Tière, Nestor de, 1856-1920 (Table P-PZ40)
6458.T4 Timmermans, Felix, 1886-1947 (Table P-PZ40)
6458.T6 Toussaint van Boelaere, Fernand Victor, 1875-1947 (Table P-PZ40)
Urk, Aug. see PT6407.B66
6458.V3853 Verbrugghen, Jo, 1931- (Table P-PZ40)
6458.V3855 Vercammen, Jan, 1906- (Table P-PZ40)
6458.V42 Vermeylen, August, 1872-1945 (Table P-PZ40)
6458.V43 Verriest, Hugo, 1840-1922 (Table P-PZ40)
6458.V44 Verschaeve, Cyriel, 1874-1949 (Table P-PZ40)
6459 Vuylsteke, Julius Pieter, 1836-1903 (Table P-PZ39)
6460 Vuy - Wil
6460.W3 Walschap, Gerard, 1898- (Table P-PZ40)
6460.W37 Wellens, René, 1914- (Table P-PZ40)
6460.W39 Weyer, D.G. (Table P-PZ40)
6461-6462 Willems, Jan Frans, 1793-1846 (Table P-PZ36)
6465 Wil - Z
Wilderode, Anton van, 1918- see PT6416.C58
6465.W4 Woestijne, Karel van de, 1878-1929 (Table P-PZ40)
6465.Z5 Zielens, Lode, 1901-1944 (Table P-PZ40)
6466-6466.36 1961-2000 (Table P-PZ29)
Here are usually to be classified authors beginning to publish about 1950, flourishing after 1960
6467-6467.36 2001- (Table P-PZ29)

PT6500-6593.36

Afrikaans literature
(South African Dutch literature)
Literary history and criticism
6500 Periodicals. Serials
6502 Societies
6507.A-Z Biography of historians and critics of Afrikaans literature, A-Z
History
6510 General works
6513 Biography (Collective)
Special forms
Poetry
6515 General works
Folk poetry see PT6545
6520 Drama
6525 Prose. Prose fiction
6530 Other. Wit and humor, letters, etc.
Folk literature
(6540) General works
see GR359.2.A47
6545 Folk poetry
6547 Children's literature (General)
For special genres, see the genre
Collections
6550 General
6553 Anthologies
6555.A-Z Translations. By language, A-Z
Special forms
Poetry
6560 General works
Folk poetry see PT6545
6565 Drama
6570 Prose. Prose fiction
6575 Other. Wit and humor, letters, etc.
6580.A-Z Local, A-Z
Individual authors or works
Subarrange each author by Table P-PZ40 unless otherwise indicated
6590 Through 1960
6590.A1A-.A1Z Anonymous works. By title, A-Z
6590.B7 Brink, Melt Jacobus, 1842-1925 (Table P-PZ40)
6590.B8 Bruggen, Jochem van, 1881- (Table P-PZ40)
6590.C2 Cachet, Jan Lion, 1838- (Table P-PZ40)
6590.C4 Celliers, Jan François Elias, 1865- (Table P-PZ40)
6590.D8 DuToit, Jacob Daniel, 1877- (Table P-PZ40)
6590.D9 DuToit, S. J., 1847-1911 (Table P-PZ40)
6590.E9 Eybers, Elisabeth, 1915- (Table P-PZ40)
6590.F3 Fagan, H.A., 1889- (Table P-PZ40)

Individual authors or works
Through 1960 -- Continued

6590.G7 Grosskopf, Johann Friedrich Wilhelm, 1885- (Table P-PZ40)
6590.H4 Heever, Christiaan Maurits van den, 1902-1957 (Table P-PZ40)
6590.L3 Langenhoven, Cornelius Jacob, 1873-1932 (Table P-PZ40)
6590.L4 Leipoldt, Christian Louis, 1880-1947 (Table P-PZ40)
6590.L59 Louw, Nicolaas Petrus van Wyk, 1906- (Table P-PZ40)
6590.M3 Malherbe, Daniel François, 1881- (Table P-PZ40)
6590.M37 Marais, Eugène Nielen, 1872-1936 (Table P-PZ40)
6590.M4 Maré, Leon, 1889- (Table P-PZ40)
6590.M5 Meurant, Louis Henri, 1812-1893 (Table P-PZ40)
6590.N55 Nienaber, Christoffer Johannes Michael, 1918- (Table P-PZ40)
6590.P5 Pienaar, Andries Albertus, 1894- (Table P-PZ40)
6590.P6 Pienaar, Pierre de Villiers, 1904- (Table P-PZ40)
6590.P75 Preller, Gustav Schoeman, 1875-1943 (Table P-PZ40)
6590.R6 Roubaix, Emanuel de, 1880- (Table P-PZ40)
6590.V3 Van Heerden, Ernst, 1916- (Table P-PZ40)
6590.V5 Visser, Andries Gerhardus, 1878-1929 (Table P-PZ40)
6590.W2 Waal, Jan H.H. de, 1871- (Table P-PZ40)
6592-6592.36 1961-2000 (Table P-PZ29 modified)

Here are usually to be classified authors beginning to publish about 1950, flourishing after 1960

6592.12 B

Boerneef, 1897-1967 see PT6592.32.A49

6592.32 V
6592.32.A49 Van der Merwe, Izak Wilhelmus, 1897-1967 (Table P-PZ40)
6593-6593.36 2001- (Table P-PZ29)

Scandinavian literature
Literary history and criticism
7001 Periodicals. Serials
(7003) Yearbooks
see PT7001
7005 Societies
7007 Congresses
Collections
7013 Monographs, studies, etc. By various authors
7014.A-Z Festschriften. By honoree, A-Z
7017 Encyclopedias. Dictionaries
7019 Theory and principles of the study of Scandinavian literature
7025 History of literary history
7029 Philosophy. Psychology. Aesthetics
Includes national characteristics in literature
Study and teaching
7035 General
7036 General special
7037.A-Z By region or country, A-Z
7038.A-Z By school, A-Z
Biography of teachers, critics, and historians
7038.5 Collective
7039.A-Z Individual, A-Z
Subarrange each by Table P-PZ50
Criticism
7045 Treatises
7047 History
7048 Special topics (not A-Z)
7049 Collections of essays in criticism
Special periods
7051 Medieval to 1540
7052 16th-18th centuries
7053 19th century
7054 20th century
7055 21st century
History of Scandinavian literature
General works
7060 Danish and Norwegian
7062 Swedish
7063 English
7064 French
7065 German
7066.A-Z Other languages, A-Z
Relations to other literatures
7071 General works
7072.A-Z Special, A-Z
e.g.

Literary history and criticism
History of Scandinavian literature
Relations to other literatures
Special, A-Z -- Continued

7072.E6 English literature
7073.A-Z Special topics, A-Z
7073.B64 Body, Human
7073.F34 Fantastic literature
Human body see PT7073.B64
7073.I55 Illegitimacy
7073.L47 Lesbianism
7073.N38 Nature
7073.O84 Other (Philosophy)
7073.S63 Social control
7073.T73 Travel
7073.W65 Women in literature
Biography, memoirs, letters, etc.
7073.3 Biography (Collective)
7073.5 Memoirs. Letters
7073.7 Iconography: Portraits, monuments, etc.
7073.8 Literary landmarks. Homes and haunts of authors
7074 Women authors. Literary relations of women
7074.5.A-Z Other classes of authors, A-Z
7074.5.P75 Prisoners
Special periods
7075 Early to 1540
7076 16th-18th centuries
19th century
7077 General works
7077.5.A-Z Special topics, A-Z
7077.5.A76 Art
7077.5.C58 Cities and towns
7077.5.N37 Narration (Rhetoric)
7077.5.N39 Nature
7077.5.P67 Portraits
7077.5.R65 Romanticism
20th century
7078 General works
7078.5.A-Z Special topics, A-Z
7078.5.I83 Italy
7078.5.M63 Modern philosophy in literature
7078.5.M64 Modernism
7078.5.R33 Radicalism
21st century
7079 General works
7079.5.A-Z Special topics, A-Z
Special forms

Literary history and criticism
History of Scandinavian literature
Special forms -- Continued
7080 Poetry
7082 Drama
7083 Prose and prose fiction
7084 Essays
7085 Letters
7086 Oratory
7087 Miscellaneous
Folk literature
see GR205+
(7088) History and criticism
(7089) Collections
Collections (in two or more Scandinavian languages)
7090 General
7091 Minor
7092.A-Z Translations. By language, A-Z
Special forms
7093 Poetry
7094 Drama
7095 Prose and prose fiction
7096 Essays
7097 Letters
7098 Oratory
7099 Miscellaneous. Wit and humor, etc.

Old Norse literature: Old Icelandic and old Norwegian
To about 1540
Literary history and criticism
7101 Periodicals. Serials
(7103) Yearbooks
see PT7101
7105 Societies
7107 Congresses
Collections
7113 Monographs, studies, etc. By various authors
7114.5.A-Z Festschriften. By honoree, A-Z
7117 Encyclopedias. Dictionaries
7119 Theory and principles of the study of Old Norse literature
7125 History of literary history
7129 Philosophy. Psychology. Aesthetics
Study and teaching
7135 General
7136 General special
7137.A-Z By region or country, A-Z
7138.A-Z By school, A-Z
Biography of teachers, critics, and historians
7138.5 Collective
7139.A-Z Individual, A-Z
Subarrange each by Table P-PZ50
Criticism
7145 Treatises
7147 History
7148 Special topics (not A-Z)
7149 Collections of essays in criticism
History of Old Icelandic and Old Norwegian literature
General works
7150 Icelandic
7151 Danish and Dano-Norwegian
7152 Landsmaal
7153 Swedish
7154 English
7155 French
7156 German
7157.A-Z Other languages, A-Z
7162.A-Z Special topics, A-Z
7162.C4 Celtic influence
7162.C46 Children
7162.C5 Christianity
7162.C55 Civilization
7162.C6 Classical influence
7162.D4 Death

Literary history and criticism
History of Old Icelandic and Old Norwegian literature
Special topics, A-Z -- Continued

7162.D7 Dreams
7162.E54 England
7162.E86 Ethics
7162.F6 Folklore
7162.F8 Funeral rites and ceremonies
7162.G7 Griselda
7162.M2 Maiden king in Iceland
7162.M25 Manuscripts
7162.M3 Mary, Blessed Virgin, Saint
7162.M34 Masculinity
7162.N3 Nature
7162.N5 Njála
7162.N67 North America
7162.S23 Sacrifice
7162.S24 Sami
7162.S63 Slavery and slaves
7162.S7 Social life
7162.S94 Supernatural
7162.W56 Witchcraft
7162.W6 Women
7163 Norway's share in Old Norse literature
Relations to other literatures
7165 General works
7166.A-Z Special, A-Z
e.g.
7166.E6 English literature
Special forms
Poetry
7170 General works
Edda poetry see PT7235
7172 Scaldic poetry
7173 Rímur
7174 Religious poetry
7175 Ballads
7176.A-Z Other special forms, A-Z
7176.E43 Elegiac
Prose
7177 General works
7178 Historical
7179 Norwegian history before Snorri
Sagas
7181 General
Historical sagas

Literary history and criticism
History of Old Icelandic and Old Norwegian literature
Special forms
Prose
Sagas
Historical sagas -- Continued
7182 General works
7183 Family sagas (Njáls saga, Egils saga, etc.)
7184 Sagas of kings (Konunga sögur)
7185 Sagas relating to Norwegian colonies (Greenland, America, etc.)
7186 Sagas relating to Denmark and Sweden
7187 Sagas relating to the Icelandic church, bishops, etc.
7188 Mythical or heroic sagas (Völsunga saga, etc.)
7189 Icelandic novels and fairy tales
Translation of foreign literature
7190 General works
7191 Romantic sagas (Tristrams saga, etc.)
7192 Religious works. Legends, etc. (Postola sögur, etc.)
7193.A-Z Other special, A-Z
7193.D42 Death
7193.R5 Riddarasögur
7193.R65 Romances
Scientific and learned literature
7195 General works
7196 Of Iceland
7197 Of Norway
Younger Edda see PT7314
7201 Philology
7203 Theology
7204 Geography
7205 Medicine
7206 Mathematics and astronomy
7207 Natural science
7208 Philosophy
Laws
7209 General works
7210 Icelandic
Cf. Class K, Law
7211 Norwegian
Cf. Class K, Law
Collections of Old Icelandic and Old Norwegian literature
7220 General
7221 Translations into foreign languages (Table PT6)
7228 Miscellaneous
Special forms

Collections of Old Icelandic and Old Norwegian literature
Special forms -- Continued
Poetry
7230 General collections
7232 Translations (Table PT6)
Special
Elder Edda or Edda Sæmundar
Class here also works containing both Eddas
7233.A1 Texts. By date
7233.A3-Z Texts. By editor
7233.5 Selections
7234 Translations (Table PT6)
7234.5 Paraphrases, adaptations, etc. (Table PT6)
7235 History and criticism
Special parts
7236 Hávamál (Table P-PZ41)
7237.A-Z Other parts, A-Z
Subarrange each part by Table P-PZ43
7237.A7 Atlamál (Table P-PZ43)
7239 Mythical lays, A-Z (Völuspá, etc.)
Subarrange each lay by Table P-PZ43
7240.A-Z Heroic lays, A-Z (Helgakviða Hjörvarðssonar, etc.)
7241.A-Z Doubtful or spurious lays, A-Z
7242 Poetry of Eddic type
Scaldic poetry
7244 Collections
7245 Translations (Table PT6)
7246.A-Z Special authors, A-Z
7246.B8 Bragi Boddason, Gamli (Table P-PZ40)
7246.E3 Egill Skallagrímsson, ca. 900-ca. 983 (Table P-PZ40)
7246.E5 Einarr Skúlason, prestr., 12th cent. (Table P-PZ40)
(7246.E9) Eysteinn Asgrímsson
see PT7329
7246.G3 Glúmr Geirason (Table P-PZ40)
7246.H3 Hallfreðr Ottarsson Vandræaskáld, ca. 967-ca. 1007 (Table P-PZ40)
7246.I9 Ívar Ingimundarson (Table P-PZ40)
(7246.L8) Loptr Guttormsson
see PT7333
7246.S5 Sighvatr Þjórðarson, d. 1045? (Table P-PZ40)
7246.T4 Þjóðólfr hinn Hvinverski, ca. 870-ca. 925 (Table P-PZ40)
Cf. PT7246.Y6 Ynglingatal
7246.T47 Þorarinn Loftunga, 11th cent. (Table P-PZ40)
7246.T5 Þorbjörn Hornklofi (Table P-PZ40)

Collections of Old Icelandic and Old Norwegian literature
Special forms
Poetry
Special
Scaldic poetry
Special authors, A-Z -- Continued
7246.Y6 Ynglingatal (Table P-PZ40)
Younger Edda (Snorra Edda) see PT7312
Rímur
7250.A1 General
7250.A5-Z Special
Religious and learned poetry
7252.A1 General
7252.A5-Z Special
Prose literature
Collections
7255 General
7256 Translations (Table PT6)
7257 Religious literature
Historical literature
7258 General collections
7259 Translations (Table PT6)
7260.A-Z Special collections. By name, A-Z
7260.E3-.E5 Eirspennill (Table P-PZ42a)
7260.F3-.F5 Flateyjarbók (Table P-PZ42a)
7260.F6-.F8 Fornmanna sögur (Table P-PZ42a)
7260.F91-.F93 Fríssbók (Table P-PZ42a)
7260.H3-.H5 Hauksbók (Table P-PZ42a)
7260.H6-.H8 Hulda (Table P-PZ42a)
7260.I6-.I8 Íslendínga sögur (Table P-PZ42a)
7260.O35-.O37 Ögmundar báttr dytts (Table P-PZ42a)
Sagas
7261 General
7261.5 Quotations
7262 Translations (Table PT6)
7262.5.A-Z Special collections. By name, A-Z
For collections of special types of sagas, see the type of saga, e.g. PT7269.A1, Sagas relating to Icelandic families; PT7271, Sagas relating to the Icelandic church and its bishops, etc.
7262.5.M63-.M633 Möðruvallabók (Table P-PZ43)
Individual sagas and historical works
Subarrange one number works by Table P-PZ41 unless otherwise specified
Subarrange authors or works with three successive Cutter numbers by Table P-PZ42 unless otherwise specified

	Individual sagas and historical works -- Continued
	Íslendíngabók
7263.A1	Texts. By date
7263.A3-Z	Texts. By editor
7264	Translations (Table PT6)
7265	Criticism
	Landnámabók
7266	General works
7267	Translations (Table PT6)
7268	Criticism
7269	Sagas relating to Icelandic families
7269.A1	General collections
7269.A2-.A39	Translations. By language, alphabetically
7269.A2	Danish and Norwegian
7269.A25	English
7269.A4	History and criticism
7269.A5-Z	Special sagas. By name
7269.B3-.B5	Bandamanna saga (Table P-PZ42a)
7269.B6-.B63	Bjarnar saga Hítdaelakappa (Table P-PZ42)
7269.D5-.D7	Droplaugarsona saga (Table P-PZ42a)
7269.E2-.E4	Egils saga Skallagrímssonar (Table P-PZ42a)
7269.E5-.E7	Eyrbyggja saga (Table P-PZ42a)
7269.F18-.F183	Fljótsdaela saga (Table P-PZ42)
7269.F2-.F4	Flóamanna saga (Table P-PZ42a)
7269.F5-.F7	Fóstbrœðra saga (Table P-PZ42a)
7269.G3-.G5	Gísla saga Súrssonar (Table P-PZ42a)
7269.G6-.G8	Grettis saga (Table P-PZ42a)
7269.G84-.G86	Gull-þóris saga (Table P-PZ42a)
7269.G9-.G93	Gunnlaugs saga (Table P-PZ42)
7269.H2-.H23	Hænsa-þóris saga (Table P-PZ42)
7269.H3-.H33	Hallfreðar saga. Hallfreðar Þáttr Vandræðaskálds (Table P-PZ42)
7269.H36-.H38	Harðar saga (Table P-PZ42a)
7269.H4-.H43	Hávarðar saga Ísfirðings (Table P-PZ42)
7269.H7-.H9	Hrafnkels saga Freysgoða (Table P-PZ42a)
7269.K6-.K8	Kormáks saga (Table P-PZ42a)
7269.L3-.L5	Laxdœla saga (Table P-PZ42a)
7269.N3-.N5	Njála (Table P-PZ42a)
7269.S6-.S8	Stúfs saga (Table P-PZ42a)
7269.S84-.S86	Svarfdœla saga (Table P-PZ42a)
7269.T5-.T7	Þorgils saga ok Hafliða (Table P-PZ42a)
	Þorskfirðinga saga see PT7269.G84+
7269.V17-.V19	Valla-Ljóts saga (Table P-PZ42a)
7269.V24-.V26	Vápenfirðinga saga (Table P-PZ42a)
7269.V3-.V33	Vatnsdœla saga (Table P-PZ42)
7269.V5-.V7	Víga-Glúms saga (Table P-PZ42a)

	Individual sagas and historical works
	Sagas relating to Icelandic families
	Special sagas. By name -- Continued
	Víga-Styrs saga
7269.V8	Texts. By date
7269.V8A-.V8Z	Texts. By editor, A-Z
7269.V81A-.V81Z	Translations. By language, A-Z Further subarrange by date
7269.V82A-.V82Z	Criticism
	Sturlunga saga
7270.A2	Texts. By editor, A-Z
7270.A6-Z	Criticism
	Sagas relating to the Icelandic church and its bishops
7271	Collections. Biskupa sögur
7272.A-Z	Special, A-Z
7272.A6-.A8	Árna saga biskups þorlákssonar (Table P-PZ42a)
7272.G6-.G8	Guðmundar saga Arasonar (Table P-PZ42a)
7272.H6-.H8	Hungrvaka (Table P-PZ42a)
7272.K6-.K8	Kristnisaga (Table P-PZ42a)
7272.P37-.P373	Pals saga biskups (Table P-PZ42)
7274.A-Z	Icelandic annals, A-Z
7274.K4-.K6	Konungs annáll (Table P-PZ42a)
	Sagas of kings (Konunga sögur)
	Heimskringla (by Snorri Sturluson, 1178-1241)
7276.A1	Texts. By date
7276.A3-Z	Texts. By editor
7277	Translations (Table PT6)
7278	Criticism
7278.5.A-Z	Special parts, A-Z
7278.5.Y5	Ynglingasaga
7279.A-Z	Other special, A-Z
7279.A2-.A4	Ágrip af Nóregs konunga sögum (Table P-PZ42a)
7279.B4-.B43	Bergsbók (Table P-PZ42)
7279.B64-.B643	Boglunga sogur (Table P-PZ42)
7279.F2-.F4	Fagrskinna (Table P-PZ42a)
7279.H2-.H4	Hákonar saga Gamla Hákonarsonar (by Sturla Þorðarson) (Table P-PZ42a)
7279.H68-.H683	Hrafns saga Sveinbjarnarsonar (Table P-PZ42)
7279.H7-.H73	Hreiðars Þáttr (Table P-PZ42)
7279.H78-.H783	Hryggjarstykki (Table P-PZ42)
7279.M3-.M5	Morkinskinna (Table P-PZ42a)
	Ólafs saga Helga
7279.O3-.O33	Oldest version (Table P-PZ42)
7279.O35-.O37	Short or legendary saga (Table P-PZ42a)
7279.O4-.O6	Great or historical Olafs saga (Table P-PZ42a)
7279.O63-.O633	Rauðúlfs Þáttr (Table P-PZ42)

Individual sagas and historical works
Sagas of kings (Konunga sögur) -- Continued
Ólafs saga Tryggvasonar

7279.O65-.O67	The Great Saga (Table P-PZ42a)
	Oddr Snorrason version
	See also Olaf's life in the Heimskringla
7279.O7	Texts. By date
7279.O7A-.O7Z	Texts. By editor, A-Z
7279.O71A-.O71Z	Translations. By language, A-Z
	Further subarrange by date
7279.O72A-.O72Z	Criticism
7279.S3-.S5	Sigurðar Þáttr Hranasonar (or Þinga Þáttr) (Table P-PZ42a)
7279.S6-.S8	Sverris sage (Table P-PZ42a)
7281.A-Z	Sagas relating to the Norwegian colonies, A-Z
7281.E4-.E6	Eiríks Þáttr Rauða (Table P-PZ42a)
7281.F2-.F4	Færeyinga saga (Table P-PZ42a)
7281.G6-.G8	Grœnlendinga Þáttr (Þorfinns saga Karlsefnis) and Eiríks þáttr Rauða) (Table P-PZ42a)
7281.O6-.O8	Orkneyinga saga (Table P-PZ42a)
7282.A-Z	Sagas relating to Denmark and Sweden, A-Z
7282.A1	Collections
7282.A1S6	Sögur Dana-konunga
7282.A4-.A6	Ambales saga (Table P-PZ42a)
7282.J5-.J7	Jómsvíkinga saga (Table P-PZ42a)
7282.K6-.K8	Knýtlinga saga (Table P-PZ42a)
7282.Y6-.Y8	Yngvars saga Víðförla (Table P-PZ42a)
	Mythical sagas
	Including sagas mainly on Scandinavian subjects
7285	Collections
7287.A-Z	Special, A-Z
7287.A3-.A5	Áns saga bogsveigis (Table P-PZ42a)
7287.A6-.A8	Ásmundar saga Kappbana (Table P-PZ42a)
7287.B6-.B8	Bósa saga (Table P-PZ42a)
7287.E2-.E4	Egils saga Einhenda ok Ásmundar Beserkjabana (Table P-PZ42a)
7287.E5-.E7	Eiríks saga Víöförla (Table P-PZ42a)
7287.F33-.F35	Frá Fornjóti ok ættmönnum hans (Table P-PZ42a)
7287.F4-.F6	Friöþjófs saga hins Frœkna (Table P-PZ42a)
	For Tegnér's poem see PT9830+
	Fundinn Noregr see PT7287.F33+
7287.G3-.G5	Gautreks saga (Table P-PZ42a)
7287.G6-.G8	Göngu-Hrólfs saga (Table P-PZ42a)
7287.H16-.H18	Hálfdanar saga Brönufóstra (Table P-PZ42a)
7287.H21-.H23	Hálfdanar saga Eysteinssonar (Table P-PZ42a)
7287.H32-.H34	Hálfs saga ok Hálfsrekka (Table P-PZ42a)

Individual sagas and historical works
Mythical sagas
Special, A-Z -- Continued

7287.H57-.H59 Hervarar saga ok Heiðrekskonungs (Table P-PZ42a)
7287.H66-.H68 Hjálmtérs saga ok Ölvis (Table P-PZ42a)
7287.H83-.H85 Hrólfs saga Gautrekssonar (Table P-PZ42a)
7287.H87-.H89 Hrólfs saga Kraka (Table P-PZ42a)
7287.H91-.H93 Hrómundar saga Greipssonar (Table P-PZ42a)
7287.I3-.I5 Illuga saga Gríðarfóstra (Table P-PZ42a)
7287.K3-.K5 Ketils saga hængs (Table P-PZ42a)
7287.K6-.K8 Krákumál (Table P-PZ42a)
7287.N67-.N673 Nornagests páttr (Table P-PZ42)
7287.O6-.O8 Orvar-Odds saga (Table P-PZ42a)
7287.R2-.R4 Ragnars saga Loöbrókar ok sana hans (Table P-PZ42a)
7287.R83-.R85 Ragnarssona Þáttr (Table P-PZ42a)
7287.S6-.S8 Sturlaugs saga starfsama (Table P-PZ42a)
7287.T5-.T7 Þorsteins saga Víkingssonar (Table P-PZ42a)
7287.U5-.U7 Úlfhams saga (Table P-PZ42a)
7287.V6-.V8 Völsunga saga (Table P-PZ42a)
7288.A-Z Novels and fairy tales, A-Z
7288.A1 Collections
7288.A7-.A9 Auðunar þáttr vestfirzka (Table P-PZ42a)
7288.B2-.B4 Bárðar saga Snæfellsáss (Table P-PZ42a)
7288.F3-.F5 Finnboga saga Ramma (Table P-PZ42a)
7288.J6-.J8 Jökuls Þáttr Búasonar (Table P-PZ42a)
7288.K3-.K5 Kjalnesínga saga (Table P-PZ42a)
7288.K6-.K8 Króka-Refs saga (Table P-PZ42a)
7288.T4-.T6 Þórðar saga Hreðu (Table P-PZ42a)
7288.T73-.T75 Þorgríms saga prúða ok Víglundar Væna (Table P-PZ42a)
Víglundar saga see PT7288.T73+
7291 Þáttir
Cf. PT7279.S3+ Sigurðar Þáttr Hranasonar
Cf. PT7281.G6+ Grœnlendinga Þáttr
Cf. PT7287.R83+ Ragnarssona Þáttr
Cf. PT7288.A7+ Auðunar þáttr vestfirzka
Sagas with subjects from Southern sources
Includes romantic and historical sagas adapted or imitated from the Latin, French, etc.
7294 General
7296.A-Z Special, A-Z
7296.A23-.A25 Addónius saga (Table P-PZ42a)
7296.A31-.A33 Ála Flekks saga (Table P-PZ42a)
7296.A37-.A39 Alexanders saga (Table P-PZ42a)
7296.B25-.B27 Barlaams saga ok Josaphats (Table P-PZ42a)
7296.B56-.B58 Bevers saga (Table P-PZ42a)
7296.B82-.B84 Breta sögur (Table P-PZ42a)

Individual sagas and historical works
Sagas with subjects from Southern sources
Special, A-Z -- Continued

7296.C6-.C8 Clarús saga (Table P-PZ42a)
7296.D5-.D53 Dínus saga drambláta (Table P-PZ42)
7296.D6-.D8 Drauma-Jóns saga (Table P-PZ42a)
7296.E4-.E6 Elis saga ok Rosamundu (Table P-PZ42a)
7296.E7-.E9 Ereks saga Artúskappa (Table P-PZ42a)
7296.F62-.F64 Flóres saga ok Blankiflúr (Table P-PZ42a)
7296.F66-.F68 Flovents saga (Table P-PZ42a)
7296.G6-.G8 Gyðinga saga (Table P-PZ42a)
7296.H4-.H6 Hektors saga (Table P-PZ42a)
7296.I9-.I93 Ivents saga Artúskappa (Table P-PZ42)
7296.K2-.K4 Karlamagnús saga (Table P-PZ42a)
Kirialax saga
7296.K5 Texts. By date
7296.K5A-.K5Z Texts. By editor, A-Z
7296.K51A-.K51Z Translations. By language, A-Z
Further subarrange by date
7296.K52A-.K52Z Criticism
7296.K6-.K8 Konráðs saga keisarasonar (Table P-PZ42a)
7296.M2-.M4 Mágus saga (Table P-PZ42a)
7296.M6-.M8 Mírmans saga (Table P-PZ42a)
Möttuls saga
7296.M9 Texts. By date
7296.M9A-.M9Z Texts. By editor, A-Z
7296.M91A-.M91Z Translations. By language, A-Z
Further subarrange by date
7296.M92A-.M92Z Criticism
Parcevals saga Artúskappa
7296.P2 Texts. By date
7296.P2A-.P2Z Texts. By editor, A-Z
7296.P21A-.P21Z Translations. By language, A-Z
Further subarrange by date
7296.P22A-.P22Z Criticism
Partalópa saga
7296.P3 Texts. By date
7296.P3A-.P3Z Texts. By editor, A-Z
7296.P31A-.P31Z Translations. By language, A-Z
Further subarrange by date
7296.P32A-.P32Z Criticism
7296.R3-.R5 Rémundar saga keisarasonar (Table P-PZ42a)
7296.S4-.S6 Sigurðar saga þögla (Table P-PZ42a)
7296.S7-.S9 Strengleikar (Table P-PZ42a)
Thidreks saga
7296.T4 Texts. By date

Individual sagas and historical works
Sagas with subjects from Southern sources
Special, A-Z
Thidreks saga -- Continued
7296.T4A-.T4Z Texts. By editor, A-Z
7296.T41A-.T41Z Translations, By language, A-Z
Further subarrange by date
7296.T42A-.T42Z Criticism
Tristrams saga
7296.T7 Texts. By date
7296.T7A-.T7Z Texts. By editor, A-Z
7296.T71A-.T71Z Translations. By language, A-Z
Further subarrange by date
7296.T72A-.T72Z Criticism
Trójumanna saga
7296.T8 Texts. By date
7296.T8A-.T8Z Texts. By editor, A-Z
7296.T81A-.T81Z Translations. By language, A-Z
Further subarrange by date
7296.T82A-.T82Z Criticism
7296.V2-.V4 Valdimars saga køngs (Table P-PZ42a)
7296.V5-.V7 Veraldar saga (Table P-PZ42a)
7296.V8-.V83 Viktors saga ok Blávus (Table P-PZ42)
Religious works
Heilagra manna sögur (Legends of the saints)
7298.A1 Texts. By date
7298.A3-Z Texts. By editor
7299.A-Z Special saints, A-Z
7299.B7-.B9 Brandanus saga (Table P-PZ42a)
7299.J3-.J5 Játvarðar saga Helga (Table P-PZ42a)
7300 Postola sögur (Legends of the apostles)
7301.A-Z Special apostles, A-Z
Biskupa sögur see PT7271+
7302 Maríu saga, Maríu Jartegnir (Legends of the Virgin)
7304 Icelandic Homilíubók
7305 Norwegian Homilíubók
7306 Stjórn (Old Norse Bible stories)
7309.A-Z Other, A-Z
Gyðinga saga see PT7296.G6+
7309.V57 Visio Tnugdali
Scientific and learned literature
7312 Edda Snorra Sturlusonar (Younger Edda or Prose Edda)
7312.5 Selections
7313 Translations (Table PT6)
7314 History and criticism
Grammatical treatises

Scientific and learned literature
Grammatical treatises -- Continued
7315 Skálda (The Shorter Skálda)
For Skáldskaparmál, second part of the Younger Edda see PT7312
7316.A-Z Others, A-Z
7318.A-Z Other scientific and learned works, A-Z
7318.A3-.A5 Alfræði íslenzk
7318.A6-.A8 Leiðarvísir
7318.R5-.R7 Rímbegla
7320.A-Z Other miscellaneous works, A-Z
7320.C6-.C8 Codex 1812
7320.K7-.K9 Konungs skuggsjá (Speculum regale)
7320.R4-.R6 Reykjaholts máldagi
7320.R7-.R73 Roeða móti biskupum (Speech against the bishops)
Varnarræda móti biskupum see PT7320.R7+
7321 Icelandic and Norwegian laws
Class here language studies only
Cf. Class K, Law
7323 Modern imitations. Icelandic apocrypha
7323.H7 Hrana saga Hrings
Individual authors or works before 1540
Subarrange Cutter number authors by Table P-PZ40 unless otherwise specified
Subarrange one number authors by Table P-PZ39 unless otherwise specified
For Skaldic poetry see PT7246.A+
For individual sagas and historical works see PT7263+
7326 A - Ar
7327 Ari Þorgilsson Fróði, 1068?-1148 (Table P-PZ39)
7328 Ar - Ey
Catonis disticha see PT7330.H8
7328.E45 Einar Hafliðason, 1307-1393. Laurentius saga biskups
7328.E47 Einar Skúlason, ca. 1090-1165 (Table P-PZ40)
7329 Eysteinn Ásgrímsson, 14th cent. (Table P-PZ39)
7330 Ey - Ka
7330.H8 Hugsvinnsmál
Translation of Catonis disticha
7331 Karl Jónsson, abbot, d. 1213 (Table P-PZ39)
Cf. PT7279.S6+ Sverris saga
7332 Ka - Lo
7333 Loptr Guttormsson, d. 1432 (Table P-PZ39)
7334 Lo - Sn
7334.S3 Sæmundr Sigfússon Froði, 1056-1133 (Table P-PZ40)

Individual authors or works before 1540 -- Continued

7335 Snorri Sturluson, 1178-1241 (Table P-PZ39)

Cf. PT7276+ Heimskringla

Cf. PT7312 Edda Snorra

7336 Sno - St

7337 Sturla Þróarson, 1214-1284 (Table P-PZ39)

Cf. PT7270.A+ Sturlunga saga

Cf. PT7279.A+ Hákonar saga Gamla Hákonarsonar

7338 St - Z

7338.V5 Visio Pauli (Table P-PZ40)

Modern Icelandic literature
Literary history and criticism
7351 Periodicals. Serials
(7353) Yearbooks
see PT7351
7355 Societies
7357 Congresses
Encyclopedias, dictionaries see PT7117
Philosophy, aesthetics see PT7129
Study and teaching
7370 General
7371 General special
7372.A-Z By region or country, A-Z
7373.A-Z By school, A-Z
7374.A-Z Biography of teachers, critics, and historians, A-Z
Criticism
7380 Treatises
7382 History
7383 Special topics (not A-Z)
7384 Collections of essays in criticism
History of modern Icelandic literature
7390 General
Special periods
16th-18th centuries
7395 General works
7397.A-Z Special topics, A-Z
19th-20th centuries
7400 General works
7402.A-Z Special topics, A-Z
7402.D43 Death
7402.L68 Love
21st century
7403 General works
7404.A-Z Special topics, A-Z
7405 Translation of Icelandic literature (as subject)
7407 Biography, memoirs, letters, etc. (Collected)
7409 Women authors. Literary relations of women
Special forms
7410 Poetry
7411 Drama
Prose
7412 General works
7413 Fiction
7414 Oratory
7415 Letters
7416 Essays
7417 Wit and humor

Literary history and criticism
History of modern Icelandic literature
Special forms
Prose -- Continued
7418 Miscellaneous
Folk literature
For general works on and collections of folk literature see GR215
History
(7420) General works
Special forms
7425 Poetry
(7426) Prose
Collections
(7430) General
7431 Chapbooks
7432 Poetry. Ballads, songs, etc.
Prose tales. Legends
(7433) General works
(7434.A-Z) By locality, A-Z
(7435) Fairy tales
(7436.A-Z) Special characters, persons, etc., A-Z
(7437.A-Z) Individual tales, A-Z
(7438.A-Z) Translations. By language, A-Z
7442 Juvenile literature (General)
For special genres, see the genre
Collections of modern Icelandic literature
General and comprehensive
7450 Periodicals. Serials
7451 Collections before 1801
7452 Collections, 1801-
7453 Selections. Anthologies
Translations into foreign languages
7456 Polyglot collections
7457 Danish and Norwegian
7458 Swedish
7459 English
7460 French
7461 German
7462.A-Z Other. By language, A-Z
Special forms
Poetry
7465 General
7466 Selections. Anthologies
7467.A-Z Translations. By language, A-Z
Drama
7470 General
7471 Selected plays. Anthologies

Collections of modern Icelandic literature
Special forms
Drama -- Continued
7472.A-Z Translations. By language, A-Z
Special forms
7473 Tragedies
7474 Comedies
7476.A-Z Minor, A-Z
7476.F2 Farces
7477 Amateur drama. Juvenile plays
Prose
7480 General
7481 Minor
Prose fiction
7485 General
7486 Selections. Anthologies
7487.A-Z Translations. By language, A-Z
Other forms of prose
7489 Oratory
7490 Letters
7491 Essays
7492 Wit and humor
7493 Fables
7495 Miscellaneous
Individual authors or works
16th-18th centuries

7500 Anonymous works (Table P-PZ28)
7501.A-Z Authors, A-Z
Subarrange individual authors by Table P-PZ40 unless otherwise indicated
7501.E25 Eggert Ólafsson, 1726-1768 (Table P-PZ40)
7501.G85 Gunnar Pálsson, 1714-1791 (Table P-PZ40)
7501.H28 Hallgrímur Pjetursson, 1614-1674 (Table P-PZ40)
7501.J6 Jón Steingrímmsson, 1728-1791 (Table P-PZ40)
7501.J63 Jón Þorlaksson, 1744-1819 (Table P-PZ40)
7501.S52 Sigurður Pjetursson, 1759-1827 (Table P-PZ40)
7501.S65 Snorri Bjarnarson, 1710-1803 (Table P-PZ40)
7501.S654 Stefán Olafsson, ca. 1620-1688 (Table P-PZ40)
7501.T6 Þorleifur Halldórsson, 1683?-1713 (Table P-PZ40)
19th-20th centuries
7510 Anonymous works (Table P-PZ28)
7511.A-Z Authors, A-Z
Subarrange individual authors by Table P-PZ40 unless otherwise indicated
7511.A83 Ásmundur, víkingur, 1874-1919 (Table P-PZ40)
Bjarni Thorarensen, 1786-1841 see PT7511.T4
7511.B59 Bólu-Hjálmar, 1796-1875 (Table P-PZ40)

Individual authors or works
19th-20th centuries
Authors, A-Z -- Continued

7511.B7 Breiðfjörð, Sigurður Eiríksson, 1798-1846 (Table P-PZ40)
7511.E3 Eðvarð Ingólfsson, 1960- (Table P-PZ40)
7511.E38 Einar Benediktsson, 1864-1940 (Table P-PZ40)
Einar Hjörleifsson Kvaran, 1859-1938 see PT7511.K8
7511.E94 Eyjólfur Guðmundsson, 1870-1954 (Table P-PZ40)
7511.G4 Gestur Pálsson, 1852-1891 (Table P-PZ40)
7511.G7 Gröndal, Benedikt Jónsson 1762-1825 (Table P-PZ40)
7511.G877 Guðmundur Finnbogason, 1873-1944 (Table P-PZ40)
7511.G88 Guðmundur Friðjónsson, 1869-1944 (Table P-PZ40)
7511.G882 Guðmundur Frímann (Table P-PZ40)
Guðmundur Guðmundsson, 1874-1919 see PT7511.A83
7511.G884 Guðmundur Hjaltason, 1853-1919 (Table P-PZ40)
7511.G885 Guðmundur Jónsson (Table P-PZ40)
Guðmundur Kamban, 1888-1945 see PT7511.K3
Guðmundur Magnússon, 1873-1918 see PT7511.J557
7511.G9 Gunnarsson, Gunnar, 1889-1975 (Table P-PZ40)
7511.G93 Gunnsteinn Eyjólfsson, 1866-1910 (Table P-PZ40)
Halldór Laxness, 1902- see PT7511.L3
Hjálmar Jónsson, 1796-1875 see PT7511.B59
7511.H8 Hugrùn (Table P-PZ40)
7511.I5 Indriði Einarsson, 1851-1939 (Table P-PZ40)
7511.J52 Jökull Jakobsson (Table P-PZ40)
(7511.J5287) Jóhann Magnús Bjarnason, 1865-1945 (Table P-PZ40)
see PT7545.B62
7511.J534 Johannessen, Matthias, 1930- (Table P-PZ40)
7511.J535 Jón Arnason, 1819-1888 (Table P-PZ40)
7511.J538 Jón frá Ljárskógum, 1914-1945 (Table P-PZ40)
7511.J556 Jón Thoroddsen, 1818-1868 (Table P-PZ40)
7511.J557 Jón Trausti, 1873-1918 (Table P-PZ40)
7511.J56 Jón úr Vör (Table P-PZ40)
7511.J572 Jónas Hallgrímsson, 1807-1845 (Table P-PZ40)
7511.J573 Jónas Jónasson, 1856-1918 (Table P-PZ40)
7511.J85 Júlíana Jónsdóttir, 1838-1918 (Table P-PZ40)
7511.K3 Kamban, Guðmundur, 1888-1945 (Table P-PZ40)
Cf. PT8175.K3 Danish
7511.K687 Kristján Jónsson, 1842-1869 (Table P-PZ40)
7511.K8 Kvaran, Einar Gísli Hjörleifsson, 1859-1938 (Table P-PZ40)
7511.L3 Laxness, Halldór Kiljan, 1902- (Table P-PZ40)
7511.M29 Matthías Jochumsson, 1835-1920 (Table P-PZ40)
Matthías Johannessen, 1930- see PT7511.J534
7511.O46 Ólöf Sigurðardóttir á Hlöðum, 1857-1933 (Table P-PZ40)
7511.P18 Páll Olafsson, 1827-1905 (Table P-PZ40)
Sigurður Breiðfjörð, 1798-1846 see PT7511.B7

Individual authors or works
19th-20th centuries
Authors, A-Z -- Continued
7511.S5887 Sigurður Gunnarsson, 1812-1878 (Table P-PZ40)
7511.S5955 Sigurjón Friðjónsson, 1867-1950 (Table P-PZ40)
7511.S7177 Stein Sigurðsson, 1872-1940 (Table P-PZ40)
7511.S733 Steingrímur Thorsteinsson, 1831-1913 (Table P-PZ40)
7511.S735 Steinn Jónsson, 1861- (Table P-PZ40)
7511.S736 Steinn Steinarr (Table P-PZ40)
7511.S77 Stephan G. Stephansson (Stephan Guðmundsson Stephansson),1853-1927 (Table P-PZ40)
7511.T4 Thórarensen, Bjarni Vigfússon, 1786-1841 (Table P-PZ40)
7511.T63 Þorgils Gjallandi, 1851-1915 (Table P-PZ40)
Thóroddsen, Jón Þórðarson, 1818-1868 see PT7511.J556
7511.T635 Þorsteinn Erlingsson, 1858- (Table P-PZ40)
7511.T637 Þórunn Elfa Magnúsdóttir (Table P-PZ40)
7511.V62 Vigdis Grimsdóttir (Table P-PZ40)
21st century
7512 Anonymous works (Table P-PZ28)
7513.A-Z Authors, A-Z
Subarrange individual authors by Table P-PZ40 unless otherwise indicated
Icelandic literature: Provincial, local, foreign
Provincial, local, etc.
7520.A-Z By region, A-Z
7521.A-Z By place, A-Z
Icelandic literature outside of Iceland
7525 General
Special
North America
Literary history and criticism
7526 General works
7527 General special
7529 Biography (Collective)
Special periods
7530 19th century
7531 20th century
7531.2 21st century
7532 Poetry
7533 Drama
7534.A-Z Other special forms, A-Z
Collections
7536 General
7537 Poetry
7538 Drama

Icelandic literature: Provincial, local, foreign
Icelandic literature outside of Iceland
Special
North America
Collections -- Continued

7539.A-Z Other special forms, A-Z

7540.A-Z Local, A-Z

7545.A-Z Individual authors, A-Z
Subarrange each author by Table P-PZ40
e.g.

7545.B62 Bjarnason, Jóhann Magnús, 1865-1945 (Table P-PZ40)

7550.A-Z Other regions or countries, A-Z

	Faroese literature
	Literary history and criticism
7581	General works
7582	General special
7584	Biography (Collective)
	Special periods
7586	To 1800
7587	19th century
7588	20th century
7589	21st century
	Special forms
7590	Poetry
7591	Drama
7592.A-Z	Other, A-Z
	Collections
7593	General
7594	Poetry
7595	Drama
7595.5	Fiction
7596.A-Z	Other special forms, A-Z
7596.G46	Ghost stories
7596.S65	Songs
7596.5.A-Z	Translations into foreign languages. By language, A-Z
7597.A-Z	Local, A-Z
	Individual authors or works
7598	Anonymous works (Table P-PZ28 modified)
7598.A1A-.A1Z	Works without any indication of author, either by symbol or initial. By title, A-Z
	Sjúrðar kvaeði
7598.A1S5	Texts. By date
7598.A1S6	Criticism. By date
7599.A-Z	Authors, A-Z Subarrange individual authors by Table P-PZ40

Danish literature
Literary history and criticism
7601 Periodicals. Serials
(7603) Yearbooks
see PT7601
7605 Societies. By place
7607 Congresses
Collections
7613 Monographs, studies, etc. By various authors
7614.A-Z Festschriften. By honoree, A-Z
7619 Encyclopedias. Dictionaries
7621 Theory and principles of the study of Danish literature
7625 History of literary history
7629 Philosophy. Psychology. Aesthetics
Includes national characteristics in literature
Study and teaching
7640.A-.Z8 General
7640.Z9 Catalogs of audiovisual materials
7641 General special
7642.A-Z By region or country, A-Z
7643.A-Z By school, A-Z
Biography of teachers, critics, and historians
7643.5 Collective
7644.A-Z Individual, A-Z
Subarrange each by Table P-PZ50
Criticism
7650 Treatises. Theory
7652 History
7653 Special topics (not A-Z)
7654 Collections of essays in criticism
History of Danish literature
General works
7660 Danish and Dano-Norwegian
7661 Landsmaal
7662 Swedish
7663 English
7664 French
7665 German
7666.A-Z Other languages, A-Z
7669 Outlines, syllabi, etc.
Miscellaneous special subjects
7673 Relation to history, civilization, etc.
7675.A-Z Relation to other literatures, A-Z (as subject)
7680 Translation of other literatures into Danish (as subject)
7681 Translation of Danish literature (as subject)
7683 Other special aspects
Treatment of special subjects

Literary history and criticism
History of Danish literature
Treatment of special subjects -- Continued

7685.A-Z Special topics, A-Z
7685.B44 Belief and doubt
7685.H64 Holocaust, Jewish (1939-1945)
7685.L65 Love
7685.N3 Nature
7685.R4 Religion
7685.T7 Travel
7690.A-Z Special countries and races, not limited to one period or form, A-Z

Under each country:

.x General
.x2A-.x2Z Local, A-Z

Denmark
7690.D4 General
7690.D5A-.D5Z Local, A-Z
7690.D5S5 Sjælland
7693.A-Z Special classes, A-Z
7693.C44 Children
7693.F6 Fools and jesters
7693.P4 Peasants
7693.P5 Pharmacists
7693.P7 Priests
7693.W6 Women
7695.A-Z Special characters, persons, etc., A-Z

Biography, memoirs, letters, etc.
7700 Biography (Collective)
7702 Memoirs. Letters
7703 Relations to women, love, marriage, etc.
7705 Literary landmarks. Homes and haunts of authors
7710 Women authors. Literary relations of women
7715.A-Z Other classes of authors, A-Z
7715.L3 Laboring class authors

Special periods
Medieval to 1500. Old Danish
7721 General works
7723.A-Z Special subjects, A-Z
7723.E4 Education
7723.G3 Games. Amusements
7723.M3 Magic. Occultism
(7725) Historical literature

see DL; PT7738

(7726) Medical literature

see class R

Literary history and criticism
History of Danish literature
Special periods
Medieval to 1500. Old Danish -- Continued

(7727) Legal literature
see class K

(7729) Religious literature
see class B

Other special forms

(7733) Proverbs
see PN6484

7734 Heroic legends

7735 Ballads (Folkeviser)

7737 Prose romances

7738 Rimed chronicles
Cf. DL147 Danish history

16th-18th centuries

7741 General works

7743.A-Z Special topics, A-Z

Sub-periods

7744 Reformation (1500-1550)

7745 Learned period (1550-1700)

7746 Age of Holberg (1700-1750)

7747 Period of Rationalism (1750-1800)

19th century

7751 General works

7753.A-Z Special topics, A-Z

7753.B54 Biedermeier

7753.C65 Don Juan

7753.E53 Engineering

7753.H57 Historical fiction

7753.O75 Orientalism

7753.S9 Success

7753.S93 Symbolism

Sub-periods

7755 Romanticism (1800-1860)

7756 Realism (ca. 1860-ca. 1890)

20th century

7760 General works

7762.A-Z Special topics, A-Z

7762.F37 Fascism

7762.F45 Feminism

7762.H65 Homosexuality

Literature and society see PT7762.S63

7762.M46 Men

7762.M56 Middle class

7762.M6 Modernism

Literary history and criticism
History of Danish literature
Special periods
20th century
Special topics, A-Z -- Continued
7762.N38 National socialism
7762.P6 Politics
7762.R4 Realism
7762.S63 Society and literature
21st century
7765 General works
7766.A-Z Special topics, A-Z
Special forms
Poetry
7770 General works
7772.A-Z Special topics, A-Z
7772.E35 Ebbesen, Niels, d. 1340
7772.P3 Patriotic poetry
Special periods
(7774) Medieval
see PT7721+ PT7735+
16th-18th centuries
7775 General works
7777 Special topics (not A-Z)
19th century
7780 General works
7782 Special topics (not A-Z)
20th century
7785 General works
7787 Special topics (not A-Z)
21st century
7788 General works
7789 Special topics (not A-Z)
Special forms
7790 Epic poetry
7791 Popular poetry. Ballads, songs, etc.
Cf. PT7735
7792 Lyric poetry
7793.A-Z Other special forms, A-Z
7793.D5 Didactic
7793.E4 Elegiac
7793.L69 Love
7793.P3 Pastoral
7794.A-Z Special subjects, A-Z
7794.M6 Modernism
7794.N3 Nature
7794.R4 Religion

Literary history and criticism
History of Danish literature
Special forms -- Continued
Drama
History of the Danish stage see PN2740+
7800 General works
7802.A-Z Special topics, A-Z
Special periods
Medieval
7805 Origins
7807 Mysteries, moralities, miracle plays
16th-18th centuries
7810 General works
7812.A-Z Special topics, A-Z
19th century
7815 General works
7817.A-Z Special topics, A-Z
20th century
7820 General works
7822.A-Z Special topics, A-Z
21st century
7823 General works
7823.2.A-Z Special topics, A-Z
Special forms of drama
7824 Tragedy
7825 Comedy
7827 Tragicomedy
7828 Vaudeville
7829 Romantic drama
7830 Melodrama
7831 Farce
7832.A-Z Other special, A-Z
7832.C45 Children's plays
Prose
7835 General works
Special periods
(7837) Medieval
see PT7721+
Modern
7840 General
7841 16th-17th centuries
7842 18th century
7843 19th century
7844 20th century
7845 21st century
Special forms
Prose fiction

Literary history and criticism
History of Danish literature
Special forms
Prose
Special forms
Prose fiction -- Continued
7847 General works
Special topics
7851 Romanticism
7852 Historical fiction
7853 Realism
7854 Naturalism
7855.A-Z Other, A-Z
7855.B56 Biography
7855.C46 Detective and mystery stories
7855.F35 Fantastic fiction
7855.W67 World War II
Special periods
7860 17th-18th centuries
7861 19th century
7862 20th century
7863 21st century
7865 Oratory
7866 Letters
7867 Essays
7868 Wit and humor
7869 Miscellaneous
Folk literature
For general works on and collections of folk literature, see GR209+
History
(7900) General works
Special periods
7905 Origins. Middle Ages
(7906) Later
Special forms
7909 Poetry
Cf. PT7735 Ballads
(7910) Prose
Collections
(7915) General
7917 Chapbooks
7919 Poetry. Ballads, songs, etc. (Folkeviser)
Prose tales. Legends (Folkesagn)
7921 General works
(7922) Special localities
(7924) Fairy tales

	Folk literature
	Collections -- Continued
(7926.A-Z)	Special characters, persons, etc., A-Z
(7928)	Individual tales
(7930.A-Z)	Translations. By language, A-Z
7935	Juvenile literature (General)
	For special genres, see the genre
	Collections of Danish literature
	General
7945	Periodicals. Serials
7950	Collections before 1801
7951	Collections, 1801-
7953	Medieval literature (Old Danish)
7954	Selections. Anthologies
7954.5.A-Z	Special classes of authors, A-Z
7954.5.P43	Peasants
7954.5.W65	Women
7955.A-Z	Special topics (Prose and verse), A-Z
7955.A43	Alcoholics
7955.C47	Childhood
7955.C5	Christmas stories
7955.C62	City and town life
7955.D4	Denmark
7955.E75	Erotic literature
7955.F67	Forests
7955.G7	Greece
7955.H35	Happiness
7955.H64	Holberg, Ludvig
7955.I74	Israel
7955.J43	Jealousy
7955.J8	Jutland
7955.K57	Kissing
7955.M6	Mothers
7955.N65	Norway
7955.O43	Old age
7955.S5	Skagen (Denmark)
7955.S63	Socialism
7955.S79	Students
	Town life see PT7955.C62
7955.W64	Women
7955.W66	Work
	Translations into foreign languages
7961	Polyglot
7965	English
7966	French
7967	German
7968	Swedish

PT7601-8260

Collections of Danish literature
General
Translations into foreign languages -- Continued
7970.A-Z Other. By language, A-Z
Poetry
7975 Collections before 1801
7976 Collections, 1801-
For medieval see PT7953
7978 Selections. Anthologies
7979 Selections from women authors
Translations into foreign languages
7983.A2 Polyglot collections
7983.A5-Z By language, A-Z
e.g.
7983.E5 English
Subarrange by editor or title, A-Z
Special forms and subjects
7990 Ballads. Songs
7991 Sonnets
7992 Historical. Patriotic. Political
7993 Satire
7994.A-Z Other, A-Z
7994.D4 Denmark
7994.K63 Køge (Denmark)
7994.L6 Love
7994.M57 Months
7994.M6 Mothers
7994.R4 Religious
7994.R6 Roads
7994.S4 Sea
7994.S5 Silk
Drama
7999 Collections before 1801
8000 Collections, 1801-
8005 Selected plays. Anthologies
8006.A-Z Translations. By language, A-Z
Special forms
8010 Mysteries, moralities, miracle plays
8012 Tragedies
8013 Comedies
8015 Farces, vaudevilles, etc.
8018 Amateur drama. Juvenile plays
8020.A-Z Other special, A-Z
Prose
8021 General
Fiction
8022 General

Collections of Danish literature
Prose
Fiction -- Continued
8023 Minor. Selections. Anthologies
8024.A-Z Translations. By language, A-Z
8027 Oratory
8030 Letters
8033 Essays
8037 Wit and humor
8040 Fables
(8043) Proverbs
see PN6484
8046 Miscellaneous
Individual authors or works
Medieval (ca. 1100-ca. 1540). Old Danish
8050.A-Z Individual authors or works, A-Z
8050.D3-.D32 Danske rimkrønike
8050.G4-.G42 Gammeldanske krøniker
8050.G7-.G72 Grimilds hævn
8050.K3-.K32 Karl Magnus krønike
8050.M3-.M32 Mariaviserne
8050.S3-.S32 Saxo Grammaticus, fl. 1200
8050.S48-.S482 Sjælens og kroppens trætte
16th-18th centuries
Subarrange Cutter number authors by Table P-PZ40 unless otherwise indicated
8060 Anonymous works (Table P-PZ28)
8061 A - E
8061.A7 Arrebo, Anders Christensen, 1587-1637 (Table P-PZ40)
8061.B5 Biehl, Charlotta Dorothea, 1731-1788 (Table P-PZ40)
8061.B6 Bording, Anders, 1619-1677 (Table P-PZ40)
8061.B66 Brorson, Hans Adolf, Bp., 1694-1764 (Table P-PZ40)
8063 Ewald, Johannes, 1743-1781 (Table P-PZ39)
8064 E - Hol
8064.F34 Falster, Christian, 1690-1752 (Table P-PZ40)
8064.H25 Hammer, Morten, 1739-1809 (Table P-PZ40)
8064.H3 Hansen, Christiern, fl. 1531 (Table P-PZ40)
8064.H44 Hegelund, Peder Jensen, 1542-1614 (Table P-PZ40)
8064.H5 Heiberg, Peter Andreas, 1758-1841 (Table P-PZ40)
8064.H6 Hiøring, Anders Matthisen, 1609-1678 (Table P-PZ40)
Holberg, Ludvig, baron, 1684-1754
Bibliography see Z8414.2
8070 Collected works. By date
8071.A-Z Selected works. By editor, A-Z
8072 Selections. Anthologies
Translations
8073 English

Individual authors or works
16th-18th centuries
Holberg, Ludvig, baron, 1684-1754
Translations -- Continued
8074 French
8075 German
8076 Swedish
8077.A-Z Other. By language, A-Z
Poetical works
Collected works
8079.A1 By date
8079.A3-Z By editor, A-Z
Special
8080 Peder Paars (Table P-PZ41)
8081 Fire skjemtedigte (Table P-PZ41)
Comedies
Collected works
8082.A1 By date
8082.A3-Z By editor, A-Z
8083.A-Z Translations. By language, A-Z
8084.A-Z Individual comedies, A-Z
e.g.
8084.A7 Det arabiske pulver
8084.B3 Barselstuen
8084.D4 Diderich v. Menschenschreck
8084.D6 Don Ranudo de Colibrados
8084.E5 Den ellevte juni
8084.E7 Erasmus Montanus (Table P-PZ43)
8084.H4 Henrich og Pernille
8084.H5 Hexerie
8084.H7 Den honnette ambition
8084.H8 Huus-spøgelse
8084.J2 Jacob von Tyboe
8084.J3 Jean de France
8084.J4 Jeppe paa Bierget
8084.J8 Jule-stue
8084.K5 Kilde-reisen
8084.L8 Det lykkelige skibbrud
8084.M3 Mascarade
8084.M5 Mester Gert Westphaler
8084.P3 Den pantsatte bondedreng
8084.P4 Pernilles korte frøkenstand
8084.P7 Den politiske kandestøber
8084.S7 Den stundesløse
8084.U6 Ulysses von Ithaca
8084.U8 De usynlige
8084.V3 Den vægelsindede

Individual authors or works
16th-18th centuries
Holberg, Ludvig, baron, 1684-1754 -- Continued
8085.A-Z Other special works, A-Z
e.g.
8085.E5-.E6 Epigrammata
8085.E5 Latin texts. By date
8085.E52 Danish translations. By date
8085.M6-.M63 Moralske fabler
8085.M7-.M73 Moralske tanker
8085.N5-.N6 Nicolai Klimii iter subterraneum
8085.N5 Latin texts. By date
8085.N52 Danish translations. By date
8085.N53-.N59 Other translations. By language (alphabetically)
8085.N54 English
8085.N56 French
8085.N57 German
8085.N6 Criticism
8085.5 Imitations, paraphrases, etc.
8085.7 Dictionaries, indexes, etc.
Biography and criticism
8086 Memoirs, letters, etc.
Ad virum perillustrem epistolae
8086.A3 Texts. By date
8086.A35-.A49 Translations. By language (alphabetically)
8086.A5 Criticism
Epistler
8086.A6 Collections. By date
8086.A7-Z Collections. By editor, A-Z
8086.5.A-Z Translations. By language, A-Z
8087 General works. Life and works
8088 Homes and haunts
8089 Anniversaries. Celebrations. Festschriften
Subarrange by date letters, using .B for 19th century, .C for 20th century, .D for 21st century, etc., e.g. 1822 = .B22; 1934 = .C34
8089.Z5 Memorials, testimonials (other than anniversaries)
8089.Z7 Iconographies, museums, exhibitions, monuments, portraits
Criticism
8090 General works
8091 Sources
8092 Influence in general
8093.A-Z Holberg in special countries, A-Z
e.g.
8093.G3 Germany
8093.S8 Sweden

Individual authors or works
16th-18th centuries
Holberg, Ludvig, baron, 1684-1754
Biography and criticism
Criticism -- Continued
8094 Language. Grammar
8094.5 Dramatic representation of Holberg's plays
8096 Hol - St
8096.K5 Kingo, Thomas Hansen, 1634-1703 (Table P-PZ40)
8096.K6 Kok, Laurids Olufsen, 1634-1691 (Table P-PZ40)
8096.P3 Paulli, Joachim Richard, 1691-1751 (Table P-PZ40)
8096.P4 Pedersen, Christiern, 1480?-1554 (Table P-PZ40)
8096.R3 Ranch, Hieronymus Justesen, 1539-1607 (Table P-PZ40)
8096.R4 Reenberg, Toger Clausen, 1656-1742 (Table P-PZ40)
8096.R6 Rostgaard, Frederik, 1671-1745 (Table P-PZ40)
8096.S6 Sneedorff, Jens Schielderup, 1724-1764 (Table P-PZ40)
8096.S7 Sthen, Hans Christensen, ca. 1540-1610 (Table P-PZ40)
8097 Stub, Ambrosius, 1705-1758 (Table P-PZ39)
8098 St - Z
8098.T45 Terkelsen, Soren, d. 1656 or 7 (Table P-PZ40)
8098.T5 Thaarup, Thomas, 1749-1821 (Table P-PZ40)
8098.W5 Wessel, Johan Herman, 1742-1785 (Table P-PZ40)
8098.W6 Wolf, Jacob Jacobsson, 1554-1635 (Table P-PZ40)
19th century
Subarrange Cutter number authors by Table P-PZ40 unless otherwise indicated
Subarrange one number authors by Table P-PZ39 unless otherwise indicated
8100 Anonymous works (Table P-PZ28)
8101 A - An
8101.A3 Aarestrup, Emil, 1800-1856 (Table P-PZ40)
8101.A4 Abrahamson, Werner Hans Frederik, 1744-1812 (Table P-PZ40)
Andersen, Hans Christian, 1805-1875
8102 Collected works. By date
8103 Selected works. Minor works: Posthumous works, fragments, etc.
Selections. Anthologies
8104.A1 By date
8104.A2 By editor
Translations
8105 English
8106 French
8107 German
8108 Swedish
8109.A-Z Other. By language, A-Z

	Individual authors or works
	19th century
	Andersen, Hans Christian, 1805-1875 -- Continued
8110.A-Z	Prose works, A-Z
8110.B5-.B52	Billedbog uden billeder
8110.I5-.I52	Improvisatoren
8110.K8-.K82	Kun en spillemand
	Poetry
8111	Collected. By date
8112.A-Z	Separate, A-Z
	Drama
8113	Collected. By date
8114.A-Z	Separate, A-Z
	Fairy tales
8115	Collected. By date
8116.A-Z	Translations. By language, A-Z Limited to scholarly editions Juvenile editions are classed in PZ8, PZ24, PZ34, etc. Rare Book Room editions are treated similarly
8117.A-Z	Special tales, A-Z
8117.5	Translation as subject
8118	Autobiography. Memoirs. Letters
8118.A2-.A5	Autobiography. By date
8118.A6	Memoirs, diaries, etc.
8118.A7A-.A7Z	Letters. By editor, A-Z
8118.A71-.A79	Translations
8118.A8-.Z8	Special correspondents, A-Z
8118.Z9	Drawings by Andersen
	Biography
8119	General works
8119.8	Iconography: Portraits, monuments
8119.82	Journeys
8119.9	Museums. Institutions. Exhibitions. Relics Subarrange by author
8120	Criticism
8121	An - Bag
8122	Baggesen, Jens, 1764-1826 (Table P-PZ39)
8123	Bag - Bl
8123.B3	Bang, Herman Joachim, 1857-1912 (Table P-PZ40)
8123.B4	Bauditz, Sophus Gustav, 1850-1915 (Table P-PZ40)
8123.B45	Benzon, Carl Otto Valdemar, 1856-1927 (Table P-PZ40)
8123.B5	Bergsøe, Vilhelm, 1835-1911 (Table P-PZ40)
	Bernhard, Carl, 1798-1865 see PT8165.S2
8124	Blicher, Steen Steensen, 1782-1848 (Table P-PZ39)
8125	Bl - Dr
8125.B6	Boeck, Christopher Nyholm, 1850- (Table P-PZ40)
8125.B63	Bodtcher, Ludwig Adolph, 1793-1874 (Table P-PZ40)

Individual authors or works
19th century
Bag - Bl -- Continued
8125.B7 Bournouville, Auguste, 1805-1879 (Table P-PZ40)
Cf. Class M, Music
8125.B8 Brandes, Georg Morris Cohen, 1842-1927 (Table P-PZ40)
8125.B85 Bredahl, Christian Hviid, 1784-1860 (Table P-PZ40)
8125.C6 Christiansen, Arne Einar, 1861-1939 (Table P-PZ40)
8126 Drachmann, Holger Henrik Herholdt, 1846-1908 (Table P-PZ39)
8127 Dr - Gj
8127.E4 Eltzholtz, Alberta, 1846-1934 (Table P-PZ40)
8127.E6 Esmann, Gustav Frederik, 1860-1904 (Table P-PZ40)
8127.E8 Ewald, Carl, 1856-1908 (Table P-PZ40)
8127.E9 Ewald, Herman Frederik, 1821-1908 (Table P-PZ40)
8127.F54 Fibiger Mathilde, 1830-1872 (Table P-PZ40)
8128 Gjellerup, Karl Adolph, 1857-1919 (Table P-PZ39)
8129 Gj - Gr
8129.G5 Goldschmidt, Meir, 1819-1887 (Table P-PZ40)
8130 Grundtvig, Nicolai Frederik Severin, 1783-1872 (Table P-PZ39)
8131 Gr - Hau
8131.G7 Grundtvig, Svend Hersleb, 1824-1883 (Table P-PZ40)
8131.G9 Gyllembourg-Ehrensvärd, Thomasine Christine (Buntzen), 1773-1856 (Table P-PZ40)
8131.H36 Hansen, Mâds, 1834-1880 (Table P-PZ40)
8132 Hauch, Johannes Carsten, 1790-1872 (Table P-PZ39)
8133 Hau - Hei
8134 Heiberg, Johan Ludvig, 1791-1860 (Table P-PZ39)
8135 Hei - Her
8136 Hertz, Henrik, 1798-1870 (Table P-PZ39)
8137 Her - In
8137.H7 Holst, Hans Peter, 1811-1893 (Table P-PZ40)
8137.H8 Hostrup, Jens Christian, 1818-1892 (Table P-PZ40)
8138 Ingemann, Bernhard Severin, 1789-1862 (Table P-PZ39)
8139 In - Ja
8140 Jacobsen, Jens Peter, 1847-1885 (Table P-PZ39)
8141 Ja - Kier
8141.J83 Juel-Hansen, Erna (Table P-PZ40)
8141.K2 Kaalund, Hans Vilhelm, 1818-1885 (Table P-PZ40)
8142 Kierkegaard, Soren Aabye, 1813-1855 (Table P-PZ39)
8143 Kier - Oehl
8143.K6 Kruse, Laurids, 1778-1839 (Table P-PZ40)
For works in German see PT2388.K63
8143.L34 Lassen, Rasmus Kruuse, 1811-1886 (Table P-PZ40)
8143.M6 Møller, Carl Emanuel, 1844-1898 (Table P-PZ40)

	Individual authors or works
	19th century
	Kier - Oehl -- Continued
8143.M62	Møller, Niels Lauritz, 1859-1941 (Table P-PZ40)
8143.M65	Møller, Poul Martin, 1794-1838 (Table P-PZ40)
8143.M68	Molbech, Christian, 1783-1857 (Table P-PZ40)
8143.M7	Molbech, Christian Knud Frederik, 1821-1888 (Table P-PZ40)
8143.N8	Nyrop, Kristoffer, 1858-1931 (Table P-PZ40)
	Oehlenschläger, Adam Gottlob, 1779-1850
8145	Collected works. By date
8146.A-Z	Selected works. By editor, A-Z
8147.A-Z	Selections. Anthologies. By editor, A-Z
8148.A-Z	Translations. By language, A-Z
	Poetry
8149	Collected. By date
8150.A-Z	Separate, A-Z
	Drama
8151	Collected. By date
8152.A-Z	Separate, A-Z
	e.g.
8152.A5-.A52	Aladdin
8152.A8-.A82	Axel og Valborg
8152.C6-.C62	Correggio
8152.H3-.H32	Hakon jarl hiin Rige
8152.P3-.P32	Palnatoke
8153.A-Z	Other works, A-Z
8155	Memoirs, letters, etc.
	Biography
8156	General works
8156.8	Iconography: Portraits, monuments
8157	Criticism
8160	Oehl - Pal
8160.O4	Østergaard, Vilhelm, 1852-1928 (Table P-PZ40)
8162	Paludan-Müller, Frederik, 1809-187 (Table P-PZ39)
8163	Pal - Plo
8163.P2	Paludan-Maller, Johannes Nathanael, 1853- (Table P-PZ40)
8164	Ploug, Carl, 1813-1894 (Table P-PZ39)
8165	Plo - Win
8165.R3	Rahbek, Knud Lyne, 1760-1830 (Table P-PZ40)
8165.R35	Ravnkilde, Adda, 1862-1883 (Table P-PZ40)
8165.R5	Richardt, Christian, 1831-1892 (Table P-PZ40)
8165.S2	Saint-Aubain, Andreas Nicolai de, 1798-1865 (Table P-PZ40)
8165.S27	Schack, Hans Egede, 1820-1859 (Table P-PZ40)

Individual authors or works
19th century
Plo - Win -- Continued
8165.S3 Schandorph, Sophus Christian Frederik, 1836-1901 (Table P-PZ40)
8165.S4 Scharling, Carl Henrik, 1836-1920 (Table P-PZ40)
8165.S7 Staffeldt, Adolph Wilhelm Schack von, 1769-1826 (Table P-PZ40)
8165.S8 Suenssen, Fanny, 1832-1918 (Table P-PZ40)
8165.T54 Thiele, Vilhelm (Table P-PZ40)
8165.T62 Timm, Herman Andreas, 1800-1866 (Table P-PZ40)
8165.T7 Topsøe, Vilhelm Kristian Sigurd, 1840-1881
8165.V54 Viersøe, Severin, 1814-1897
8166 Winther, Christian, 1796-1876 (Table P-PZ39)
8167 Win - Z
1900-1960
Here are usually to be classified authors beginning to publish about 1890, flourishing after 1900
8174 Anonymous (Table P-PZ28)
8175.A-Z Authors, A-Z
Subarrange individual authors by Table P-PZ40 unless otherwise indicated
8175.A12 Aabye, Karen, 1904- (Table P-PZ40)
8175.A2 Aakjaer, Jeppe, 1866-1930 (Table P-PZ40)
8175.A26 Abildgaard, Ove, 1916- (Table P-PZ40)
8175.A29 Agerskov, Michael (Table P-PZ40)
8175.A43 Andersen, Knud, 1890- (Table P-PZ40)
8175.A45 Andersen, Vilhelm Rasmus Andreas, 1864- (Table P-PZ40)
Andersen Nexø, Martin see PT8175.N4
8175.A5 Anker-Larsen, Johannes, 1874- (Table P-PZ40)
8175.B37 Becker, Knuth, 1891- (Table P-PZ40)
8175.B45 Benzon, Peter Eggert, 1857-1925 (Table P-PZ40)
8175.B48 Bergstedt, Harald Alfred, 1877- (Table P-PZ40)
8175.B5 Bergstrøm, Hjalmar, 1868-1914 (Table P-PZ40)
8175.B53 Bergstrøm, Vilhelm, 1886- (Table P-PZ40)
8175.B543 Bjarnhof, Karl, 1898- (Table P-PZ40)
8175.B5444 Bjørnvig, Thorkild, 1918- (Table P-PZ40)
8175.B545 Blixen, Karen, 1885-1962 (Table P-PZ40)
8175.B55 Bønnelycke, Emil, 1893- (Table P-PZ40)
8175.B6 Børup, Marinus, 1891- (Table P-PZ40)
8175.B65 Bomhalt, Julius, 1896- (Table P-PZ40)
8175.B73 Bramson, Karen (Adler), 1875-1936 (Table P-PZ40)
8175.B743 Branner, Hans Christian, 1903- (Table P-PZ40)
8175.B75 Bregendahl, Marie, 1867- (Table P-PZ40)
8175.B755 Breum, Sophie, 1870-1935 (Table P-PZ40)
8175.B79 Brun, Annette (Table P-PZ40)

Individual authors or works
1900-1960
Authors, A-Z -- Continued

8175.B8 Bruun, Laurids Valdemar, 1864-1935 (Table P-PZ40)
8175.B9 Buchholtz, Johannes, 1882- (Table P-PZ40)
8175.B92 Bukdahl, Jørgen, 1896- (Table P-PZ40)
8175.C4 Cederstrand, Ditte, 1896- (Table P-PZ40)
8175.C5 Christmas, Walter, 1861-1924 (Table P-PZ40)
8175.C65 Claussen, Sophus, 1865-1931 (Table P-PZ40)
8175.D26 Dahlsgaard, Marius, 1879 (Table P-PZ40)
Dinesen, Isak, 1885-1962 see PT8175.B545
8175.D5 Ditlevsen, Tove Irma Margit, 1918- (Table P-PZ40)
8175.D6 Dons, Aage, 1903- (Table P-PZ40)
8175.D75 Drachmann, Povl, 1887- (Table P-PZ40)
8175.E27 Egeberg, Edvard, 1855-1938 (Table P-PZ40)
8175.E5 Eilersgaard, Charlotte (Møller), 1858-1922 (Table P-PZ40)
8175.F47 Fischer, Leck 1904- (Table P-PZ40)
8175.F5 Fleuron, Svend, 1874- (Table P-PZ40)
8175.F65 Freuchen, Peter, 1886- (Table P-PZ40)
8175.G35 Gandrup, Richardt, 1885- (Table P-PZ40)
8175.G38 Garff, Alex, 1904- (Table P-PZ40)
8175.G45 Gelsted, Otto, 1888- (Table P-PZ40)
8175.G7 Gravlund, Thorkild, 1879-1939 (Table P-PZ40)
8175.G745 Gress, Elsa, 1919- (Table P-PZ40)
8175.G9 Gunnarson, Gunnar, 1889-1975 (Table P-PZ40)
For his work in Icelandic see PT7511.G9
8175.H29 Hansen, Aase, 1893- (Table P-PZ40)
8175.H3 Hansen, Carl, 1860-1916 (Table P-PZ40)
8175.H33 Hansen, Martin Alfred, 1909-1955 (Table P-PZ40)
8175.H34 Hansen, Peter Christian Valdemar, 1869-1927 (Table P-PZ40)
8175.H35 Hansen, Robert, 1883- (Table P-PZ40)
8175.H3534 Harthern, Ernst, 1884-1969 (Table P-PZ40)
8175.H38 Henningsen, Agnes Kathinka Malling (Andersen), 1868- (Table P-PZ40)
Herdal, Ditte (Cederstrand) see PT8175.C4
8175.H387 Herdal, Harald, 1900- (Table P-PZ40)
8175.H5 Hjortø, Knud, 1869-1931 (Table P-PZ40)
8175.H6 Hoeck, Johannes, 1869-1922 (Table P-PZ40)
8175.H63 Hørlyk, Lucie (Koch), 1870-1912 (Table P-PZ40)
8175.H65 Holm, Anders Wilhelm Sandberg, 1878- (Table P-PZ40)
8175.H66 Holst, Bertha, 1881-1929 (Table P-PZ40)
8175.H67 Holstein, Ludvig Ditlef, greve, 1864-1943 (Table P-PZ40)
8175.H7 Houmark, Christian, 1869-68 (Table P-PZ40)
Hoyer, Niels see PT8175.H3534

Individual authors or works
1900-1960
Authors, A-Z -- Continued

8175.J3 Jacobsen, Vigo Valdemar Ludvig Emil, 1876-1918 (Table P-PZ40)

Jacobson, Ludwiz, 1884-1969 see PT8175.H3534

8175.J355 Jaeger, Frank, 1926- (Table P-PZ40)

8175.J483 Jensen, Erik Aalbaek, 1923- (Table P-PZ40)

8175.J5 Jensen, Johannes Vilhelm, 1873-1950 (Table P-PZ40)

8175.J55 Jensen, Maria Kirstine Dorothea, 1876-1975 (Table P-PZ40)

Jensen, Thit, 1876-1975 see PT8175.J55

8175.J57 Jeppesen, Niels, 1882- (Table P-PZ40)

8175.J73 Jørgensen, Johannes, 1866- (Table P-PZ40)

8175.J8 Juel, Axel, 1883- (Table P-PZ40)

8175.K3 Kamban, Guðmundur, 1888-1945 (Table P-PZ40)

Cf. PT7511.K3 Icelandic

8175.K5 Kidde, Astrid Ehrencron (Müller), 1872- (Table P-PZ40)

8175.K515 Kidde, Harald, 1878-1918 (Table P-PZ40)

8175.K52 Kielgast, Ellinor (Table P-PZ40)

8175.K53 Kirk, Hans, 1898- (Table P-PZ40)

8175.K58 Knudsen, Erik, 1922- (Table P-PZ40)

8175.K6 Knudsen, Jakob Christian Lindberg, 1858-1917 (Table P-PZ40)

8175.K68 Korch, Morten, 1876- (Table P-PZ40)

8175.K73 Kristensen, Erling, 1893- (Table P-PZ40)

8175.K78 Kristensen, Tom, 1893- (Table P-PZ40)

8175.L2 LaCour, Paul, 1902-1956 (Table P-PZ40)

8175.L25 Lange, Sven, 1868-1930 (Table P-PZ40)

8175.L26 Lange, Thor Naeve, 1851-1915 (Table P-PZ40)

8175.L3 Larsen, Karl Halfdan Eduard, 1860-1931 (Table P-PZ40)

8175.L33 Larsen, Thøger, 1875-1928 (Table P-PZ40)

8175.L35 Lauesen, Marcus, 1907- (Table P-PZ40)

8175.L36 Lemche, Gyrithe (Frisch), 1866- (Table P-PZ40)

8175.L4 Leopold, Svend, 1874- (Table P-PZ40)

8175.L45 Levin, Poul Theodor, 1869-1929 (Table P-PZ40)

8175.L6 Løkken, Thomas Olesen, 1877- (Table P-PZ40)

8175.M2 Madelung, Aage, 1872- (Table P-PZ40)

8175.M23 Madsen, Johanne, 1877- (Table P-PZ40)

8175.M27 Magnussen, Julius Eugène Ove, 1882- (Table P-PZ40)

8175.M3 Malling, Mathilda (Kruse), 1864- (Table P-PZ40)

For biography and works in Swedish see PT9875.M3

8175.M5 Michaëlis, Karin, 1872- (Table P-PZ40)

8175.M6 Michaëlis, Sophus August Berthel, 1865-1932 (Table P-PZ40)

8175.M62 Mikkelsen, Ejnar, 1880- (Table P-PZ40)

8175.M7 Molbech, Oluf Christian, 1860-1927 (Table P-PZ40)

Individual authors or works
1900-1960
Authors, A-Z -- Continued

8175.M74 Mortensen, Chr. Fr., 1879-1933 (Table P-PZ40)
8175.M84 Munk, Kaj Harald Leininger, 1898-1944 (Table P-PZ40)
8175.N17 Nalbandiàn, Inga (Collin), 1879-1929 (Table P-PZ40)
8175.N2 Nansen, Peter, 1861-1918 (Table P-PZ40)
8175.N3 Nathansen, Henri, 1868-1918 (Table P-PZ40)
8175.N4 Nexø, Martin Andersen, 1869- (Table P-PZ40)
8175.N47 Nielsen, Harald Charles Christian Anton, 1879-69 (Table P-PZ40)
8175.N48 Nielsen, Jørgen, 1902- (Table P-PZ40)
8175.N5 Nielsen, Laurits Christian, 1871-1930 (Table P-PZ40)
8175.N535 Nielsen, Morten, 1922-1944 (Table P-PZ40)
8175.N55 Nielsen, Zakarias, 1844-1922 (Table P-PZ40)
8175.N7 Nordentoft, Severin, 1866-1922 (Table P-PZ40)
8175.N9 Nygaard, Fredrik, 1897- (Table P-PZ40)
8175.O5 Olson, Christian (Table P-PZ40)
8175.P33 Paludan, Jacob, 1896- (Table P-PZ40)
8175.P413 Pedersen, Sigfred, 1903- (Table P-PZ40)
8175.P45 Petersen, Lauritz, 1878- (Table P-PZ40)
8175.P48 Petersen, Nis, 1897-1943 (Table P-PZ40)
8175.P6 Pontoppidan, Henrik, 1857-1943 (Table P-PZ40)
8175.P7 Poulsen, Frederik, 1876- (Table P-PZ40)
8175.R3 Rasmussen, Emil, 1873- (Table P-PZ40)
8175.R33 Rasmussen, Halfdan Wedel, 1915- (Table P-PZ40)
8175.R4 Recke, Ernst Frederik Vilhelm von der, 1848-1933 (Table P-PZ40)
8175.R57 Rode, Edith (Nebelong), 1879- (Table P-PZ40)
8175.R58 Rode, Helge, 1870-1937 (Table P-PZ40)
8175.R59 Rønberg, Georg, 1877- (Table P-PZ40)
8175.R6 Rørdam, Valdemar, 1872- (Table P-PZ40)
8175.R7 Rosenkrantz, Palle Adam Vilhelm, baron, 1867- (Table P-PZ40)
8175.R8 Rung, Otto, 1874- (Table P-PZ40)
8175.S3 Sandemose, Aksel, 1899-1965 (Table P-PZ40)
Cf. PT8950.S23 Norwegian
8175.S5 Sick, Ingeborg Maria, 1869- (Table P-PZ40)
8175.S55 Sigurjónsson, Jóhann, 1880-1919 (Table P-PZ40)
Cf. PT7511.S5955 Icelandic
8175.S58 Skjoldborg, Johan Martinus Nielsen, 1861-1936 (Table P-PZ40)
8175.S63 Søiberg, Harry, 1880- (Table P-PZ40)
8175.S64 Sørensen, Carl, 1875- (Table P-PZ40)
8175.S66 Soya, Carl Erik, 1896- (Table P-PZ40)
8175.S7 Stender, Adolph (Table P-PZ40)
8175.S72 Stinus, Erik (Table P-PZ40)

Individual authors or works
1900-1960
Authors, A-Z -- Continued
8175.S8 Stuckenberg, Viggo Henrik Fog, 1863-1905 (Table P-PZ40)
8175.T3 Tandrup, Harald, 1874- (Table P-PZ40)
8175.T45 Thuborg, Anders, 1887- (Table P-PZ40)
8175.W5 Wied, Gustav Johannes, 1858-1914 (Table P-PZ40)
8175.W64 Wivel, Ole, 1921- (Table P-PZ40)
8175.W7 Woel, Cai Mogens, 1895- (Table P-PZ40)
8175.W8 Wulff, Johannes, 1902- (Table P-PZ40)
8176-8176.36 1961-2000 (Table P-PZ29 modified)
Here are usually to be classified authors beginning to publish about 1950, flourishing after 1960
8176.18 H
Høyer, Lis, 1935- see PT8176.23.O725
8176.23 M
8176.23.O725 Mortensen, Lis, 1935 (Table P-PZ40)
8177-8177.36 2001- (Table P-PZ29)
Danish literature: Provincial, local, foreign
The works and biography and criticism of individual authors (provincial and local) are to be classified in PT8050+
Provincial, local, etc.
8205.A-Z By region, A-Z
Subarrange individual places by Table P-PZ26
8206.A-Z By province, A-Z
Subarrange individual places by Table P-PZ26
8207.A-Z By place, A-Z
Subarrange individual places by Table P-PZ26
Danish literature outside of Denmark
8210 General
Special
Danish West Indies. Virgin Islands of the United States
8211 General works
8212 General special
8214 Biography (Collective)
Special periods
8216 To 1800
8217 19th century
8218 20th century
8219 21st century
Special forms
8220 Poetry
8221 Drama
8222.A-Z Other, A-Z
Collections
8223 General

Danish literature: Provincial, local, foreign
Danish literature outside of Denmark
Special
Danish West Indies. Virgin Islands of the United States
Collections -- Continued
8224 Poetry
8225 Drama
8226.A-Z Other special forms, A-Z
8228.A-Z Local, A-Z
Subarrange individual places by Table P-PZ26
8229.A-Z Individual authors, A-Z
Subarrange each author by Table P-PZ40
North America
8231 General works
8232 General special
8234 Biography (Collective)
Special periods
8236 To 1800
8237 19th century
8238 20th century
8239 21st century
Special forms
8240 Poetry
8241 Drama
8242.A-Z Other, A-Z
Collections
8243 General
8244 Poetry
8245 Drama
8246.A-Z Other special forms, A-Z
8248.A-Z Local, A-Z
Subarrange individual places by Table P-PZ26
8250.A-Z Individual authors, A-Z
Subarrange each author by Table P-PZ40 unless otherwise specified
8250.A5 Andersen, Rasmus, 1848-1930 (Table P-PZ40)
8250.C5 Christensen, Cai Løve, 1878- (Table P-PZ40)
Enebo, Bror see PT8250.C5
8250.K55 Kildsig, J.J. (Table P-PZ40)
8250.M7 Mortensen, Enok, 1902- (Table P-PZ40)
8250.O4 Østergaard, Kristian, 1855-1931 (Table P-PZ40)
8260.A-Z Other countries, A-Z
Subarrange individual places by Table P-PZ26

Norwegian literature
Literary history and criticism
8301 Periodicals. Serials
(8303) Yearbooks
see PT8301
8305 Societies
8307 Congresses
Collections
8313 Monographs, studies, etc. By various authors
8316.A-Z Festschriften. By honoree, A-Z
8317 Encyclopedias. Dictionaries
8319 Theory and principles of the study of Norwegian literature
8325 History of literary history
8329 Philosophy. Psychology. Aesthetics
Includes national characteristics in literature
Study and teaching
8340 General
8341 General special
8342.A-Z By region or country, A-Z
8343.A-Z By school, A-Z
Biography of teachers, critics, and historians
8343.5 Collective
8344.A-Z Individual, A-Z
Subarrange each by Table P-PZ50
Criticism
8350 Treatises. Theory
8352 History
8353 Special topics (not A-Z)
8354 Collections of essays in criticism
History of Norwegian literature
General works
8360 Danish and Dano-Norwegian
8361 Landsmaal
8362 Swedish
8363 English
8364 French
8365 German
8366.A-Z Other languages, A-Z
8369 Outlines, syllabi, etc.
Miscellaneous special aspects
8380 Relation to history, civilization, culture, etc.
8383 Relation to foreign literatures
8388 Translations of other literatures into Norwegian (as subject)
8389 Translation of Norwegian literature (as subject)
8391 Other special aspects (not A-Z)
Treatment of special subjects

Literary history and criticism
History of Norwegian literature
Treatment of special subjects -- Continued
8395.A-Z Special topics, A-Z
8395.C55 Cities and towns
8395.F3 Fascism
8395.N3 Nature
8395.R35 Realism
8395.R4 Religion
8396.A-Z Special countries and races, A-Z
8396.N6 North America
8397.A-Z Special classes, A-Z
8397.P7 Priests
8397.W6 Women
8398.A6-Z Special characters, persons, etc., A-Z
Biography, memoirs, letters, etc.
8405 Biography (Collective)
8407 Memoirs. Letters
8408 Relation to women, love, marriage, etc.
8410 Literary landmarks. Homes and haunts of authors
8415 Women authors. Literary relations of women
Special periods
(8420) Medieval to about 1540
see PT7101+
16th-18th centuries
8425 General works
8427.A-Z Special topics, A-Z
Sub-periods
8428 16th-17th centuries
8429 Age of Holberg (ca. 1700-1750)
8430 Period of Rationalism (1750-1814)
19th century
8435 General works
8437.A-Z Special subjects, A-Z
8437.B64 Body, Human
8437.D63 Decadence (Literary movement)
8437.G67 Gothic revival
8437.H65 Homosexuality
Human body see PT8437.B64
8437.M64 Modernism
8437.M95 Mysticism
8437.N3 Nature
8437.W6 Women
Sub-periods
8438 Romanticism (ca. 1814-1865)
8439 Realism (ca. 1865-1890)
Maalstraev. Landsmaal movement see PT9000+

Literary history and criticism
History of Norwegian literature
Special periods -- Continued
20th century
8450 General works
8452.A-Z Special subjects, A-Z
8452.F37 Fascism
8452.I45 Immoral literature
8452.T76 Tromsø (Norway)
21st century
8455 General works
8456.A-Z Special subjects, A-Z
Special forms
Poetry
8460 General works
8462.A-Z Special topics, A-Z
Special periods
(8465) Medieval
see PT7101+
16th-18th centuries
8470 General works
8472 Special topics (not A-Z)
19th century
8475 General works
8477 Special topics (not A-Z)
20th century
8480 General works
8482 Special topics (not A-Z)
21st century
8483 General works
8484 Special topics (not A-Z)
Special forms
8485 Epic poetry
8486 Popular poetry. Ballads, songs, etc.
Cf. PT8609 Folk poetry
8487 Lyric poetry
8488.A-Z Other special forms, A-Z
8488.D5 Didactic
8488.E4 Elegiac
8488.P3 Pastoral
8489.A-Z Special subjects, A-Z
8489.N3 Nature
8489.R4 Religion
Drama
For history of the Norwegian stage see PN2760+
8500 General works
8502.A-Z Special topics, A-Z

Literary history and criticism
History of Norwegian literature
Special forms
Drama -- Continued
Special periods
Medieval
8505 Origins
8506 Mysteries, moralities, miracle plays, etc.
16th-18th centuries
8510 General works
8512 Special topics (not A-Z)
19th century
8515 General works
8517 Special topics (not A-Z)
20th century
8520 General works
8522 Special topics (not A-Z)
21st century
8523 General works
8524 Special topics (not A-Z)
Special forms
8525 Tragedy
8526 Comedy
8528 Tragicomedy
8529 Vaudeville
8531 Romantic drama
8532 Melodrama
8533 Farce
8534.A-Z Other special, A-Z
Prose
8540 General works
Special periods
(8545) Medieval
see PT7101+
Modern
8550 General
8551 16th-18th centuries
8552 19th century
8553 20th century
8554 21st century
Special forms
Prose fiction
8555 General works
Special topics
8560 Romanticism
8561 Historical fiction
8562 Realism

Literary history and criticism
History of Norwegian literature
Special forms
Prose
Special forms
Prose fiction
Special topics -- Continued
8563 Naturalism
8564.A-Z Other, A-Z
8564.C45 Christianity
8564.D4 Detective and mystery stories
8564.N46 Neorealism
Special periods
8565 17th-18th centuries
8566 19th century
8567 20th century
8568 21st century
8570 Oratory
8571 Letters
8572 Essays
8573 Wit and humor
8574 Miscellaneous
Folk literature
For general works on and collections of folk literature, see GR220+
History
(8600) General works
Special periods
8605 Origins. Middle Ages
(8606) Later
Special forms
8609 Poetry
(8610) Prose
Collections
(8615) General
8617 Chapbooks
(8618.A-Z) Special localities, A-Z
8619 Poetry. Ballads, songs, etc. (Folkeviser)
Prose tales. Legends (Folkesagn)
(8621) General works
(8623.A-Z) Special localities, A-Z
(8625) Fairy tales
(8628.A-Z) Special characters, persons, etc., A-Z
(8631) Individual tales
(8635.A-Z) Translations. By language, A-Z
(8637) Proverbs
see PN6486

8640 Juvenile literature (General)
For special genres, see the genre
Collections of Norwegian literature
General
8645 Periodicals. Serials
8650 Collections before 1801
8651 Collections, 1801-
8653 Selections. Anthologies
8653.5.A-Z Special classes of authors, A-Z
8653.5.C48 Children
8653.5.W65 Women
8654.A-Z Special topics (Prose and verse), A-Z
8654.B52 Bible
8654.F6 Forests
8654.L3 Labor. Working class
8654.L6 Lofoten
8654.M96 Mysticism
8654.R4 Religion
8654.S4 Sailors
8654.S46 September 11 Terrorist Attacks, 2001
8654.S57 Sogn (Norway)
8654.S6 Sørlandet
8654.U54 United States
8654.W57 Women
Working class see PT8654.L3
8654.W6 World War II
Translations into foreign languages
8660 Polyglot
8661 English
8662 French
8663 German
8664 Swedish
8665.A-Z Other. By language, A-Z
Poetry
8675 Collections before 1801
8676 Collections, 1801-
8678 Selections. Anthologies
8678.5 Anthologies of poetry for children
8680 Selections from women authors
Translations into foreign languages
8683.A2 Polyglot collections
8683.A5-Z By language
Subarrange by editor or title
Special forms and subjects
8690 Ballads. Songs
8691 Sonnets
8692 Historical. Patriotic. Political

Collections of Norwegian literature
Poetry
Special forms and subjects -- Continued

8693 Satires
8695.A-Z Other, A-Z
8695.F65 Foresters
8695.L3 Labor. Working class
8695.L7 Love poetry
Norway see PT8692
8695.P75 Protest poetry
8695.R34 Railroads
8695.R4 Religious poetry
8695.S32 Seasons
8695.T74 Trees
Working class see PT8695.L3

Drama
8699 Collections before 1801
8700 Collections, 1801-
8705 Selected plays. Anthologies
8706.A-Z Translations. By language, A-Z
Special forms
8710 Mysteries, moralities, miracle plays
8712 Tragedies
8713 Comedies
8714 Farces, vaudevilles, etc.
8716 Amateur drama. Juvenile plays
8718.A-Z Other special, A-Z
8718.O53 One-act plays

Prose
8719 General
Fiction
8720 General
8721 Selections. Anthologies
8722.A-Z Translations. By language, A-Z
8723.A-Z Special subjects, A-Z
8723.C5 Children
8723.D4 Detective and mystery stories
8723.S3 Science fiction
8723.W65 Women

8725 Oratory
8726 Letters
8727 Essays
8728 Wit and humor
8730 Fables
(8731) Proverbs
see PN6486
8733 Miscellaneous

Individual authors or works
Medieval see PT7326+
16th-18th centuries
Subarrange Cutter number authors by Table P-PZ40 unless otherwise indicated
Subarrange one number authors by Table P-PZ39 unless otherwise indicated

8750 Anonymous works (Table P-PZ28)
8751 A - Bru
8751.A6 Anker, Bernt, 1746-1805 (Table P-PZ40)
8751.B34 Bang, Marcus Frederik, 1711-1789 (Table P-PZ40)
8752 Brun, Johan Nordahl, 1745-1816 (Table P-PZ39)
8753 Bru - Das
8754 Dass, Petter, 1647-1708 (Table P-PZ39)
8755 Das - Fal
8755.D6 Dorothe Engelbretsdatter, 1634-1716 (Table P-PZ40)
8757 Falsen, Enevold de, 1755-1808 (Table P-PZ39)
8759 Fasting, Claus, 1746-1791 (Table P-PZ39)
(8761) Friis, Peder Claussøn, 1545-1614
see DL445.7.F7
8763 Frimann, Claus, 1746-1829 (Table P-PZ39)
8765 Frim - Hol
(8766) Holberg, Ludvig
see PT8070+
8768 Hol - Tul
8768.S7 Storm, Edvard, 1749-1794 (Table P-PZ40)
8770 Tullin, Christian Brauriman, 1728-1765 (Table P-PZ39)
8772 Tul - Zet
8774 Zetlitz, Jens, 1761-1821 (Table P-PZ39)
8775 Zet -

19th century
Subarrange Cutter number authors by Table P-PZ40 unless otherwise indicated
Subarrange one number authors by Table P-PZ39 unless otherwise indicated

8800 Anonymous works (Table P-PZ28)
8801 A - As
8802 Asbjørnsen, Peter Christen, 1812-1885 (Table P-PZ39)
8803 As - Bjer
8803.B4 Bergh, Hallvard Ellestad, 1850-1922 (Table P-PZ40)
8804 Bjerregaard, Henrik Anker, 1792-1842 (Table P-PZ39)
8805 Bjer - Bjør
Bjørnson, Bjørnstjerne, 1832-1910
Collected works
8807 By date
8808.A-Z Translations. By language, A-Z
Selected works

Individual authors or works
19th century
Bjørnson, Bjørnstjerne, 1832-1910
Selected works -- Continued
8809 By editor
Translations
8811.A-Z English. By translator, A-Z
8812.A-Z Other. By language, A-Z
8813 Selections. Extracts. Quotations
8814 Poetry (Table PT7)
8816 Drama (Table PT7 modified)
8816.A5-Z Separate works. By title, A-Z
8816.F3 En fallit
8816.M3 Maria Stuart
8816.R4 Redaktøren
8816.S5 Sigurd Slembe
8817 Novels and tales (Table PT7 modified)
8817.A5-Z Separate works. By title, A-Z
8817.A9 Arne
8817.F5 Fiskerjenten
8817.G5 En glad gut
8817.M2 Magnhild
8817.M3 Mary
8817.S8 Synnøve Solbakken
8818 Speeches, addresses, etc. (Table PT7)
8819 Dictionaries. Indexes
8820 Memoirs. Letters. Autobiography
8820.A2 Memoirs. Autobiography. By date
8820.A3 Letters (Collections). By date
8820.A3A-.A3Z Translations. By language, A-Z
8820.A4-Z Letters to and from particular individuals. By correspondent, A-Z
8821 Biography and criticism. General works
8822 Relation to contemporaries
8823 Homes and haunts. Local associations. Landmarks
8824 Iconography. Portraits. Monuments
8825 Authorship. Manuscripts. Followers
Criticism and interpretation
8826 General works
8827 Language
8828 Versification
8829 Bjør - Boy
8829.B7 Botten-Hansen, Paul, 1824-1869 (Table P-PZ40)
(8830) Boyesen, Hjalmar Hjorth, 1848-1895
see PS1115+
8831 Boy - Bu
8831.B4 Brinkman, Karl Gustav von, 1764-1847 (Table P-PZ40)

Individual authors or works
19th century
Boy - Bu -- Continued
Brun, Johan Nordahl, 1745-1816 see PT8752
8834 Bull, Jacob Breda, 1853-1930 (Table P-PZ39)
8835 Bu - Cas
8836 Caspari, Theodor, 1853-8838 (Table P-PZ39)
8838 Cas - Col
8839 Collett, Camilla (Wergeland), 1813-1895 (Table P-PZ39)
8840 Col - Dah
8840.D8 Dahl, Jonas Anton, 1849-1919 (Table P-PZ40)
8841 Dahl, Konrad Neumann Hjelm, 1843- (Table P-PZ39)
8842 Dah - Diet
8843 Dietrichson, Lorentz Henrik Segelcke, 1834-1917 (Table P-PZ39)
8844 Diet - El
8844.D92 Dybfest, Arne, 1869-1892 (Table P-PZ40)
8845 Elster, Kristian Mandrup, 1841-1881 (Table P-PZ39)
8846 El - Fin
8847 Finne, Gabriel, 1866-1899 (Table P-PZ39)
8848 Fin - Han
8848.F2 Flatabø, Jon, 1846-1930 (Table P-PZ40)
8848.G2 Garborg, Arne, 1851-1924 (Table P-PZ40)
Cf. PT9070 Landsmaal
8848.G3 Garborg, Hulda (Bergersen), 1862-1934 (Table P-PZ40)
Cf. PT9071 Landsmaal
8849 Hansen, Mauritz Christopher. 1794-1842 (Table P-PZ39)
8850 Han - Ib
Ibsen, Henrik, 1828-1906
Bibliography see Z8431
Collected works
8851 By date
8852.A-Z Translations. By language, A-Z
e.g.
8852.E5 English. By translator or editor
Selected works
8853 By editor
Translations
8854 English. By translator or editor
8855.A-Z Other. By language, A-Z
8856 Selections. Extracts. Quotations
Dramatic works
Collected see PT8851+
Separate works
8858 Brand (Table P-PZ41)
8859 Bygmester Solness (The master builder) (Table P-PZ41)

Individual authors or works
19th century
Ibsen, Henrik, 1828-1906
Dramatic works
Separate works -- Continued

8860 Catilina (Table P-PZ41)
8861 Et dukkehjem (A doll's house) (Table P-PZ41)
8862 En folkefiende (An enemy of the people) (Table P-PZ41)
8863 Fru Inger til Østråt (Lady Inger of Østraat) (Table P-PZ41)
8864 Fruen fra havet (The lady from the sea) (Table P-PZ41)
8865 Gengangere (Ghosts) (Table P-PZ41)
8866 Gildet paa Solhaug (The feast at Solhaug) (Table P-PZ41)
8867 Hærmaemdene paa Helgeland (The vikings (or warriors) at Helgeland) (Table P-PZ41)
8868 Hedda Gabler (Table P-PZ41)
8869 John Gabriel Borkman (Table P-PZ41)
8870 Kejser og Galilaeer (Emperor and Galilean) (Table P-PZ41)
8871 Kjaemrlighedens komedie (Love's comedy) (Table P-PZ41)
8872 Kongs-emnerne (The pretenders) (Table P-PZ41)
8873 Lille Eyolf (Table P-PZ41)
8874 Naar vi døde vaagner (When we dead awaken) (Table P-PZ41)
8875 Olaf Liljekrans (Table P-PZ41)
8876 Peer Gynt (Table P-PZ41)
8877 Rosmersholm (Table P-PZ41)
8878 Samfundets støtter (Pillars of society) (Table P-PZ41)
8879 Sancthansnatten (St. John's eve) (Table P-PZ41)
8880 De unges forbund (The league of youth) (Table P-PZ41)
8881 Vildanden (The wild duck) (Table P-PZ41)
8882.A-Z Other, A-Z
Subarrange individual works by Table P-PZ43

Poetry
Collections
8883.A1 By date
8883.A2 By editor
Translations
8883.A3A-.A3Z English. By translator, A-Z
8883.A4A-.A4Z Other. By language, A-Z
8883.A5-Z Separate works
8884 Letters

Individual authors or works
19th century
Ibsen, Henrik, 1828-1906
Letters -- Continued
Collections
8884.A1 By date
8884.A2 By editor
Translations
8884.A3A-.A3Z English. By translator, A-Z
8884.A4-Z Other. By language, A-Z
8885 Speeches and addresses
Collections
8885.A1 By date
8885.A2 By editor
Translations
8885.A3A-.A3Z English. By translator, A-Z
8885.A4-Z Other. By language, A-Z
8886 Imitations. Parodies
8887 Dictionaries. Indexes
8890 Biography and criticism. General works
8890.A1 Periodicals, societies, etc.
8891 Relation to contemporaries
8892 Homes and haunts. Local associations. Landmarks
8892.5 Anniversaries. Celebrations
8893 Iconography. Portraits. Monuments
8894 Authorship. Manuscripts. Followers
Criticism and interpretation
8895 General works
8896 Characters, plots, scenes, time
8897.A-Z Treatment and knowledge of special subjects, A-Z
8897.A4 Anarchism
8897.D4 Death
8897.D7 Drama technique
8897.F6 Folklore
8897.N3 Nationalism
8897.P3 Philosophy
8897.P7 Psychology
8897.R4 Religion
8897.S3 Science
8897.W7 Women
8898 Language, versification, etc.
8899 Dramatic representation of Ibsen's plays
Ibsen in foreign countries
8900.A1 General
8900.A2-Z Special countries, A-Z
8901 Ib - Jan
8901.J5 Jaeger, Hans Henrik, 1854-1910 (Table P-PZ40)

Individual authors or works
19th century -- Continued
8902 Janson, Kristofer Nagel, 1841-1917 (Table P-PZ39)
Cf. PT9075 Landsmaal
8903 Jan - Kiel
8903.J84 Juell, Dagny, 1867-1901 (Table P-PZ40)
8904 Kielland, Alexander Lange, 1849-1906 (Table P-PZ39)
8905 Kiel - Lie
8905.K7 Koren, Charlotte Amalie, 1831-1909 (Table P-PZ40)
Lie, Jonas Lauritz Idemil, 1833-1908
8906 Collected works. By date
8907.A-Z Selected works. By editor, A-Z
8908.A-Z Translations. By language, A-Z
8909 Drama (Table PT7)
8910 Poetry (Table PT7)
8911 Novels (Table PT7)
8913 Fairy tales (Table PT7)
8914 Biography and criticism
8915 Lie - Mel
8916 Meltzer, Harald, 1814-1862 (Table P-PZ39)
8917 Mel - Moe
8918 Moe, Jørgen Engebretsen, 1813-1882 (Table P-PZ39)
8919 Moe - Mu
8920 Munch, Andreas, 1811-1884 (Table P-PZ39)
8921 Mu - Pry
8921.N5 Nilsen, Anthon Bernhard Elias, 1855-1936 (Table P-PZ40)
8921.O2 Obstfelder, Sigbjørn, 1866-1900 (Table P-PZ40)
8921.P38 Pavels Hielm, Peter, 1781-1846 (Table P-PZ40)
8922 Prydz, Alvilde, 1848-1922 (Table P-PZ39)
8923 Pry - Rei
8923.R3 Randers, Kristofer, 1851-1917 (Table P-PZ40)
8924 Rein, Jonas, 1760-1821 (Table P-PZ39)
8925 Rei - Rol
8926 Rolfsen, Nordahl, 1848-1928 (Table P-PZ39)
8927 Rol - Skr
8928 Skram, Amalie (Alver), 1846-1905 (Table P-PZ39)
8932 Skr - Wel
8932.T5 Thoresen, Magdalene, 1819-1903 (Table P-PZ40)
8933 Welhaven, Johan Sebastian Cammermeyer, 1807-1873 (Table P-PZ39)
8934 Wel - Wer
Wergeland, Henrik Arnold, 1808-1845
8935 Collected works. By date
8936.A-Z Translations. By language, A-Z
Poetry
Collections

Individual authors or works
19th century
Wergeland, Henrik Arnold, 1808-1845
Poetry
Collections -- Continued
8937.A1 By date
8937.A2 By editor
Translations
8937.A3A-.A3Z English. By translator, A-Z
8937.A4A-.A4Z Other. By language, A-Z
8937.A5-Z Separate works, A-Z
Drama
Collections
8938.A1 By date
8938.A2 By editor
Translations
8938.A3A-.A3Z English. By translator, A-Z
8938.A4A-.A4Z Other. By language, A-Z
8938.A5-Z Separate works, A-Z
8939 Miscellaneous works
8940 Biography
Includes his Hasselnødder
8941 Criticism
8942 Wer - Z
8942.W2 Wergeland, Nicolai, 1780-1848 (Table P-PZ40)
1900-1960
Here are usually to be classified authors beginning to publish about 1890, flourishing after 1900
8949 Anonymous works (Table P-PZ28)
8950.A-Z Authors, A-Z
Subarrange individual authors by Table P-PZ40 unless otherwise indicated
8950.A2 Aanrud, Hans, 1863- (Table P-PZ40)
8950.A22 Aars, Sophus Christian Munk, 1841-1931 (Table P-PZ40)
8950.A4 Aikio, Matti, 1872-1929 (Table P-PZ40)
8950.A5 Andersen, Tryggve, 1866-1920 (Table P-PZ40)
8950.A6 Anker, Nini (Roll), 1873- (Table P-PZ40)
8950.A7 Ansteinsson, Ove Arthur, 1884- (Table P-PZ40)
8950.A75 Arnesen, David Dietrichs Swensen, 1884- (Table P-PZ40)
8950.A77 Aslagsson, Olai, 1885- (Table P-PZ40)
8950.B4 Benneche, Olaf, 1883-1931 (Table P-PZ40)
8950.B47 Bjerke, André, 1918- (Table P-PZ40)
8950.B5 Bjerke, Ejlert Osvald, 1887- (Table P-PZ40)
8950.B6 Bojer, Johan, 1872-1959 (Table P-PZ40)
8950.B63 Bolander, Asta (Grash), 1861- (Table P-PZ40)
Borg, Otto see PT8950.B75

Individual authors or works
1900-1960
Authors, A-Z -- Continued

8950.B713 Borgen, Johan, 1902- (Table P-PZ40)
8950.B73 Braaten, Oskar, 1881-1939 (Table P-PZ40)
8950.B75 Breda, Olaus Caspersen, 1866- (Table P-PZ40)
8950.B78 Brinchmann, Alexander, 1888- (Table P-PZ40)
8950.B8 Broch, Lagertha Olea Sofie, 1864- (Table P-PZ40)
8950.B85 Bull, Olaf Jacob Martin Luther, 1883-1933 (Table P-PZ40)
8950.B9 Butenschon, Hanna (Døderlein) Andresen, 1851-1928 (Table P-PZ40)
8950.C5 Christensen, Hjalmar, 1869-1925 (Table P-PZ40)
8950.C55 Christiansen, Sigurd Wesley, 1891- (Table P-PZ40)
8950.D3 Dal, Signe (Greve), 1867- (Table P-PZ40)
Dickmar, Helene see PT8950.B9
8950.E3 Ebbell, Bendix Joachim, 1869-1937 (Table P-PZ40)
8950.E4 Egge, Peter, 1869- (Table P-PZ40)
8950.E5 Elster, Kristian, 1881- (Table P-PZ40)
8950.E6 Elvestad, Sven, 1884-1934 (Table P-PZ40)
8950.F2 Fabricius, Sara, 1880- (Table P-PZ40)
8950.F3 Falkberget, Johan, 1879- (Table P-PZ40)
8950.F35 Fangen, Ronald, 1895- (Table P-PZ40)
8950.F55 Fønhus, Mikkjel, 1894- (Table P-PZ40)
Garborg, Arne see PT8848.G2
Garborg, Arne (works in Landsmaal) see PT9070
8950.G32 Geelmuyden, Hans, 1906- (Table P-PZ40)
8950.G34 Geijerstam, Gösta af, 1888- (Table P-PZ40)
8950.G4 Gierløff, Christian Per Gronbeck, 1879- (Table P-PZ40)
8950.G45 Gjesdahl, Katharina, 1885- (Table P-PZ40)
8950.G5 Gløersen, Kari (Hansen), 1871- (Table P-PZ40)
8950.G7 Grane, Anna, 1879- (Table P-PZ40)
8950.G76 Grieg, Nordahl, 1902- (Table P-PZ40)
8950.H23 Haalke, Magnhild, 1886- (Table P-PZ40)
8950.H25 Hagen, Ingeborg Refling, 1895- (Table P-PZ40)
8950.H258 Hagerup, Inger (Halsør), 1905- (Table P-PZ40)
8950.H26 Hagerup, Jens, 1884- (Table P-PZ40)
8950.H3 Hamsun, Knut, 1859-1952 (Table P-PZ40)
8950.H32 Hansen, Lars, 1869- (Table P-PZ40)
8950.H33 Harbitz, Alf, 1880- (Table P-PZ40)
8950.H34 Hauge, Yngvar, 1899- (Table P-PZ40)
8950.H35 Haukland, Andreas, 1873-1933 (Table P-PZ40)
8950.H38 Hegna, Hans, 1863- (Table P-PZ40)
8950.H4 Heiberg, Gunnar Edvard Rode, 1857-1929 (Table P-PZ40)
8950.H483 Hellesnes, Lars, b. 1865 (Table P-PZ40)
8950.H5 Hilditch, Jacob, 1864-1930 (Table P-PZ40)

Individual authors or works
1900-1960
Authors, A-Z -- Continued

8950.H55 Hiorth-Schøyen, Rolf, 1887-1932 (Table P-PZ40)
8950.H57 Hjermann, Audun, 1892- (Table P-PZ40)
8950.H58 Hoel, Sigurd, 1890- (Table P-PZ40)
8950.H6 Holme, Edin, 1865-1927 (Table P-PZ40)
8950.H72 Holt, Kåre, 1917- (Table P-PZ40)
8950.I3 Ibsen, Sigurd, 1859-1930 (Table P-PZ40)
8950.J4 Jessen, Burchard, 1871-1925 (Table P-PZ40)
8950.J6 Jølsen, Ragnhild, 1875-1908 (Table P-PZ40)
8950.J8 Juuhl, Johan Christian Walhammer, 1867- (Table P-PZ40)
8950.K32 Keilhau, Carl (Table P-PZ40)
8950.K4 Kielland, Jens Zetlitz, 1873-1926 (Table P-PZ40)
8950.K5 Kinck, Hans Ernst, 1865-1926 (Table P-PZ40)
8950.K6 Kjaer, Nils, 1870-1924 (Table P-PZ40)
8950.K65 Kjølstad, Lars, 1861-1923 (Table P-PZ40)
8950.K7 Klaeboe, Hallfrid Ravn, 1878- (Table P-PZ40)
Knudsen, Anna see PT8950.G7
8950.K75 Koren-Wiberg, Christian, 1870- (Table P-PZ40)
8950.K8 Krag, Thomas Peter, 1868-1913 (Table P-PZ40)
8950.K85 Krag, Vilhelm Andreas Wexels, 1871-1933 (Table P-PZ40)
8950.K89 Kristiansen, Kristian, 1909- (Table P-PZ40)
8950.K897 Kristmann, Guömundsson, 1901- (Table P-PZ40)
8950.L3 Larsen, Helmik (Table P-PZ40)
8950.L5 Lie, Bernt Bessesen, 1868-1916 (Table P-PZ40)
8950.L55 Lie, Erik Roring Møinichen, 1868- (Table P-PZ40)
8950.L6 Lieblein, Severin, 1866-1933 (Table P-PZ40)
8950.L7 Løken, Haakon, 1859-1923 (Table P-PZ40)
Lønn, Leo see PT8950.M35
8950.L75 Lossius, Kitty, 1892- (Table P-PZ40)
8950.L8 Lyche, Hans, 1885- (Table P-PZ40)
8950.L85 Lykke-Seest, Peter, 1868- (Table P-PZ40)
8950.M32 Mahrt, Haakon Bugge, 1901- (Table P-PZ40)
8950.M35 Mathiesen, Sigurd, 1871- (Table P-PZ40)
8950.M37 Maurer, Axel, 1866-1925 (Table P-PZ40)
8950.M4 Meidell, Hjalmar Sigvard, 1871- (Table P-PZ40)
8950.M66 Møller, Ingeborg, 1878- (Table P-PZ40)
8950.M7 Mork, Per, 1877- (Table P-PZ40)
8950.N47 Nilsen, Ernst, 1898- (Table P-PZ40)
8950.N7 Normann, Regine, 1867- (Table P-PZ40)
8950.O2 Øberg, Edith, 1895- (Table P-PZ40)
8950.O4 Øverland, Arnulf, 1889- (Table P-PZ40)
Orvil, Ernst see PT8950.N47
8950.P3 Parelius, Fredrik Arnoldus, 1879- (Table P-PZ40)

Individual authors or works
1900-1960
Authors, A-Z -- Continued
Pettersen, Amalie see PT8950.W65
8950.R3 Ramm, Minda, 1859-1924 (Table P-PZ40)
8950.R33 Rasmussen, Egil, 1903- (Table P-PZ40)
8950.R4 Rein, Sigmun, 1873- (Table P-PZ40)
8950.R6 Ring, Barbra, 1870- (Table P-PZ40)
Riverton, Stein see PT8950.E6
Roberts, Roy see PT8950.B78
8950.R74 Rongen, Bjørn, 1906- (Table P-PZ40)
8950.S2 Saeter, Ivar, 1864- (Table P-PZ40)
8950.S23 Sandemose, Aksel, 1899-1965 (Table P-PZ40)
Cf. PT8175.S3 Danish
8950.S4 Scott, Gabriel, 1874- (Table P-PZ40)
8950.S5 Sinding, Holger, 1853-1929 (Table P-PZ40)
8950.S55 Singdahlsen, Ole Christopher Lie, 1877-1926 (Table P-PZ40)
8950.S6 Skramstad, Adolf Hedevard, 1865-1927 (Table P-PZ40)
8950.S63 Skredsvig, Christian, 1854-1924 (Table P-PZ40)
8950.S7 Sparre, Christian, 1859-1940 (Table P-PZ40)
8950.S85 Stenersen, Rolf, 1899- (Table P-PZ40)
8950.T524 Thornaes, K.O., 1874-1945 (Table P-PZ40)
8950.T53 Thorstensen, Nora, 1874- (Table P-PZ40)
8950.T57 Thrane, Nanna, 1854- (Table P-PZ40)
8950.T8 Trøan, Jens, 1883-1911 (Table P-PZ40)
8950.U4 Ulvig, Elisa (Table P-PZ40)
8950.U5 Undset, Sigrid, 1882-1949 (Table P-PZ40)
8950.V3 Valstad, Otto, 1862- (Table P-PZ40)
8950.V5 Vinsnes, Johan Frederik, 1866-1932 (Table P-PZ40)
8950.V6 Vogt, Nils Collett, 1864-1937 (Table P-PZ40)
8950.W4 Weedon, Sara Helene (Petersen), 1875-1925 (Table P-PZ40)
Wiberg, Christian Koren see PT8950.K75
8950.W442 Wessel, Ellisif, 1866-1949 (Table P-PZ40)
8950.W45 Wiborg, Julli (Landmark), 1880- (Table P-PZ40)
8950.W6 Wiers-Jenssen, Hans, 1866-1925 (Table P-PZ40)
8950.W65 Wiers-Jenssen, Rigmor Nikolowna (Danielsen), 1874- (Table P-PZ40)
8950.W7 Wildenvey, Herman, 1885- (Table P-PZ40)
8950.Z8 Zwilgmeyer, Dikken, 1859-1913 (Table P-PZ40)
8951-8951.36 1961-2000 (Table P-PZ29 modified)
8951.13 C
Subarrange Cutter number authors by Table P-PZ40 unless otherwise indicated
8951.13.A44 Camillo, Don (Table P-PZ40)

	Individual authors or works
	1961-2000 -- Continued
8951.32	V
	Subarrange Cutter number authors by Table P-PZ40 unless otherwise indicated
	Vatne, Hans see PT8951.13.A44
8952-8952.36	2001- (Table P-PZ29)
	Landsmaal or New Norwegian (Nynorsk) literature
	Literary history and criticism
9000	General works
9003	General special
9005.A-Z	Works in foreign languages, A-Z
	Special periods
9007	19th century
9009	20th century
9010	21st century
	Special forms
9013	Poetry
9015	Drama
9017	Prose fiction
9019.A-Z	Minor forms, A-Z
9019.E5	Essays
9019.W5	Wit and humor
	Collections
9025	General
9026	Minor
9029.A-Z	Translations into foreign languages, A-Z
	Special forms
	Poetry
9035	General works
9036	Minor collections
9039.A-Z	Translations into foreign languages, A-Z
	Drama
9040	General works
9041	Minor collections
9044.A-Z	Translations into foreign languages, A-Z
	Fiction
9045	General works
9046	Minor collections
9049.A-Z	Translations into foreign languages, A-Z
9055.A-Z	Other forms, A-Z
9055.E7	Essays
9055.F3	Fairy tales
9055.W4	Wit and humor

Landsmaal or New Norwegian (Nynorsk) literature -- Continued
Individual authors
Subarrange Cutter number authors by Table P-PZ40 unless otherwise indicated
Subarrange one number authors by Table P-PZ39 unless otherwise indicated
For their works in Riksmaal, see PT8801+

9064 Anonymous works (Table P-PZ28)
9065 A - Aas
9066 Aasen, Ivar Andreas, 1813-1896 (Table P-PZ39)
9067 Aas - Be
9068 Bergh, Hallvard Ellestad, 1850-1922 (Table P-PZ39)
9069 Be - Gar
9069.D8 Duun, Olav, 1876-1939 (Table P-PZ40)
Egnund, Ivar Mortensson see PT9081
9069.E5 Eldegard, Sigurd, 1866- (Table P-PZ40)
9069.F6 Floden, Halvor, 1884- (Table P-PZ40)
9070 Garborg, Arne, 1851-1924 (Table P-PZ39)
9071 Garborg, Hulda (Bergersen), 1862-1934 (Table P-PZ39)
9072 Gar - Hov
9072.G8 Gullvåg, Olav, 1885- (Table P-PZ40)
9072.H3 Handagard, Idar Antonius, 1874 (Table P-PZ40)
9072.H4 Heggstad, Magne, 1881- (Table P-PZ40)
9072.H7 Holm, Hans Henrik, 1896 (Table P-PZ40)
9073 Hovden, Anders Karlson, 1860-1943 (Table P-PZ39)
9074 Hov - Jan
9075 Janson, Kristofer Nagel, 1841-1917 (Table P-PZ39)
9076 Jan - Løl
9076.K7 Krohn, Henrik, 1826-1879 (Table P-PZ40)
9076.K75 Krokann, Inge, 1893- (Table P-PZ40)
9077 Løland, Rasmus, 1861-1907 (Table P-PZ39)
9078 Løl - Mor
9078.M3 Matre, Kristian, 1877- (Table P-PZ40)
Moren, Halldis see PT9088.V57
9079 Moren, Sven, 1871-1938 (Table P-PZ39)
9080 Mor - Mort
9081 Mortenson, Ivar Julius, 1857-1934 (Table P-PZ39)
9082 Mort - Sel
9082.O4 Ørjasaeter, Tore, 1886- (Table P-PZ40)
9083 Seland, Hans Andreas Johannesson, 1867- (Table P-PZ39)
9084 Sel - Siv
9085 Sivle, Per, 1857-1904 (Table P-PZ37)
9086 Siv - Tv
9086.S33 Skagestad, Tomod, 1920- (Table P-PZ40)
9086.S4 Sletto, Olav, 1886- (Table P-PZ40)
9087 Tvedt, Jens, 1857-1935 (Table P-PZ39)

Landsmaal or New Norwegian (Nynorsk) literature
Individual authors -- Continued
9088 Tv - Vi
9088.U6 Uppdal, Kristofer, 1878- (Table P-PZ40)
9088.V2 Vaa, Aslaug, 1889- (Table P-PZ40)
9088.V57 Vesaas, Halldis Moren, 1907- (Table P-PZ40)
9088.V6 Vesaas, Tarjei, 1897-89 (Table P-PZ40)
9089 Vik, Oddmund Jakobson, 1858-1930 (Table P-PZ39)
9090 Vi - Vin
9091 Vinje, Aasmund Olavsson, 1818-1870 (Table P-PZ39)
9092 Vin - Vis
9093 Vislie, Vetle, 1858-1933 (Table P-PZ39)
9094 Vis - Z
Norwegian literature: Provincial, local, foreign
For the works and biography and criticism of individual authors, except American, see PT8750+
Provincial, local, etc.
9100.A-Z By region (Valley, parish, etc.), A-Z
Subarrange individual places by Table P-PZ26
9101.A-Z By province, A-Z
Subarrange individual provinces by Table P-PZ26
9102.A-Z By place, A-Z
Subarrange individual places by Table P-PZ26
Norwegian literature outside of Norway
9105 General
North America
9131 General works
9132 General special
9134 Biography (Collective)
Special periods
9136 To 1800
9137 19th century
9138 20th century
9139 21st century
Special forms
9140 Poetry
9141 Drama
9142.A-Z Other, A-Z
Collections
9143 General
9144 Poetry
9145 Drama
9146.A-Z Other special forms, A-Z
9148.A-Z Local, A-Z
Subarrange individual places by Table P-PZ26

Norwegian literature: Provincial, local, foreign
Norwegian literature outside of Norway
North America -- Continued

9150.A-Z Individual authors, A-Z

Subarrange Cutter number authors by Table P-PZ40
e.g.

9150.A4 Ager, Waldemar Theodor, 1869-1941 (Table P-PZ40)
9150.B7 Bratager, Laura (Ringdal), 1862- (Table P-PZ40)
9150.B8 Buslett, Ole Amundson, 1855-1924 (Table P-PZ40)
9150.C37 Carlsen, Berntine Stover (Table P-PZ40)
9150.F6 Folkestad, Sigurd, 1877- (Table P-PZ40)
9150.F7 Foss, Hans Andersen, 1851-1929 (Table P-PZ40)
9150.G77 Grundysen, Tellef, b. 1854 (Table P-PZ40)
9150.H5 Henning Hommefoss, Lise Bentsen, 1862- (Table P-PZ40)
9150.J6 Johnson, Simon, 1874- (Table P-PZ40)
9150.K65 Kolkin, N. (Table P-PZ40)
9150.M28 Martinson, Embret (Table P-PZ40)
9150.M3 Mason, A.H. (Table P-PZ40)
9150.R55 Rølvaag, Ole Edvart, 1876-1931 (Table P-PZ40)
9150.S5 Sether, Gulbrand, 1869- (Table P-PZ40)
9150.S6 Sneve, Ole Svendsen, 1846-1913 (Table P-PZ40)
9150.S7 Stenholt, Lars A. (Table P-PZ40)
9150.T4 Teigen, Knut Martin Olson, 1854-1914 (Table P-PZ40)
9150.W4 Wergeland, Agnes Mathilde, 1857-1914 (Table P-PZ40)
9150.W5 Wist, Johannes Benjamin, 1864-1923 (Table P-PZ40)

9155.A-Z Other regions or countries, A-Z

Subarrange individual countries by Table P-PZ26

Swedish literature
Literary history and criticism
9201 Periodicals. Serials
(9203) Yearbooks
see PT9201
9205 Societies
9207 Congresses
Collections
9213 Monographs, studies, etc. By various authors
9214.5.A-Z Festschriften. By honoree, A-Z
9217 Encyclopedias. Dictionaries
9219 Theory and principles of the study of Swedish literature
9225 History of literary history
9229 Philosophy. Psychology. Aesthetics
Includes national characteristics in literature
Study and teaching
9240 General
9241 General special
9242.A-Z By region or country, A-Z
9243.A-Z By school, A-Z
Biography of teachers, critics, and historians
9244 Collective
9245.A-Z Individual, A-Z
Subarrange each by Table P-PZ50
Criticism
9250 Treatises
9252 History
9253 Special topics (not A-Z)
9254 Collections of essays in criticism
History of Swedish literature
General works
9260 Swedish
9261 Danish and Dano-Norwegian
9262 Landsmaal
9263 English
9264 French
9265 German
9266.A-Z Other languages, A-Z
9269 Outlines, syllabi, etc.
Miscellaneous special aspects
9280 Relation to history, civilization, etc.
Relation to other literature
9283 General works
9285 Icelandic and Old Norse
9286.A-Z Other, A-Z
9288 Translation of other literatures into Swedish (as subject)
9289 Translation of Swedish literature (as subject)

Literary history and criticism
History of Swedish literature
Miscellaneous special aspects -- Continued
9291 Other special aspects (not A-Z)
Treatment of special subjects
9295.A-Z Special topics, A-Z
9295.A3 Agricultural laborers
9295.F5 Fires
9295.H5 History
9295.L2 Labor. Working class
9295.L37 Law
9295.L6 Love
9295.M8 Mythology
9295.N3 Nature
9295.P37 Pastoral literature
9295.R3 Realism
9295.R4 Religion
9295.R44 Renaissance
Working class see PT9295.L2
9297.A-Z Special countries and races, not limited to one period or form, A-Z
Under each country:
.x General
.x2A-.x2Z Local, A-Z
Sweden
9297.S8 General
9297.S9A-.S9Z Local, A-Z
9297.S9U3 Uddevalla
9299.A-Z Special classes, A-Z
9299.P7 Priests
9299.W6 Women
9300.A-Z Special characters, persons, etc., A-Z
Biography, memoirs, letters, etc.
9305 Collective biography
9307 Memoirs. Letters. Interviews
9308 Relations to women
9310 Literary landmarks. Homes and haunts of authors
9312 Travel
9315 Women authors. Literary relations of women
Special periods
Medieval to about 1540. Old Swedish
9320 General works
9325.A-Z Special topics, A-Z
9325.E4 Education
9325.G3 Games, amusements, etc.
9325.M3 Magic. Occult

Literary history and criticism
History of Swedish literature
Special periods
Medieval to about 1540. Old Swedish -- Continued

(9330) Historical literature
see DL

(9331) Medical literature
see class R

(9332) Legal literature
see class K

(9333) Religious literature
see class B

Other special forms
Cf. PT9509+ Folk literature

(9335) Proverbs
see PN6487

(9337) Ballads
see PT9401

9339 Prose romances

16th-18th centuries

9345 General works

9349.A-Z Special topics, A-Z

Sub-periods

9355 Reformation period, ca. 1520-ca. 1611

9357 Empire (or Learned period), 1611-1718

9359 Age of Liberty (Frihetstiden), 1718-1772

9361 Gustavian period, 1872-1809

19th century

9365 General works

9367.A-Z Special topics, A-Z

9367.C48 Childhood

9367.D43 Decadence (Literary movement)

9367.L3 Labor. Working class

9367.N36 Nationalism

9367.N37 Natural history

9367.P4 Peasants

9367.R7 Romanticism

9367.S65 Society and literature

9367.W67 Women

Working class see PT9367.L3

20th century

9368 General works

9370.A-Z Special subjects, A-Z

9370.A73 Archetype (Psychology)

9370.B87 Bureaucracy

9370.F34 Faith

9370.F37 Fascism

Literary history and criticism
History of Swedish literature
Special periods
20th century
Special subjects, A-Z -- Continued
9370.G4 General strike, Sweden, 1909
9370.L33 Labor. Working class
9370.M67 Modernism
9370.N48 Neutrality
9370.P65 Politics
9370.S6 Social conditions
9370.S94 Symbolism
9370.T43 Technology
9370.U54 Universities and colleges
Working class see PT9370.L33
21st century
9372 General works
9373.A-Z Special subjects, A-Z
Special forms
Poetry
9375 General works
9377.A-Z Special topics, A-Z
9377.B5 Bible
Special periods
(9380) Medieval
see PT9320+
16th-18th centuries
9385 General works
9387.A-Z Special topics, A-Z
19th century
9390 General works
9392.A-Z Special topics, A-Z
9392.P57 Poets, Latin
20th century
9395 General works
9397.A-Z Special topics, A-Z
9397.N54 Nihilism
21st century
9398 General works
9399.A-Z Special topics, A-Z
Special forms
9400 Epic poetry
9401 Popular poetry. Ballads, songs, etc.
Cf. PT9519 Folk poetry
9402 Lyric poetry
9403.A-Z Other special forms, A-Z
9403.D5 Didactic

Literary history and criticism
History of Swedish literature
Special forms
Poetry
Special forms
Other special forms, A-Z -- Continued
9403.E4 Elegiac
9403.E65 Epigrams
9403.H85 Humorous
9403.O33 Occasional verse
9403.P3 Pastoral
9403.S65 Sonnets
9404.A-Z Special subjects, A-Z
9404.C4 Cemeteries
9404.N3 Nature
9404.P6 Politics
9404.R3 Realism
9404.R4 Religion
Drama
History of the Swedish stage see PN2770+
9415 General works
9417.A-Z Special topics, A-Z
9417.S72 Stage directions
Special periods
Medieval
9420 Origins
9421 Mysteries, moralities, miracle plays, etc.
16th-18th centuries
9425 General works
9427.A-Z Special topics, A-Z
9427.A8 Authorship, Disputed
9427.C53 Cities and towns
9427.C6 Comedy
9427.S3 School and student plays
Towns see PT9427.C53
19th century
9430 General works
9432.A-Z Special topics, A-Z
20th century
9435 General works
9437.A-Z Special topics, A-Z
21st century
9438 General works
9439.A-Z Special topics, A-Z
Special forms
9440 Tragedy
9441 Comedy

Literary history and criticism
History of Swedish literature
Special forms
Drama
Special forms -- Continued

9443 Tragicomedy
9444 Vaudeville
9445 Romantic drama
9446 Melodrama
9447 Farce
9449.A-Z Other special, A-Z

Prose

9460 General works

Special periods

(9465) Medieval
see PT9320+

Modern

9470 General
9471 16th-17th centuries
9472 18th century
9473 19th century
9474 20th century
9475 21st century

Special forms
Prose fiction

9480 General works

Special topics

9483 Romanticism
9484 Historical fiction
9485 Realism
9486 Naturalism
9487.A-Z Other, A-Z
9487.A87 Autobiographical fiction
9487.C67 Country life
9487.D4 Detective and mystery stories
9487.L3 Labor. Working class
9487.L68 Love stories
9487.P66 Popular literature
9487.S35 Science fiction
9487.S5 Short stories
9487.W4 Welfare state

Working class see PT9487.L3

Special periods

9490 16th-18th centuries
9491 19th century
9492 20th century
9493 21st century

Literary history and criticism
History of Swedish literature
Special forms
Prose
Special forms -- Continued
9495 Oratory
9496 Letters
9497 Essays
9498 Wit and humor
9499 Miscellaneous
Folk literature
For works on and collections of folk literature, see GR224+
History
(9509) General works
Special periods
9515 Origins. Middle Ages
(9516) Later
Special forms
(9519) Poetry
see PT9401
(9520) Prose
Collections
(9525) General
9527 Chapbooks
9529 Poetry. Ballads, folk songs, etc. (Folkvisor)
Prose tales. Legends
(9531) General works
(9533.A-Z) Special localities, A-Z
(9535) Fairy tales
(9538.A-Z) Special characters, persons, etc., A-Z
(9540.A-Z) Individual, A-Z
(9542.A-Z) Translations. By language, A-Z
9544 Juvenile literature (General)
For special genres, see the genre
Collections of Swedish literature
9547 Periodicals. Serials
9550 General
9552 Medieval. Old Swedish
9555 Selections, anthologies, etc.
9556.A-Z Special classes of authors, A-Z
9556.J48 Jews
9556.W65 Women
Special topics (Prose and verse), A-Z
9558.B4 Bleking län (Sweden)
9558.B63 Bohuslän (Sweden)
9558.B66 Books and reading
9558.E5 Entertaining

Collections of Swedish literature
Special topics (Prose and verse), A-Z -- Continued

9558.F38 Fathers
9558.G6 Göteborg (Sweden)
9558.G63 Gotland (Sweden)
9558.G76 Grönköping (Imaginary place)
9558.H3 Hallands län (Sweden)
9558.J65 Jörn (Sweden)
9558.K6 Kolmården (Sweden)
9558.L8 Lund (Sweden)
9558.N67 Norroköping (Sweden)
9558.O42 Öland (Sweden)
9558.O67 Österlen (Sweden)
9558.S3 Sailing
9558.S53 Skåne
9558.S57 Småland (Sweden)
9558.S76 Stockholm
9558.S95 Sweden
9558.T43 Teenagers
9558.U66 Uppsala (Sweden)
9558.V37 Västmanland (Sweden)
9558.V5 Vietnam War, 1961-1975
9558.W6 Women

Translations into foreign languages

9565 Polyglot
9566 Danish and Norwegian
9567 English
9568 French
9569 German
9570.A-Z Other. By language, A-Z

Poetry

9580 Collections before 1801
9581 Collections, 1801-
9582 Medieval. Old Swedish
9583 Selections, anthologies, etc.
9585 Selections from women authors

Translations into foreign languages

9590.A2 Polyglot
9590.A5-Z By language, A-Z
Subarrange by translator or title

Special forms and subjects

9595 Ballads. Songs
9596 Sonnets
9597 Historical. Patriotic. Political
9598 Satires
9599.A-Z Other, A-Z
9599.R44 Religious

Collections of Swedish literature -- Continued
Drama
9605 Collections before 1801
9606 Collections, 1801-
9609 Selections, anthologies, etc.
9612.A-Z Translations. By language, A-Z
Special forms
9615 Mysteries, moralities, miracle plays
9617 Tragedies
9618 Comedies
9620 Farces, vaudevilles, etc.
9623 Amateur drama. Juvenile drama
9625.A-Z Other special, A-Z
Prose
9626 General
Fiction
9627 General
9628 Selections
9629 Selections from women authors
9630.A-Z Translations. By language, A-Z
9631.A-Z Special subjects, A-Z
9631.I55 Immigrants
9631.S43 Sea
9633 Oratory
9633.5 Diaries
9634 Letters
9635 Essays
9636 Wit and humor
9637 Fables
Proverbs see PN6487.A2+
9639 Miscellaneous
Individual authors or works
Medieval to about 1540. Old Swedish
9650 Anonymous works
9650.E5 Engelbrektskroniakn
9650.E7 Erikskrönikan (Table P-PZ43)
9650.G8 Guta saga
9650.I9 Ivan Lejonriddaren
9650.K3 Karl Magnus
9650.K66 Konungastyrelsen
9650.S64 Södermannalagen
9651.A-Z Authors, A-Z
Subarrange individual authors by Table P-PZ38

Individual authors or works -- Continued

16th-18th centuries

Subarrange Cutter number authors by Table P-PZ40 unless otherwise indicated

Subarrange one number authors by Table P-PZ39 unless otherwise indicated

9674 Anonymous works

9674.A1H6 Holofernes och Judit

9675 A - Ast

9676 Asteropherus, Magnus Olai, d. 1647 (Table P-PZ39)

9677 Ast - Bel

9678 Bellman, Carl Michael, 1740-1795 (Table P-PZ39)

9679 Bel - Bren

9680 Brenner, Sofia Elisabet (Weber), 1659-1730 (Table P-PZ39)

9681 Bren - Creu

9681.C7 Columbus, Samuel, 1642-1679 (Table P-PZ40)

9682 Creutz, Gustaf Philip, greve, 1731-1785 (Table P-PZ39)

9683 Creu - Dal

9683.D7 Dalstierna, Gunno Eurelius, 1661-1709 (Table P-PZ40)

9684 Dalin, Olof von, 1708-1763 (Table P-PZ39)

9685 Dal - Env

9686 Envallsson, Carl Magnus, 1756-1806 (Table P-PZ39)

9687 Env - Gyl

9688 Gyllenborg, Gustaf Fredrik, greve, 1731-1808 (Table P-PZ39)

9689 Gyl - Kel

9689.H5 Hjärne, Urban, 1641-1724 (Table P-PZ40)

9689.H7 Holmström, Israel, 1660-1708 (Table P-PZ40)

9689.H75 Horn, Agneta, 1629-1672 (Table P-PZ40)

Johansson, Lars, 1638-1674 see PT9697.L8

9690 Kellgren, Johan Henrik, 1751-1795 (Table P-PZ39)

9691 Kel - Len

9691.K6 Kolmodin, Israel, 1643-1709 (Table P-PZ40)

9691.K63 Königsmarck, Aurora von, 1662-1728 (Table P-PZ40)

9691.L3 Lagerlöf, Petrus, 1648-1699 (Table P-PZ40)

9691.L5 Leijoncrona, Christoffer, 1662-1710 (Table P-PZ40)

9692 Lenngren, Anna Maria (Malmstedt), 1754-1817 (Table P-PZ39)

9693 Len - Leo

9694 Leopold, Carl Gustaf af, 1756-1829 (Table P-PZ39)

9695 Leo - Lid

9696 Lidner, Bengt, 1757-1793 (Table P-PZ39)

9697 Lid - Mod

9697.L3 Lillienstedt, Johan Paulinus, greve, 1655-1732 (Table P-PZ40)

9697.L8 Lucidor, Lasse, 1638-1674 (Table P-PZ40)

Individual authors or works
16th-18th centuries
Lid - Mod -- Continued
9697.M5 Messenius, Johannes, 1579-1636 (Table P-PZ40)
9698 Modée, Reinhold Gustaf, 1698-1752 (Table P-PZ39)
9699 Mod - Mör
9700 Mörk, Jakob Henrik, 1714 or 5-1763 (Table P-PZ39)
9701 Mör - Nor
9702 Nordenflycht, Hedvig Charlotta, 1718-1763 (Table P-PZ39)
9703 Nor - Od
9704 Odel, Anders, 1718-1773 (Table P-PZ39)
9706 Od - Rud
9706.O6 Oxenstierna, Johan Gabriel, greve, 1750-1818 (Table P-PZ40)
9706.O7 Oxenstierna, Johan Thuresson, greve, 1666-1733 (Table P-PZ40)
9706.P7 Prytz, Andreas Johannis, 1590-1655 (Table P-PZ40)
9706.R6 Rosenhane, Gustaf, friherre, 1619-1684 (Table P-PZ40)
9708 Rudbeck, Olof, 1630-1702 (Table P-PZ39)
9709 Rud - Sti
9709.R4 Rudeen, Torsten, 1661-1729 (Table P-PZ40)
9709.R5 Runius, Johan, 1679-1713 (Table P-PZ40)
9709.S6 Skogekär, Bergbo (Table P-PZ40)
9709.S7 Spegel, Haqvin, 1645-1714 (Table P-PZ40)
9710 Stiernhielm, Georg, 1598-1672 (Table P-PZ39)
9711 Sti - Thor
9711.S94 Swedenmarck, Catharina Charlotta, 1744-1813 (Table P-PZ40)
9711.T5 Tessin, Carl Gustaf, greve, 1695-1770 (Table P-PZ40)
9712 Thorild, Thomas, 1759-1808 (Table P-PZ39)
9713 Thor - Wra
9713.W3 Wallenberg, Jacob, 1746-1778 (Table P-PZ40)
9713.W46 Westerberg, Mats, b. 1691 (Table P-PZ40)
9713.W5 Wivallius, Lars, 1605-1669 (Table P-PZ40)
9714 Wrangel, Erik, 1686-1765 (Table P-PZ39)
9715 Wra - Z
19th century
Subarrange Cutter number authors by Table P-PZ40 unless otherwise indicated
Subarrange one number authors by Table P-PZ39 unless otherwise indicated
9725 Anonymous works (Table P-PZ28)
9726 A - Ahr
Ahlgren, Ernst see PT9733
9727 Ahrenberg, Johan Jacob, 1847-1914 (Table P-PZ39)
9728 Ahr - Alm
9729 Almquist, Carl Jonas Love, 1793-1866 (Table P-PZ39)

Individual authors or works
19th century -- Continued

9730 Alm - Arv
9731 Arvidsson, Adolf Ivar, 1791-1858 (Table P-PZ39)
9732 Arv - Ben
9732.A5 Atterbom, Per Daniel Amadeus, 1790-1855 (Table P-PZ40)
9732.B54 Bäckström, Eduard, 1841-1886 (Table P-PZ40)
9733 Benedictsson, Victoria Maria (Bruzelius), 1850-1888 (Table P-PZ39)
9734 Ben - Bl
9735 Blanche, August Teodor, 1811-1868 (Table P-PZ39)
9736 Bl - Bre
9736.B45 Böttiger, Carl Vilhelm, 1807-1878 (Table P-PZ40)
9736.B5 Bondeson, August, 1854-1906 (Table P-PZ40)
9736.B7 Braun, Wilhelm August Detlof von, 1813-1860 (Table P-PZ40)
9737 Bremer, Fredrika, 1801-1865 (Table P-PZ39)
9738 Bre - Caj
9738.B4 Brinkman, Karl Gustav von, 1764-1847 (Table P-PZ40)
Brn, J-y see PT9782
9739 Cajanello, Anna Carlotta (Leffler) Edgren, 1849-1892 (Table P-PZ39)
9740 Caj - Car
Carlén, Emilie (Smith) Flygare see PT9746.F6
9742 Car - Dah
9742.C4 Cederbrogh, Fredrik, 1784-1835 (Table P-PZ40)
9743 Dahlgren, Carl Fredrik, 1791-1844 (Table P-PZ39)
9744 Dah - Fah
9744.D3 Dahlgren, Fredrik August, 1816-1895 (Table P-PZ40)
9744.E7 Estlander, Carl Gustaf, 1834-1910 (Table P-PZ40)
9745 Fahlcrantz, Christian Erik, Bp., 1790-1866 (Table P-PZ39)
9746 Fah - Fra
9746.F6 Flygare-Carlén, Emilie (Smith), 1807-1892 (Table P-PZ40)
9747 Franzén, Frans Michael, Bp., 1772-1847 (Table P-PZ39)
9748 Fra - Geijer
9749 Geijer, Erik Gustaf, 1783-1847 (Table P-PZ39)
9750 Geijer - Geijerst
9751 Geijerstam, Gustaf af, 1858-1909 (Table P-PZ39)
9752 Geijerst - Ham
9753 Hammarskjöld, Lorenzo, 1785-1827 (Table P-PZ39)
9754 Ham - Hed
9754.H43 Hebbe, Wendela, 1808-1899 (Table P-PZ40)
9755 Hedberg, Frans Theodor, 1828-1908 (Table P-PZ39)
9756 Hed - Hei
9757 Heidenstam, Verner von, 1859-1940 (Table P-PZ39)

Individual authors or works
19th century -- Continued
9758 Hei - Lag
9758.H45 Hill, Carl Fredrik, 1849-1911 (Table P-PZ40)
Lagerlöf, Selma Ottiliana Lovisa, 1858-1940
9759 Collected works
9760 Selected works
9761 Selections
Translations
9762 Danish
9763 English
9764 French
9765 German
9766.A-Z Other. By language, A-Z
9767.A-Z Separate prose works, A-Z
Subarrange individual works by Table P-PZ43
Mårbacka see PT9770.A1+
Poetry
9768 Collected works
9769.A-Z Separate works, A-Z
Biography. Memoirs
9770.A1-.A6 Autobiography, memoirs, letters
9770.A7-Z General works
9771 Criticism
9773 Lag - Liv
Leffler, Anne Charlotte, 1849-1892 see PT9739
9774 Livijn, Clas, 1781-1844 (Table P-PZ39)
9775 Liv - Lun
9776 Lundegård, Axel Wilhelm, 1861-1930 (Table P-PZ39)
9777 Lun - Mol
9777.L25 Lundin, Claës, 1825-1908 (Table P-PZ40)
9777.L3 Lundquist, Ernst Gustaf, 1851- (Table P-PZ40)
9778 Molander, Harald, 1858-1900 (Table P-PZ39)
9779 Mol - Nic
9779.M3 Molin, Pelle, 1864-1896 (Table P-PZ40)
9780 Nicander, Karl August, 1799-1839 (Table P-PZ39)
9781 Nic - Öd
9781.N5 Nordin, Johan Albert Erhard, 1863- (Table P-PZ40)
9782 Ödmann, Jenny Maria (Braun), 1847-1917 (Table P-PZ39)
9783 Öd - Pal
9783.O6 Oscar II, King of Sweden, 1829-1897 (Table P-PZ40)
9784 Palmblad, Vilhelm Fredrik, 1788-1852 (Table P-PZ39)
9785 Pal - Run
9785.P5 Pihlstrand, Ragnar, 1850-1914 (Table P-PZ40)
9786 Runeberg, Johan Ludvig, 1804-1877 (Table P-PZ39)
9787 Run - Ryd
9788 Rydberg, Viktor, 1828-1895 (Table P-PZ39)

Individual authors or works
19th century -- Continued
9789 Ryd - Sch
9790 Schwartz, Marie Sofie (Birath), 1819-1894 (Table P-PZ39)
9791 Sch - Sno
9791.S5 Sjöberg, Erik, 1794-1828 (Table P-PZ40)
9791.S57 Slotte, Alexander, 1861-1927 (Table P-PZ40)
9792 Snoilsky, Karl Johan Gustaf, greve, 1841-1903 (Table P-PZ39)
9793 Sno - Stag
9794 Stagnelius, Erik Johan, 1793-1823 (Table P-PZ39)
9795 Starbäck, Carl Georg, 1828-1885 (Table P-PZ39)
9797 Star - Str
9797.S37 Stenback, Lars, 1811-1870 (Table P-PZ40)
Strindberg, Johan August, 1849-1912
Bibliography see Z8850.2
9800 Collected works. By date
9801 Selected works
9802 Selections. Anthologies
Translations
9803 Danish and Norwegian
9804 English
9805 French
9806 German
9807.A-Z Other. By language, A-Z
Poetry
Collections
9809.A1 By date
9809.A2 By editor
Translations
9809.A3A-.A3Z English. By translator, A-Z
9809.A4A-.A4Z Other. By language, A-Z
9810.A-Z Separate, A-Z
Drama
Collections
9811.A1 By date
9811.A2 By editor
Translations
9811.A3A-.A3Z English. By translator, A-Z
9811.A4A-.A4Z Other. By language, A-Z
9812.A-Z Separate, A-Z
9812.A4-.A42 Advent (Table P-PZ43a)
9812.B6-.B62 Brända tomten (After the fire) (Table P-PZ43a)
9812.B7-.B72 Brott och brott (There are crimes and crimes) (Table P-PZ43a)
9812.D4-.D42 Debet och kredit (Table P-PZ43a)
9812.D6-.D62 Dödsdansen (Dance of death) (Table P-PZ43a)

Individual authors or works
19th century
Strindberg, Johan August, 1849-1912
Drama
Separate, A-Z -- Continued

9812.D7-.D72 Drömspelet (The dream play) (Table P-PZ43a)
9812.E7-.E72 Erik XIV (Table P-PZ43a)
9812.F3-.F32 Fadren (The father) (Table P-PZ43a)
9812.F4-.F42 Folkungasagen (Table P-PZ43a)
9812.F5-.F52 Första varningen (The first warning) (Table P-PZ43a)
9812.F6-.F62 Fordringsägare (Creditors) (Table P-PZ43a)
9812.F7-.F72 Fritänkaren (Table P-PZ43a)
9812.F8-.F82 Fröken Julie (Countess Julie; Miss Julia) (Table P-PZ43a)
9812.G5-.G52 Gillets hemlighet (The secret of the guild) (Table P-PZ43a)
9812.G7-.G72 Gustaf Adolf (Table P-PZ43a)
9812.G8-.G82 Gustaf Vasa (Table P-PZ43a)
9812.H4-.H42 Hermione (Table P-PZ43a)
9812.H5-.H52 Herr Bengts hustru (Table P-PZ43a)
9812.H6-.H62 Himmelrikets nycklar (The keys of the Kingdom of Heaven) (Table P-PZ43a)
9812.I5-.I52 Inför döden (Facing death) (Table P-PZ43a)
9812.K3-.K32 Kamraterna (Comrades) (Table P-PZ43a)
9812.K34-.K342 Karl XII (Table P-PZ43a)
9812.K67-.K672 Kristina (Table P-PZ43a)
9812.K7-.K72 Kronbruden (The bridal crown) (Table P-PZ43a)
9812.L4-.L42 Leka med elden (Playing with fire) (Table P-PZ43a)
9812.L8-.L82 Lycko-Pers resa (Lucky Peter's travels) (Table P-PZ43a)
9812.M3-.M32 Master Olof (Table P-PZ43a)
9812.M5-.M52 Midsommar (Table P-PZ43a)
9812.M6-.M62 Moderskärlek (Mother love) (Table P-PZ43a)
9812.N3-.N32 Näktergalen i Wittenberg (Table P-PZ43a)
9812.O7-.O72 Oväder (The thunderstorm) (Table P-PZ43a)
9812.P3-.P32 Påsk (Easter) (Table P-PZ43a)
9812.P4-.P42 Paria (Table P-PZ43a)
9812.P5-.P52 Pelikanen (Table P-PZ43a)
9812.S3-.S32 Samum (Simoom) (Table P-PZ43a)
9812.S6-.S62 Spöksonaten (The spook Sonata) (Table P-PZ43a)
9812.S7-.S72 Stora landsvagen (Table P-PZ43a)
9812.S8-.S82 Svanehvit (Swanwhite) (Table P-PZ43a)
9812.T5-.T52 Till Damaskus (Table P-PZ43a)
9813.A-Z Other prose works, A-Z
9813.B5-.B52 En blå bok (Zones of the spirit) (Table P-PZ43a)
9813.F6-.F62 Författaren (Table P-PZ43a)
9813.G5-.G52 Giftas I & II (married) (Table P-PZ43a)

Individual authors or works
19th century
Strindberg, Johan August, 1849-1912
Other prose works, A-Z -- Continued

9813.G6-.G62 Götiska rummen (Table P-PZ43a)
9813.G7-.G72 Gröna säcken (Table P-PZ43a)
9813.H3-.H32 Han och hon (Table P-PZ43a)
9813.H4-.H42 Hemsöborna (Table P-PZ43a)
9813.H5-.H52 Historiska miniatyrer (Table P-PZ43a)
9813.I4-.I42 I hafsbandet (Table P-PZ43a)
9813.I45-.I452 I vårbrytningen (Table P-PZ43a)
9813.I5-.I52 Inferno (Table P-PZ43a)
9813.K56-.K562 Klostret (Table P-PZ43a)
9813.L5-.L52 Lilla katekes för underklassen (Table P-PZ43a)
9813.N7-.N72 Det nya riket (Table P-PZ43a)
9813.N8-.N82 Nya svenska öden (Table P-PZ43a)
9813.R6-.R62 Röda rummet (The red room) (Table P-PZ43a)
9813.S3-.S32 Sagor (Table P-PZ43a)
9813.S5-.S52 Skärkarlslif (Table P-PZ43a)
9813.S6-.S62 Svarta fanor (Table P-PZ43a)
9813.S7-.S72 Svenska folket i helg och söken (Table P-PZ43a)
9813.S8-.S82 Svenska öden och äfventyr (Table P-PZ43a)
9813.T28-.T282 Taklagsöl (Table P-PZ43a)
9813.T3-.T32 Tal till svenska nationen (Table P-PZ43a)
9813.T6-.T62 Tjensteqvinnans sön (The son of a servant) (Table P-PZ43a)
9813.T7-.T72 Tschandala (Table P-PZ43a)
9813.U7-.U72 Utopier i verkligheten (Table P-PZ43a)
9814.A-.Z3 Autobiography. Memoirs

e.g. En dåres forsvarstal (The confession of a fool); Legender (Legends)

Letters

9814.Z4 Collected letters
9814.Z5 Selected letters
9814.Z6A-.Z6Z By correspondent
9814.5 Dictionaries. Indexes
9815 Biography

Criticism

9816 General works
9817.A-Z Special topics and subjects, A-Z
9817.A7 Art
9817.B65 Books and reading
9817.D53 Dialogue

Drama see PT9817.T54

9817.E94 Expressionism
9817.F5 Film adaptations
9817.L47 Letter writing

Individual authors or works
19th century
Strindberg, Johan August, 1849-1912
Criticism
Special topics and subjects, A-Z -- Continued
9817.L58 Literary form
9817.L59 Literature and society
9817.M87 Music
9817.N67 Nordiska musset
9817.R37 Realism
9817.R4 Religion
9817.S45 Senses and sensations
9817.S7 Stockholm
9817.T54 Theater. Drama
9817.T73 Translations
9817.W6 Women
9818 Str - Teg
9818.T4 Tavaststjerna, Karl August, 1860-1898 (Table P-PZ40)
Tegnér, Esaias, 1782-1846
9820 Collected works. By date
9821 Selected works
9822 Selections. Anthologies
Translations
9823 Danish and Norwegian
9824 English
9825 French
9826 German
9827.A-Z Other. By language, A-Z
Poetry
9828 Collected works
9829.A-Z Translations. By language and translator, A-Z
e.g.
9829.E5 English
9829.G5 German
Separate
Frithjofs saga
9830 Text. By date
9831.A-Z Translations. By language, A-Z
e.g.
9831.E5 English
9831.G5 German
9832 Criticism
9833.A-Z Other poems, A-Z
9833.A7-.A72 Axel
9834 Speeches
9835 Letters
9836 Memoirs

Individual authors or works
19th century
Tegner, Esaias, 1782-1846 -- Continued
9837 Biography
9838 Criticism
9840 Teg - Top
9840.T6 Törneros, Adolf
9841 Topelius, Zakarias, 1818-1898
9842 Top - Wad
Vitalis see PT9791.S5
9843 Wadman, Johan Anders, 1777-1837 (Table P-PZ39)
9844 Wad - Wal
9845 Wallin, Johan Olof, abp., 1779-1839 (Table P-PZ39)
9846 Wal - Wallm
9846.W34 Wallengren, Axel, 1865-1896 (Table P-PZ40)
9847 Wallmark, Peter Adam, 1777-1858 (Table P-PZ39)
9848 Wallm - Wen
9848.W4 Wecksell, Josef Julius, 1838-1907 (Table P-PZ40)
9849 Wennerberg, Gunnar, 1817-1901 (Table P-PZ39)
9850 Wen - Z
9850.W4 Wetterbergh, Carl Anton, 1804-1889 (Table P-PZ40)
9850.W5 Wikner, Carl Pontus, 1837-1888 (Table P-PZ40)
9850.W54 Wirsén, Carl David af, 1842-1912 (Table P-PZ40)
9850.W7 Wranér, Henrik, 1853-1908 (Table P-PZ40)
1900-1960
Here are usually to be classified authors beginning to publish about 1890, flourishing after 1900
9870 Anonymous works (Table P-PZ28)
9875 Authors, A-Z
Subarrange individual authors by Table P-PZ40 unless otherwise indicated
9875.A29 Agrell, Alfhild, 1849-1923 (Table P-PZ40)
9875.A33 Ahlin, Lars Gustav, 1915- (Table P-PZ40)
9875.A46 Alving, Barbro, 1909- (Table P-PZ40)
9875.A63 Anderberg, Bengt Niklas, 1920- (Table P-PZ40)
9875.A7 Arnér, Sivar, 1909- (Table P-PZ40)
9875.A83 Aspenström, Werner, 1918- (Table P-PZ40)
9875.A9 Aurell, Tage, 1895- (Table P-PZ40)
9875.B35 Barthel, Sven Christian, 1903- (Table P-PZ40)
9875.B43 Bengtsson, Frans Gunnar, 1894-1954 (Table P-PZ40)
9875.B45 Berg, Bengt Magnus Kristoffer, 1885- (Table P-PZ40)
9875.B5 Berger, Henning, 1872-1924 (Table P-PZ40)
9875.B52 Bergman, Bo, 1869- (Table P-PZ40)
9875.B53 Bergman, Hjalmar Fredrik Elgerus, 1883-1931 (Table P-PZ40)
9875.B563 Beskow, Elisabeth Maria, 1870-1928 (Table P-PZ40)
9875.B59 Björling, Gunnar Olof, 1887- (Table P-PZ40)

Individual authors or works
1900-1960
Authors, A-Z -- Continued

	Brenner, Arvid see PT9875.H45
9875.B75	Browallius, Irja, 1901- (Table P-PZ40)
9875.C514	Chronwall, J.H. (Table P-PZ40)
9875.D12	Dagerman, Stig Halvard, 1923-1954 (Table P-PZ40)
9875.D2	Dahlbäck, Sigurd, 1866-1932 (Table P-PZ40)
9875.D5	Didring, Ernst, 1868-1931 (Table P-PZ40)
9875.D53	Diktonius, Elmer Rafael, 1896- (Table P-PZ40)
9875.E514	Ekelöf, Gunnar, 1907- (Table P-PZ40)
9875.E53	Ekelund, Vilhelm, 1880-1949 (Table P-PZ40)
9875.E574	Enckell, Rabbe Arnfinn, 1903- (Table P-PZ40)
	Fahlman, Erik see PT9875.D2
9875.F3	Fallström, Karl Daniel, 1858-1937 (Table P-PZ40)
9875.F6	Fogelqvist, Torsten, 1880-1941 (Table P-PZ40)
9875.F788	Fridegård, Jan, 1897- (Table P-PZ40)
9875.F8	Fröding, Gustaf, 1860-1911 (Table P-PZ40)
9875.G75	Gripenberg, Bertel Johan Sebastian, friherre, 1878- (Table P-PZ40)
9875.G767	Gullberg, Hjalmar Robert, 1898- (Table P-PZ40)
9875.G8	Gustaf-Janson, Gösta, 1902- (Table P-PZ40)
9875.H2	Hallström, Per August Leonard, 1866- (Table P-PZ40)
9875.H3	Hansson, Ola, 1860-1925 (Table P-PZ40) Cf. PT2615.A58 German literature
9875.H39	Hedberg, Olle, 1897- (Table P-PZ40)
9875.H4	Hedberg, Tor Harald, 1862-1931 (Table P-PZ40)
9875.H45	Heerberger, Helge, 1907- (Table P-PZ40)
	Heidenstam, Verner von see PT9757
	Heller, Frank see PT9875.S4
9875.H5	Hellström, Gustaf, 1882-1953 (Table P-PZ40)
9875.H6	Högberg, Olof, 1855-1932 (Table P-PZ40)
9875.H67	Höijer, Björn-Erik, 1907- (Table P-PZ40)
9875.J3	Janson, Gustaf, 1866-1913 (Table P-PZ40)
9875.J6	Johnson, Eyvind, 1900- (Table P-PZ40)
9875.K2	Karlfeldt, Erik Axel, 1864-1931 (Table P-PZ40)
9875.K47	Kjellgren, Josef Bertil, 1907-1948 (Table P-PZ40)
9875.K6	Koch, Martin, 1882-1940 (Table P-PZ40)
9875.K8	Kuylenstierna-Wenster, Elisabeth, 1869-1933 (Table P-PZ40)
9875.L2	Lagerkvist, Pär Fabian, 1891- (Table P-PZ40)
9875.L3	Larsson, Hans, 1862- (Table P-PZ40)
9875.L4	Levertin, Oscar Ivar, 1862-1906 (Table P-PZ40)
9875.L5	Lidman, Sven, 1882- (Table P-PZ40)
9875.L55	Lilja, Gertrud Linnea, 1887- (Table P-PZ40)
9875.L64	Ljunggren, Hjalmar (Table P-PZ40)
9875.L67	Lo-Johansson, Ivar, 1901- (Table P-PZ40)

Individual authors or works
1900-1960
Authors, A-Z -- Continued

9875.L72 Lundegard, Erik Ewald Wilhelm, 1900- (Table P-PZ40)
9875.L74 Lundkvist, Artur, 1906- (Table P-PZ40)
9875.L8 Lybeck, Mikael, 1864-1925 (Table P-PZ40)
9875.L9 Lyttkens, Alice (Cronquist), 1897- (Table P-PZ40)
9875.M3 Malling, Mathilda (Kruse), 1864- (Table P-PZ40)
9875.M323 Malmberg, Bertil, 1889-1958 (Table P-PZ40)
9875.M39 Martinson, Moa, 1890- (Table P-PZ40)
9875.M4 Mattson, Gustaf Otto, 1873-1914 (Table P-PZ40)
9875.M5 Moberg, Vilhelm, 1898- (Table P-PZ40)
9875.M58 Mörne, Arvid, 1876-1946 (Table P-PZ40)
9875.M6 Mörner, Birger, greve, 1867-1930 (Table P-PZ40)
Myrberg, Anna see PT9875.S847
9875.N49 Nisser, Peter William, 1919- (Table P-PZ40)
9875.N6 Nordström, Ludvig Anselm, 1882-1942 (Table P-PZ40)
9875.N87 Nyblom, Lennart (Table P-PZ40)
9875.O64 Österling, Anders, 1884- (Table P-PZ40)
9875.O765 Olsson, Hagar, 1893- (Table P-PZ40)
9875.O8 Ossian-Nilsson, Karl Gustaf, 1875- (Table P-PZ40)
Red Top see PT9875.N87
Runa see PT9875.B563
9875.S23 Salminen, Sally, 1906- (Table P-PZ40)
9875.S262 Sandel, Maria, 1870-1927 (Table P-PZ40)
9875.S27 Sandgren, Gustav Emil, 1904- (Table P-PZ40)
9875.S274 Schildt, Runar, 1888-1925 (Table P-PZ40)
9875.S28 Schutt, Bertil Fredrik, 1909- (Table P-PZ40)
9875.S4 Serner, Gunnar, 1886-1947 (Table P-PZ40)
9875.S43 Setterlind, Bo, 1923- (Table P-PZ40)
9875.S5 Siwertz, Sigfrid, 1882- (Table P-PZ40)
9875.S54 Sjoberg, Birger, 1885-1929 (Table P-PZ40)
9875.S6 Söderberg, Hjalmar Emil Fredrik, 1869- (Table P-PZ40)
9875.S617 Södergran, Edith Irene, 1892-1923 (Table P-PZ40)
9875.S62 Söderhjelm, Alma, 1870-1949 (Table P-PZ40)
9875.S7 Stjernstedt, Marika, 1875-1954 (Table P-PZ40)
9875.S75 Stolpe, Sven, 1905- (Table P-PZ40)
Strand, Jol see PT9875.L64
9875.S847 Svarta masken, 1878-1931 (Table P-PZ40)
9875.T8 Tuominen, Mirjam Irene, 1913- (Table P-PZ40)
9875.V35 Vennberg, Karl Gunnar, 1910- (Table P-PZ40)
9875.V4 Vetterlund, Fredrik Mauritz, 1865- (Table P-PZ40)
9875.V5 Viksten, Albert, 1889- (Table P-PZ40)
9875.W33 Warburton, Thomas Henry, 1918 (Table P-PZ40)
9875.W45 Wilhelm, Prince of Sweden, 1884- (Table P-PZ40)

Individual authors or works -- Continued
9876-9876.36 1961-2000 (Table P-PZ29)
Here are usually to be classified authors beginning to publish about 1950, flourishing after 1960
9877-9877.36 2001- (Table P-PZ29)
Swedish literature: Provincial, local, foreign
For works and biography and criticism of individual authors, except North American see PT8645+
Provincial, local, etc.
9950.A-Z By region or country, A-Z
Subarrange individual places by Table P-PZ26
9951.A-Z By province, A-Z
Subarrange individual places by Table P-PZ26
9952.A-Z By place, A-Z
Subarrange individual places by Table P-PZ26
Swedish literature outside of Sweden
9955 General
Special
Finland
Literary history and criticism
9958 Periodicals. Serials
9960 General works
9961 General special. Minor
9963 Biography (Collective)
Special periods
9964 Origins
9965 To 1800
9966 19th century
9967 20th century
9967.2 21st century
9968 Poetry
9969 Drama
9970.A-Z Other special forms, A-Z
Collections
9971 General
9972 Poetry
9973 Drama
9974.A-Z Other, A-Z
9974.F5 Folklore
9974.S5 Short stories
9975.A-Z Local, A-Z
Subarrange individual places by Table P-PZ26
(9976) Individual authors
see PT9650+
North America
Literary history and criticism
9980 General works

Swedish literature: Provincial, local, foreign
Swedish literature outside of Sweden
Special
North America
Literary history and criticism -- Continued

9981	General special. Minor
9983	Biography (Collective)
	Special periods
9984	19th century
9985	20th century
9985.2	21st century
9986	Poetry
9987	Drama
9988.A-Z	Other special forms, A-Z
	Collections
9990	General
9991	Poetry
9992	Drama
9993.A-Z	Other special forms, A-Z
9994.A-Z	Local, A-Z Subarrange individual places by Table P-PZ26
9995.A-Z	Individual authors, A-Z Subarrange each author by Table P-PZ40 unless otherwise specified
9995.B5	Bloom, Fredrik Arvid, 1867- (Table P-PZ40)
9995.H6	Holmes, Ludvig, 1858-1910 (Table P-PZ40)
9995.O55	Olsson, Anna, 1866- (Table P-PZ40)
9995.R8	Ryden, Peter, 1857-1941 (Table P-PZ40)
9995.S7	Strömberg, Leonard, 1871-1941 (Table P-PZ40)
9995.W5	Wermelin, Alfred, 1857 (Table P-PZ40)
9999.A-Z	Other regions or countries, A-Z

.A1 Collected works

.A3 Selections, anthologies

Arrange alphabetically by editor

.A4 Poems

Arrange alphabetically by translator

.A5 Prose works

Arrange alphabetically by translator

.A7-.Z Separate works, A-Z

Subarrange by translator

.xA1	Collected works
.xA3	Selections, anthologies Arrange alphabetically by editor
.xA4	Poems Arrange alphabetically by translator
.xA5	Prose works Arrange alphabetically by translator
.xA7-.xZ	Separate works, A-Z Subarrange by translator

.xA1	Collected works
.xA2	Dramatic works
.xA3	Poems
.xA4	Prose works
.xA43	Letters
	Separate works
.xA5	Emilia Galotti
.xA53	Fables
.xA55	Faust
(.xA57)	Laokoon see N64
.xA6	Minna von Barnheim
.xA7	Nathan the wise
.xA8-.xZ	Other In case of works on special subjects, see the subject in classes A-Z

TABLES

.x	Collected works. By date
.x1-.x9	Separate works. By original title and translator
	e.g.
.x2	Einsame Menschen
.x25	Das Friedensfest
.x3	Fuhrmann Henschel
.x4	Hanneles Himmelfahrt
	Parsival
	see PZ8.1
.x7	Die versunkene Glocke
.x75	Vor Sonnenaufgang
.x8	Die Weber

	History
0.A1-.A5	Periodicals. Societies. Collections
0.A6-Z	General works
1	Biography (Collective)
2	Poetry. Folk songs
3	Drama
4	Other special
	Collections
5	General
6	Poetry
	For folk songs, see PT1205.A+
6.Z5	Translations
7	Drama
7.5.A-Z	Other forms, A-Z
7.5.S4	Short stories
7.5.W5	Wit and humor

	History
0	Periodicals. Societies. Collections
1	General works
2	General special
4	Biography (Collective)
5	Origins
6	Early to 1800
7	19th century
8	20th century
10	Poetry. Folk songs
11	Drama
12	Other special
	Collections
13	General
14	Poetry For folk songs, see PT1205.A+
14.A2	Early to 1800
14.Z5	Translations
(15)	Folk literature see GR99.6+
16.A-Z	Other special, A-Z
16.A43	Aliens' writings
16.D47	Detective and mystery stories
16.D5	Dialect literature
16.D8	Drama
16.F2	Fantastic fiction
16.F3	Farmers' writings
16.F5	Fiction
16.J48	Jewish authors
16.L32	Laboring class writings
16.L68	Love stories
16.P7	Prose
16.R33	Radio plays
16.S34	Science fiction
16.S4	Short stories
16.W5	Wit and humor
16.W65	Women authors
	Local
17.A-Z	States, regions, etc., A-Z
18.A-Z	Cities, towns, etc., A-Z

.A1	Polyglot
.A2	Dano-Norwegian
.A3	Landsmaal (New Norwegian)
.A5	Swedish
.A6-.Z	Other languages, A-Z. By translator or editor, A-Z
.E5	English
.E8	Esperanto
.F7	French
.G5	German

TABLES

	Collections
.A1	By date
.A2A-.A2Z	By editor, A-Z
	Translations
.A3A-.A3Z	English. By translator, A-Z
.A4A-.A4Z	Other. By language, A-Z
.A5-.Z	Separate works. By title, A-Z

.xA1-.xA129	Collected works. By editor or translator (alphabetically)
.xA13-.xA199	Selections, anthologies. By editor (alphabetically)
	Poems (including selections)
.xA2	Anonymous. By date
.xA21-.xA29	By translator (alphabetically)
	Special poems
	Das lied von der glocke (Song of the bell)
.xA3	Anonymous translations. By date
.xA31-.xA329	By translator (alphabetically)
.xA33-.xA339	Other poems. By title and translator (alphabetically)
	Dramatic works
.xA4-.xA499	Collections. By translator or editor (alphabetically)
	Separate works see PT8 .xA8+
	Prose and prose fiction
.xA5-.xA599	Collections. By translator or editor (alphabetically)
	Separate works see PT8 .xA8+
	Correspondence
.xA6	General collections
.xA7	Correspondence with Goethe
.xA71-.xA79	Correspondence with other persons (alphabetically)
.xA8-.xZ	Separate works. By original title, A-Z
	Expand the final Cutter number to subarrange each by translator
.xD5	Don Carlos
.xG4	Der geisterseher
.xJ7	Die jungfrau von Orleans
.xK3	Kabale und liebe
.xM3	Maria Stuart
.xN3	Der neffe als onkel
.xR3	Die räuber
.xT3	Tell (Wilhelm Tell)
.xV2	Der verbrecher der verlorner ehre
.xV4	Die verschwörung des Fiesko
.xW3	Wallenstein
.xW4	Wallensteins lager
.xW5	Die Piccolomini
.xW6	Wallensteins tod

.xA1	Collected works. By date
.xA2	Selections, anthologies, quotations. By date
.xA3	Collected poems. By date
.xA4-.xA49	Individual poems (alphabetically)
.xA5	Dramatic works (Collections). By date
.xA7-.xZ	Separate works, A-Z

A

INDEX

E

INDEX

L

INDEX

INDEX

INDEX

INDEX

U

GPO U.S. GOVERNMENT PRINTING OFFICE: 2009–350–024/60033